Junko's story is every woman's story. It is a story about the pain and splendor of a woman giving birth to herself by opening up the interior world of her own knowing and being. That hidden world is the only place to be that is safe when gender norms, cultural codes and family values dictate when a woman must sacrifice herself. Junko has reflected, probed and analyzed this secret world that creates the space for woman to be other than, different from, what her society or culture makes her. What makes this story so powerful is the searing honesty of her self-knowing and the political crucible in which she forges the words to speak to us. Junko's story is set against the deep connections to nature fostered by Shintoism, the strenuous disciplines of femininity for women of the Imperial court, and the confusion of revered Japanese traditions being overrun by American modernity. All these play out against the terrifying backdrop of nuclear war, the trauma of the authoritarian military state and the social upheaval of occupation. There are 1000 reasons to read this book.

> —**Karen Torjesen**, author of *When Women Were Priests*, and currently working to eradicate gender violence in the Congo.

There are those who regard foreign nations, other cultures, with suspicion or contempt and those who idealize them. With regard to Japan, Junko Chodos' rich and various achievement provides a cure for both conditions, for it reveals the history and customs of that country through a kaleidoscopic approach that deepens our understanding and surprises our expectations. But primarily this is story of a life, and in the telling Chodos explores language, dreams, the awakening of the artistic spirit, and the struggle for identity within a family and within a culture. Many of the vignettes haunt the imagination—that one, for example, about her first husband trained by the Japanese military as a suicide bomber but never required to complete a mission. The author discovers that on many nights he rises secretly and slips out into the cold, into the garden, to begin digging a hole for compost, a hole, says Chodos, that seems shaped like his own grave. It's this intersection of cultural knowledge, first-hand experience and poetry that makes *Out of the Mansion of the Motoyasu* a striking exploration.

—Suzanne Lummis is a widely published, award-winning poet whose poems have appeared in *The New Yorker* and many other publications.

The work engages from its very first sentence with remarkable narrative momentum, slowing just long enough for the
cultural or anthropological insights that enrich it along the
way. We are seeing its world initially through the eyes of a
child, but what eyes! The pictorial imagination at work is just
beautiful. I am deeply impressed by this account of the
making of an exceptional artist.

—Jack Miles, Pulitzer Prize-winning author of
God: A Biography

OUT OF THE MANSION OF THE MOTOYASU

Junko Chodos

GIOTTO MULTIMEDIA

Out of the Mansion of the Motoyasu
© 2017 by Junko Chodos

Published by:

Giotto Multimedia
P.O. Box 995
Malibu, CA 90265
United States of America

ISBN 978-0-9994408-2-7

Library of Congrress Information on File with Publisher.

Hardback Museum Edition 978-0-9994408-0-3

E-book ISBN 978-0-9994408-1-0

Visit us on the web!
GiottoMultimedia.com

CONTENTS

Part	Chapter	Page
One	One	1
	Two	32
	Three	52
	Four	72
Two	Five	89
	Six	117
	Seven	139
	Eight	175
	Nine	201
	Ten	223
Three	Eleven	255
	Twelve	296
	Thirteen	342
	Fourteen	375
	Fifteen	412
	Sixteen	432
	Epilogue	458
	Acknowlegments	463
	Artist Biography	469

Detailed Table of Contents

by Paragraph Number

PART ONE

Chapter One [Page 1]:

1-4 Memories of the Mansion. 5-7 Language.
8-12 The Mansion described. 13-17 History of the Edo Period.
18 The family name, Motoyasu. 9 The black ships. 20-28. The
Meiji Period begins. Great Grandfather's life changes. 29 The Secret
Christians. 30-38. After Great Grandfathers' death, Grandfather's
life and Christianity. 39-40 Mother's childhood. 41 The uncle who
was a doctor. 42 The uncle who left for Manchuria. 43-45 The
three young Korean men. 46-47 Grandfather the Healer.
48-50 Grandmother's household. 51 Grandfather dies.

Chapter Two [Page 32]:

1-2 Pearl Harbor and WWII begins. 3-16 Grand-mother's
Christianity and Uncle's love marriage. 17-30 The wedding party.
31-33 Deaths in the war. 34-35. Grandmother alone in the
bomb shelter.

Chapter Three [Page 52].

1 Escape from Tokyo to hospital owned by father's elder brother. 2
The toilet upstairs. 3-11 Hiding from the bombs. Beethoven's Ninth
Symphony. 12-14 Death everywhere. 15-17 The red sandals.
18-19. The executed bird. 20 Bombings. 21-23 Mother escapes from
the underground shelter in the railroad station. We all escape to a
small country village.

Chapter Four [Page 72]:

1-3 Life in the country village. 4 The silkworms. 5 The bath.
6 Making straw sandals. 7 The small shrine. 8-9 Father's
craftsmanship. 10-11 The Shining Princess. 12-16 Hardships in the
country.   17 The airplane fires bullets at us. 18-22 We start to live
as cave people. The atomic bombs fall.

PART TWO

Chapter Five [Page 89]:

1-5 Japan surrenders. 6-8 The American occupation begins.
9-23 We return to Tokyo. 24 The second son returns.
25-28 The church. 29 My father's medical office opens.
30-31 The thirst for culture. 32-46. Tuberculosis. Jane Eyre.
The priest.

Chapter Six [Page 117]:

1-9 At the school for the Emperor's children. 10-12 Classes in fine
art and crafts. 13 Classes in literature. 14-18 The Emperor as
Shinto god. 19-22 The world outside the school. The market of
darkness. Father's medical office. 23-31 Recovering from
tuberculosis. Trying to understand the meaning of it.

Chapter Seven [Page 139]:

1-8 Visiting the mansion after the war. 9-13 Trip to the beach.
Making rice cakes and cooking vegetables. 14-15 At school, the
essay contest: writing about the sickness. 16- 29 The Story of Q.
30 My essay wins. 31- 35 The painting competition. "A woman in
yellow." 36-38 Being honest to herself. Enduring the shame.
39-51 Graduating from elementary school and entering the junior
high division. Segregation of boys and girls. Activism and then the
shunning. 52-53 Grandmother visits Tokyo.

Chapter Eight [Page 175]:

1-5 Visiting Grandmother at the Mansion. 6-7 Thinking about her art, her illegitimate child. 8-9 Western Art is introduced into Japan. Paul Klee. Protecting her art. 10-11 The new school of music. 12-19 Violin lessons. Shame at school. 20-32 Life at home. Storytelling. The stolen blouse. No justice: justice and harmony. 33-41 The cult of talent. 42-44 The young man, Mendel, stays in the house.

Chapter Nine [Page 201]:

1-12 Mother's life as a foreigner in her own country. Her piano. Her Christian background. Her marriage.   13-16 Reaching out to father. 17-24 The brilliant young man visits. Casablanca. 25-31 At home: abuse, injustice, the cult, jealousy.

Chapter Ten [Page 223]:

1-3 Transferring to a new school. 4-9 The math teacher. The library. Reading Rilke. 10-11 The home room teacher. 12-24 Relationship with the math teacher. 25-29 The relationship cut. 30-45 The home room teacher comes closer. His home, family and church. The confessions. Betrayal and guilt. 46-48 The crumbling cathedral. Proposal of marriage. 49-51 Transfer of custody.

PART THREE

Chapter Eleven [Page 255]:

1 Monologue. 2-3 The two sources of her despair. 4-6 Home life deteriorates. Escape from that home becomes urgent. 7-11 Home room teacher offers her a different life. 12-15 The church and its

community. 16-22 The exhibition of Western art. 23-30 Struggling to survive. Considering the options. 31-32 Decision to accept the marriage proposal. Preparing to rebuild. 33-38 Toson Shimazaki's The Broken Commandment. My secret. My confession becomes a declaration. 39-41 Announcing the decision to marry. 42-47 The wedding ceremony. The father-in-law and the liberal Christian church. Starting to build a new life.

Chapter Twelve [Page 296]:

1-6 The church garden. The parents-in-law and their journey. Liberal Christianity. Life in the new home. 7-8 The tall, skinny woman. 9-14 The young girl from the snow-covered mountains. Daily tasks. 15-16 Sisters win scholarships to Julliard and leave to America. 17-18 Husband digging holes in the garden.
19-20 Images of the collapsing cathedral and of the horseshoe crab.
21-23 Teaching Sunday School. 24-29 The Dean's Fourth Wife.
30-35 The Woman in Yellow and the tall, skinny woman; the living and the dead. 36-43 Closer contact with America. The cathedral reappears. Husband leaves to attend postgraduate divinity school in America. I follow him. 44-46 Arriving at husband's apartment in America. Being encouraged to audit classes at the postgraduate school. 47-50 The mock therapy class. Freud. The uses of language in America, versus its uses in Japan. 51 Traveling across America. 52-53 The kind classmate and the foreign language. 54-57 The sea voyage back to Japan. 58-63 The welcome home dinner. Deciding to divorce.

Chapter Thirteen [Page 342]:

1 Divorce. 2-5 A visit to the mysterious priest. 6-7 Return to parents' home. Accepted at a top university in Japan.
8-16 Extracurricular study at a school of dessein. Reading Herbert Read and the philosophy of art. 17-18 Studying mysticism with a professor who translated Buber into Japanese. 19-24 Encounter with

Marxism. Daring to be oneself. 25-27 Younger sister's glorious
Comeback Home Recital, followed immediately by her elopement.
The family cult collapses. 28-31 Return to America. Studying art at
SUNY-Buffalo. 32-39 Planning a new life. Proposal of marriage
from a young American man.

Chapter Fourteen [Page 375]:

1-5 Our house in Boston. 6-9 Language difficulties.
10-15 Encouragement from an unexpected source. 16-17 Art shows
in Boston and New York. 18-23 The old woman in New Hampshire
and remembering the tall, skinny woman in the church.
24-26 The teacher dies. 27 William James. The upside-down nature
of religious experience. 28 Mother visits the New York show.
29-35 One-person shows in Tokyo and Osaka. Math teacher visits
the show in Tokyo. 36-39 The priest's son, the abbot, visits the
show in Osaka. 40-43 We move to Los Angeles and my husband
sets up his law practice. Thinking seriously about Judaism.

Chapter Fifteen [Page 412]:

1-3 Driving through Topanga Canyon. We purchase a home there.
Welcome party with the neighbors. 4-8 Therapy: being a client.
9-13 The bird decanter, remembering fascism. 14-21 Creating the
series, Requiem for an Executed Bird. 22-27 The phobia
transcended; the art show curated by my husband. 28-29 New art
rushes out of me. Lecturing about my art, and the different way
language functions in American culture. 30 My husband's first
book, and his most recent book: struggling with religion.

Chapter Sixteen [Page 432]:

1-2 Driving through the mountains and along the beach.
Constellations. 3-9 "Spiritual refugee"   10 The illegitimate baby is
now strong. 11 Taking a turn back to Japan. 12-13 Grandmother
demolishes the old mansion and sells it for a parking structure. She
builds a small home in Tokyo and starts a new life when she was
over 80 years old. 14-17 Last visit with Grandmother.
18-19 Reflections on marriage to an American, and on death.
20-24 Visiting mother and playing Chopin's Nocturne. 25-26 The
brilliant young man, now suffering from a stroke, visits, and dies
soon after. 27-30 The mayor of Nagasaki and the Black Hole of
Japan. The Emperor dies and his son becomes the next Emperor.
31-33 Mother talks about Mendel's visit. 34-35 The creative artist
and the performing artist. 36-41 Mother reminisces about the
garden of the Motoyasu. The letters exchanged. Father dies.
41-42 Mother's funeral. 43-44 Everything is gone except the
memories. The Presence.

Epilogue [Page 458]:

1 My first husband's book, and his death. 2 My mother-in-law
dies. 3 My studio across the mountains. 4-6 Fascism, its roots and
the rumbling of the volcano today.

PART ONE

CHAPTER 1

1   I am not allowed to go inside the Emperor's palace that sits in the middle of Tokyo, shaped like a gigantic black snake coiled, covered with a dark, ancient forest—so ancient that it is said that some life-forms are still alive there long after they became extinct in the rest of the world, isolated by a moat, dimly shining, green with water weeds—to see the small attached castle where my ancestors used to live. But the mansion which they built in the quiet village 200 miles away from Tokyo, after the last Shogun gave back his power to the Emperor, I remember very well. I can reconstruct that mansion in every detail in my mind's eye. Still, as for some of the images of what happened there, it is not clear whether they are memories or dreams; they seem to float in between.

2   One of those images is of when I was about three years old. I woke up in the middle of the night and found myself alone lying on a beautiful *futon* in a large *tatami* room—a Japanese-style floor made of tightly-woven straw—far away from the living quarters. The room was surrounded by silk sliding doors and all those doors themselves were huge panel paintings. This was the room where a masterpiece by an Edo-period artist was displayed which the Shogun had given our family as a gift of honor. I do not remember the artwork itself but I felt as if something came out of the huge painting and enveloped me in the dim light. It was not the image painted in the artwork: it was an unexplainable existence, a spirit, or a presence of art you might say. It was a solemn and frightening experience. But looking back, isn't it rather unlikely that I would be sleeping alone as a little child in a place that was so much like a museum? I still wonder if this really happened. I no longer have any way of finding out the name of the artist who painted the silkscreen: the work is gone and all the people who might have known his name are gone.

3 Another image is of many lanterns lit up in the garden and people strolling along the winding paths on the little hills and on the red bridge over the pond. This scene was confirmed as a memory when I asked my grandmother whether it actually happened. But her enthusiastic confirmation makes me feel on the contrary that my memory might be the image I created in my childhood by listening to her telling me over and over how beautiful it was when they opened their garden to the public on some summer evenings.

4 These images belong to a time more than half a century ago, and belong to a land which the infinite ocean used to isolate from the rest of the world. Beyond the horizon was the place where the dead live, we were told. I am writing this now from the other side of the Pacific Ocean, six thousand miles away, from the west coast of America, from that very land.

5 I just took a long ride along Mulholland Highway through the Santa Monica Mountains to the beach. The yellow center line on the highway winds, stretches, climbs, and slides down the slopes through mountain after mountain where the dry sun-drenched soil is covered with shrubs and bushes clinging to it. Approaching the end of the highway, suddenly between the mountains you see the ocean spread out in front of you. It is always a surprise when I come to this spot. I turn onto the Pacific Coast Highway where all the cars run fast, their windows rolled up, each with its own short, crisp shadow dragging right below it, each keeping a measured distance from the others; even if I ever cried aloud in my car, no one would notice. I hear the sound of the rolling ocean waves coming over me, but it isn't: it is the sound of the cars. The ocean to my left is spread out like a sheet of hammered metal, shining in silence. I have never caught even a glimpse of the horizon without thinking that I am looking at it now from the other side of the ocean.

6 I have started writing these images from my childhood in the foreign language I struggled to learn in order to live here but which is yet still so remote from my deepest feeling, and in which I still cannot quite touch the reality of each word. I utter the words but I cannot see how they describe a parabola in the air and fall into someone's soul. I feel as if I am throwing the words into darkness: I cannot see where they end up. For those images I described were formed and recalled over and over in my mind only in Japanese words, in which language the name of every person, the name of every tree, even every murmur or sigh evokes something strong in me immediately. It can evoke a cry in the ancient forest to summon god to descend through the trees; it can evoke the whisper of that love poem written at the dawn of Japan and still with us, by the unknown sea soldier rowing his little wooden boat who, seeing the seaweed swaying deep in the water as he looked down, thought of his loved one's long black hair spread out on the pillow. Now such things must all be evoked in English.

7 It seems that the sense of reality of each word comes to you only through someone to whom you feel deeply attached: when that someone talks to you and listens to you, when he comes all the way from the edge of the universe and fills in the unfathomable dark gap of your fear and hesitation when you are at a loss, overcomes your apprehension of failing to reach him by his strong imagination and by the confidence of his own language, and suddenly knows what you have said, and smiles. Only then does the word cease to be just a sign and it is born in you as a word, alive. It must have happened the same way when, as infants, we learned our mother tongue and started to speak. But for foreigners it comes only after the decades of deep silence, craving to express it with words and failing to express it. The gap between inner silence and outer words is so unfathomably, disproportionately unbalanced, it would bring you to the edge of disintegration of character. But now, with those precious words which were born in me one by one like drops of water over decades in America, I am trying to write this in English. It is my language now through which I am experiencing the world and through which I want to reach the souls that have become precious to me—not as an infant does, but rather as a person who feels as if she has crossed over the boundary of death, and who already belongs to the world of the dead, to the land of eternity, and looks back at this world—who finally feels that we can figure out and reveal what we have experienced in life and what it really meant, what all that has really been revealing to us.

8 When the deep morning mist started to lift, the Mansion of the Motoyasu which my great grandfather built in the quiet village emerged from it in a higher place than you anticipated through the mist. It was built on a hillside where the first Shogun often came to enjoy his falconry. It was a dignified traditional Japanese-style home surrounded by a high stone wall. When the tall wooden doors of the gate, which were decorated with iron nails, were opened to both sides you could see a long path graveled with smooth, gray pebbles, still wet with the morning mist. It reminded you of the pebbled path into a Shinto shrine and it had the same intriguing feeling which made you whisper or fall silent when you walked slowly towards the entrance. Just as with a shrine, this was considered the entrance to a sacred realm, the home, where everyone, without exception, had to take off his shoes. A manicured Japanese lawn was spread around the mansion, and perfectly trimmed pine trees stood together creating a deep, shadowy wood still dripping with dew. Here and there in the woods stood white azalea trimmed round like some mysterious big birds sleeping in the shade.

9 But the most impressive things were the big stones which were placed to look as if they were part of those woods from the beginning of time. They were carefully chosen by the artist according to the traditional aesthetics of a long history of appreciation of rocks and stones, and they were carried in from distant mountains. Some of them were much taller than a man's height, some were smaller; some were deep black and smooth, some had rough surfaces with complicated patterns. Every one of them radiated a strong presence there and pulled all who looked at them into a meditative state of mind, as if they still carried the air of the deep mountains where the gods dwell.

10 Only the light poles which stood in regular intervals outside the stone walls were of European style: they were made of iron and big, round, glass light bulbs were attached to them with elaborate iron ornaments. They lent the mansion the magnificent European style of the new Meiji period. The light poles were already converted to electricity from gaslights as early as I can remember them. The high wall provided the best seats for the village children to sit on; I was there among them. I remember someone pushing me to the top of the stone wall high enough to see the parade of the Shinto festival in harvest time approaching from far away, when only the beat of drums and the faint melody of bamboo flutes could be heard on the street.

11   But at the back of the mansion there was a different world: a soft, delicate garden provided a peaceful life for the family. A rather large pond shaped loosely like a figure-8 lay in the middle of the garden. Well-trimmed pine trees were carefully structured into dramatic forms and stretched their shiny green branches towards the pond low enough almost to touch the surface of the water and yet curved slightly up at their ends, which made the whole movement of each tree more intense. At the narrow neck of the pond, near the middle of the 8, there was a red-gem-colored bridge powerfully shaped like a big drum cut in half. Small gentle hills surrounded the pond. And at the far side of the hills stood a terrace made of bamboo and a bamboo bench was placed inside, ready for the people who strolled through the garden. When spring came, deep purple wisteria blossomed in clusters on the bamboo shelf. They grew long, and as if they could not bear their own weight they grew straight down towards the ground without ever trembling in the wind.

12   When you walked up the few steps at the opposite end of the garden a somewhat unexpectedly wild field spread open from which you could see the gentle mountains far away without your view being interrupted by any trees. At knee height, wild bush-cloves were spread; when autumn came these bore small delicate flowers whose white petals embraced bright purple or red centers, and they trembled and swayed in the wind and the whole field seemed like waves in the ocean. When you stood there alone you could almost hear in the wind the sound of horses galloping and neighing, and the voices of the samurai and their dogs excited at their falconry, and you could almost see the great eagles stretch their wings in the sky above you and suddenly swoop down from the sky at high speed towards the game in the bush. It was like unfolding an old picture scroll.

13   My ancestors on my mother's side had been the Shogun's doctors for seventeen generations: from the time that the first Tokugawa accomplished the greatest unification of Japan in history, established the feudal government *Bakufu* in Edo and received the title of Shogun from the Emperor, all the way up to the time that the last Tokugawa gave back his power to the Emperor in 1863 and the modern Japanese nation began under the Meiji Emperor.

14   The Shogun established a huge political, financial, and military hierarchy and placed strict regulations on top of it and controlled all of Japan. He was at the top of the elite class of warriors, the samurai, and below them all the other social strata were distinctly classified and strictly regulated. He controlled 250 domains throughout Japan, each of which had its own hierarchy with a Daimyo on top as its feudal lord. Each delivered measured packages of rice to the Shogun and each maintained his own kingdom.

15   The samurai elite were honored to have family names—not like commoners who were allowed to have only first names—and their households were inherited with pride. The most distinct difference between them and commoners was that they were allowed to wear two swords, one long and one short. These swords symbolized the fact that they owned and controlled force in society: they had the right to kill others (under certain strict regulations) and they had as well the right to kill themselves in the ritual of *seppuku*—for this too was an honor, that you owned your own life.

16 The *Bakufu* government prohibited all of Japan to have any contact with foreign countries except in Dejima, a little piece of reclaimed land in Nagasaki harbor which was constructed for only one purpose—so that the Dutch trading house could be allowed to operate there. The Dutch were not allowed to go outside of that island. Under this isolation from all foreign countries, Japan enjoyed more than 260 years of peace and prosperity. There were samurai for domestic fights, but there was no military system to defend or attack outside of country. Edo had a population of one million and was the biggest city in the world, twice as big as London and Paris at that time. The literacy level was very high, including among women. The whole nation was secure and documents show that even a woman could safely travel alone on long trips of many days and months. The development of technology and of the transportation system had reached the highest level to such a point that only the Industrial Revolution could bring it higher.

17 During this long peaceful period, the culture of the aggressive samurai warrior gained sophistication. The discipline of force, sensitivity towards killing, and death were internalized and gave the culture an intensity and vitality. Many cultural styles and artifacts that are now considered typically Japanese, such as *ukiyoe, haiku, kabuki,* flower arrangement, tea ceremony—all these flourished in this period and all of them show this quality underneath their refined and gentle surface.

18   The first Shogun gave my ancestors the special family name Motoyasu. This is the name which belonged to the first Shogun when he was an ambitious, tormented young man winning battles after spending thirteen years of his childhood as a hostage in the enemy's hand. This name, to which he must have had a strong emotional attachment, was given to my ancestor as his family name as an honor and it was allowed only to our family to use it. We do not know what made the Shogun give this name to his doctor rather than to one of the warriors who took great risk of their lives to support him in their youth and later received high positions in his government. But my ancestors responded to this extraordinary honor and personal affection by taking care of the Shogun's health with the highest excellence and utmost loyalty while they lived in a small castle inside the Shogun's own castle for more than 260 years.

19   My great grandfather remembered very well as a young man the devastating incident which occurred in 1853. Commodore Perry appeared in Tokyo Bay from America with four black ships, two of them warships, and demanded that the Japanese open up their country and sign a treaty with America. It was a great shock for it was obvious that these "barbarians" had some unbelievable technology and that their threat had validity to it. They demanded an unfair treaty: Japan was not to have jurisdiction over its own territory, and a system of tariffs was to be established which gave America and its allies enormous advantages in international trade. The Americans backed up their demands with threats of violence. For Japan, these threats offended its pride and evoked fear and concern for the lives of the citizens. But the black ships evoked enormous curiosity as well: records show that some whose curiosity was bigger than their fear swam out to the ships, which were anchored far away from the shore secretly at night to see how iron could float on water and how the ships could move without sails.

20 For the West, this sudden visit of Commodore Perry was part of an aggressive colonization movement: all the western nations, The Great Powers as they were called, were ganging up on the East as they struggled to win the competition of capitalism, gaining resources for their products and markets into which they could sell them. All of this was required by the Industrial Revolution. In Japan, turmoil and friction arose between those who wanted to open the country up to the West and those who insisted on shaking off these "barbarians." Friction between those for and those against opening up the nation took the form of friction between *Bakufu*, the Shogun's government, and the daimyos who viewed the Emperor as the highest representative of Japan. Throughout history the Emperor had been the highest priest of all the shrines of Japan as well as a politician, but by that time his political power had declined. Japan saw that all other nations in Asia had already undergone a rapid, aggressive sweep of colonization by The Great Powers. China, the proudest nation, who believed her culture was the highest and that she was the center of the world, refused to sign the unfair treaty with England. But her action brought unexpected consequences: China was trapped and fell into the abyss of opium. England wanted silver from China, and they got it by exporting huge quantities of opium to China in return. In this way, opium poured into China, and when China tried to put a stop to it, England launched a violent war in 1842, the first Opium War. In the end, England was victorious and took Hong Kong from China and China was forced to sign the unfair treaty with England. In 1858, after the Indian Rebellion the preceding year, England assumed direct control of India by establishing the new British Raj.

21 Japan saw enough with its own eyes and understood what colonization actually involved. It was a force rooted to the same belief system that allowed Westerners to systematically tear people from their lands in Africa and bring them to America as slaves in order to make a profitable enterprise of the growing of cotton. That was in the time of mercantilism; now, in the age of industrial capitalism, the Westerners needed resources and markets, and for those they came to the East. Their project of colonization was based on their unshakeable belief in both the absolute superiority of the white man, and in all the glory of Christianity, modern technology and science. France offered its support to the *Bakufu* government, and England offered its support to the Emperor. It was obvious that Japan would soon be thrown into an aggressive power struggle among America, Holland, Russia, England, and France, and that it would be chopped up into pieces to become prey for the Western vultures, The Great Powers, just as had happened to all other Asian nations. It was the most serious crisis in Japan's history.

22 In 1868 the Shogun yielded his power and without a fight returned the title of Shogun to the Emperor. In this way, Japan was able to avoid the fate of being colonized and was able to keep her independence. It was the biggest revolution Japan ever went through, and yet the process of transition went relatively smoothly. The 15-year-old Emperor moved in from Kyoto; Edo became Tokyo, the East Capital;

the Meiji period began; and modern Japan opened the country up to the outside world. The whole clan of the Shogun left Tokyo "for the honor of the Emperor," and my great grandfather, the doctor of the Shogun, left with them. That was the time that he moved to the quiet village and built the mansion of the Motoyasu there. And since then, the castle that the Shogun vacated in Tokyo has been the Emperor's palace.

23 My great-grandfather refused to see any patients after he moved there. "My hands took His Highness' pulse," he said, "They cannot touch a commoner!" This was his expression of loyalty and pride, and it was the last fortress to protect his identity as a amurai elite. The memory of the Shogun's parade in which he had participated was still too vivid for my great grandfather. This was the parade to the tomb of the first Shogun where he was worshipped as one of the deities. This parade was a tradition carried on throughout the reign of the Shoguns. The parade started with demonstrations of military power: tall colorful banners, archers carrying long bows and arrows, and soldiers carrying guns and boxes of gunpowder were followed by gorgeously decorated horses carrying the Shogun and the government dignitaries, all of them wearing spectacular costumes. It was six o'clock in the morning when the first parts of the parade pressed through the gates of the castle, and it was ten o'clock at night when the end of the parade came through the gate. According to written records, the number of horses reached more than 320,000 and the number of people who were in the parades was even greater. My great grandfather used to look out through the window of the little carriage in which he rode, which was carried through the parades by four porters. He saw commoners sitting all along the road with their knees folded on the dusty ground, both hands neatly placed on the ground in front of their knees and their faces almost touching the ground bowing, as if their faces were buried between their hands.

24 He withdrew to the world of calligraphy in which he had been known to a certain circle of cultured people for the dignity and serenity of his style. People saw him sitting in his study early every morning holding *sumi* and sliding it along the stone pallet to make *sumi* ink. When the temperature in the room was cold, the black color of the *sumi* ink intensified, so he had to do this work in the early morning before it became warm. He dipped his brush in the little dent in the pallet and put it on the rice paper while controlling his breath. He practiced calligraphy by writing Chinese classical poems, which have the same connotation for the Japanese as Latin has for Westerners. The Chinese poets who had gone through so many rises and falls over five thousand years of their own history caught his mind, which was now filled with the shock of witnessing the collapse of the samurai hierarchy. This was an avalanche which he and his ancestors had never anticipated, and he found himself in the midst of it sliding down and becoming buried in it, living in a world where his most honorable right, the right to kill himself with dignity in the solemn ritual of *seppuku*, no longer had any meaning at all: it would simply be called a suicide if he did it.

25 The Meiji government, afraid that the Shogun's political power might be restored, confiscated considerable assets from most of the members of the Shogun's circle in order to keep them powerless. Some of them fell into poverty immediately, some launched new businesses and failed. But I heard the story of the dinner my great grandfather took every evening, which became a sort of family legend. The fish on the cutting board had to be fully alive; while it was still jumping and slapping the board with its tail the chef quickly cut it into pieces small enough that his master's chopsticks could easily pick them up. It was prepared in a special way so that the fish was still breathing under its own skin when it was served on the beautifully ornamented plate; my great-grandfather would never eat dead fish. It was served with forty other exquisite dishes, of which his chopsticks touched only a very few. The chef went down to the seashore every day at dawn to select the best live fish that the fisherman had caught. And many other servants worked hard as well to keep their master's lifestyle as close as possible to the old one in the old castle since that was the only way he knew how to live. He brought the whole family deep into debt.

26 Under the unfair treaty with America and other Great Powers that Japan had been coerced into signing, huge amounts of gold were taken out of Japan and transported to Europe to make dazzling profits for the Europeans. To establish an equal relationship with these countries and to avoid being colonized by them became the most urgent concern of the Meiji government. "Catch up to the West and surpass it!" became a slogan. A new educational system was established. The government invited excellent foreign scholars to teach science, technology, medicine, law and all other cultural endeavors such as singing, playing new musical instruments, drawing with perspective, and oil painting. Those were taught not as superficial skills, but along with the aesthetics behind them and their long histories. New foreign languages were taught and in order to translate them correctly many new words were created in the Japanese language. But Japan did not want to rely on foreign scholars to stay in Japan forever: they did not want all the professors to be foreigners and the Japanese to be students forever. They wanted all studies to raise the level of the whole population. So Japanese studied and learned foreign languages as quickly as they could. They produced professors in all fields of study, as soon as possible. They wanted to establish Japanese universities in Japan, where Western things could be taught in Japanese for Japanese people. In this way Japan is fundamentally different from the many other colonized Asian countries: its educational system remained Japanese.

27 In 1889 the new constitution was set. The national military was formed and it was the first time that citizen soldiers rather than elite samurai who were proud of their art were called upon to defend the country and fight against outsiders. Men and women cut their hair, started wearing Western clothes, riding bicycles, and eating meat. Everything was done almost overnight. It was also the first time that they all had to put on shoes, and found out that shoes have to fit to the size of your feet; Japanese clothes and footwear are one-size-fits-all. Political parties were organized, and the Diet, the cabinet, opened in1898. The Japanese flag and national anthem were created for the first time. Incidentally, the curiosity of the Japanese to see the "black ships" bore fruit: they succeeded in creating iron ships of their own by imitating these "black ships" and eight years later a group of one hundred Japanese crossed the Pacific Ocean in iron warships made in Japan, to "inspect" America. Since then shipbuilding has become one of the major industries in which Japan was determined to surpass the West.

28 Some Westerners and other Asian countries laughed at the Japanese—for imitating the West like monkeys, for lack of self-respect and lack of integrity. But all these changes of the Japanese were based on the single assumption that Japan's independence and an equal relationship with Western nations could be established only by doing things in their way: better to accept humiliation now, before the core of self-respect would be taken away so that it would take hundreds of years to recover. Among "their ways," the most crucial was winning in the competition of capitalism. As a country without natural resources with a huge population, it became clearer and clearer that Japan needed a strong military to expand its land so that the population could thrive and provide resources. In 1894 Japan started the Sino-Japanese War and won. In 1904 Japan started a war with Russia and won. In the second decade of the 20th century, Korea became one of the Japanese colonies. It appeared that Japan had become one of the imperial nations among The Great Powers, the only imperial nation of the modern world which was built by non-whites and non-Christians. Finally in 1911, the unfair treaty with America was corrected after tenacious nego-tiations ever since Perry had come in 1853, and other Western nations followed America's lead. Japan took this as proof that military power was required to make the Western powers accept fair treaties.

29 Even though the Tokugawa period is known as a peaceful period, it is also known as the most terrifying period of Japanese persecution of Christians. Be-tween 1549, when Francis Xavier, a Catholic missionary, arrived in Japan and the early 17th century, the Christian population reached 750,000. The Tokugawa Shogun—who was convinced that the Western nations used a pattern of sending missionaries to the target nations first, and a few steps later, taking over the nation itself—tried hard to eradicate Christianity from Japan.

But in spite of passing the most detailed, strict regulations yet, which required everyone to register as a Buddhist, and in spite of a spy network which covered all of Japan, and in spite of the cruelest persecution and torture—from burning and crucifixion to spearing children in front of their parents—they did not succeed. Persecution continued under the Meiji government: records from 1869 show that 3,300 Christians were arrested and exiled during that one year. "Even though we will learn everything from the West, and catch up and surpass it, we will never sell our soul," was the Meijis' commitment. They maintained their anti-Christian policies despite aggressive reproaches from the West. But Christians remained disguised as Buddhists and survived.

30 My grandfather became one of the first physicians trained in Western, German-style medicine in Japan. After my great-grandfather died, he practiced in the office at the front quarter of the mansion. He opened the doors to everyone who came and to everyone he could reach—including people at the bottom of the social hierarchy who he knew had no ability to pay. He and his young wife, my grandmother, fired all the servants and worked extremely hard by themselves. Before dawn, their mansion's big front lawn was covered with sick people waiting for him, some leaning against the stones in the little woods where the darkness still hovered, waiting for him to get up. Not even one night during their married life, my grandmother said, did he sleep through without being awakened by a loud knock and the cry that someone's baby was dying. Then he rushed out with a paper-and-bamboo lantern in his hand, on which the letters of Motoyasu were written with *sumi* ink. Sometimes he went over the mountain to the patients' houses. From far away the light of his lantern could be seen flickering through the woods as he ran up the dark mountain.

31 Here is a book, the paper is slightly yellowed, though it is well preserved considering that it is 226 years old. Drawn on the cover are two human figures standing like columns. In the middle of the cover it says "*Kaitaishinsho*" in Japanese. I encountered this book in the rare book collection of a university in America near where I live. It is the very book in which I was told that my ancestor was deeply involved. In 1774 a man name Sugita Gempaku, along with other scholars, translated and published "*Kaitaishinsho*"—a translation of a Dutch anatomy book, *Tafel Anatomia*, published in Amsterdam in 1734, which was originally written in Latin. They were given this Dutch book from the Dejima and translated it without the assistance of any dictionary or interpreter; it was a hard task. One of my ancestors in the Motoyasu family was involved in this task and is mentioned in some related document as the Shogun's doctor. This whole project is considered to have been the beginning of Western-style science in Japan, and the story of this accomplishment is known to every elementary schoolchild in Japan as a heroic story of the passion for scientific truth and of the painstaking effort of teamwork to search for it. The passion for Western science which my ancestors gained from this project formed their identities as doctors: they were more scientists and scholars than traditional Eastern medicine men.

32 My grandfather rebuilt his household from deep debt to prosperity. And he brought all kinds of new surprising things to his village such as a piano, a violin, and a phonograph, none of which had ever been seen before by the people in that village. It was part of the Meiji revolution that Western culture rushed into Japan like a storm, and he became one of the breezes carrying culture from the West to his village. He wore a three-piece suit just like a Victorian gentleman in Europe. He organized small record concerts regularly with some young people, and he played records of European classical music which was so new to everyone—among which Chopin's Nocturnes were listened to over and over, I was told. He had a standing order at the store that an Englishman had opened to serve European customers in Tokyo to collect records of as many different performances of Chopin as could be obtained. Emil Cortot was his favorite pianist. Sometimes he even played the violin himself—how and when he learned to play I don't know but he surprised everyone with joy.

33   But the most surprising thing he ever did to everybody was that he and his wife converted themselves to Christianity, becoming Episcopalians. It was a totally different kind of surprise from the Western music. The memory of the terror of hunting Christians was still vivid. Although Christianity had finally ceased to be illegal by that time, Shinto was still the national religion and socially being a Christian was a risky thing to do. As far as his family was concerned, it was considered a clearly traitorous act. The Shogun had given the family a statue of Buddha housed in a special chest to worship, on the cover of which their family crest was inlaid in gold—also a gift from the Shogun's own symbol, as was the family name. The Shogun's crest, consisting of three hollyhock leaves, had been admired and feared throughout Japan as a symbol of power and glory, and two leaves from this crest had been given as a crest to the Motoyasu. Only one generation had passed since the Shogun lost his power, and now the son of his most loyal doctor had become a Christian. How shocking it must have been to the entire family and clan of the former Shogun, and how could my grandparents have fought against all the pride of the family and the outrage that came from it?

34 I heard from my grandmother that he kept in his room one of the original wooden signs that the Shogun had put in the town square during the 17th century. The sign says that anyone who knows of a Christian should report it to the authorities. Also he collected some material on the Secret Christians who disguised them-selves as Buddhists for more than 300 years and lived underground. The Tokugawa government found out who was Christian by using *fumi-e*. *Fumi* means to step on, and *e* means picture; they made copper plates on which Christ's picture was drawn in relief—later on they found that a picture of the Virgin Mary with the Christ child was more effective than his alone—and they ordered people to step on these pictures. Anyone who refused or hesitated to step on the picture was considered to be a Christian and cruel torture and execution awaited him. But some disguised themselves as Buddhists, hid themselves underground, and continued to recite the Latin mass.

35 I saw one of those *fumi-e* in the Tokyo National Museum long ago. The copper plate was the exact size needed for one pair of feet to stand on. Their feet must have been bare when people stepped on Jesus' figure. His face was worn down and had become round at the edges and made smooth by the thousands of feet that had stepped on it. You could not see any expression on his face any more; only from his arms stretched on the cross could you tell who he is. Was it easier for them to step on him when his face lost his alertness and became dull like this, or was it harder to do when you saw him so worn out that it became like a flat, ugly, rotten piece of meat shining black with the oil from people's feet? Many refused to step on the picture and were executed. Some heard his voice coming out of this copper plate whispering, "Step on me, step on me and survive!" And they did.

36 Christians living underground made wooden statuettes of Buddha, inside of which a cross was secretly engraved. They believed that if they patiently waited for seven generations (no one knows why it was seven), Western missionaries would come and save them from this darkest isolation. After more than seven generations had passed, in the Meiji period when Catholic missionaries actually did come to Japan, again being allowed to give mass only to Christian foreigners who were residing in Japan, the Secret Christians approached them and revealed their secret, their faith, to them. But the missionaries could not recognize them as Christians because their Latin sounded like nothing but Japanese to them. And their translation of the teachings of the Catholics, which had been passed down through the generations, contained elaborate code. The Catholic missionaries could not read it nor were they interested in it. It was my grandfather's desire to investigate this topic and to put it in some form which he could leave to history; he had done some research on it.

37 I don't know if my grandparents went to church; I don't even know if there was a church in those early days in that district. But I remembered they had a special room where a little statue of a half-naked man was hanging on the wall. It was a statue of a man who was hung by his hands nailed on a horizontally stretched piece of wood, which was supported with a vertical piece of wood. His body was twisted in agony and his head hung down sideways without strength. It was a shocking and frightening little statue. How totally different a feeling it evoked in me from the feeling that all the other artifacts I was familiar with evoked: the lacquer boxes on which delicate lines suggested the waves of the ocean moving, with inlaid mother of pearl, in which a scroll of soft rice paper was placed; or bronze cranes that stretched their wings and were just about to fly into the sky; or countless beautiful porcelain flower vases on whose surface a little poet standing under a pine tree was painted—all of which were placed in the alcoves in the rooms of the mansion with careful attention so that all of them looked alive and enjoyed their peaceful lives in the little imaginary universe of alcoves as a symbol of our own lives. But this statue of a half-naked man was different. It was obvious that he had suffered the effects of brutality and cruelty. What was done to him was done not by any disaster like a storm or an earthquake—we all knew how frightening they can be—but by human beings with hostility and force and in a way I had never yet known. What exactly did people do to this man? Was he tortured to death? Was he executed? What did he do to deserve this? And why on earth was such a horrible thing in this beautiful mansion? It was a terrible intrusion of a gruesome, cruel, dark image into the beautiful life we were having. And yet the deep sense of sorrow that the statue radiated filled the entire room. I thought I saw something I was not supposed to see, but I could not wipe the image of the statue from my mind.

38   I also saw a mysterious man with a white collar and black robe there. He was familiar to me; I saw him often in the mansion. He looked alone even when he was talking and laughing among the family.

He reminded me of a master of the sword in the old Japanese story I read whose training of the sword was so severe that he gained some sorcery powers. He was tall and skinny, with sharp eyes, and looked dignified just as I imagined the swordsman in that story. People told me that he was a priest of Christianity and also our distant relative. But his name was neither Motoyasu nor any of the other relatives' names I was familiar with.

39 My grandparents raised three children of their own. The first one was a daughter, my mother, who was the last woman to be called a princess in the family according to tradition. When she was a little girl she became known as a prodigy for her playing of the koto, the beautiful harp-like instrument. It is played on the *tatami*. Placed in front of her folded knees, the player bends over the wooden body of this instrument which looks like a boat. With ivory nails on her fingers and the long sleeves of her kimono spread on the *tatami*, she looks like a butterfly dancing around the big trunk of some fallen tree. My mother soon moved to the piano, which demanded more challenging technique and offered broader, more complicated avenues of emotional and intellectual expression. She studied with the man who gave the first piano recital in Japan after studying in Europe. She inherited the passion for music, but not for religion, from her father. She had a hard time being away from the piano to learn the other things which aristocratic ladies were so busy with. My grandmother told me of a little episode: My mother came back from her flower arrangement lessons with a bouquet of flowers in her hands which she used as material for lessons in the teacher's house and was supposed to use for reviewing at home. But she never had any flowers on the stems, because she ran home all the way from the teacher's house as fast as possible to play the piano at home and her kimono sleeves were flying in the air, and all the flowers flew off the stems. Soon she became known as a prodigy pianist too after some concerts she gave in the cities. She was sent to the mission school in the city closest to home where she could continue practicing her piano, and later she entered the music school in Tokyo, which disappointed her bitterly because its level was not sufficiently advanced. Her parents arranged a "perfect marriage" for her before she went too far outside the mold of the traditional lady.

40   The one chosen for her marriage was a doctor, with the highest qualifications and license in German medicine, highly literate in Chinese classics and a black-belt third-*dan* in judo—a strong, big man, the ninth son of the landlord who had governed some district. Following the aristocratic tradition, her parents investigated the prospective groom thoroughly in the areas of morals, accomplishments, and physical records—not only his but also those of his family all the way back to his ancestors. A bronze statue of one of these ancestors was still standing in the capital town of that district in honor of his having saved the whole district from famine years ago. The family had been producing doctors for generations including one of his sisters, a most extraordinary accomplishment for a woman in those days. And in fact, she was there in the *miai* marriage interview as a proxy for his mother, who was supposed to be there. She added a cheerful, gentle, sophisticated touch to the whole *miai* interview. My grandparents did not find any horrible diseases or mental illness episodes in the family history. They made sure that the man loved music, and the good news was that he even played some traditional instruments himself as a cultured gentleman. My mother did not dare to lift her eyes to look at him during the *miai*, for such a thing was not appropriate at the marriage interview. But her parents were deeply impressed by the bridegroom candidate's polite and respectful manners. Besides, his family did not have a high aristocratic title even though he was proud of the fact that his family had been allowed to keep the family name and to carry two swords for hundreds of years. There would not be too much hard work to maintain the appropriate level of status, coming as my mother did from the Motoyasu. And he had already lost his parents, and he was much older than she was, so in short, she would have maximum freedom—which my grandparents knew she needed.

41 The second child was a son, the first son of the family. In Japan, that position itself carries great weight in any family but particularly so in the Motoyasu. He was prepared to be the 19th-generation Motoyasu doctor from the day he was born. His commitment to being a doctor like his father, a doctor who helped people who needed help, was never shaken in his mind. He was an accomplished artist as well, a master of the tea ceremony and of flower arrangement and he also developed an interest in oil painting. Much later, I saw one of his paintings hanging in a dark hallway of the mansion: I was astonished by its refinement and accomplished skill. There was not the slightest harshness or awkwardness in the work; it was completed at a highly professional level. It reminded me of some works of Vermeer, the 17th-century artist in Holland, in the way it dealt with light and shadow. Did he happen to study oil painting with the artist who learned that Dutch tradition from the artist who came from Holland to Japan to teach painting in the Meiji period? Was he a first- or second-generation student perhaps? It might be said that the highly accomplished style showed some limitation in his being a strong, big-scale character of his own, but the art itself showed honesty and sensitivity. It was a painting of flowers in a vase, and the vulnerability and strength of living things were clearly captured.

42 The third child, the second son, was a rebel and adventurer: he was against all traditions at home and he loved to climb mountains alone. He quit the excellent private school in Tokyo when he was 20 years old and left Japan to go to the empire of Manchuria which Japan built as a colony on the Asian continent between China and Siberia — a new nation, with a target population of three million. Under the new modern nation plan, huge beautiful cities were constructed, and many Japanese industrial companies and banks had already moved in; they needed many energetic pioneers to settle there. Moving from the Japanese mainland to Manchuria was like moving from England to the new vast continent of America. It was a dreamland for many people in Japan who wanted an entirely new life without the fetters of tradition: for that, they did not mind severe work in the severe, cold climate. What else could my uncle have done to establish his own identity against his brother, a brilliant born doctor, with a good mind and good-looking too, with all the qualities and talents an aristocrat was expected to have, and who received all the respect from people as he deserved?

43 My grandparents also took care of three brilliant Korean young men at home, and supported them all the way through medical school until all of them became doctors and went back to their homeland. The rampant nationalism of Japan treated Korea, its colony, with extreme cruelty. When the Tokyo earthquake occurred in 1923, the rumor spread like a plague that Koreans had taken advantage of the disaster by putting poison into all the wells in Tokyo. Based only on these rumors, the Japanese military, the police, and civilian groups slaughtered an estimated 6,000 Koreans on the street. Japan seemed to choose Korea as the target on which to project all of its own pain of humiliation, fear, and indignation which it suffered at the hands of the Westerners and had to swallow, and which it could not afford to express directly ever since Commodore Perry had arrived and forced them to sign the unfair treaty with America. It was my grandparents' belief that Korea should be free from Japan, and for that, good, brilliant young men trained in the helping professions were needed to make their country strong from the inside.

44   I remember only one of them; I think I used to call him my elder brother in the affectionate words of a child. He and I were crouching in the barn which stood in the field of bush clove one afternoon. He took out a log from the piles and made a boat for me to play with, using his tools with extremely skill. It was not a warship but a big ship with lots of windows which he carved out of the wood one by one. I don't remember if he was telling me that he came to Japan by boat and that some time not too far ahead, he was going to go back to his homeland by boat. But thoughts of boats filled my mind while I watched the fascinating process of the boat taking shape in his hands. Japan is made up of islands, three thousand of them. Everything comes to us, and everyone leaves us, by boat, including the dead who live far away over the horizon.

45   For my grandparents to have helped the young Korean men based on such an idealistic thought was an extraordinary thing to do. Japanese people were excited about the idea that in order to escape from the fate of being colonized by Western nations, Japan had to become a nation with a colony of its own. They had to do just as the Western nations were doing, and this was the only way to compete in the arena of world capitalism as a latecomer. To have Korea as colony was a big part of it. Japan's hysterical exuberance went sky-high to the ambition of conquering all of Asia under one empire, to rescue them from the violent domination of the West. Under this idea, the empire of Manchuria was built by Japan at the northern edge of where Russia expanded her land to China: it was completely a puppet nation of Japan. A hysterical idealism played the role of justifying this invasion of China. Under these circumstances, where did my grandparents get ideas so opposite from those of their own government and most of the Japanese people? And how did they get the strength to manifest such ideas so steadily in their everyday lives over decades? The secret police's activity had become increasingly intense around that time. They kept an eye on the individuals who were considered to have dangerous thoughts; the maximum penalty for criticizing the Emperor was death. Critics of the government were arrested and some had been tortured to death in jail.

46   The rumor started that babies were cured just by being held by Dr. Motoyasu. Soon the reputation of a saintly doctor and a miracle healer spread widely and people from faraway districts came into the village by steam engines to see him, and that made his life unbearably busy. I was one of the babies saved by him, I was told. I became seriously ill and no doctors in Tokyo, including my father, could tell what was wrong with me. I did not eat and I became skinnier and weaker, I looked like I was about to die. My mother took me to my grandfather all the way from Tokyo. As the story goes, a few weeks later when my mother came to see me, I was strong and healthy without having received any particular medical treatment. All my grandfather did was to hold me: every night he put me between himself and my grandmother when they slept, just as many parents used to do in Japan in those days. Although this story must be true, I cannot help thinking that something is missing from it, something that people did not tell me. Without there being any clear connection, I think about the faint, almost invisible scar I have around my left ankle like a ring; I was told that it was caused by the rubber band of the baby socks which my nanny left around my ankle and forgot about for many days or weeks, so that it ate into my flesh as I grew. "You almost lost your left foot," people told me. But didn't anyone hear my cry—a cry like that of a little animal whose ankle is caught in a trap? Something dark must have been happening in my family around that time, and because of that my grandfather held me all night.

47 He worked hard by day and at night he studied medicine to catch up with medical developments in the world. Even though he was far away from Tokyo, and even farther away from the world outside of Japan, his sense of responsibility as a doctor, as a scientist in the modern world, was firm. He never let his reputation as a "miracle doctor" influence him. His quest for scientific truth was still burning in his mind, and that respect for the West which motivated his ancestors to work so hard to translate the Dutch anatomy book was still burning in him.

48 My grandmother ran the household in an orderly and efficient manner. She was in charge of managing the employees who came in considerable numbers at that certain time in her life. Nurses in long, white, Western uniforms were swiftly walking around and handling patients and assisting her husband in the front part of the mansion while in the family quarter, maids and other male and female employees were walking, almost running, and sliding on the shining wood floors with white *tabi*, kimono socks. Many workers were in and out of the mansion to maintain the gardens, to craft and trim the trees, to clean the pond, to cut the bamboo and logs, to sharpen the knives, to dye the fabrics and design the kimonos—an amazing variety of workers. There were always some people who had just lost a husband or needed help for some other reason, and who were staying in the mansion temporarily. My grandmother, dressed sharply in a subdued silk tweed kimono and a narrow *obi*, spent her time sitting upright and making decisions and giving instructions, listening to their complaints, solving their problems, and working hard among these people.

49 In spite of the affluent lifestyle they were enjoying, there was some of the samurai mentality in her which was to remain detached from all luxury, as if she needed to prepare and train herself for the severe life of the battlefield, where one's real life is and where one's real strength is tested. But more than any of those ideas, her sense of mission and her belief that she was doing God's work was here, and this invisible belief made her handle every trivial task, and all of the concerns and troubles which inevitably surfaced every day in such a large household, calmly and decisively. That is what made others feel that there was something very different in her, something they had never quite experienced before.

50   She taught many things to her employees besides housekeeping: their language became clearer; their greetings became more warm and polite; they started writing more intelligent letters, their way of wearing the kimono made them somehow look smarter, their body movements lost their awkwardness and gained some touch of confidence and elegance. My grandmother's personal care and strict discipline were known to people. Having worked in the mansion of the Motoyasu gave them high credentials for future work and for a good marriage. The household seemed like a good and healthy body, well nourished, actively metabolized, fully functioning and growing strong with the fullness of my grandmother's love.

51   In order to catch up with his busy schedule, my grandfather acquired a car, the first car in the village, and he hired a chauffeur who was given one of the little houses in the garden of the mansion to live in. But in order to traverse the narrow country roads, he still had to walk or ride his bicycle on midnight emergency calls. One afternoon he said to one of his patients, "Let me take a little rest, I will be with you shortly," and retired to his room. A little later when my grandmother went into the room to wake him, she found him dead on the *futon*. It was in 1941: he was 52 years old.

CHAPTER 2

1 The Great Japanese Empire spread its wings ever more broadly in the world. It joined World War I as a member of the victorious allies, and it was seated as one of the five great powerful nations at the Versailles Peace Conference in 1919. Japan was the first and only nation of non-whites, and non-Christians, allowed such status. But in the 1920s and '30s, the situation changed drastically. A serious depression struck America and spread over the world. Japan's aggressive tactics of gaining control of markets and resources met with severe reprisals. Economic sanctions were imposed. America, which had provided 70 percent of Japan's oil until then, started to refuse to sell oil to Japan. It also refused all immigration from Japan, and the immigrants who were already there were deprived of some of their educational and financial rights. America demanded that Japan give up its Manchurian Empire entirely. Japan found that it was in complete isolation in the world and had no way out. In 1941, out of desperation, Japan attacked Pearl Harbor—despite the opposition of a small group of rational people who knew that America was a nation of limitless resources against which the war could not succeed. Japan carried out the attack as if it was rolling down a steep slope—unable to stand and unable to control the fall.

2 A storm of fascism swallowed up the whole of Japan. At first, news of victories in the Pacific Islands was reported every day. East Asia had been colonized by America, England, Holland, and France. The Japanese official motto of the war was, "We will release our brother Asians from the oppressive power of the West!" The idea of the "Greater East Asia Co-Prosperity Sphere" seemed to be working, fantastically—the Japanese army was welcomed by enthusiastic Asians as a rescuing army, or so the Japanese media reported. But after only half a year, it all came to an abrupt end as a result of the complete depletion of all the resources—gasoline, food, medicine and everything else the army needed to keep on fighting—was all gone. War seems to be made possible only when the project of concealing the truth from the citizens is carefully managed. No one in Japan knew the truth; the only thing we knew was the glorification of death. The young men who were drafted stood up on the train platforms of their villages to go to the war. The young man who listened in tears while Chopin's Nocturnes, played on a record player—a recording of my grandfather performing the classic in concert—was there too, saying, "I will die bravely for the honor of the Emperor." Everybody, including their mothers, waved flags and screamed "Banzai" ("glory forever") holding both hands up with pride and ecstasy. Japan was rapidly rolling even further down the slope of war.

3 The first son of the Motoyasu, who had just become a doctor, now became the head of the entire family, as the 19th successor of generations of Motoyasu doctors. He had to go to war, too, and the possibility of his coming back from it alive was slim. My grandmother surprised everybody by fighting and winning a severe fight—a very small one, as far as history goes, but personally a significant one. She fought against all the relatives of her late husband and against the whole aristocratic clan of the Shogun who had tried to prepare an arranged marriage for her son. Assuring the succession of the household was their most serious concern and the arrangement of an appropriate marriage was the responsibility of the entire household, so important that the young couple who were to actually marry had to be kept out of the decision-making process.

4 The Christian vows of matrimony, "Do you take this woman to be your lawful, wedded wife…," if those relatives ever heard them, would seem the most ridiculous, offensive idea to them. Who would ask two lambs if they wanted to be sacrificed? It was beyond comprehension. "Marriage shall be based only on the mutual consent of both sexes… " Thus spoke the heavenly voice of the new constitution, which now they are enjoying in Japan, but this came many years later and only after costing the death of three million Japanese.

5 An urgent meeting was set. My grandmother knew that her son was in love with a woman whom he had met at an art exhibition, an exhibition of oil paintings. In that fascistic society, love marriage was considered not only scandalous, but also a dangerous, anti-social, rebellious action—like a crime. Even a married couple, or brothers and sisters, walking together closely on the street, aroused the attention of the police. Falling in love was a fatal mistake.

6 The fascist idea supported the traditional view of marriage in Japan, which is that a man should not bring love into the serious realm of morality, order, and family honor. Love belongs to a different realm where the most elaborate culture of sensuality flourished: it has a different tradition of its own. It was not considered a sin but mixing up the two worlds was a sin. My grandmother, recently widowed and the only woman in the meeting, fought for a marriage between her son and the woman he loved against all the men who had no doubt of their authority over the morality of what the aristocratic man should do. To give any thought to the sensuous world where the honor of the family was concerned was out of the question. The bottom line was that even though they could accept the fact that the woman came from a non-titled family, the fact that she was the kind of woman who went to a Western art exhibition—not flower arrangement or calligraphy, but oil paintings—was totally unacceptable. After a few days of intense meetings, my grandmother won—not by convincing them but rather by making them furious—and anyway, the threat of bombing was too imminent to allow the meeting to continue: they had to go to their own homes to protect their families. They gave up. Her final words were, "I will take the whole responsibility for the consequences of my decision. I will never give you any problem."

7 Her victory was a final emotional separation from the entire household, from the aristocracy, from the world of tradition. Her determination to support her son's love marriage came not only from natural love towards her son as a mother eager to fulfill her son's wish, which very well might be his last, but was also supported by her strong belief in the integrity of love. Her son was in love; for her, love did not belong simply to the realm of sensuality anymore: love was a serious matter in the inner world where one talks to God: honesty, conscience, and integrity all mattered there. She respected her son's love, his inner world: it was precious to her. This frame of reference of the inner world is something she got from Christianity, and this is the thing that was beyond the rest of the family's comprehension.

8 I doubt seriously that she knew how the idea of love between man and woman had been conceived in the long, severe history of Christianity. She might have been surprised to find that her idea of the integrity of love which she had developed through her life as a Christian in Japan might not be exactly what the Western Christian church had in mind. The separation between the world of sensuality and the world of morality with which she did not feel comfortable in traditional Japanese culture is in fact presented in Christianity in a much more severe way than in the Japanese culture.

9 The land of Japan was born form the sexual union of a god and goddess, and that sexual union must continue to be celebrated among us. The two worlds of sensuality and morality were joyfully harmonized for a long time in Shinto. Esoteric Buddhism showed the powerful unity between the two under the Tantra tradition imported from India. Other forms of Buddhism lost some of their severity as they grew in Japan: the strict rule of priestly celibacy was deleted from the rules. The separation came much later, mainly from the feudal sociological need, supported by Confucianism, to keep the household intact. But in Christianity it goes far beyond that: it is a matter of central importance; it is about spirit versus flesh.

10 How difficult it must have been for her to understand the concept of love, or the God of Christianity. Until the Meiji period Japanese did not even have a word for "love", which they use now in the translation of the Bible. The word "love" was created by a committee of the Meiji government as one among many other words such as "justice", "individual", "rights", "society", and simple words like "you", "He", and "she", they created when they struggled to translate works of Western literature that rushed into Japan like a flood. This made-up new word "love", as an official translation for "love" in English, retains some touch of the awkwardness of a made-up word even now—some in Japan might hesitate to use it in a delicate situation. Still, it was a good thing to have because all the other Japanese words used throughout history for the feelings between man and woman had an all-too-strong sexual connotation. That feeling had never been viewed as anything beyond sexual desire, and Japan had never strived to go beyond that, even though its rich variety of poetic vocabulary shows delicate differences of nuance in the realm of desire throughout history. Those historical words for love could not have been used to translate romantic literature that grew out of the conflict between spirit and flesh in Christian culture, which was completely foreign to the Japanese. And needless to say, those words could not have been used to translate the Bible either.

11 All other words for love between parents and children, siblings, friends, teacher and disciple, and so on, had different independent words. And they reflect the strict and complicated hierarchy of status, position, and the degree of closeness between the people involved: lower person to higher person, insider to outsider, or vice versa—they all require different nouns and verbs, just like any other words in the Japanese language. Even the new word for "love" has a tone implying speech from a higher position to a lower position. "I love God" always sounds a little like a contradiction in terms. Simple words like "you", "he", or "she" turned out to be not so simple to use under this strict system of hierarchy. I have never said "you", for example, to my mother, even in a casual question like "What do you think?"

12   But no confusion is bigger than the confusion caused by the translation of "God" itself. After much trial and error, in the early years of the Meiji period it was decided to use the word *"kami"* as the translation of "God" in Western literature. This is the word that Shinto has been using from the beginning of history to refer to all nature itself: we use it for animals, rocks, trees, mountains, and rivers, and for what lies behind all those things, anything that arouses strong feelings of awe in us. Emperors and mythological deities are part of that something. All are called *kami* they are not too distant from people, nor did they create the universe. Using the word *kami* for the Christian "God" brought nothing but chaos into the minds of Japanese. Later on, the word *"Kami"* itself took on a life of its own: rather than reducing the Christian God to the status of the many deities, the word took on the sense of Absolute Authority from Christianity and helped aggrandize the Emperor.

13   And yet, in spite of all this unfathomable confusion, I believe that my grandmother's intuitive insight into Christianity was sharp. She gained the power of individuality from Christianity and that power allowed her to fight against the absolute authority of the feudal system of the household. Christianity reached the concept of the human as a being separated from nature by conquering nature in the human being. By going through a strict, severe ascetic life, humans were able to transcend the mere status of beings in nature; only after that could the individual appear who has his own inner world, who goes beyond tribalism and the tie of blood. If the separation between man and nature were not made, there could be no intrinsic difference between the death of a tree and the death of a human, as is the case in Shinto. There could be no love other than mere sexual desire, no matter how beautifully and elaborately developed that might be. This separation from nature, from blood, is the base of individuality, the place where the integrity of love occurs. My grandmother sensed this in Christianity and assimilated these ideas in her own way.

14 Her aristocratic relatives could not believe what they were seeing: that this well composed, disciplined lady could talk about something so embarrassing and disgusting without seemingly being ashamed of herself. And that made them furious. If she had simply fallen apart out of a mother's love and begged for permission from the depths of shame, and cried for forgiveness for the love marriage of her son, they would have not changed their belief, but they would have tried sweetly to calm her down since she was just a woman.

15 This was the completion of her and her husband's declaration of conversion to Christianity. What came naturally to her, the sense of value beyond tribal tradition, beyond blood and soil, was incomprehensible to others. The sanctity of the aristocracy depends essentially on blood. But behind her quiet manners, they sensed something much bigger and more dangerous than they could comprehend: the concept of individuality, if I may use the contemporary vocabulary here. It was the power to allow her to have her own inner world. Individuality was the strength to allow her to talk to God face to face, the power to make her break the taboos of her own tribal tradition, and the strength to undergo persecution for what she believed. It was the very thing, the very power, which made all the successive Tokugawa Shoguns and the Meiji government so frightened that it drove them to the cruelest persecution of Christians. They sensed the concept of individuality without knowing any of the vocabulary for it and they saw that because of it, Christianity would erode the society composed by feudal authority and Emperor worship, from the inside.

16 The last time she had made such a statement she was with her husband. Now she was alone, and the only person who supported her from the bottom of his heart, her son, was expected to die. In order to stand up for what she really cared for, what she believed in, she had to let the whole system go: the very system which she, a helpless widow, might need for help and support in the most vulnerable, fearful times ahead.

17 The mansion looked grim for the first time on the evening of the wedding party. The largest room in the mansion was lit up with standing lanterns instead of electric lights for this particular occasion: they were lined up every few feet in front of the silk sliding panels which surrounded the room. And in front of those lanterns, small black lacquered tables with four little legs each with gold family crests inlaid were lined up on the *tatami*—one for each guest, each set with sake bottles and many lacquered bowls, and baked fish carefully shaped as if they were alive and springing out of the ocean right this moment, waving their bodies powerfully and their eyes staring at the sky, their fins and tails standing upright on the dish. Only men were invited there except for my grandmother and a few others whom I did not recognize.

They were sitting in front of those tables, according to the strict order of their complicated ranks and ages. All other women and children were served a few rooms away. Between those two rooms the house remained dark, and only maids who were carrying the heavy trays went in and out of the dark. The darkness outside the sliding paper doors of the hall which surrounded the room, and the darkness of all the other rooms in the mansion, made this banquet room look like a stage.

18 The men wore black silk kimonos and kimono jackets over them with big trousers hanging down to their white socks. On each man's back, just below his neck, and on each sleeve front and back, the white family crest was brightly dyed out. Women, too—all the married women—carried their husbands' family crests as an honor on the same places that men did. The difference from the men was that they did not wear trousers or jackets on their kimonos. Instead, subdued and restrained gold and silver, or other soft-colored patterns, were dyed, painted, or embroidered on their black kimonos: for young wives, it was patterns which started from the feet going up and reached to the shoulder; and for older ones, the patterns stayed lower; and for some really old ladies, it was grayish patterns staying below the knees. Only young women not yet married were allowed to be in colorful kimonos, and they were.

19 My mother surprised everyone by appearing in a deep rose-colored kimono instead of a black kimono with patterns. On her back and both sleeves she had a family crest too, but it was the Motoyasu crest, not the crest of my father's family that she was supposed to carry. And what's more, she was wearing one extra family crest of the Motoyasu made of agate in front as an ornament to hold her *obi*. I don't know if this sudden action of breaking tradition shocked and offended all the relatives or whether instead they understood instantly the meaning of her appearance—though it was rather eccentric—that she was celebrating her younger brother's love union and saying farewell to him without words. Being one of the few who knew her brother's intense loathing of the war, she wanted to do both of those things as his only sister, as the only princess of the Motoyasu—not as a representative of her husband's family.

20   Three years old, I walked towards the panel doors which we kept open and stood with half of my body hiding behind them and watched the banquet room from the dark room where all maids shuffled in and out to serve the guests. I was wearing a white silk Western dress with subtle blue embroidery. Because of my mother's dislike of children's kimonos—they are too decorative and vulgar, she said—she had my dress made by a special French designer who happened to be in Japan at the time. It made me feel so out of place among the people who were all in kimonos that I felt like I was a girl who turns the pages of a picture book and the characters in the picture book are unable to see me.

21   The gold *byôbu*, the partitions, stood solemnly and reflected the dull light in the dark at the back of the room where the bride and bridegroom were sitting in silence. According to Japanese custom, they should never smile during their wedding but still this bride looked unusually tense; she cast down her face as if she could not hold the weight of her own black hair, which was mounted high with oil paste. Her painted white neck and white cheekbones and small red lips, which were painted much smaller than her own in order for them to look like a bud rather than flower petals, were barely visible. Her formal kimono, which had the design of an ancient royal carriage and of a crane with wings widely spread, of winding pine trees and waving clouds, and every possible symbol of long life and happiness embroidered with gold and fire-like red thread on black, wrapped her heavily. Her wide gold *obi* wound a few times tightly around her chest and waist almost to the shoulder joint over her undergarment, which was prepared by winding long fabric over and over tightly, like making a mummy, in order to hide her natural womanly curves.

22 When people talked about their love marriage, many years later they still talked with some touch of mystery. "They saw each other at an exhibition of oil painting for the first time. In that peculiar Western art she saw something, and that something drove her wild, something she could not find in any other place; the young man saw it in her flaming eyes and he fell in love with her. They were not the same since then." What kind of oil painting did they see? What was it she saw in a painting to drive her wild? She was a young girl who lost her mother some years before and lived with a strict father who was a school principal. Why on earth did she go to see the peculiar Western oil paintings all by herself in the first place? Was it her loneliness, her craving for love, or her despair and anger that touched her and set her afire? No one knew. With all her secrets inside, she was bound and wrapped with heavy silk, and she was sitting there quietly. Only the delicate, dewdrop-like ornaments hanging from her piled hair were reflecting the light and trembling all through the ceremony, as if they were appealing to the people who were sitting and drinking almost in silence "I am alive here, young warm blood gushing through my veins. I have to breathe."

23 But when it comes to my young uncle's secret, my imagination has a little more solid base. Many decades after that wedding I saw some of his sketches. They were not drawn on paper, they were on canvasses with oil, diluted with a lot of turpentine so the effect was as if they were drawn with watercolors. The canvasses were small pieces not stretched on wood frames, just fabric. And they were in bundles tied together with strings, obviously not created for display. The images on those canvasses showed each stage of the process from naturalistic images to abstract images, showing the serious effort to go inside the deep part of the mind. "Oh, he was going to create abstract painting!" I exclaimed in my heart at that time. It occurs to me that he must have followed the art movement of the 20th century which started in Europe, the biggest revolution in art history, which landed on Japanese shores and survived for only a very short period, for the war closed the gate on Japan's shores, history said. These sketches were nothing like the 17th-century paintings which I thought he created under the Dutch influence some years before, like the one I saw hanging in the dark hallway of the mansion. Abstract art was not the art which sought to describe the world around us any more, it was art looking inward into the depths of our inner world—into our self.

24 Abstract art was born very much from the spirit of introspective art, and it became the leading art of the modern period. In 1937, the year Japan started the war with China, in that same year Picasso hung the huge painting "Guernica" on the wall of the Expo in Paris—the work which was inspired by the destruction of the city of Guernica in the Spanish Civil war. He expressed the terror, the agony, and cruelty of the war with abstractly distorted images; he expressed the misery of the war instead of aggrandizing it; he expressed anger against the war instead of pride and glory. It was a prophetic painting of the doom that was coming. It was one of the first paintings of war presented as misery after countless huge paintings with glorious images of war filled countless museums across the world and throughout history. Two years later, in 1939, the German army invaded Poland and World War II started. This is the year in which I was born.

25 Was my uncle a man who was aware of where he was standing in the course of history? Did he know that his bundle of abstract sketches had its significance? Apart from the question of whether he was recognized or not, he had his place in history. He protested in his mind against the overwhelming current of aggrandizing war and he tried to reach the deeper part of his mind honestly, through art, even though his bundle of sketches was so tiny and no one paid attention to it. European Modern Art artists played the role of bringing people to the top of the volcano, to let them see the magma boiling—flaming in the unfathomable pit of their own world. What did my uncle see in those oil paintings in the exhibition and in his own pit? Did he see his own anger and despair at being forced to be killed by an irrational power? Love for that young girl had made his anger and despair even more intolerable. Love, despair and anger—those were the very emotions strictly forbidden and deeply repressed by Japanese government. He should certainly keep them secret.

26 The way of the bridegroom's sitting was correct. His back was straight and the way he folded his knees in the thin-striped kimono trousers showed a perfect mastery of the tea ceremony: the fingers of both his hands were stretched together and placed outside of his knees so that his arms hung down in a most manly way. He was tense and yet, in the way that only a man who was used to many ceremonies and knew exactly what was expected can be, he was elegant. This was the "coronation" which he had prepared for all his life, and which now had finally come, to act as the head of the family for the first time, and at the same time he knew this might be his last time to be with his family. One of the guests proceeded towards him by sliding with his knees kept folded and poured sake onto his lacquer place. He received it with both his hands, politely bowed, and drank. He was calm and dignified, as the joy of being united with his loved one and the thought of his impending death flamed in his heart.

27   A spectacular flower arrangement was placed behind them, so that people could see it between the bride and bridegroom. The gnarled trunk of an old pine tree was winding upward, powerfully twisted by age, but the young branch stretching out its arm had fresh young green pine needles pointing towards Heaven. It was arranged in the bronze vase at its base by the bridegroom himself. He did not do it for his wedding party decoration; so many people in the Motoyasu mansion had excellent flower-arranging skills and would have done it for him proudly if that was the purpose. He did it for the purpose which is the same as the reason that the flower arrangement was born out of its origins in an ancient mythological age, at the dawn of Shinto: to create a pole through which god can descend. He was the only one in the mansion of the Motoyasu who had a special talent to invoke this power of art, by which he could conjure up the power of the universe and condense it into a timeless space and participate in the process that went on in that space: the process of a branch of a tree transforming itself into the sacred pole that god will descend through. God should come down to the mansion of Motoyasu while he is away. It was his prayer, and it did not contradict in his mind at all the prayer to the foreign God he had offered in the wedding ceremony performed earlier that day in the chapel, in the room where the half-naked man was hanging, by that mysterious priest I had seen often in the mansion with only my grandmother as a witness.

28 "This wedding is a funeral" was on everybody's mind. It was a funeral: a funeral for the glory of the aristocratic world, and a funeral for the relationship between my grandmother and the other relatives. Now that she had stood up once for her love, for her faith, she was not afraid of anyone there anymore. She was the one who could see the two worlds where they stood clearly, and she could see the depth of the gap between them, but they could not. She felt strong; she would protect this young daughter-in-law from the dark forces of the aristocratic family, from tradition, and from other darkness if it should fall on her. Everyone there was filled with unspoken emotions: indignation, reproach, hurt, remorse, and strong fear of the future. My father, who had lost his parents at an early age, strongly believed that for a man who is expected to die to marry, only to make the woman a widow and to produce a fatherless child, was the most irresponsible act a man could carry out. He refused to be a part of any justification of it, and he was not there.

29 Every funeral is the birth of a new life: something completely different was about to be born. But it seemed like it was taking a long time to unfold. We all had to go through something tremendously frightening before that, something which none of us, nor our ancestors in the 2,000 years of Japanese history, had experienced. My family was going to the countryside to escape from the bombing: after this wedding party we might not see anybody who was here ever again.

30   The song of the wedding celebration started; the men in the banquet room changed the position of their knees from tightly folded to the more relaxing pose of the lotus position. A man's low voice slowly started singing. "May the couple live a long life together until their hair turns white just like the snow which covers Mt. Fuji" resounded through the rooms, and the sharp high sounds of a small drum echoed throughout the rooms. It was as if it was hitting and penetrating the thick wall which stood between the world of the living and the world of the dead. Suddenly, the whole scene made sense. This room was the space where the living and the dead meet. Just like the theater of the Noh play, where the dead quietly tell the story of their remorse, their love never fulfilled in the world of the living, and the living, wearing masks, respond by telling their own story of lost love. Their dance together is slow and quiet, their movements are tense and sometimes not even visible to the audience, and yet their deep, stormy emotions reach out to them. So this banquet room was the stage of a Noh play in which the samurai who had lived close to death were the players and which they offered to god since hundreds of years before the Edo period. The bride's white-painted face was a mask, not expressive. Only slight changes of angle revealed the depth of her passion. The bride's and bridegroom's restricted movements showed that they were already inhabitants of this timeless space. As the music continued, all the ancestors of the Motoyasu family rose up from the ground and walked on this stage to attend the last wedding of the glorious family. I was a weird little thing, trembling and sobbing, clinging to my mother in her deep-rose-colored kimono, covering half of my face with its cold smooth silk sleeve, murmuring, "Ghosts are in this room there and in that dark corner over there." Being scolded by her to behave, my fear was intensified.

31   Two months after the wedding, my young uncle was sent to the jungles in the Philippines as an army doctor. He was sent without any medicine or medical equipment: the army could not afford them anymore. It took me some time to realize that what he was expected to do there was not to treat the suffering—which he had prepared to do all his life and for which he had become a doctor—but to give them grenades so they could commit suicide when their injuries were so severe that they could not fight anymore, to avoid the humiliation of becoming war prisoners in the enemy's hands. No one knows if he ever received the letter about his wife's pregnancy. When his baby boy was born, we were already notified that his army troop was completely destroyed; they called it the "Shattered Jewel."

32   The three Korean doctors whom my grandparents supported died in Korea one after another some time ago—all of them, including the one who made a boat for me, from tuberculosis. Everything my grandfather cared for seemed washed away. The mansion was selected as an evacuation center by the military. The big room that housed the masterpiece was filled with people and their feet poked through the masterpiece, and they pasted old newspapers on the artwork in order to prevent drafts coming through. Soon the masterpiece was completely covered with old newspapers. Cement was poured into the pond so that more people could train more efficiently to relay buckets of water to extinguish the fires of incendiary bombs that were often dropped, and for training in bamboo spearing—in case the enemy came to the land, every woman and child was instructed to poke them with a spear before committing suicide to avoid humiliation. The documents on the Secret Christians which my grandfather collected disappeared in that confusion without any book being produced from them. No one seemed to care.

33 The young bride, who was now the young widow destined to serve her mother-in-law for the rest of her life, left the mansion. My grandmother did not know her young daughter-in-law's decision not to come back when she gently put her baby in her mother-in-law's arms and went out. The succession of the household belonged to the husband's family. A letter arrived from the father of her daughter-in-law, the school principal, written politely with *sumi* ink and brush: "Deeply apologize" and "begging your forgiveness" for my shameful daughter's not fulfilling the obligations of a daughter-in-law, and "the kindness you showed my daughter will never be forgotten." This letter made clear without saying so specifically that it was all over. Perhaps she would have a new life. It might be the case that her son would never be able to see his mother again. He would never have any direct memory of his father nor of his mother throughout his life. The time had already come that grandmother's words, "she would take full responsibility for the consequences, I will never give you a burden," were starting to be realized when her son's death became a reality, and now reality became even more severe. She would raise her grandson, a newborn baby, by herself in the decayed mansion. All the nurses, maids, and the chauffeur had left—all the men to the army, the younger women to the military factories and the other women to heavy labors to meet their quotas in the rice fields while taking care of their children and the elderly in the houses the men had left.

34   The money her husband had left her rapidly lost its value and became literally trash during the war. Because everybody knew without illusion, in crises like that, that a bottle of milk is far more precious than lacquer boxes inlaid with mother-of-pearl, and that a silk-embroidered kimono is a far inferior material to washed-out cotton for baby's diapers, bartering was difficult.

35   She sat many long nights in the bomb shelter which the neighbors and former patients came and dug for her. It was a small hole underground; she crawled into it with the baby in her arms. No lights, no heaters were allowed, only the little square cut-out entrance which she crawled into framed the night sky. Illumination bombs flushed the entire sky in bright blue, and grenades fell and exploded somewhere far away, and the big black roofs of the Mansion of Motoyasu looked as if they were slanting and sliding towards her at a strange angle in the square patch of sky which had just returned to darkness.

CHAPTER 3

1 Our family escaped from Tokyo to another city where my father's elder brother owned a hospital and practiced. He kept his office open but the sick wards were all empty due to a lack of young doctors. We rented some of the rooms upstairs and downstairs at the end of the long building to live in. A long hallway ran through the hospital: on one side were many doors to the sick wards; the other side of the hallway was a wall covered with windows. But pieces of paper were glued on every window to prevent fragments of glass from scattering in case of an explosion. The hallway was dark and eerie. A skinny man with a small head whose shape reminded me of a light bulb often stood at the end of the hallway. I knew that he did not belong to this world: he must have been a patient in one of these wards who died here—I somehow knew it. I never mentioned him to anyone; I knew he wanted to be left alone and I did not want to be bothered by having to explain him to others. Besides, he did not scare me at all. My mother had a piano placed at the end of that long hallway. It was during this time that my mother started teaching piano seriously to my two sisters. As for me, I could not be away from crayon and paper: when she pulled me to the piano I started drawing on the keyboard, so my mother gave up and left me alone.

2 There was one place I was scared of in our new residence. It was the upstairs toilet. For some reason it was the only toilet that our family of five had to use. From the porcelain bowl on the floor (the Japanese traditional toilet was basically a hole in the floor decorated with a porcelain bowl), a long iron pipe about seven inches in diameter stretched from the second story to the ground and even farther underground. The inner wall of that pipe was visible: darkened, dirty, dimly shining with all mixed colors almost all the way down, then beyond that, complete darkness. "This is the crack, the beginning of the long passage to the underground world," I thought. "Probably I will never fall in–it is small enough, unless I were sucked into it by the power of some vacuum." When I look back at my memory of this pipe, I could say immediately that it was a symbol of the passage to the unconscious world and that I was afraid of the unconscious, and it is true that I could talk about that forever. But at the same time, I was thinking about the real underground. I was aware that there is such a thing, an underground world right beneath our feet—and not only as a metaphor for the unconscious world. It must exist very clearly and strongly in this physical world. Where else would the bodies of people who were killed in the shelters in the underground go after the huge bombings? Where would the things like family pictures which people bury to shelter them from the bombings go after the people had died! Are there any people who secretly live underground to avoid the whole bombing? Were they living together secretly? Are there any passages to those worlds? Is this iron pipe which we are using every day one of them?

3 Darkness, fear, misery, and worries crept into our lives and quickly they took over our entire life. We lived in darkness because we draped black cloth over the small lights in our rooms in order not to let any light leak out lest the enemy find us as a target, for we knew that one single light all by itself could wipe out the entire town. We lived in fear because bomb attacks became frequent: in the middle of the night we were often awakened by my parents and told to put on the jackets on which our names, address, and blood types were written in big black letters; then we entered the bomb shelter which my father had dug in the yard in compliance with the government's instructions. It was a damp, smelly, tunnel-like hole under the ground into which we had to crawl one by one. We spent many nights sitting tightly together in the dark—with no lights, nor water—waiting for the sound of the B-29 bombers to fade away. And it was miserable because we were hungry, cold, and tired. And I was in constant worry that when the time came, my father would carry my young sister on his back, because she was still a baby, and my older sister would hold my mother's hand and run, because she was alert and strong, but I would be left alone because I would not be quick or strong, and I would be lost in the crowd of people running away in all directions screaming and crying in the dark night, in fire and smoke.

4 There were neighbors' groups organized by the government: about six families to each group. Through these groups, information flowed quickly and efficiently: messages could be sent from one end of the network to the other very fast, and through these networks the government could receive any information about its citizens that it wanted. We were thus part of a strict spy network with our neighbors. We helped each other by checking on every detail of each other's lives and by passing on every bit of information: how tightly we blocked the windows with black cloth to prevent light leaks, how we distributed the small amount of food the government allocated to each family according to each member's age. At the same time, different kinds of information spread quickly but secretly: why was her hair not jet-black and straight as all pure Japanese are supposed to be? Why did her clothes retain some beautiful color when we were instructed to throw away all luxury from our lives in order to serve the Emperor full-heartedly? We paid attention to every detail of our own lives to avoid arousing suspicion. To look "different" or behave differently was the most dangerous thing: anyone with a different appearance or different behavior was viewed as a "non-citizen"—but because being a citizen in Japan had traditionally meant being the Emperor's retainer, to be a non-citizen was to be accused as a betrayer of the Emperor— and anything could happen to you then.

5 I had secret treasures. They were cards, bunches of paper carefully cut into the size of the credit cards we have today. I divided each rectangle of paper into four sections like a window and each section I colored different colors. I worked on them all the time; I carried these cards with me into the bomb shelter. Paper was scarce so they had to be portable. And crayons were scarce, too, though I figured out how to mix three crayons, which were all I had, to make limitless tones. But if I used those up I would probably never get another crayon in my whole life, so I thought that cutting paper into this size was a brilliant solution. It was many years later, of course, that I learned that the four part images are an important symbol of integration in the mind. Religious art such as mandalas repeatedly show the division of the pictorial space into four sections and provide an object of contemplation to help the viewer reach the integration of his mind. The image of four comes when one's soul has something hard to take in: it comes to you often by your own creation, without your knowing or contemplating the images of other art; it is a help to all who suffer. It was much later that I found that Jung wrote about it. I was tremendously busy every minute of my life to create four-sectioned art, if I can call it art, to hold myself together as one unit in the midst of that insane world.

6 When the bombs fell in the town, my father would go out to treat the injured, riding in the truck that the town sent to pick him up. During those long nights, my mother and her three daughters would often sit huddled in the near darkness, the small lights covered with cloth. Then my mother often played the phonograph at its lowest volume. "I want you to know the most beautiful thing that mankind has ever produced before you end your short lives." She wound the handle of the phonograph slowly and turned the records over, and changed the records continuously to play all that were in the thick album with the dark green cover with an embossed European decorative pattern, and which contained so many LP records for just one piece of music. She carried this extremely heavy album on her back in the crowded train when we moved to this city in order to escape the bombs – instead of carrying potatoes or rice like everyone else was doing. It was Beethoven's *Ninth Symphony*.

7 We could not afford to turn the volume up to a proper level because we were afraid the sound might leak outside. Western music was prohibited and neighbors were obligated to be government spies against each other. So it was like listening to a whisper coming from a faraway world. I remember listening to the words "to joy—*an die Freude*" repeated over and over in chorus as the sounds of bombs exploded outside. I listened to each note with the utmost concentration, following the beautiful linear curve of the string lines, the frightening sound of the drums. It seemed almost comical in the beginning, but suddenly the music welled up as from the bottom of the world and erupted like lava from a volcano, the demonic rhythms pulsing through to the final chorus. I saw a complicated architecture—now I see it as a cathedral, but I don't know if I had ever seen even a picture of a cathedral then—but I saw myself inside it and I saw layers upon layers of structure within structure and I touched the texture of every intricacy of detail in that building. The music itself existed exactly as a form of architecture. My mother said that we should all experience this before we die. But I was looking up at the domed and vaulted ceiling and I heard different words, "You should all construct your own architecture, a cathedral such as this, for that is what mankind has been put on earth to do." I felt there was something I had to do if I survived, something I came here for, and it must be something intensely serious and frightening.

8 When I listen to this piece now I wonder, why did my mother choose this as the final piece? This music strikes me as more difficult the older I grow. I cannot identify with the emotion of this piece. I cannot let my feelings go deeply and fully into this piece. It seems that the music itself refuses that very sort of desire in the listener. From the beginning of the first movement, a subtle and serene string melody suddenly, almost out of place, tries to merge into the main current of the movement which has already started: was I exposed to such profoundly complicated phrases at such an early time of my life? I am always aghast—but as if this melody were some sort of dangerous temptation, how quickly the strings are quieted down. They try again and again, but they don't succeed in coming in; they were not invited there to become part of the structure of the whole piece yet. Many other themes and phrases, one after another, try to do the same throughout the three movements before the final choral movement is reached—and yet how quickly, how definitely, sometimes how violently they are interrupted, broken, fragmented, or cut abruptly. It is only a long emotional preparation, you might say, for the final movement where all the tenacious attempts are carried through and finally transcend and join in a miraculous expression of joy. But still the cynicism, the self-doubt, the ambivalence, the prohibition against self-complacency never disappear: they are essential. Even while the most joyful final melody of the last part of this piece is sung by the chorus, the exact same melody of that joy is rolling at a faster speed, and a demonic rhythm, underneath it.

9   There should be a visual artwork in the 20th century, at the dawn of the 21st century, which I always imagine, that is like this piece. I have almost seen such a work: a huge work made of collage each part of which refuses to continue and be developed into a coherent integrated part of the image. Breaking is everywhere: not only is the flow of images broken, but also the canvas itself is torn in the middle as part of the work. There is profound and fundamental doubt, the destruction of the stage itself in the middle of the play as part of the script. But this work too reaches a final resolution, a sublime resolution. Only the meaning of *resolution* is far different from what the masters of the past ever dreamed of.

10 Once, much later on, my mother said to me that if you listen to Beethoven you don't have to go to church. I knew that she was talking about the transcendence—the transcendence through art, which is the theme of the Ninth Symphony and that is exactly what she believed in. She did not intend to die in an ecstasy which would blind her mind by losing herself in glorious music, she wanted to accept her life and death as a joy, no matter how dark and miserable they both looked at that time, and she wanted to reach a state of mind that would allow her to accept them as they were, a joy. For her, music was the only thing that showed a possible way to that place.

11 I sometimes think how very different this piece is from the others, for example from the St. Matthew Passion by Bach. That piece, without cynicism, allows the listener to go in deeply, to identify with its emotion, and even to be intoxicated with God. Bach's resolution did not come out of original struggle and conflict that had to be resolved: polarization of the mind is not an antecedent of his resolution. For Bach, resolution is something to receive from Heaven as bliss, not something to struggle for and reach as in Beethoven's case. I sometimes think that if my mother had chosen the St. Matthew Passion instead of the Ninth Symphony for her final piece, if she were the kind of person who did that, she would have been much happier.

12 Death passed by. My father came back. I sometimes awoke hearing my parents talking to each other in low voices: "I just stitched back two arms that were blown from her little body," my father was saying to my mother. "Her mother could not see that her daughter was already dead, she kept asking me, 'Please stitch them back so that she will be all right.' I stitched them back, and I told her that now she is perfect, and with this perfect figure she can go to the Pure Land. The Mother suddenly realized what I meant, and bowing towards me with deep gratitude she left with her daughter in her arms." Did I really overhear this story? I often wondered because I know that as soon as he jumped on the truck the city sent for him to take him to the burning town he was plunged into chaos. Distinguishing the injured who still could survive from those for whom there was no hope or who were already dead was itself hard work: everything had to be decided in a split second, and medical equipment and materials were extremely scarce. Compared to a scene like that, this story of the little girl and her mother had an out-of-this-world quality: time was stopped, it had the somewhat quiet tone of a Buddhist parable. But it is possible that when he arrived, everybody in the town was already dead and there was nothing he could do, and a woman who had escaped death appeared and they had an encounter in a moment of eternity–a moment when there was a crack in this world and eternity gushed in. "He saw his own children in that dead girl," people would say; and for myself, just four years old, this dead girl was me. Death went through my whole body as I lay my body on the *futon* holding my breath in the room next to my parents'. But most of the time, my father would come back plunged in the deep silence known only to the person who has seen horrendous pain and cruelty and who has fully experienced his own powerlessness to prevent it.

13 Suddenly epidemics spread in the town. As if the worst part of the violence had not yet unfolded, this new violence was finally unleashed. Families were separated into the group not touched by the epidemic and the group which had to be quarantined. My two sisters fell ill. My father was in a faraway place as an army doctor at that time. My mother stayed to take care of her two daughters under strict quarantine in our own home, which ironically was once a sick room of the hospital. There was no one else in the big hospital except at the far end of the building where my uncle, who owned the hospital, lived with his wife. He came to visit our quarters to examine the sick and decided that because I was the only child not contaminated, I should be sent to his living quarters and that my mother should stay with my two sisters until the epidemic subsided—and no one knew how long that would be.

14   One of my uncle's nurses, whom I had never met, led me to my uncle's residence one day through the long corridor of the empty hospital. It was dark, the building being under strict regulation of light. A strong smell of creosol was soaked into the walls and floor—that smell that was so much a part of my life. In the mansion of the Motoyasu, when I noticed this smell I always knew that I had gotten lost in the big mansion somewhere in my grandfather's office area. And my family house always had this smell: when my father was wearing a white doctor's smock, we were prohibited to touch him because dangerous germs were on it, we were told, and his smock had this strong odor. But now it definitely felt like it was the smell of death. "I will never see my mother again," I feared. My whole body was almost exploding with fear. "When we die, we all die together, so there is nothing to be afraid of," our mother would whisper every time the sounds of the bombings thundered loud over the shelter while embracing the three of us. It was a strange sweet moment. Now it became different: we each had to die alone without knowing what happened to the others.

15 When I stepped into my uncle's living room, a quiet Japanese-style room, he was lying down on the *tatami* on his stomach and his wife, my aunt, was massaging his back, but her left hand was on her own stomach pressing hard and only her right hand was on his back massaging. I realized she was in enormous pain and yet she was continuing to massage her husband, her whole body bent over and her face distorted with pain and sweat. The moment she realized that I had come in she took her right hand away from her husband, and put her index finger on her lips begging me to keep silent. I left the room quietly. I did not know if she was saying to me not to come in to see him because he was not in the mood for it, or simply not to tell him that she was in pain. I saw my aunt had a sweet face, though she was in pain and desperate. The early-old-age couple's household was quiet. My uncle was in charge of everything in the community: he was powerful and strict in strengthening the network of spies. People were afraid of him—his wife, his nurses, and his patients—and they seemed to handle their fear by being full of secrets and lies. He seldom talked to me, but on some occasions when I had to answer him, I saw my aunt's concerned face watching me and hoping that this little girl would not say anything to upset him.

16   One day my aunt took me to a small storeroom and took out a wooden box from the high shelf. "Try these on," she said. They were the most beautiful wooden sandals I ever saw: enameled red, and on the place hidden under the soles were painted pink flowers. "These are festival sandals!" I whispered. When girls reached the age of seven they dressed up in kimonos and went to the shrine to show their gratefulness to the gods. These sandals were for that occasion. "My daughter, your cousin, wore them many, many years ago for the festival—you are right, but now I will give them to you." I hadn't seen any colorful thing like these for a long time. They fit me perfectly. The only thing I wanted to do with them was to go to see my mother to show her how I looked wearing them. "Oh she would be so thrilled and pleased. She likes beautiful things: she was a princess herself, a real princess." Of course the door to the hospital corridor was closed: no one could go into the quarantine area, but I exclaimed in my mind, I can go near there through an outside route—between the fences, beyond the bushes, the path that only children knew about—I would go that way. Suddenly I felt strong—the many days of dark depression seemed to be over. "But you know that you cannot let anyone see you wearing them, they will put you into real trouble. You know all about it, don't you?" she lowered her voice. "Yes, of course I know, Aunty, don't worry," I replied. I knew she was referring to the network of neighbors spying on each other, which was not a small matter at all, and I knew that wearing luxurious clothes was considered a betrayal of the Emperor, who prohibited all luxury during such a serious war. Even a little child could be humiliated, tortured, and excommunicated as a traitor in the schools, or even put into jail and tortured. I had heard many terrifying stories. But my mother was not 'anyone': I wouldn't show myself to anyone else, and I knew the secret way to her place. "No one will see me," I told myself.

17   I flew out like a bird wearing the red sandals, these sandals made of special fancy wood. The wood has an amazing effect on how the sandals work: they were light and fit my feet perfectly, and above all they had some kind of special slightly bouncing, springing quality. It

was like flying. I ran between fences over bushes and crawled through the cracks of broken walls, all secret pathways no one knew, and I found myself standing just under the second-story window where we lived, and my mother was taking care of my two sisters. I stood there looking up, not knowing what to do to let my mother know that I was here: the window was closed and paper was pasted over it. Suddenly the windows opened and my mother appeared like a miracle. Our eyes met, but she did not smile. That moment the idea hit me that she might be crying. That was when I burst out crying, though we did not say anything to each other. Come to think of it, it was only the second floor, so it was easy to carry on a short conversation between a person sticking her head through the upstairs windows and a person standing on the ground looking up. Why did we not speak? Some huge sense of secrecy, darkness, some sense of terrifying restriction, some prohibition overtook us. My mother seemed to look back only halfway over her shoulder, as if someone had said something behind her. She was hiding the fact that I came to visit her. She closed the window, I stood there a little while, then I turned and walked back. I was sobbing all the way to my uncle's residence missing my mother. But probably more than that I felt some heavy darkness like a spear thrust into my chest. That evening, I started imagining that someone might have seen that I was wearing red sandals. "Didn't you see a little girl with red sandals flying over the bushes like a bird?" This chant was repeated in my dreams all that night. I felt like a traitor.

18   I came into my uncle's living room the next day. There, I confronted right in my face a hen hanging upside down from an exquisitely carved beam. The hen's head had been chopped off, blood was dripping into a bucket carefully placed on the straw mat below. Splashed with blood, her white feathers still looked warm and trembling. The wings opened in the air without any strength. The bird had been executed, punished by my uncle just because she enjoyed her freedom, she enjoyed flying. She deserved to be executed not because she had done something wrong but because of what she was. She was enjoying what she was. This is what people kept telling me ever since I can remember: "Don't enjoy your life, don't be yourself, don't be free, don't let anyone see you are wearing red sandals, or you will be executed." I was surrounded by a dark heavy cloud all the time: this is what people were warning me about, I realized. Of course I did not know the word "fascism" at such a young age, but the essence of fascism—hating freedom, hating one who is himself, hating life itself— I understood more than I could have from any book I might read. The bird was dead, and that bird was me, wearing the red sandals and flying. This is the first time I really confronted my own death. People tried so hard to run away from death: every night being awakened, putting on jackets and running to the cold smelly ditch, everybody lowering their voices, "So-and-so died"; women sobbing in the corner of our kitchen, huge dark clouds constantly running after us day and night. Our whole life as far as I remember was nothing but effort after effort to run away from it. That is death and that is war. This bird's killing did not happen in the butcher's shop as it might have on some other occasion: it happened in my uncle's living room. Now for the first time, I saw the clear picture. How soft the white feathers looked, how easy to be killed, one slash of the knife and she died. The vulnerability of life shook me deeply.

19 Something extraordinary happened that day. Imagine you have innocently walked into some empty theater: it is a stage with heavy curtains closed in front of you, and behind the curtain, everything is carefully planned to disclose each scene, one after the other, according to a carefully constructed scenario. But suddenly for some peculiar reason the curtain was slashed and dropped on the floor and a strange scene that was supposed to appear much later is suddenly there: a final scene appearing unexpectedly out of sequence. Everything was exposed out of order, and once it appeared there was no way to hide it any more. War, fascism, cruel death—things you should be forced to face only gradually—are right in front of you. Things you should only encounter after you grow up when all your faculties are ready to handle it—probably only after decades—exposed themselves suddenly. I saw the essence of these things appearing not as they were supposed to be: the bird was *executed* because she loved freedom, because she was herself. Fascism will torture and execute you if you reveal your real self. My uncle's room was not a beautiful room as it seemed before—instead it was a torture chamber and an execution chamber under strong stage lights in the empty theater. And it is true that the living room of my uncle was full of lies and secrets, because that is the only way to survive if you live under fascism. I saw through it. I was forced to figure out the whole meaning of it in a flash: things far too difficult and heavy for a 4-year-old to figure out. But I did, I figured it out amazingly sharp relief. And an intense phobia started in me that day and lingered: a phobia of birds. I could not see birds in any form. It took me five decades to recover from it. I had lost my childhood innocence. The camouflage was taken away from me. Childhood was gone. And yet at some level I continued to live the child's life as if I were pretending to be a child, but I felt always at some deeper level that I was seeing a hidden reality underneath.

20 The epidemic was over. Many died but not my sisters. Our father came back home from the army medical mission in the faraway city, seriously sick. At first the enemy's air attacks had targeted soldiers and military facilities, but the enemy changed its strategy and began random bombings of major cities where only women and children and the elderly remained. Besides the bombings in which many victims were instantly killed, more than two hundred thousand incendiary bombs were dropped like rain in the city overnight: fire formed gigantic waves, the city became an ocean of flame, and it swallowed people up. People who tried to run away saw huge pillars of fire standing up to the sky preventing them from running in whatever direction they faced. Under extreme heat, people jumped into the concrete containers filled with water which each house had prepared for an occasion like this, for bucket relays to put out fires. But fire wrapped the containers, the water boiled instantly, and boiled dead bodies, swollen, spilled onto the ground. Hundreds of thousands of people lost their lives overnight. One by one, major cities were bombed and the death toll piled up to a million. With only some exceptions, all of them were women, children, and the elderly. Responding to these devastating tactics, the Japanese government announced that it would send its own airplanes to plunge into enemy airplanes: they carried gasoline only for attacking and never carried any for returning. They were called kamikaze pilots: *kami* means God and *kaze* means wind. This word came from an incident of 1274, the only time Japan was ever attacked in her history, when unexpected winds sunk the 900 fighting boats of Genghis Khan. In addition to this response, the government also decided that all children past the fourth grade in school had to be separated from their families, isolated from the environment, and sent out to the remote places, the backwaters, where no enemy could reach them, with young schoolteachers, in order to keep future soldiers, future heroes, intact. But whatever the government said, the groups of children, age nine and older, torn away from their families in this most frightening time, looked like nothing but sacrificial offerings to evil, insane hero worship.

21 My mother made a one-day trip to the village in the countryside in a further district, by getting permission and a ticket from the military office. By that time, trains were scarce and extremely crowded and passengers were required to have a convincing reason to get a ticket. My mother wanted to find another place for our family to escape to, so leaving her sick husband and three children behind, she went out. On the way back home, when her train was approaching the station, an air alert siren sounded which indicated that enemy bombers were approaching. The moment the train arrived at the station, a group of military police with pistols in their hands led all the passengers— hundreds of them—down to the station's huge underground shelter. It was dimly lit, constructed with concrete walls and floor, and two doors in front and back. Another group of military police stood there with rifles, making it clear that any disorderly act would be met with gunshots to avoid triggering a mob uprising. Hundreds people were ordered to sit down on the concrete floor to make it easier for the military police to control the mobs. My mother instantly saw this was the worst place to be and thought, *I have to run away from this place.*

She found that the back door was locked and she tried to see how she could reach the front door by getting through the crowds sitting tightly on the concrete floor. She watched the police officers' eye movements intently. Suddenly she heard a young girl next to her whispering in her ear, "If you are thinking about running away from this place, please take me with you—give me a sign." – "Now!" mother whispered. At the same time, both stood up and dashed to the front door and up the steps to the street. Sharp, alarmed voices and the outcries of the military guards echoed but she knew they would not follow them as soon as they got outside, because outside the shelter was not the territory for which they were responsible. Now she saw another group of military police standing outside with rifles pointed at them. They ran. Voices and gunshots followed but they kept running. Here and there in the empty town, military police were standing: they believed that any movement would attract the enemy's attention and if it was people who moved they had to be killed. But my mother and the young girl did not stop, they kept running, as gunshots and the sounds of bombing followed them. Then the girl said with a clear but sweet voice to my mother, "I will turn right here, my house is on this street. Thank you very much for taking me with you!" My mother replied, out of breath and without even looking back at her, "Good luck." She kept running alone to our home, to our shelter, where a sick father and three daughters were crying with worry. "I was an excellent runner and won a prize for it in the girls' school so I knew I could go through it," she said with a smile.

22 The next morning the newspaper reported that the underground shelter of the biggest station in our district was bombed and there were no survivors. The newspaper reports of bad news, however, were kept as brief as possible to keep the citizens' fears at a minimum. "I was thinking about yesterday's incident over and over last night," my mother said. "The little girl thanked me very politely, but I was the person who had to say thank you to her. If I had run by myself, it certainly would have looked as though a hysterical woman who became panicked had jumped out and was running, and it would have made the military police think they had to control me, otherwise a hysterical reaction would spread. But a mother and daughter—we looked like that I am sure—was a little different. And she looked very composed: even though loud men's terrifying voices threatened us with guns many times, she never cried nor panicked. She ran very fast, she ran alongside me, just a little bit behind me and a little to my left, so I did not have to look back to make sure she was with me. All through it she was keeping the same distance, the same speed. It looked like a loyal daughter following her mother, the way her mother told her to do. It must have made the police hesitate for a second, to kill one of us or both of us. I can see now that she was a help for me. Even her steady, composed running might have helped me to keep myself calm, come to think of it. Yet I don't even know her name. I never saw her face. I heard her whisper in the dim shelter and after that she ran right behind me. I thought she might be on her way home from factory work. Just recently I heard the girls' age limit for factory work was lowered from fourteen years old to twelve and older. She might be one of that extended group."

23   Our escape from there to a faraway country village was done rather quickly as we were overcome by the urge to escape. Hurriedly we took only a few belongings with us. A few weeks later my mother went back to get the things we had left behind. She got off at the station, half destroyed but still barely functioning, and walked towards the hospital where we had lived. It was a burnt field. She walked to the spot she thought was the place where the girl had said, "I will turn right here, my house is on this street," and no houses were there, no person was there, only dark ashes covering the bare field. She walked in the direction where she thought our house was. She could not find even the ruins of the hospital. Suddenly she saw near her feet piano wires, twisted and tangled on the burnt field like arteries and veins cut from wounded flesh, and exposed, indicating the place where we used to live. When she looked inside our bomb shelter she found our neighbors sitting there instead of us, sitting just like we used to. They were like statues made of ashes, every one of them completely as they were, some with babies in their arms and recognizable without mistake. They kept their shapes until the first breeze would blow them away.

CHAPTER 4

1 In the country, the whole bamboo forest was buzzing with swarms of black mosquitoes near where the farmer from whom we rented his guestrooms lived. In a district where we knew no one, in a village we had never heard of, my mother found a farmer whose house had a rather big gate which had a black-tiled roof of its own. She knew that this kind of roof was allowed only to the first son of the original family who had inherited the household: they were usually well-to-do and had extra rooms and occupied a position of some responsibility to take care of the community. So she went inside and asked if she could rent rooms for our family. The moment she mentioned that her husband was a doctor, they instantly decided to accept us as tenants. There were no doctors in that village, and they desperately needed one. There were two rooms with *tatami* and one toilet, but no kitchen, no bath, no running water. But they said they would allow us to cook outside and use their wells, and once a week they allowed us to use their family bath. The little path to the farmer's house, along the edge of the bamboo forest, was dark and cold even in the middle of the brightest day. My straw sandals became moist and cold to my soles when I came to that spot. I often ran along that path to the gate of the farmer's house. In the middle of their front yard, straw mats were spread out and many kinds of grain were set out on them to dry. The square yard was trimmed with bright red cannas flowers, and the pigs in the nearby sty were always making squeaking sounds.

2 When you walked along a little path near the back of the house, through the small woods, suddenly you saw a great rice field which spread to the sky. On the surface of the swamp-like deep soil, clear water reflected the sky with a dull light. The green rice plants were planted by the farmers by hand as they stood in the water with bare feet, bending over to put their fingers in the swamp to plant them one by one. Slowly walking backwards with their backs always bent, they would plant the rice at exact intervals with amazing geometric accuracy. The field was divided into many sections by bridge-like paths so narrow that barely anyone could walk along them, and small edamame beans were planted on either side of these bridges so as not to waste even an inch of land. The water was perfectly clean: there were no yellowed or dried leaves, no weeds anywhere to be seen. The thousands of young green rice plants were standing upright with the translucent edges of their blades pointing straight to Heaven. The rice field is a sacred place: it had been sacred since the beginning of human history and nature's god had delegated the work of planting and harvesting the rice to human farmers. It was a sacred entrustment and as long as we keep it sacred, Japan will remain god's own country. The farmers in the village worked hard to keep the rice field beautiful even as the hard-working young men among them were taken away to the army.

3 There was a square hole made of concrete just outside the front door—three feet by three feet, just as some houses might have a little pond filled with koi fish. But this hole was there for a completely different purpose: it was filled with human excreta. All the family members—men, women, young, and old—used this hole as a toilet. It had no partition around it, no lid to cover it, and it was always open at the front of the house so that anyone wearing working clothes and heavy shoes covered with dirt did not have to take them off to go into the house and interrupt his work. The contents of that hole were carefully drawn out by dippers into two small barrels and the men carried these barrels suspended from the edges of bars laid across their shoulders to the vegetable fields to use as fertilizer. This system had been used in Japan ever since the Edo period. In town it was somehow hidden from our eyes and camouflaged by the pretty interiors of the houses. But here this great natural recycling system was functioning openly and directly and the villagers blessed it as the symbol of the limitless abundance that Nature provides. The openness of this whole system saved me from the dark and horrific memory of the hospital toilet we all used and its mysterious black pipe. Here, if someone fell into this pit—which happened once a while—we laughed and laughed and took him to the well nearby and poured a bucketful or two of cold water over his head.

4   In the attic of their house lived silkworms—thousands of them. They lived on the many layers of shelves constructed like bunk beds in the low-ceilinged room and each of the shelves was covered with mulberry leaves. The worms were soft and gentle: they lifted their heads in the air like babies' fingers trying to grasp something. Through their opaque skin shone an illumination of pale green as if the deep-green-colored mulberry leaves they were digesting were shining through them. When I stood at the head of the alley formed by those shelves, in the room where the only light had to come through the rice paper covering on the small window at the other end, I was enveloped by the sound of thousands of worms making small holes in the mulberry leaves—munching on them and crawling on them and scratching their soft bodies against them. The family called the worms by a special name, okaikosan, just as you might call girls. When I heard them talking about them for the first time I thought they were talking about some beautiful girls who lived upstairs. But they were not girls: they were gods! The farmers worshipped them and thanked them every day in front of the little Shinto shrine they displayed in their living room. I was excited when the old lady in the house allowed me to help in the holy task of snipping off the mulberry leaves in the field and offering them to the worms. I was told that the work was holy, but of course I would not have known then that still today it is part of the sacred work of the Empress to take care of a small kaiko bed. These worms spun cocoons of the purest white silk, spinning the cocoons around themselves and closing themselves off until it was impossible for them to ever come out. Then the farmer boiled the cocoons while the worms were still inside—boiled gods! And then they took them to the factory where silk thread was made. This thread used to be woven into kimonos for the samurai families because the farmers themselves were forbidden to wear silk. But now the silk was sent to the army in order to make parachutes, they said.

5   In the long evenings when the farmer invited us to the bath, we went to the living room and waited our turn. The old man and his wife, their grown daughter, and other relatives were always there. We all used the same bathwater, which was carried in from the well outside bucket by bucket. This was not a sanitary practice but it was the only way we could clean ourselves and we could not skip this opportunity. The old man went first, and then my father, and then all the other men, and after them the women, and then my mother and her children—the four of us together were always the last to bathe. The living room was rather large and the whole family sat together in the room to save electricity. The family was all very quiet and almost never talked to each other. They all had some work to do, such as knitting or mending clothes.

6 I watched the old man stretch his legs towards the fireplace cut out of the center of the living room floor. The iron kettle, hung from the high ceiling blackened by smoke, was always steaming there. He was making straw sandals using his own toes as guides to weave the straw, and in this way he made the sandals to perfectly fit the size of his own feet. I learned how to make sandals myself by watching him intently: I was not supposed to waste any straw so I practiced making sandals in my imagination over and over when I was alone. One evening the old man piled a bunch of straw in front of me and I stretched my leg out in front of me and folded the other leg just like the old man did, and by using my own toes I wove the straw quickly just as I had practiced it in my mind. Soon, a perfect pair of little sandals was made which fit my feet perfectly. The old man did not say anything but I saw a satisfied smile come over his face. Pleasure spread in my chest.

7 There was a Shinto shrine in that room, a miniature of a real shrine made of simple unpainted wood, sitting in the corner at the place where the walls and ceiling met. The old lady would offer rice in a little container to god and would pray for the safety of their son who was in the army at that time. There was also a Buddhist shrine in the next room, painted black, and inside of it many tomb-like wooden stands were placed, and on each of them was written, in gold letters, the name of one of their family's ancestors. They worshipped at that shrine every morning. They seemed to believe that god would take care of the living and Buddha would take care of the dead.

8   My father, who was working as a doctor at a weapon-making company, seemed to have more time at home in the country. He created various fantastic things for the three of us. He used the old cardboard boxes in which his medicines came and created a tiny, marvelously intricate working tricycle. He made each of the three wheels with two pieces of cardboard glued together, and they each had tires made of cardboard. In order to make the wheels perfectly straight he put each wheel under a pile of medical books and left it overnight. The glue he used he made out of rice, which he saved by skipping a few meals, and then he cooked the rice for a long time to make it into a strong adhesive. The handle turned smoothly and I pushed the little pedals with my fingers, the tricycle moving in all directions.

9 I watched every step as he made it. The most impressive part came first when he made a plan: when he saw any three-dimensional thing he immediately started analyzing how to translate it onto a two-dimensional surface. His mind kept moving between three-dimensional and two-dimensional visualizations, back and forth. This process was mysterious and intriguing. It affected me so strongly that I started seeing everything in a different way: I started thinking, How can I make this into a two-dimensional world, and by assembling things how can

I make them into three dimensions? I kept thinking, thinking until my brain almost exploded. So it seemed did my father's, for when he started making those things he often skipped dinner because he was lost in thought. He looked quiet and unapproachable during his "thinking time," but I liked him so much when he was that way.

10 I watched someone cutting bamboo in the forest, even though I was not allowed to cut it myself. When the strong green trunk of the bamboo was cut, it was always a surprise how fresh a fragrance came out, and the smooth, pale, slightly yellowish-white interior of the bamboo was unexpectedly quiet. It was hard to believe that the interior was dark before it was cut open. It was as if an intense emptiness existed there which was filled with a light that came from the very beginning of the ancient forest. I knew the story of the Shining Princess: An old man, walking in the bamboo forest, saw one stalk of bamboo shining between two of its joints. The old man cut the bamboo and found a tiny Shining Princess sitting inside. The old man and his wife raised this princess and she grew up to become a most beautiful woman. Many men proposed to her but she never accepted any of them. The Daimyo himself proposed to her. But with a sad countenance she would look up constantly at the moon and finally she said that she belonged to the moon and that she would have to return to the moon, that a special carriage would come to pick her up and take her back to the moon. The Daimyo prepared an army of warriors armed with bows and arrows and positioned them on the roof of the nearby house with instructions to shoot the carriage when it arrived. But when it did arrive, all the soldiers were transfixed and could not move. The Shining Princess stepped into the carriage and instantly forgot everything that happened to her on earth, and she was not sad anymore. The carriage, with her in it, flew back to the moon.

11 Perhaps I was disappointed not to find the Shining Princess inside the bamboo whenever it was cut, and it was this disappointment which inspired such intense curiosity in me about the hollowness of the bamboo. I walked around the bamboo forest thinking about that shining emptiness: could I keep that emptiness intact and send it back to Heaven? Could I make an airplane out of bamboo? Why didn't people make airplanes out of bamboo instead of metal? How could I construct a vehicle which could reach Heaven? But the question of how she could forget everything that happened to her on this earth as soon as she got into the vehicle struck me deeply. How sad it must have been for the people who loved her, and how cruel for the princess to lose all memory of her life here on the earth. Often I could not eat because these questions overwhelmed me: just like my father did, instead of sitting at the table to eat, I had to rush out of the house. My father often told my mother who was wondering why: "It is OK. She needs thinking time." I walked around the fields and the forest all by myself, thinking until the sky became red in the sunset and then until the darkness fell in the bamboo forest, though light floated on the fields, and people said, "Here she goes again!"

12 The whole place was magical—even though the bath water was always low when our turn came in the small bathroom which had no electric light; even though only a little window was open to the evening sky and our soles always felt lots of sand at the bottom of the tub; even though there was always the strong smell of human excreta and urine; and even though there were frequent attacks of swarms of black mosquitoes which came into our house from the forest and surrounded us like a huge black smoke with their buzzing filling our house right outside the mosquito nets we hung from the ceiling and stayed inside all night long.

13   But material things for everyday life had become scarce. Soap, matches; any kind of candle to substitute for electric lights; any kind of paper, pencil, crayon; any kind of clothes or shoes to keep us warm, Band-Aids and medicines—all were beyond our reach. Being an outsider in the food-producing community was hard. The farmers were under strict orders to give all the food they produced to the government after taking the minimum amount necessary to sustain their own families. Selling food or bartering it was forbidden by law. The government allocation for a non-food-producing family was, in fact, much less than what was required to sustain life. A handful of grain for one family did not last long. We made gruel with it to fill our stomachs but it became almost water-thin. Soon we could not find any grain in our soup bowls at all. Rice was sacred: it is not only the main foodstuff for which other things were just a garnish or a substitute when rice was not available, it is a spiritual substance. When we could not eat rice we felt our spiritual strength decline before the lack of nourishment affected our physical being. People in the village sometimes brought us vegetables and homemade miso and some soy sauce, and exchanged these things for my father's medical treatment. But it was not appropriate to rely on them for food. My mother took her kimono to a farmer in a faraway village and tried to trade it for food so we could survive. She visited strangers' houses like a door-to-door salesman or a fugitive: some days it worked and she was given a sack of potatoes in exchange for a kimono, but often it didn't.

14 She took me on one of those trips on her bicycle. All morning her efforts failed: we were waved off as if we were beggars or stray dogs. Before noon we entered a rather large farmhouse. An old woman opened the door: her head was wrapped in a washed-out cloth to prevent it from bothering her work. She invited us to sit at the edge of the wooden walkway which opened up on the courtyard where many straw mats were spread with grain drying on them—mirroring the process that the farmers used where we were living. When my mother opened up the cotton furoshiki, the wrapping cloth, and carefully lifted the innermost rice paper, the old woman swallowed her breath. Pale pink cherry blossoms sprang up from the package—hundreds of cherry blossoms swaying in the wind on branches which stretched out and curved in the warm spring sky. They were not buds or young, hesitating blossoms: they were proudly open, intoxicated with their own beauty, knowing that at any moment the spring wind would blow and they would become part of the flower storm. They would be blown away, scattered into thousands of petals, and fill the sky until the sky would turn dark—just like snow turns the sky black in a wild snowstorm. The old woman stared at the kimono for a long time, stretched out her hand with its big joints, and slowly touched the surface of the kimono. The silk made a faint squeaking sound and seemed to shrink from her shining skin. She withdrew her hand as if she had touched something hot by mistake. And then she stared for a while at the family crest embroidered with gold thread on the sleeves right near the branches reaching into the hazy sky. She took the cloth off her head and crumpled it up in her big hand and thanked my mother for having shown her this kimono and said there was no one in her family who could wear this kimono: the last wedding had finished long ago. But she wanted us to be her guests for lunch because her eyes were deeply honored to have seen such beauty.

15 "Nothing here will suit your taste, I am afraid." She placed a tray on the floor before us. With a slightly sweet fragrance the rice was forming round, fluffy shapes in the rice bowl. Each grain of rice was soft and firm and shining white, standing against the other grains of rice moist and soft and none sticking to the other. Big chunks of carrots, yams, and gobo roots boiled in soy sauce were sticking out of the edge of a handmade pottery bowl. We had not seen such an abundance of food for a long time. We bowed and thanked her and took off our wooden sandals as was suggested to us, and we folded our legs on the bare wooden floor and ate. At her gate my mother looked at me and sighed deeply. "Why didn't you eat more than a few mouthfuls? I don't know what to do with your shyness. We probably will not be able to eat white rice like that any more, at least not for a long, long time. Unless you drop your shyness, you will never survive in this world." My heart sank. I sensed fully my mother's desire for me to eat a lot while we were sitting as this woman's guests, and I wanted to show my gratitude to this old woman by eating enough I wanted to do the right thing. But the more I wanted to do it, the more tightly my throat closed. I thought my mother's premonition must be right: I would not live long.

16 The situation of the war turned drastically worse. Even in this small village we were attacked from the sky day and night. It soon became clear without a doubt that the enemy's targets were not military facilities and not soldiers. Indiscriminate overnight "carpet bombing" was carried out by thousands of B-29s over multiple cities. No men who could be soldiers were left in the country, for all men aged 18 to 45 were gone. There was even a plan to expand the draft from 15 to 60 years old. There was no material to make weapons and no gasoline to fly airplanes in all of Japan. Our hands and feet started to swell and bleed like rotten tomatoes with frostbite from lack of material to keep ourselves warm: even in the summer the frostbite never healed and it ached. Our cheeks cracked and bled if we smiled because there was no elasticity in our skin due to lack of fat. By government order we preschool children got together with elementary school kids and peeled the bark off trees with bleeding fingernails in order to make fabric for the military. We worked many hours every day to fill our daily quotas, then we went to the fields to catch locusts with our hands to fill our families' stomachs with them and to get the calcium we needed—a taste we never got used to. And even there, in the locust fields, we were targeted by machine-gun fire from low-flying airplanes.

17 One afternoon I was walking along a dusty road at my mother's side from the fields back toward the house. Suddenly I saw an enemy plane emerge in front of my eyes. I saw a young man, the enemy pilot, laughing at me through the front window of the plane. I wonder now whether it was possible for me to see so much detail but I remember his face vividly. A straight line of machine-gun bullets ran along the road directly at my feet, raising a smoke of dust. At the same instant, my mother grabbed me and threw the two of us into the field at the side of the road. The plane flew away. As I felt my mother's warm and heavy body on top of me, I felt the strong smell of grass and I was watching a miniature pink lotus flower trembling in the grass beside the road. I heard that evening that a baby boy was hit by a machine gun's bullets while he was lying in a bamboo basket. His older brother had set him down to fill his school's quota in the bamboo forest just across the road from where my mother and I had jumped out of the airplane's path. The enemy could not possibly have seen that baby boy through the thick bamboo forest: the bullets meant for me must have hit him.

18 In 1945 the enemy finally landed on the island at the edge of Japan, Okinawa, with 1,457 parent ships and 183,000 soldiers. Gruesome stories of what happened spread rapidly despite the army's strict regulation of information. Altogether, 110,000 Japanese soldiers and 100,000 civilians were killed. Included in those numbers were a great number of deaths by mass suicide and by family suicide, and the deaths of those who were forced by our own Japanese army to avoid humiliation by tying themselves together in order to use one precious grenade to kill them all at once.

19 In our village we started digging caves deep in the mountains. We decided to live in hiding from the enemy and probably from our own army. Because 75 percent of the Japanese islands are uninhabitable mountains where the saints and pilgrims of Shinto and Buddhism had roamed for severe training and meditation without being seen by other people throughout history, it seemed possible to hide ourselves from any outsider for a long time. We had to go deeper into the forests, as deep as possible and for as long as possible, and live as primitive cave dwellers. I would be in the first generation in more than 1,500 years of Japanese history who would never know school and I would grow up in a cave if we should ever survive long enough. My father determined to teach his daughters as well as the community of the village anything that he knew which might prevent us from falling into a caveman existence and which might keep civilization alive in our hands.

20   His teaching to us of reading and writing became more intense. But what was he really thinking? To keep civilization going is not a simple matter: no one individual nor any small community can carry out such a project. He prepared a bunch of books for us to read, but our whole library inventory was extremely small because we had lost almost everything in the firebombing at the hospital residence. I remember clearly only one book: a book of Greek mythology in a young adult version that was picked up with other things, perhaps by mistake, and carried in one of our backpacks. That was one of the books grandmother had sent us before the war became so severe: they were the books my mother had read when she was a child. This book of Greek mythology had survived and was carried into this faraway village. Now it was going to be carried inside a primitive cave. What could this book do for all of us?

21   I was sitting on the ground while people were digging a cave out of the rocky hillside. No young men were there anymore. Some skilled women swiftly wove straw baskets that could carry the soil out of the cave, many using pickaxes. Some, including my mother though her physical strength was limited, prepared humble food for them. I was drawing on the cardboard on my lap, which came from the medicine boxes my father stored for his patients: paper was not available and even cardboard was scarce. I drew over the drawings that I had already made, over and over. I was feeling strangely powerful. As long as I had paper and pencil or a substitute for them, I could create; I could produce anything in the world. I was in a special state of consciousness, like an ancient shaman would have been in the cave, drawing figures of animals on the wall of the cave and believing that the drawing could conjure up the power to bring sustenance for the people.

22   And then the atomic bombs were dropped in Hiroshima and Nagasaki. People saw what hell actually is right in front of their eyes for the first time in the entire history of mankind: violence, pain, hopelessness, total destruction. All that we had experienced up to that time was nothing compared to this. It was programmed to destroy mankind itself, a destruction meant to last forever through generations, a death that still continues today and which will continue as long as mankind lasts, if it ever lasts.

PART TWO

CHAPTER 5

1 When the voice of the Emperor was broadcast over the radio on August 15, 1945, it was the first time Japanese ever heard their Emperor's voice. I had been told that if you ever saw the Emperor in person you would become blind. I did not know if one would become deaf if he heard the Emperor's voice in person or if the same principle would apply to the voice heard over the radio.

2 It was an unusual tone of voice, not the low sound usually associated with a great man's voice: it was a high sound and it did not sound like any human voice at all. It was like the sound of wind coming from a dark, ancient forest on a stormy night or of some big bird unexpectedly crying and breaking the silence of the forest and evoking the depth of silence even more deeply. There were many ancient words, classic poetic expressions, in his speech. But most of all, no one had ever heard any Japanese spoken in this intonation: the closest thing to it was the tone of a Shinto priest chanting the ancient prayers in the shrine. Because the Emperor had been the highest priest of Shinto, that would make sense. That voice seemed to have come from a place where the sounds of nature formed language, where the magical power of nature moved into language and still dwelled in it. Language has never been Logos in Japan. And ironically because of this inhuman quality, it had a strong tone of mournfulness, which hit all of us deeply.

3 People could not comprehend what he actually said, and there was confusion all over Japan that day. Some interpretations contradicted others and serious arguments were waged over whether Japan had won or lost. After the broadcast was over, the village people, one after another, gathered at our house to ask my father, whom they respected, what the Emperor had said. My father interpreted it for them: it was the Emperor's decision that Japan had accepted the demand from the Allies to end the war and that the Emperor said that he felt our pain and our sacrifice and our feelings—and then using a dignified classic Chinese metaphor—said it was as if all his organs were slashed into pieces; but that considering that the recent atomic bombs, which were used now for the first time in history, were the most destructive for all mankind itself, continuing the fight would bring total destruction not only to Japan, but to humanity and to all mankind's civilization and to future generations as well. He said that we deeply regret that we could not bring liberation to the East Asian brothers and could not build the Greater East Asia Co-Prosperity Sphere, as we had promised. To accomplish that goal as a way of reaching world peace was the whole purpose of this war in the first place. And the Emperor wanted us to make an effort from now on to do our best to bring peace into the world from generation to generation for all eternity.

4 And then, my father concluded that because we had lost the war, it was perhaps an unconditional surrender: we should accept anything America demanded, there was no room for any negotiation with them, and we did not even know what would happen to us; but whatever it was we would have to go through it because we surrendered. None of us knew if the time had finally come for all of us to move to the cave, or whether we could finally start living like human beings. The village people cried quietly, standing still without moving their bodies at all in the farmer's courtyard, cannas flowers flaming red under the beating sun of the August noon. It was out of respect for the Emperor and intense empathy with his pain which made their desire to sacrifice their lives for him even more intense. Suicides started after this: 600 suicides in a few months. Five years old at that time, I caught only three words of the Emperor's speech: "Bear the unbearable." Those words rang in my ears for a long time after that.

5   Two weeks later, on September 2, 1945, on the deck of the Americans' battleship *Missouri* in Tokyo Bay, an official representative of Japan signed the documents of surrender. My father's words were right: this was an absolute unconditional surrender and our destiny was now in America's hands. It was the end of four years of war, but for the Japanese, it was the end of the "fifteen years war" which had started with the war in China. And more precisely, it was the end of 92 years of absolute turmoil since Commodore Perry appeared from America in 1853 with black ships looming on the horizon and demanded that Japan open the country and sign the unfair treaty. Under the coercion of force they did sign. The turmoil began then: in order to get out of the most humiliating situation Japan had ever found herself in, in order to have an equal and fair relationship with America and the other Western nations, Japan had fought throughout 92 years on the biggest global scale and had built a gigantic empire in the Pacific Ocean, and as a latecomer had entered in the most violent, bloody competition between Capitalism and Imperialism. Now, Japan's representative had to sign the documents of surrender—documents far more unequal and far more humiliating than the treaty they had signed 92 years earlier.

6 The day after the broadcast, my mother started teaching us English—the language that had been strictly prohibited for anyone to study, as during the war, even uttering a single word such as "elevator" or "baseball" could be very dangerous. As a former student of a mission school in her youth, she knew all along that Westerners were not the monsters they were called during the war. She never revealed this "knowledge" to us or even revealed that she knew some English. To let little children like us know this kind of secret would have been fatal to the family. She did not conceal her joy at the end of the war anymore, her joy at the end of fascistic Japan, and her joy at the victory of America. I did not realize for a long time how heavy her secret had been; how frightening to have a secret like this in a society where hysterical nationalism swirled and any indication of being against that nationalism resulted in torture, imprisonment, and execution. She was on the enemy's side: she wanted America to win and come to save her from fascism, just like the Secret Christians had longed for Christian missionaries to come to rescue them from the oppression of the Tokugawa *Bakufu* for three hundred years. My mother told us that America would be good to us and that finally the time had come that we would be free, that we could learn anything we wanted. America would be the best place in the world for a long time ahead, so we should study hard and someday go to America to get the highest education. We would go back to Tokyo and start a new life. People in the village thought she had finally gone out of her mind because of the shock of the news of the surrender of Japan.

7 America did not betray my mother's trust: we realized that she was right as soon as General Douglas MacArthur and a few thousand Americans marched into Japan and the Allied Occupation started. The paper reported that they marched through Tokyo in long parades of Jeeps, with soldiers who looked well fed, with dazzling clean, creased uniforms and shining shoes. They held rifles but they did not shoot us, they did not rape women or kill men and children as we had feared, they were orderly, and surprisingly, they were very friendly. They waved from the Jeeps, smiling at the children who were seeing Caucasians and blacks for the first time in their lives. Soon, packages of used clothes which American charity organizations sent us began arriving. They were shockingly—sometimes almost embarrassingly—colorful, but they came steadily and efficiently. We sensed that some incredibly generous, good, strong minds were behind them as well as wealth to a degree we had never seen before.

8 They tried everything to eradicate the roots of fascism, feudalism, and militarism. They even prohibited calligraphy from being taught in school, out of suspicion that its spirit might have something to do with the essence of fascism. They gave us a new democratic constitution in which war and the military were forever discarded from the structure of Japan. Shinto lost its position as the state religion and freedom of religion was established. They gave equal rights to women: the new constitution said that marriage should be based only on the mutual consent of both sexes and should be maintained through mutual cooperation with the equal rights of husband and wife as its basis, and the right to choose one's husband and the right to divorce him as well as equal rights in property and inheritance were all established. Women throughout Japan read about those things and some repeated them over and over and some locked themselves in their bathrooms to hide from their husbands while they read the articles describing the new laws. Everyone read those articles with profound emotion.

9 My mother persuaded my father to return to Tokyo, saying that she would be the first woman to use the new rights of divorce which America gave her if he did not come back to Tokyo to start a new life with her and to educate their daughters in the best circumstances. My father was ambivalent, having been begged to stay in the country village as its first doctor. The people in the village offered him and his family a house and an office. They loved him, and they loved his leadership. My father unexpectedly grew to love them too after going through the most difficult times together. There was something in the relationship between him and the farmers that reminded him of his original family, which had maintained a sort of parental status with their own village's people as great leaders for generations and generations, and that made him comfortable.

10 But the decision was made: we were going back to Tokyo. My parents built a most humble little house in Tokyo: it was called a barrack in those days, with my father's small office attached to it. My father went to Tokyo alone, and for a month he lived and slept on a pile of lumber every night—under the stars on the bombed-out field just like a homeless person—in order to protect the lumber from looting. His black belt in judo was the only thing our family had to rely on.

11 The train to Tokyo was already packed when it entered the station closest to our village with an enormous head of steam and black smoke. We saw people clinging to the roof of the train: they looked like they were burned black because every time it went through a tunnel, smoke filled the train. We saw people holding the handles on the train tightly as they stood on the couplers between the cars. My mother shouted and spoke bluntly to two men who were standing between two seats near the window—as if she were giving them orders—and told them to pull her daughters into the train through the window and squeeze them in where people were standing between the knees of the people who were sitting to save space. Then she pushed us through the high windows of the train one by one, from the murderously crowded platform. These men kindly did what she asked them to do. She managed to squeeze herself in through the door just before the train started to move. People were packed everywhere—even in the restroom whose doors were never closed because they were packed full of people. The whole train was filled with crying and screaming and loud voices.

12 The train passed tunnel after tunnel in the mountainous country, with people riding on the roof. It stopped often and waited due to the destruction of the railroad tracks: the tracks had to be used for traffic running in both directions. Sometimes this happened in a pitch-black tunnel filled with smoke. When it became dark outside, silence filled the train—and silence stirred memories in everyone's minds. Everyone had memories they wanted to forget but those memories came back repeatedly and flashed back. The face of a young American soldier laughing as he tried to kill me kept coming back to me: I might run into him in Tokyo, I thought. Thoughts of the baby boy who died instead of me in the bamboo forest: I had never even seen him, yet why did his face flash back to me? The train proceeded in the darkness. Many people became ill, some collapsed because of exhaustion and hunger. Some could not make it to the restroom because it was so crowded: the train was filled with the smell. And yet no one knew how long it would take to reach Tokyo, even after fifteen hours or so had passed.

13 It was like a cattle car –but different: the people who were there were not packed in against their will, nor forced to be there, they were all in the train because they had decided to take a risk. It was a dangerous risk, but they were all willing to take it. Now everybody was burned out, and they all had lost their assets. Money lost all of its value because of the abnormal rate of inflation: the government took away all financial power from the established aristocracy by instituting drastic land reforms and by deconstructing the *Zaibatsu*. The hierarchy of class and aristocracy had all ended—except for the Emperor's direct family. However miserable we might have looked, we were all equals standing at the very bottom line of poverty, and we were all free. Everything we believed, everything we had been taught—the ultimate victory we would win, the divinity of the Japanese nation, all authority, all heroes (for we had all read in our school textbooks that Adolf Hitler was one of the greatest heroes), the value of death and suicide—all this was turned upside down overnight. We had nothing to believe in anymore; we had to build our lives believing only in ourselves. We would start a new life in Tokyo, the land of the clean slate.

14 When the morning mist lifted, the first scene we saw from the train window was a burnt field spreading all the way to the horizon, with fragments of gray concrete, burnt bricks, and distorted, twisted iron pipes covering it. There was only a trace of old streets still discernible in all the rubble—stretching like a chessboard all the way to the horizon in every direction. It was as if a black-and-white photograph of the former streets had been printed on tracing paper and laid over the scene of the debris and ruin. "It was a carpet bombing," everyone in the train whispered. Fear struck us: was it possible to live in a place like this? Ruins of buildings stood here and there. People stared at them to try to find anything familiar, anything recognizable, but they couldn't. When they finally saw a narrow plume of smoke rising from a pile of debris that looked like a hut, people in the train exclaimed aloud, "Oh, someone is preparing breakfast! We can make it!" Gradually we saw that this was not a dead city devoid of inhabitants: instead people had gathered burnt tin and bricks and were living in dwellings made of those materials. We saw some clothes hanging on burnt pipes here and there, near those huts made of debris.

15   Our new house was in a field in the middle of which stood a burned-out black tree without leaves. Neighbors called it the hanging tree because someone who had come back from the army found that his whole family was dead and he hung himself on this tree. There was a bomb shelter still left—just a hole underground, neatly swept around the mouth of the hole, where a mother who had a daughter my own age were living. When it rained, water rushed into that hole. Another family lived in a shack made of burnt tin which the whole family had collected from the burnt field: a mother and daughter and babies. Every evening the daughter went out to support the family, wearing heavy makeup and a permanent wave. Some evenings we saw her walking arm-in-arm with a tall American soldier with a pink face. People never greeted her and tried not to let their eyes meet hers.

16   I was aware all the time that our house was built on ground where someone else had lived and died. When the strong rain fell sometimes things in the ground revealed themselves: beautiful dishes piled neatly and boxes full of photo albums with pages stuck to each other. When I tried to open these pages once, only blue faces showed themselves between those sticky pages. I was frightened that at any moment dead bodies swollen with rain would push themselves up through the surface of the ground—the dead bodies which had those blue faces.

17   In the underground hallways of a ruined subway station in Tokyo, I saw hundreds and hundreds of children. Some were hobbling around, some were crouching down, some were laying down and stretched their bodies out on the dirty concrete floor. They were sprayed with the white powder of DDT from head to toe to prevent the spread of lice. Under the dim light, they looked literally like a squadron of ghosts. They were the boys who were torn from their parents and their siblings when they reached nine years old during the war, and isolated, and whom the Japanese government had sent out to the backwaters in order to train them as future soldiers. They came back at the end of the war and could not find their parents or their homes, or they found that their parents were dead. Their wide-open eyes in their ghost-like white figures showed intense fear and desperation: they stared at me and my mother whose hand I held tightly.

18   What my father had told the village people on the day of the Emperor's broadcast was correct: our destiny was in America's hands. The War Crimes Trials conducted by the Americans and their victorious allies commenced in 1946, in Tokyo, and continued for more than two-and-a-half years. Fundamental questions were raised even among the judges of the Allied nations whether that court, in which the winners of the war were judging the loser, could maintain any legitimacy; and whether the Allies had the right to vindicate the concept of a crime against peace, or of a crime against humanity, since the Allies themselves had violated those laws themselves in the most violent ways. But all the questioning voices were ignored by the Americans: 984 defendants received capital punishment, 475 were given life sentences, and 2944 were given limited prison terms. Executions continued for many years; many war crimes defendants died in prison, and many stayed in prison for a long, long time. Black smoke from the extraordinarily high chimneys of the crematoriums to which the dead war criminals were sent rose and covered Tokyo's sky for five years.

19 We were prohibited from having contact with any foreign countries, nor could we carry on any trade outside of Japan. Japan was forced to be closed off again from all foreign countries, just as it had been until Commodore Perry arrived 92 years earlier. And all assets outside the country which Japanese had accumulated in business in the colonies were totally confiscated directly from their banks. People who had worked outside the country all their lives, and even those who had been born abroad, were forced to come back to Japan after abandoning everything—and were allowed to carry only a few belongings with them. The huge expenses required to support the American Occupation all had to be paid with taxes on the Japanese; and astronomical compensation to the nations to which Japan had caused damage also had to be paid through a heavy tax on all Japanese. Those taxes seemed beyond the capacity of any of us because most of our small islands are just volcanoes, and every corner had already been cultivated right up to the tops of the mountains and we had no excess natural resources of any kind. For us to stand up as any form of independent nation someday in this capitalistic world seemed impossible. And this was exactly what America's intention for us seemed to be: let them survive but never let them grow to be a threat to the world again. Severe censorship was instituted: any criticism, any negative view of America or the American Occupation was strictly eradicated from public speaking and publishing. The presence of the powerful military force was always there to remind us, "Do whatever America says or you will be destroyed." We did not know at that time that this occupation would last almost twice as long as the war itself.

20 And for me, it was still frightening to see the procession of Jeeps and army trucks every day. It was a demonstration of absolute, nonnegotiable physical force. My mind became dark every time I saw them: it reminded me of the Japanese fascistic army, of irrational authority, of hatred of the individual, of the demand for blind obedience, and of hysteria—even though I knew these Jeeps and trucks were different, that they were symbols of freedom and democracy. The clearest demonstration of nonnegotiable power they had over us was the trains that all of us had to use every single day to go to work, to school, or to get food. Every train was divided into two parts—a special boxcar for Americans and the rest for the Japanese. The boxcars for Americans were spacious and clean, and plenty of seats were empty. The rest were for Japanese, crowded to the point of being a danger to life, especially for children, the pregnant, and the old. Some people squeezed themselves out of the boxcars and threw up on the platform: so real was the danger of being crushed and suffocated inside the overcrowded boxcars.

21   I saw American women on the street for the first time in my life. Their sharpened fingernails frightened me; they looked as if they put their fingernails into infant flesh, and I fantasized that was why their fingernails became red with blood. But instead they put their fingers into the brown paper bags that they held in their arms and ate popcorn from those bags while they were walking on the street. I wondered why they were doing it: we had never eaten anything on the street, not only because it is bad manners but also because it hurt the starving people. If we had to eat in a public place like a long-distance train, we were very careful not to make those who were starving suffer, and many times I heard mothers tell their little children not to watch others eating. They looked in a different direction because they were afraid their eyes might betray their hunger in spite of their pride. GIs were tossing chocolate bars and chewing gum from the Jeeps so that children could catch them; it was shocking to see many children of my own age stretching out their arms to catch them. And I was aware that grownups did not say anything about those children, nor about Americans eating on the street.

22   Many things that we had been told strictly not to do did not seem to matter anymore and some things that had been considered normal or even good now had to be banned. A mother having a baby in her arms and breast-feeding had been considered a beautiful scene: whether it was done in private place or in a public place, we respected it. But Japanese found out that Americans thought it was a sexually provocative act so the Japanese government prohibited mothers from breast-feeding in public. That was a deeply offensive shock. Many Japanese felt that their own mothers were insulted: such a belief sounded like a blasphemy of motherhood, or at least in its most mild expression, it sounded like sexual deviancy or perversion. The authority of grownups was somehow fading quickly every day and now we had to follow everything the Americans said. Where was all that pride which we had done anything to keep? Was it just a reverse expression of the feeling of inferiority? Were we inferior to white people? We all seemed to believe that now: we lost and they won. Something must be deeply wrong with us.

23 Now the Japanese Empire, the only empire in the world built by non-whites and non-Christians, was gone, and Japan became small again. Korea, Taiwan, and all the South Asian nations, which had already been colonies of European countries or America and all of which Japan took and expanded during the Imperial period, were again taken away. The empire of Manchuria, with its 13 years of glory, disappeared from the earth like a hallucination of history. To this shrunken Japan, in the small miserable islands where everybody was sick or starving, people who had built their lives in the colonies, and who were born there, and soldiers who were drafted there, all were sent back by boats one after another abandoning everything they had built, some even forced by the situation to leave their own babies there, with only a few belongings in their hands. Japan shrunk back to the same size it was when Commodore Perry found it 92 years before, a small exquisite peaceful island. Now the land was destroyed, everyone was starved, only the population had doubled.

24 One day a skeleton-like man who looked like a beggar, wrapping his filthy body with a shredded army cloth, stood at the door of the kitchen of the mansion of Motoyasu, which looked like a ghost house by that time. At the sight of my grandmother, who opened the door for him, he collapsed on the floor and went into a coma. He was the second son of Motoyasu who had left home for an adventurous new life when he was 20 years old. His coma lasted two months. People who heard the news and visited the house to see him all expressed remorse and regret at his bedside that it was he who had come back, and not the first son, the doctor, the 19th successor of the Motoyasu family.

25 A new life had started. A church was built in grandmother's district, and she started becoming involved in church activities and having many friends. Her second son started a business: making ice for industrial and residential refrigerators. It required his own physical labor immediately after recuperating from his coma: he could not afford the luxury of waiting for a complete recovery. The Motoyasu relatives were all shocked and devastated, saying that he would not be welcome at the front door when he went selling ice from home to home: he had to go in the tradesman's door. How as a son of the Motoyasu could he put himself in such a position? My grandmother paid no attention to these remarks.

26 My mother took my elder sister and me to a church soon after we came back to Tokyo. It must have been one of the few churches which were built before the war and had escaped the bombing, because I saw old paintings there hung in rows on the wall, right next to the bench where I was sitting. They were painted with bright shining colors that I had never seen before. How vivid they looked after I was used to seeing burnt fields with burnt bricks and black trees without leaves, and only dusty shredded military cloth and camouflage colors. There were no paintings, books, paper, or crayons for me before, and I was afraid of the light since any single leak of light from your window might make the entire town a target of bombs. But although the paintings were bright, they were not pretty: the sense of tragedy filled every entire painting. They were paintings of a man who carried a big heavy cross on his back and he was proceeding into the clouds. In one of the paintings, I saw the sky behind him; I saw a faint red glow in it. My breath stopped.

27   It was the same red glow I had seen in the faraway sky, standing in the dark black rice fields with the village people at midnight. Over our heads countless planes were lined up keeping same distance from each other, and they welled up from the darkness on the other side of the sky one line after another, marching towards the faraway sky, and on the city under the glow they kept dropping bombs. This was carpet-bombing. The glow stood up like a huge curtain hung from Heaven. A sense of powerlessness overcame us. "It's Nagoya." Someone said the name of the city in which we all knew my father was staying that time as a doctor in the army. "Don't let your child see this," the others cried to my mother. She responded, "I want my child to see this, till she can print this sky into her mind's film so that she will never forget it."

28   *Something terribly important must be happening, since the sky glows like this*, I thought. I was staring at the painting. *I have to know what is happening here.* My sister, feeling responsible for her little sister's bad manners because I was twisting my body and stretching my neck from the pew to stare at these paintings, pinched my thigh. I did not fight with her; I was afraid if I uttered one word my mother would put me next to her on the other side and then I would not be able to look at these paintings. I somehow knew that my mother did not like to be in church. I don't think she ever went back there again, or took me to any church after that. I never saw those paintings again.

29 My mother bartered her own watch—her wedding ring had been confiscated by the military long before and her watch was literally the last thing she could barter something for—and she got a few unusual things in exchange, including a package of unusually large pieces of paper of surprisingly good quality. I still don't know where she got that paper: it was creamy white and smooth and strong enough to write on. She also got some ready-made *sumi* ink already in a bottle and a brush to write letters and a flat paintbrush and one bag of flour. On the papers she wrote the *kanji* (formal, dignified style of inscription) indicating a medical office, and my father's name. She took me into town. Using the brushes, we applied some glue which she had made out of flour to the back of the paper and my mother lifted the upper edges carefully and pasted the papers on the burnt electric poles and broken fences and on the broken shards of tin, all with careful arrows pointing the way to my father's office. My parents had spent all their money for an old upright piano and for these posters, and for the medicines and other supplies needed for my father to open his office— although he made all the furniture himself with the lumber left over from building the house: benches for the waiting room, an examination table with moving parts, and an airtight cabinet in which he kept his medicines and medical tools sanitary. If patients did not come before dinnertime, we would all go to sleep without any food at all. But patients did come: so many at once that my mother, who was doing the work of the office receptionist, had to ask them to wait outside our house. When evening fell they still came—even after it became pitch-dark, the line of waiting patients kept getting longer.

30 Someone's old upright piano that had somehow escaped the fire my parents brought in and it occupied most of our tiny living space. At night we three children spread *futons* on the floor from wall to wall, including the space beneath the piano: the piano chair had to be moved out of the way and part of the *futon* was under the keyboard, and we slept there. A plywood door separated our parents' room right next to ours. The small kitchen did not have a floor: just a door and plywood walls above the exposed soil. During the daytime, the *futons* were folded and put away so we could all sit and eat in our parents' room, and study and practice in the living room.

31 The quest for culture burst out and erupted everywhere in Japan. Japanese traditional culture was under strict restrictions promulgated by the Office of Occupation, but Western culture was encouraged. There had to be glorious confidence in the new culture in society. The strict piano practice of my two sisters continued many hours every day. They had continued practicing during the war: even after our piano was burnt, mother made special arrangements so that the poorest-quality little organ in the village school could be used for practice as a substitute for the piano. The best pianist in Japan who survived the war accepted my two sisters as her students. After I finished my first-grade year in public school, a privileged private elementary school accepted the three of us. With our new uniforms, a new school life started. Everything seemed to be going well, and finally the shadow of death seemed to have lifted its veil. The career of two prodigy pianists was just about to start.

32 But then they found out that I had been stricken by tuberculosis for quite some time: poor nourishment during the war had eroded my lungs. I laid my skeleton-like body on the *futon* that was placed on the *tatami* floor right under the upright piano; my head on the pillow almost touched the piano. That was the only position where my *futon* would not be an obstacle for other family members walking through to the kitchen or the bathroom. From my floor-height position I could see the lower side of the piano, the chair, and the back side of the keyboard. I remember that Bach's *Well Tempered Clavier* was repeated over and over for days and months just above my head until the four voices of every *fuga* finally emerged from the chaos of sounds. Each note of that music was engraved deeply into the cells of my brain. It was like surgery that is performed by torturous repetitious strokes of knives thrust into a person who powerlessly laid down her body. I was lying there for almost a year and they practiced from dawn to the time they went to school and after they came back from school until late intothe evening. Beauty and torture were inseparably woven in my mind.

33 Tuberculosis was a disease of terror—terror of the sickness with the biggest death toll in Japan in those days, and the deepest shame of something more than sickness, a sign of evil, just like pestilence or leprosy in medieval times and AIDS in our time. Not being allowed to have any kind of bath, and not being allowed to cry or laugh or talk much in order to keep my lungs quiet, in order to keep my life going, I came to resemble a dark, filthy dried-up corpse. I was a shame, a shame of the family which was just about to stretch its wings to fly into the sky with the brilliant genius pianist daughters who were now for the first time decked out in beautiful frilled dresses and ribbons in their hair after gray wartime rags. And I was a shame of our family because despite being a doctor's daughter I had this dreadful sickness which no one ever dared to name. They were afraid of me asking what was happening; they did not allow me to know the truth. Two things I figured out: the first was that they wanted to hide me from the world as if I did not exist, the second was that everyone seemed to know that I was going to die soon.

34   I was left out of the recovery of Japan, a terrible reminder of the war and of what war could do to a child. And I was a constant reminder of questions not yet answered: What was that war about? What drove us to war and kept driving us this far? What happened to that peaceful history of the Japan which was never invaded, never conquered, for thousands of years, even though it did not even have any form of military to protect it against the outside before Perry came and threatened to destroy it? And why, only several decades after opening up the nation, did it plunge into war after war? Why did Japan then commit such gruesome mass murders and exhibit such cruel and sadistic behavior as we had gradually been finding out about as if faraway rumors were reaching us as time went by? Why did we commit such acts against Japan's brothers and sisters in Asia who had been our great teachers and whose cultures we had admired all through our previous history? Is such cruelty and sadism intrinsically innate in our culture underneath this gentle, refined culture on the surface? Or had we simply not recovered from the traumatic experience of the threat of Perry and repressed our indignation, our humiliation, so deeply and hysterically carried it to such an extreme just to survive? Who would take care of the boys who could not find their parents, the ones who were still in the ruined subway underground, still now sprayed with DDT from head to toe? No one was going to think through the war anymore. No one wanted to see sick, injured, dying, desperate children, skeleton-like bodies, dirty clothes and feet swollen with frostbite. "Are you still carrying such dreadful things inside of you? Enough of it! We are now living a new life."

35 It was a dark, windy winter evening, and it was a very rare occasion that my parents invited guests into our tiny hut for dinner. The tiny room where dinner was served was only a three-*tatami* room, with just a small round folding table in the middle: I don't know how my parents and two sisters and the guests were all able to sit together on the floor. But even though the party was far beneath our former luxurious standard, there was food, plenty of it, or at least enough for everyone there, which made it a grand party since most of us were more or less on the edge of starvation. Laughing voices and the sound of clattering dishes I clearly heard from my *futon*, which was laid out in complete darkness right in the next room. There were only four folding doors made of plywood standing as a partition between the two rooms instead of a wall. I suddenly got up by myself and walked into that other room by my own sole effort.

36 I was not innocent. I knew very well that I was supposed to hide myself in the dark for a few hours without making any sound as if I had already died, or even as if I had never existed. I knew very well that my father's reputation as a doctor and my sisters' public images as prodigy pianists were important: our whole family had worked very hard for all those things and had made many sacrifices after we started a new life in this burnt field. And all that would vanish in a second if certain people found out the family had a haunted daughter imprisoned in their home. I knew very well that my parents trusted me more than most parents would trust an 8-year-old. "She understands; she is a quiet, sweet girl. She will never do anything which she is not supposed to do." Relying on me did not seem too big a risk for them.

37 But on that dark winter evening, deep down in the bottom of the ocean of despair, water rose. Water rose and soared like a huge wall into the stormy sky, and the water wall powerfully proceeded towards the shore. I did not become a victim being swept away by the *tsunami* of despair: I became the *tsunami* itself. With enormous effort, I pulled the sliding doors to the right and left with both hands at once, as if I divided and separated the ocean into two. I saw the thick steam coming from the pot in the middle of the round table filling the room. Through the steam I saw my two sisters with pink ribbons in their hair, and other people's faces—some I did not recognize—astonished, shocked, and frightened. And for the first time I realized how I looked to them. My black hair was tangled so tightly that no one seemed to be able to comb through it anymore: my hair was thick and twisted and stood up just like on Medusa's head. Oh, didn't I know the image of the Greek Gorgon, each of whose hairs was a snake and who turned anyone who looked at her into stone! This is the image I saw over and over in the country during the war in the illustration of the book my father wanted to take to the cave with us as the last book I would ever touch in my life. Now I became Medusa herself! My nightgown used to be white but now it had become an indescribable grayish color and it hung heavy with dirt and scabs from our not having enough soap available, and under the skirt of that gown, skeleton-like shins were sticking out, barely supporting my whole body. My frostbitten bare toes caused by severe cold during the war were still swollen dark and purple and squashed like a rotten tomato. Two years after the war was over they still had not healed.

38 My father stood up from the floor the moment he saw me, and lifted me in his arms: it looked like the easiest thing he could do. But my resistance was more violent than he ever anticipated: I bit his hand, I tasted his blood. I threw my head back and kicked the air with my legs and shrieked out and cried out my lungs. He slapped my face and carried me onto the *futon* in the dark next room. He slapped me hard. Was that because he was panicked and angry because I betrayed him, his trust, and revealed everything he was afraid of outsiders seeing? Or did he try to stop urgently my cry and my violence? After all, he was the one who believed and warned me that my excessive use of my lungs would lead me quickly to death. I was questioning that in my mind, but then some sedatives were injected into me; that was all, everything was over. The incident which happened that evening was never repeated.

39 After that evening, the suspicion of my madness and evilness was rooted deeply into my family. The burst of emotion I displayed that evening was even more frightening to them than tuberculosis itself. It had shaken them radically. They realized that they had now an even darker secret to hide from the whole world. Many years later, when I read part of *Jane Eyre* for the English reading curriculum in junior high school, a highly ambitious project, I was astonished to find a story similar to my own experience: the incident of that cold winter's evening dinner party which I had never forgotten. In the novel there is a mad woman imprisoned in the high tower of the mansion. She is the wife of the lord of the mansion. The secret, her madness, had been kept for many years by only one person, the servant who had been hired to take care of this woman in order to sustain her minimal physical life. The details of the little cracks of the secret were almost identical to my own experiences: the mad woman was wearing a white gown and she had long, thick black hair. When she attacked violently, with a burst of emotion, Jane, who is the main character in this story and who took care of her brother when he was visiting as a guest in that mansion, without yet knowing this family secret, found that some injuries—some bleeding cuts on his shoulder—had been made by teeth.

40   Besides those small similarities, what hit me the most was that people took the word "mad" as a word which belongs to a realm totally and absolutely outside of their responsibility. The moment that word, "mad", came out of someone's mouth, it was as if all responsibility was discharged, including questions concerning justice—"Do we have a right to put her into prison? What does she need for her well-being or to improve her situation?"—questions that are usually the first thing people have to consider. They become completely irrelevant. "Her mother was also mad." That statement in *Jane Eyre* was made by the master of the mansion, who double-secured the action by justifying the woman's madness as destiny. If anyone is imprisoned by force without any rational explanation, in a small space with no windows, without any rational or intimate trusted relationship, and is treated without any respect as a person, as a human being, and all chances and means to seek help from the outside are closed off, wouldn't that person become completely mad and violent whether she had been mad to begin with or not? That question was never asked in that book. The second thing that hit me was there was no happy ending, no way out suggested except by her possible death. If only this woman died, Jane could marry the lord of the mansion, the landlord of that village, and a grand lifestyle could prevail throughout the community. The mad woman's existence itself was the obstacle to the community's glory. "Be as if you were dead, as if you had never existed" is the next best thing. That was the ultimate message that they sent out to the mad woman.

41 Instead of all the concerns they should have had, their only concern was the safety of their secret. Their dignity, their glory in the community, had to come first, and anything that interfered with it was considered as shame. They went to elaborate lengths to hide their shame. This secrecy became the highest command in the life of the Lord of the Manor and of all the others who were involved. As soon as you became involved with his secrecy you automatically found yourself a part of a conspiracy: to reveal the secret is then betrayal and disloyalty. Many families who experience domestic violence, or sexual abuse, adopt this mechanism. The sense of guilt of the person who has to deal with the "betrayal" and "disloyalty" is heavy, and some of those people take their whole life to resolve it.

42 The despair of the person who becomes the target of shame is deep and the indignation of those who are caught up in this mechanism is powerful. The victim's despair and indignation become focused on only one point: to expose the perpetrator's lie, to expose the fact that his glory is based on his system of lies, to expose the structure of lies on which he built his whole life of glory, under which his victims are buried alive. If the victims want to fight, they will take a risk of their own lives, a risk of destroying themselves and others, not because they want that but because they want to expose the lies which are the underpinning of the perpetrators' success. Revolutionaries and criminals and terrorists all know this. They know what they have to do: let their deepest sorrow burst out and allow their own despair and indignation to flame up at the very moment the perpetrator thinks his lies are working and his illusional grandiosity is just about secure. This is exactly what I must have done on that dark winter evening when I was a lonely girl of eight years old.

43   When I read this Gothic novel when I was in my early teens, I immediately identified myself with the mad woman who had been imprisoned as evil rather than with the sensible attractive young woman, Jane—which is what all readers are supposed to do. I realized that I had started writing the same story in my mind, only from the different position, the position of the mad woman. It would be quite a different landscape that would have unfolded around the people of the grand mansion if it had been written that way. I did not write that story on paper at that time: of course it would have been far beyond my ability. But one thing I wanted to do was stand quietly beside this mad woman who was deprived of everything: whether she was really mad or not, I wanted to stand on the edge of her world, where the two worlds compete with each other, the world called normal and the world called abnormal, where complacency and desperation are competing with each other. Without escaping deeply into either world, I wanted to stand on the edge: probably for the rest of my life I will be standing on the edge, I thought. Because I once fell into the unfathomable abyss and struggled with the dark complicated mechanism of it on that stormy winter evening, I would probably be able to do it. *Jane Eyre* was written in 1860, almost 100 years before my sickness: now people's attitudes towards psychiatric patients have dramatically improved. But more than half a century ago, in my childhood, my parents' reaction towards my outburst of emotion was nothing but the terror of being shaken into realizing that they were afraid of losing glory, exactly the same as the experience of the characters in *Jane Eyre*, set in the early 19th century.

44   Death was finally internalized in me: after having experienced so many deaths as an outside phenomenon I recognized that the seed of death was planted in my own rib cage at the age of eight. I had started sensing some presence, Divine Presence, you might say, during the war. I started feeling the Presence around me and in me, more often after I got ill. And I started to talk to that Presence alone in silence, day and night, asking about death, about the meaning of my sickness, about the meaning of my life. When I felt strong enough, I put paper on my chest and I wrote my words to him while lying on the *futon*. I could not see my writing well as I wrote because I was prohibited from sitting up. Those were prayers, and now that I think of it, some might likely have been written by a kind of automatic writing. I wrote them without being taught how to pray or how to recite prayers. I did not even know there were people who could have taught me that. But I became happy being alone with God—I did not hesitate to call the Presence by that name. I was always aware that death and God were both quietly growing in my rib cage.

45 Gradually the questions quieted down and a scene appeared which I had been seeing for quite some time in my dreams and between my dreams: the most beautiful meadow surrounded by mountains. It was like the landscape I had seen so often in the countryside during the war but it was somehow different, and I was running there freely. I felt the cool moist gentleness of young grasses on my soles and I felt the soft breezes blowing against my ears. I knew I was in Heaven; I did not want to struggle and come back here anymore.

46 One day I received a visit from a man who was wearing a white collar and black coat. It was the mysterious priest whom I remembered in the mansion of Motoyasu before the war. My mother told me that I could ask him any question I wished: since I had been asking so many questions of my parents which they did not know how to answer, they decided to ask him to come to see me. Looking back, my parents might have wanted—for me and for them—to prepare for my death at that time. I don't think I asked him any questions that day, or at least I don't remember. But he prayed for me, and with me; that was the first prayer I experienced except my own constant talking to Him throughout the war and my sickness. An unexpected warmth spread through my body with big lumps moving up to my throat. I sobbed, breaking the doctor's order that I should not move my lungs, and I put my little hand in his big hand. The priest and I became "very good friends" that day, if I may use his expression.

CHAPTER 6

1 My new school was located just outside the moat of the Emperor's Palace on land still partially covered with an ancient forest. It was considered to be inside the special palace district, a part of the city which America wanted to keep intact for some special reason and did not bomb during the war. The school was built 100 years earlier, specifically so that the Emperor could give his son, the crown prince, the best and most modern education and an opportunity to make lifelong friends, and so that the girls of the aristocracy, who were educated on a different campus, could become candidates to be his wife—a future empress. But ever since, except for keeping the tradition of the Emperor's family, the whole system of the aristocracy was discarded under the new constitution. General MacArthur ordered that it should become a coeducational private school for students who could enter if they passed a thorough examination and paid the high tuition. My parents enrolled me in that school when I was seven years old, just after we had returned to Tokyo.

2 When you walked out of the little train station, which was built specially for our school, you saw a well-planned, broad, paved avenue stretch towards the Detached Palace, which itself was surrounded by woods and a tall black ornamented fence so that only its elaborate roof of copper, turned green with age, could be seen. Opposite those woods, just across the street, stood our school. In order to avoid becoming a target for the Americans' aerial attacks, the whole concrete building was painted black. With its odd but magnificent look, it stood on a small hill, surrounded by an iron gate of the same design as that which surrounded the Detached Palace. This palace was modeled after the Palace of Versailles in France; in fact it was an exact duplicate of it. The Japanese Meiji government built it for the Emperor's brother to use as his second house, thinking that Japan could show off its power to the Western nations so it could have an equal relationship with them, the most urgent concern of the Japanese government in those days. But the brother of the Emperor was furious at what he saw as a totally humiliating, perverse act of the government and he expressed his anger by refusing to step into this palace even once in his life.

3 In this way it came about that the Detached Palace was at once an extraordinary symbol of Japan's glory and of its deepest humiliation, and a symbol of strong pride between the government and the royal family—which revealed that something darker was going on, more than just innocent Emperor worship. It stood solemnly in the woods without an occupant and strangely showed a quiet beauty and harmony in concert with the dignity of this district. One side of the pavement was trimmed with maple trees planted in geometrical order and on the other side was a park surrounded by low-standing bushes which served as a fence all the way to the school building. Almost no cars went by on the street except that every morning, at a regular set time, the black Rolls Royce which carried the Emperor's daughter (two years older than I was) and her attendant was driven out of her palace, which was located nearby, and quietly proceeded to be parked in front of the gate of our elementary school.

4 It was my parents' choice as the highest-level school in which their children could get a solid, traditional education in Japan in those days. Most of the schools had either lost their buildings and equipment or the administrators and faculties had lost their confidence in teaching Japanese traditional culture. Many sunk lowin shame. Allowing "commoners" to enter the school while maintaining the high standards of which it was proud was the first serious challenge this Emperor's school ever experienced. When I applied to the school as a second-grader, at the age of seven, after finishing first grade in public school, along with the examination in arithmetic and music was a required one-hour essay on a given theme. The title given for the essay was, "My Favorite Thing to Do." What a perfect title it was for me, for my mind was still filled with the excitement of the favorite thing which I had done just before leaving home for the examination that morning. I had found a dead insect in my yard. He was showing his belly, tightly confined with amber-color armor, his crumbled legs pointed up to the sky. He seemed to have died not too long ago. I dug a hole in the yard with a little wooden stick and buried him and covered his grave with soil and put a little stone above it, and I kneeled down with my palms together, with my eyes closed, and I prayed. That is what I had been doing since I came to Tokyo: I found so many insects dead on the ground, so I kept burying them and making graves for them. I was careful not to dig too deep so that the human bodies which must have been lying deep underground would not reveal themselves.

5 This is what my favorite thing to do was. I wrote long descriptions of dead insects and careful records of the burials—hhow I buried them, how I prayed for each one—in small, careful letters. When the examination was over, I ran to my mother who was waiting at the end of the hall sitting with the other mothers to tell her what a wonderful essay I had written. Her face darkened. She did not know if this was good news or not. She said, "Let's wait until we go home and see what your father has to say about this." His face darkened, too. I knew very well that my parents had worried about whether I could pass the examination. "I wish I could be sure like I am about the other two," my mother was saying. I overheard them talking and I knew acutely that their worry increased because of what I had written about in that essay. We found out that my elder sister, although applying for entrance to the fourth grade, had been given the same theme for her essay examination, "My Favorite Thing to Do." She told us that she wrote about helping my mother in the kitchen. My parents thought that was the most appropriate thing for her to write, even though my sister had never helped our mother in the kitchen even once because she always wanted to practice piano instead. Her lie did not seem to bother my parents. I did not know what I had done wrong, but I knew I often made my parents very uncomfortable.

6 But the school accepted all three of us with good scores. I became one of the first students of this school after its revolutionary start. Can commoners respect tradition, adjust themselves to it, study it, maintain it, and carry it? Can they understand the core of the traditions, respect for authority, and do they know how to express it: through our language, our manners, our way of greeting? Can they catch up to the levels of accomplishment, academically and culturally, that the former aristocratic students and their families had reached? Will we face any problems by putting boys and girls together in one classroom, in spite of Confucius' teaching, "Boys and girls must not sit together from seven years old"? Can we teach democracy to the level of satisfying General MacArthur and yet still pay the highest respect to the Emperor at the same time? Our class would be monitored microscopically to see if the new programs could ever work. It was a laboratory of many layers of huge human development projects.

7   Each class started after a long procession through the grounds, through a long corridor to the classroom, all of us walking in a line in strict silence and with quiet steps to prepare for the concentration required to learn. I enjoyed this quiet procession. I liked the sounds of the little children's feet, the sounds of the special shoes we wore in order not to bring the outdoor dirt into the sacred place: the floor was covered by a mosaic of woodwork, beautifully varnished. And I liked the sounds of our uniforms rustling. The boys' heads were shaved like monks', and the girls' hair hung straight down to their shoulders. I liked my hair rustling against my ears. The boys' uniform was navy blue with a slight touch of scarlet in the collar, styled after army officers' uniforms. For girls, the uniform was made in the style of navy sailors, dark blue with white stripes and a collar, but a long pleated skirt, and a big scarlet bow to signify that we were students of the elementary division. On the part of the uniform just below the throat we carried the school crest: a cherry blossom was embroidered there and we were not allowed to cover that crest with any jacket, coat, or scarf, so that the whole world would see who we were wherever we were and how orderly, how gracefully, we behaved in any public place. We were trained to look straight ahead, never to the side, nor to show any emotion which might disturb the inner quietness of the little procession each morning. But I remember that when I was finally allowed to return to school on a full schedule, after a long period of recuperating from tuberculosis, it was hard for me to repress my intense pleasure and excitement at the prospect of learning new things in every class.

8   Each subject was taught by a devoted teacher who was also an authority of the first degree in his field. The class always began with a deep bow to the teacher. Fine arts and crafts were taught by different authorities in the variously equipped classrooms and were taken very seriously. I remember those rooms by their big windows facing north, which were believed to provide perfect light for the atelier. Through them we were able to see magnificent maple trees. How much I wanted to be sitting on one of those chairs in front of the drawing board desks which you could adjust to the best angle for you to work, and draw those trees for hours and hours—for as long as I wanted. And I knew that our teacher was working on his own oil painting of those trees in the back of the classroom where all the mysterious equipment was stored. Some cubes and cylinders for learning how the light creates shadow on those shapes, a strange stuffed rabbit with white spots in her brown fur as a subject for a still life, and plaster figures which were modeled by ancient masters in faraway Greece—all were neatly placed there. And there were mechanical tools on those shelves, too: when you looked into the little eyehole of one of them it showed how the little cube would look inside from a perfect Renaissance scientific perspective.

9   Often I went into that room after classes just to see those things, and sometimes I saw our teacher—a young newcomer to the school, hired as part of the commitment to the new democratic style of education and Western art—painting alone there. It was a painting of the same maple trees that fascinated me. He allowed me to watch the process by which the tree trunk gained strength little by little through the strokes of his brush, which he added behind the dazzling gold foliage he had painted on the canvas. Often I brought my sketchbook and drew people I had seen any place at all—on the street as I walked, waiting for the bus, or standing near the door of the train. I did those sketches in two or three minutes each. He taught me how to grasp the people as movement, the movement of body, and how to put them in the movement of the pictorial space. I became better and better and I came to be able to grasp them in a few seconds.

10 The craft room was located in a distant corner of the building, far away from the fine art classroom. In front of the craft room was a big old wooden case with glass in the front so you could see its contents: numerous little works of craft made by the former students of that school before the war and chosen by the teachers at the time as excellent. They were made over a period of 100 years and included works by the Emperors and some of his brothers when they were all elementary students and studied in this particular classroom when it was only for boys. One of my works was chosen to be displayed in that glass case, almost surely one of the first girls' works. It was a pencil stand made of wood with the heads of four horses on each side of the stand decorated in the colorful royal style of the Heian period, the time of the "The Tale of Genji" which had inspired me. It was such an intricate and ambitious project for a little girl like me to handle a jigsaw machine in order to cut out the wood to make it look like delicate lace. I required a long period of trial and error and plenty of the teacher's encouragement and help. It was a dream come true for me to be suddenly given the material and tools in abundance and the best equipment and great teachers after a long period of craving those things during the war.

11	When I look back at the way this school treated the teaching of fine art and craft, with such high respect for Western art tradition and with such a high expectation that elementary school students could practice and learn, I cannot help being hit by astonishment. Learning Western Renaissance perspective, and training to create cubic things in the flat pictorial space, were of course brought to Japan in the Meiji period, by Western artists and Western art historians and perhaps art philosophers. Those traditions were already old when they came to Japan: the art world in Europe at that time was in the heyday of Impressionism, which sprung from a rebellious mood against those Western traditions. But Meiji people did not take Western art as mood, exoticism, nor trend: they took it as a respectful spiritual practice just like other academic endeavors, which requires learning from tradition and authority, personal discipline and cultivation. The only difference between this classroom and the academic classroom was that it was prepared strictly for the purpose of creating and training—actually using hands and body. This school was built to provide the Crown Prince a high education so he could become a great Emperor and the highest priest of Shinto as well. Traditionally the Emperor should satisfy some canons: he should be a man of high virtue and saintly spiritual strength, as well as being capable of military leadership. This fantastic classroom with its elaborate equipment and its atmosphere of evoking the spirits showed how the Meiji people believed that creating art is part of the most fundamental training required to become a good Emperor. It had to be practiced seriously, even at the elementary school level.

12 When I think about it, the division between fine art and craft into different classrooms in this school, each with a teacher who practiced each specialty, makes me smile as well. Japan has a long history of separating art from craft and that tradition seemed to have been followed in this school, too. That distinction came from the ancient Chinese philosophy of art, which teaches that the crucial point of fine art, including calligraphy, is *Chi,* the life force. No matter how excellent the artist's skills, no matter how "spiritual" the subject or the script the artist depicts, if there is no *Chi* filling the entire space, then the art has no spiritual value. And *Chi* is something that gushes out from the artist: it flows out strongly, sometimes going beyond his careful planning and intention, beyond his preconceived idea. But the whole point of craft is how to pursue the preconceived idea: planning and intention are absolutely essential. Art's destiny is to send the artist on her own spiritual journey. Craft's destiny is to develop skill in order to be decorative and functional. In the West, in ancient times, Plato defined art as *techné*: the word meant skill, or craft. In the West, art and craft are inseparable—the opposite of what was practiced in this school.

13 Literature classes started by our reading the poetry that the teacher had prepared before we went into the classroom. Many of the poems came from the 8th-century collections compiled from all over Japan by the Emperors of that time. Without knowing the exact meaning of the words, still I saw in my imagination the people in their spectacular costumes in the beautiful ancient forests and I enjoyed the rhythm of chanting those poems in the way they did in those times. This kind of poetry education seemed most appropriate in this school, for since the time when the Emperor was like an ancient shaman, one of his most serious obligations was to keep alive the sorcery power of words, and that continued all the way to modern times. Even in the year of Japan's surrender to America, celebrations of poetry were held in the palace according to the ancient form. A competition was held which was open to everyone, as historically it has always been, and the winners were invited to the palace and their poetry was recited in the ancient chanting manner along with the poems written by the Emperor and his family. It was such an abundance to find great new poems every day on the blackboard.

14   I learned and spoke every day the special language that is used only in this school and in the Emperor's surroundings. We saw the children of the Emperor and the Empress, and sometimes the Emperor himself attended some of the school activities. On such a occasions I was often told to welcome him or her as part of a small welcoming group composed of the principal and other teachers: we would stand in the gate and make long bows according to some ritual ceremony. Every time I was told to do this I used to wonder, *Why me?* But I never asked, and still the reason remains unknown. We used that special language all the time. The children of the former aristocrats and of the Tokugawa Shogun's descendants and his relatives and the children of their followers were all there in that class; most of their families came from this school and they had all spoken this special language since they were born. They did not pronounce each other's names even among their classmates. When they said "You" they used a special form of address—a literal translation would be "This higher direction". "Your highness" might be closest, or "Your Grace" might be a good translation. And there were complications arising from the two vocabularies of polite language and honorific language: verbs would change their forms according to the distance in relationship, age, and status between the speaker and the person who was listening, and between that person and a third person they might be talking about. The relationship of the speaker to that third party and his relationship to the listener and the listener's relationship to that third party—it was all very complicated and required enormous knowledge of the degrees of respect you were supposed to show in all directions. Tremendous sensitivity was constantly required. If you made any mistake, they would instantly know that you are an outsider.

15 The Emperor's world was the source of the storm of fascism we had just gone through. The war was started in his name, fought in his name, and all the soldiers and citizens who died, died in his name. It turned out that I found myself in the midst of the very world of which I was most afraid. But at the same time, this Emperor's world is the source of Shinto. The Emperor himself was god, but at the same time, he had been the highest priest of the entire hierarchy of Shinto shrines inside Japan. The history of Shinto was formed in time immemorial. Before it was distorted by being combined with nationalism, and before it became the state religion in 1868, the first year of the Meiji period and became the basis of fascism, Shinto had been a serene, simple, unaggressive, nature-based religion. It was combined with Buddhism, which arrived in Japan from a foreign land in the sixth century, and since then, the intermingling of the two religions continued and produced a variety of religious expressions all through our history. You can see the unique, intriguing mixing of Esoteric Buddhism and Shinto around the ninth century, and that mixture was engraved in the Japanese mind deeply for a long time following. But if you go further back, further into the world of Shinto, before Buddhism ever arrived on the islands of Japan, there was a world filled with spirit in every tree, every rock, and every forest, in the waterfalls and rivers, in the storms and lightning. No statue of any deity was ever created, no man-made images were ever worshipped, not even a shrine was built—only spirit flowed everywhere. That Shinto spirit had formed the Japanese aesthetic sensibility towards nature throughout history. You can follow Shinto further back, to when the world was still too dark to form a sense of the human as separated from the world of nature, where the death of humans and the death of trees were not quite distinguished, and then to the world of mythology and poetry, and further back to the world of the darkness out of which everything is born.

16   In the labyrinth of mythology, the Emperor is connected to the Sun Goddess, *Amaterasu*, and became her descendant. It is the oldest monarchy in the world, and the only monarchy that is claimed to be directly traced to its ancient origin in blood and in the practice of rituals in their original ancient forms. Every tradition and authority in Japan can ultimately be traced to the mysterious power of this myth of history. It is a black hole that sucked everything into itself and has never been examined. It is like the Emperors' tombs themselves, which were built from early A.D. to the fifth century: they are magnificent—

one among them is the biggest in the world, bigger than the pyramids in Egypt—and it still has never been opened yet, even so long after the war. It is still covered with a forest and isolated by triple moats just like a symbol of the black hole itself. No archaeological excavation had ever been allowed, until recently, when some limited excavation started for the first time.

17 In 1946, at America's command, the Emperor made a declaration denying his divinity. He quit being God. God was gone! Who was going to replace him in the empty position of God now? To whom could they burst out their cries and their anger, they whose loved ones were tortured and slaughtered all over Asia, all over the world, in the most cruel ways by the Japanese army—the children of the Emperor, as they called themselves? To whom can we sing the requiem, we who are in deep remorse and feel the pain of guilt at having encouraged and sent our loved ones to their death for the glory of the Emperor, believing he was God?

18 One episode is deeply engraved in the Japanese mind: the historic meeting held between the Emperor and General MacArthur immediately after the war. The Emperor asked to spare Japanese citizens and take his life instead. This episode is written in MacArthur's memoirs, but oddly enough no record of the Emperor's plea has been found in any of the Japanese records, including the memoir by the translator who served the Emperor on that occasion. The Emperor himself maintained complete silence about it. America decided not to pursue the responsibility of the Emperor in the War Crimes Trials, nor did it ever discuss this issue on any other occasion. Whatever their reasons, they came to this decision: it was America's decision, and silence suited America's political strategy. But MacArthur's memoirs became known throughout Japan. So, without being prosecuted, the Emperor became the Symbol of Democracy in the new Japan: he slipped from the role of the one who had started the fascistic war to the new role of "Symbol of Democracy" without any clarification of people's confusion, without taking any responsibility for the past. Many believe that he was deceived, used by the fascistic army, that he was a peace lover from the beginning and he offered his life to the former enemy in order to save our lives. They believed that he died once and was reborn as a true Emperor. One has to die in order to be reborn, they thought, by going through the darkest dead of night. Faith in the rebirth of the Emperor became so deep that this episode of the offering of his life for the people became rich soil for growing a new myth, the myth of the Emperor's rebirth. Is the new myth so compelling to Japanese that we do not even need to validate the episode itself anymore? The huge black hole only deepens as time goes by.

19 The contrast between the world inside the school and the world outside the school was sharp. Children who lost their parents and homes, after coming back from the camps where they were forced to evacuate, were still there in the basements of the subways, but now they were picking up the cigarette butts which Americans threw away in the hallways of the ruined subway stations. Americans' cigarette butts came from expensive cigarettes and children collected them and sold them through a network of contacts. If a child could make enough capital that way, he could promote himself to the upper ground and sit on the street with a shoeshine kit, and shine the American soldiers' boots. Hundreds of children made a line on the pavement, day and night, and competed with each other to show how quickly they could shine the boots and how dazzlingly shiny they could make them, and many of them were making a living. The cars that were running on the street were all for Americans: Japanese were not allowed to buy any gasoline. But they fixed the busses and trucks in such a way that they could be driven by burning charcoal and logs in the back of the vehicles to make steam, using heat instead of gasoline as the energy source. Spewing black smoke everywhere in town, they moved for a short distance and stopped and then they threw in more logs, and they ran again for a while. We all relied on this innovation for our transportation.

20   There was an active market on the street, which they called the "market of darkness" because it opened before the sun rose, some said, and others said it was because their businesses were completely illegal. They sold crazy things at crazily inflated prices: everything from one used shoe to a bottle of whiskey made from methyl alcohol which would make you blind if you drank it. And blankets deeply soaked in blood, almost dry or still dripping, were sold: no one knew how the blankets got there, but they were sold. *Yakuza*, the Japanese Mafia, took kickbacks from the people who sold those weird things, saying that they were protecting their businesses and their merchandise from the city violence. Everyone knew that the *Yakuza* themselves were the only violent ones—so they paid.

21   My father's office was filled with women who had become prostitutes to the American soldiers in order to feed their children or take care of their elderly mothers. A daughter of one of our neighbors who lived in a house made of tin married an American soldier and left for America so she could keep sending money back to her family from there. She and her newly wedded American husband gave my father a weird brown thing in gratitude for something my father did for them when all the neighbors ignored them as if they did not exist. When we children came back from school one day, the brown thing was piled on the tray, on the table, and it looked like a little mountain of mud. Our father said it was a chocolate cake, which I ate that day for the first time in my life. It was extremely sweet: we had never had any sugar before, and it was so sweet that we had only one bite of it and could not eat any more. Men who contracted venereal disease in a dark alley for a momentary gratification after coming back from the battlefield panicked, clinging to my father. It was before penicillin was widely available. I developed a special sensitivity to be able to identify them by the desperate expressions on their faces, even on the street before they came to see my father. One night I was frightened by a loud knock at our door and the voices of a *Yakuza* and his followers shouting "Doctor, Doctor!" They were seeking help in the middle of the night because he had a knife still sticking out of his back, dripping blood at the front door. And the boss of the *Yakuza* told my father, "You don't ever have to worry about your beautiful daughters' safety, I have positioned my men in the town to protect the little ladies of our doctor!"

22 School was an entirely different world. When I went on a field trip from the school, I was inside a special shining bus, and a troop of policemen with white gloves stood respectfully for hours lined up along the streets all the way to our destination, saluting us and protecting our bus from the "filth" coming close to us, because the daughter of the Emperor was sitting with us in the bus. Different languages distinguished the two worlds most distinctly: the one used in the school and the other used outside of school. I did not feel comfortable using either of the languages even though I had become quite expert in both in a rather short period of time: I was afraid that one would slip into the other when I was using it, and would reveal to people that I never belonged to either world.

23 My recovery from tuberculosis was steady but hard work. Going to school meant walking to the crowded station, which had so many stairs, and taking the crowded train, standing all the way to the destination station, and from that little station walking to school. In the beginning of my recovery while I was still in the third grade, late in the morning in order to avoid the rush hour, my mother came with me for all of it. She stayed in school while I was attending one or two classes and we went home together, reversing the exact same steps we took in the morning. But soon I started going to school in the early morning, during rush hour, by myself.

24 I walked very slowly on the pavement from the station to the school, aiming for one of the trees that formed a colonnade along the street, as my first goal to reach where I might rest until I felt strong enough to get to my second goal. I tried to reach one goal at a time. How many more goals should I set? How many had I already conquered? I always counted accurately in order to distribute my energy wisely. Sometimes it seemed impossible to reach the school and the fear that I would faint before I got there was always present. Every time the train arrived at the station, the street was covered with uniformed students of my school; some kindly tried to walk with me, but I let them go, gently but firmly. This task of making it to school was so hard for me that I did not think I could do it without the most intense concentration, and in order to maintain that concentration I had to be left alone. The street became quiet again, and then at the next train, I heard the sound of pencil cases juggling in the students' leather backpacks as they ran close by me and passed me as they ran late to school. When I started attending the full schedule of classes, I went to the infirmary and stayed in bed there during the lunch break. I listened to the children's high voices and the sound of dodge balls hitting the ground while I stared at the white ceiling of the infirmary, pulling the blanket wrapped with starched white sheets to my chin. That became my routine for a long period of time.

25   I had feared that if I flunked one year by not fulfilling the mandated attendance days, I would have to be in the same class with my younger sister. This fear was supported by my parents' fear that my shameful sickness would brand me forever as a failure at the start of my life. Their fear was much deeper than mine and it had some legitimacy in Japan's culture, where age is one of the most crucial elements of society's order: all language patterns are determined by age. Between freshman and sophomore year, between a person employed at the company this year and one employed a year earlier, different words for "you" have to be used in addressing each other. Every sentence must express respect for one's elders: this is so deeply rooted in the culture of the Japanese that it continues through the rest of their lives. To ignore or confuse this ladder of hierarchy in Japanese society arouses embarrassment and hostility. If I were one year older than my sister and yet we were in the same grade, I would be labeled a failure for the rest of my life.

26 My parents did everything for me to help me fulfill the mandated attendance days of the school. The school must have credited me with one full day as long as I showed up once during that day because I often went to school and slept in the infirmary and then came home. My parents' fear that I might fall down from society's ladder was so overwhelming that often it blinded them to how tired I was and how often I fainted and collapsed. And this blindness of my parents made me feel that the weakness I was feeling might be just my laziness. I came to think that the problem I was suffering might be in big part due to my weak will power rather than to the weakness of my body since everyone else was handling his life admirably well with strong will power.

27 After I fulfilled the mandated attendance days somehow and was allowed to enter the fourth grade, my mother again started showing up at school and waiting for me at the gate. She was there to take me to private violin lessons at the house of a famous teacher: the house was located one hour by train from the school, requiring two transfers. She would be there outside my school holding a black violin case in standing position in her left arm just like American soldiers held their rifles: the violin was of a smaller size for the young, but it was still too heavy for me to carry. It was my mother's belief that I should start violin lessons immediately: since I had already failed in learning piano, I would miss the crucial timing of music education forever unless I started learning a new instrument right away. Now suddenly there was the additional hour of cradling the violin between my chin and shoulder, standing up for hours, twisting my left arm while moving the right arm and elbow widely, and with all this torturous physical labor, it seemed that my life of fighting against physical hardship would never end.

28 The questions I had started asking around the time of my sickness became deeper. What was the meaning of my sickness? In the solitude of which I had been given a lot during my sickness, this question triggered other more fundamental questions like, "Why did I live?" "Where did I come from?" and "Where would I go?" The feeling that God was telling me something very important became more intense, but at the same time my whole thinking process gained more delicacy and ambiguity. The physical hardship was always there for me to fight against, but it was also a continuous, perpetual reminder that my body was not quite myself, that I had to establish some reasonable relationship with it. Even some innocent pleasure such as reading books, or drawing a simple picture, or writing stories in my bed, had to be sacrificed often, and if I failed to sacrifice such pleasures even for a day, then a few days or even weeks of rest were required as a consequence.

29 In the course of repeatedly losing this battle with my physical body, I gradually learned to surrender myself to it. Then my life became more confined, more motionless, more silent and closer to something that looked like death. As I surrendered more, my sensitivity became more refined, and sharpened. From that complete silence and motionlessness, my new life gradually opened up to me. I listened to my body, to its breath, its pulse, to the delicate, unintelligible feeling flowing over my skin. The body started feeling not like something hostile to me but more as a gentle protector. The body protected me by shutting down all the activities of the outside world which I would have drowned in if my body had not stopped me, and it started to take me into the dark, deep, inner world, putting me on its back just as a little boat would float on the water leading into a cave. I felt as if I were a thin, shining, silver antenna, standing on that little boat alone.

30 But sometimes the boat, my body, smoothly traveled across a lake whose surface reflected things in the universe with deep satisfaction and joy. Sometimes the boat would float up to the sky, and I would see the white dust of the galaxy wheeling round me. No matter how far I floated I felt I was embraced by the universe, and that I was at the center of an unexplainable world. The usual everyday body seemed to be dying, and a more refined body was starting to be born. I was glimpsing a joyous world. At the same time, now that I look back, I must have been in a dangerous place where all darkness and evil which had been pushed down and hidden stood up and threatened to break up my joy and surge into it—a place reached by anyone who has practiced deep meditation, a place which requires proper guidance to go through. I was alone without anyone to help me, without having any knowledge of it.

31 It was this unspeakable world and an urgent quest for a clear understanding of it that made me separate from others, more than those physical hardships which I still had to endure. Still, I was increasingly enjoying various school projects—telling stories to the whole class that I read or created during my long sickness, sometimes with my own illustrations that I created with a quite elaborate method and for which I received many requests to publish "next installment" editions from friends and teachers. Or often discussing and debating various issues in the class. And although I even became popular in school—lots of friends waiting for me at the gate to walk with me after school and wanting to listen to the stories that went on every day—

and even as I was allowed to be more involved in those activities, still I was keenly aware that there was something planted in me like a seed along with my sickness, something I would never be able to share with friends, and that this something had been growing deeply and powerfully in my mind. And the quest to know what it was never gave me rest.

CHAPTER 7

1 Finally about two years after I got tuberculosis, the day came that I was pronounced fully recovered. Now I was strong enough to visit the mansion of the Motoyasu with my mother and two sisters over the summer vacation. My grandmother was standing on the platform of the small station in a beige-colored Western dress re-formed from her old summer linen kimono. My little cousin, who was raised by my grandmother after his mother left, his long skinny legs sticking out of his short pants, wearing wooden sandals on his bare feet, was standing beside her. How small they both looked under the orange light of the quiet station. We got in the taxi, the lone vehicle in front of the station, and my grandmother started directing the driver to the mansion from the back seat. My mother whispered to her that she did not have to do such a thing: it was enough just to say we were going to the mansion. My mother had been irritated at seeing her mother wearing a re-formed dress, unbecoming for the mistress of the Motoyasu mansion. "There are many newcomers in town," my grandmother replied. Finally the mansion's black roof appeared on the hillside, each tile reflecting the moonlight: it looked like the ocean spread under the night sky. But something looked slightly different from before, probably because there were no lights lit up on the light poles that surrounded the high stone walls of the mansion as there used to be. We entered the mansion from the dark kitchen gate.

2 The beautiful garden was not there, although the fence made of plywood was illuminated in the moonlight around the area where the garden was closest to the mansion. But the moment my grandmother opened the sliding kitchen doors, the familiar, shining, dark-brown wooden floor spread out before us. It was exactly as I remembered it, and the smell of the mansion flooded my mind with vivid memories. Two huge cupboards stood in the corner of the wooden hall in the exact same solemnity as before, containing hundreds of dishes and bowls and countless mother-of-pearl inlaid chopsticks and little pillows for the chopsticks to rest on during meals, pillows made of colorful porcelain in every conceivable pattern and color or of woven bamboo of strange shapes or of curved stones and wood. When my grandmother opened the paper screen doors to invite us into the family dining room next to the hall, the big wooden table at which we used to sit with twenty or more people was at once placed in the center of the *tatami* room just like before, still keeping its persimmon color, deep and intense.

3 My grandmother sat and, putting both of her hands before her knees, bowed in welcome saying how happy she was to see us all. My mother returned the same gesture to her, and we three children followed her example in the same manner. My cousin shyly did the same, too. To each of us my grandmother expressed her pleasure at meeting again, and to me, especially, she added her pleasure at seeing my recovery from the sickness. However embarrassing this greeting ceremony was for all her grandchildren, that was my grandmother's way, and we had to go through it. She opened the sideboard in the dining room and took out a little teapot and teacups and other little things, and made delicious tea for all of us as if we were mature ladies who knew how to appreciate these things.

4 But the conversation between my grandmother and my mother abruptly went in another direction, and the peaceful, cheerful atmosphere in the dining room was broken. I did not understand at first what was happening, but soon I realized that it was about the mansion of the Motoyasu: my grandmother had rented out a big part of the mansion and my mother was upset about it. Is some stranger living here now in the mansion of the Motoyasu? What happened to the gallery where that mysterious artwork solemnly stood? What happened to those most beautiful rooms in which the wedding was held? Where was the red gem-colored bridge? Is it still there so that I might stand on it and look down at the pond? Or was that red bridge only in my dreams? No, certainly not. It was there; I used to crouch down on it and look down at the boat, which the sweet young man whom I called my brother had made for me, floating in the pond. The bridge must still be forming a powerful arc over the quiet pond.

5 My two sisters and I started to explore the mansion. My cousin proudly guided us. The long corridor was dark. A faint light came through the smoked glass in the thick wooden lattice door of the entrance to the bathtub room. The wooden steps of the quiet staircase stretched and disappeared into the darkness of the upstairs. The closet room near the stairs was closed with the same heavy wooden doors that I remembered. Turning the corridor, we passed by rooms and rooms closed by silk screen doors on which the color of the rich *sumi* gray, black and subtle gold were visible, but the patterns on those panels were barely recognizable because of the darkness. The black metal handles on those panel doors were elaborately decorated with heavy silk tassels hanging down, looking so dignified and authoritative that they made me feel they were there only to forbid us to open the door rather than to encourage us to use them to open the doors. Only far away at the top of those doors, beautifully cut-out wood panels were framed between the lintel and the ceiling, through which the faint moonlight came and floated from the opaque rice-paper doors of the rooms to the garden outside the room. The cut-out patterns were extremely intricate, patterns of landscapes, pine trees on the sands of the beach, little sailing boats on the faraway ocean, houses, and mountains, continuing as on a scroll. Looking up from the dark corridor, up at the closed doors of the rooms against the faint moonlight, the landscape looked astonishingly real, only because at that small size I felt I was looking at it somehow through a mysterious microscope. This cut-out landscape was the one so vividly alive in my mind when I was crafting a pencilstand at the craft class at the school! Suddenly I almost screamed that I wanted to re-create this mysterious microscope effect: I had been so excited, so frustrated, and worked so hard.

6 Turning in the opposite direction from the entrance into the medical rooms, where the floor changed from dark-brown wood to old dark-green linoleum, the color of the floor I associated with the smell of creosol, I felt a suggestion of some abnormality and the urgency of being sick, of closeness to death, of experience far outside everyday life. I used to feel fear and awe there when I was little, but now the place had no smell of creosol. We came to the other corridor which led us to the entrance where two sliding doors closed from both sides. I felt this area was somehow familiar. I was almost sure that this entrance was the way to the big rooms where the wedding was held, and somewhere in the same direction there must be a gallery, and the chapel where the half-naked man was hanging might be there too, and in some of those rooms, if you opened the panel doors to the outside, must be the garden where the pond lies, and the gem-colored red bridge must still form a perfect semicircle over the pond. I walked up to the big doors. My cousin stood against the door. "No, you are not supposed to go in there," he said, and he added in a low voice, "Someone is there on the other side, you know." I withdrew my hand. No light came out from between the two doors nor from underneath them. "You have never seen those rooms over there, have you? But I have, I was there!" I whispered to him.

7   I felt as if all the rooms that I remembered had drifted away and sunken into the unfathomable darkness which spread beyond this door, the hundred lanterns with the dancing ancestors and the mysterious art along with them. I determined to put my hand on the door and tried to pull. I tried both doors. The doors were locked, more precisely they did not move nor could they be shaken, as if those doors were molded into the wall of the other side. I looked down to see the threshold and I saw my cousin's pale little bare feet standing near my white socks, but no one else's. "Where have they gone?" Suddenly, fear struck both of us. All through this exploration of the mansion, one thing was in my head: *ninja*. Just recently our history teacher had told us, "The first Tokugawa Shogun was the Shogun who used *ninja* as spies and assassins most frequently in history." Those words came back to me as we explored the big rooms behind the big sliding doors. I checked carefully around the corners of the lintel and the ceiling, because I knew that *ninja* often hid themselves in those corners, one leg spread to the right and the other to the left along the lintel, and looked down at the people coming into the room and jumped down quietly like a big black bird spreading its wings and grabbed them. I did not tell my cousin or either of my two sisters about my fantasies: I knew it was childish and that I should not scare them needlessly. But the moment I cried, only in my mind, "A *ninja* grabbed my sisters away!" my cousin jumped as if he had heard me crying aloud, and ran like a fox chased by hunters in the forest in the direction we just had come from. *I should not run,* were the first words which came to my mind. The thought of death gripped me: if I ran, I might die from the running itself, before the darkness behind the doors reached out and caught me. Because I still followed the doctor's strict orders at that time. I started walking steadily without a guide in the dark maze-like corridors. When I finally came out to the lighted area near the dining room, I heard my mother's voice from the room, "I will never come to this mansion again!" It sounded like a voice squeezed out from a throat full of pain.

8 My mother came upstairs to see if we were ready to sleep. My two sisters were already lying on their *futons* saving up their energy for the early morning piano practice. The excitement of exploring the mansion did not distract them. "What happened to the artwork?" I asked my mother from the *futon* I was lying on. "There is no such thing anymore," she replied. The memory came back to me of the old man whose house we had stayed at, in the village during the war. The left side of his body was suddenly paralyzed one day. He was lying on a *futon* when I went in the room. He was covered with a blanket and yet I saw instantly that something had happened to his body. Half his body was pulled down into the darkness, as if that part of the body did not remember anymore to whom it belonged. Doesn't his hand remember the texture of the straw he wove into sandals: how proudly he pulled the straw tight so that his right hand beautifully wove through the vertical threads? The old man tried hard to pull the heavy hanging part of his body back towards himself but he could not do it. The roof of the mansion of the Motoyasu looked different from the taxi window when we approached. It was covering the whole mansion under the shining black tiles, and yet just like the old man's body I saw instantly that something had happened to the mansion. The roof could not pull the parts back together; they had already sunk deep into the darkness. The roof could only embrace the mansion quietly so that its memories would not drift too far away.

9 The next day we were going to the beach two stations away from the mansion. My two sisters and my mother left for the elementary school nearby early in the morning where they arranged beforehand to be able to use the school piano for practice in the mornings. In the meantime my grandmother and my cousin and I were going to prepare a picnic lunch which we were going to take to the beach with us.

10 "You stretch your palm flat and touch the water in the plate, so that no rice grain will stick to your palm; and you spread salt on your palms and put hot rice on your palm, and place a pickled plum in the middle of the rice so that the salt and the plum prevent the rice from spoiling even in the long hours of the hot summer day. Close and fold your palm with the other hand and make a triangle shape, and wrap it with dried seaweed so that the person who eats this will not make his hands sticky." Plates for water, for salt, for seaweed, and for pickled plum were placed neatly on the table. My grandmother cooked rice in a big iron rice pot, then poured it into the wooden barrel to make the rice fluffy. And she cooled it with a big fan made of bamboo and paper. I made rice cakes one by one, following her careful instructions. She praised me for the perfectly triangular rice cakes I made, "Because you have long fingers." I kept making more and more, sitting next to my cousin, who was also making rice cakes only smaller and more irregular ones, his pale cheeks flushed red with excitement as if he had a fever. I kept my eyes on him because I once witnessed him licking his palms with his tongue instead of dipping his hands into the water.

11 Vegetables were cooked in a big iron pot to go with the rice cakes. Carrots were cut into the shape of flowers, lotus roots were sliced to show their enigmatic wheel-like pattern. Then, the soft cream-colored young bamboo shoots were sliced vertically, so that all the hollows between the joints were still folded and mysteriously visible. How humble these foods were compared to the dishes this table had on its surface a long time ago. And yet how beautiful those vegetables looked, and how abundant they all felt! My cousin usually sat at the corner of the table, half facing my grandmother, who sat at the edge of the table close to the kitchen at dinner. There would never have been a time that the dishes were spread edge to edge on the table like today. How quiet it must be to have dinner with grandmother alone evening after evening. My grandmother placed a bunch of bamboo skins, in which the young bamboo shoots were wrapped when they shot out of the ground, one by one on the table, with their smooth shiny sides up and their furry brown sides down, and she placed the rice cakes on them, then wrapped and tore the edge of the skin off to make string and tied each package with it. It was quick and magical. We counted forty-three rice cakes we had made. How on earth could just six of us eat all of them?

12   It was the best declaration of my complete recovery from tuberculosis—even though some people still got a shock when they saw how skinny and how pale I was, and were frightened to be near me—that I was recovered and not contagious. No one should be ashamed of me anymore, or be so deeply overwhelmed by shame and detest me just like ancient people felt about lepers; they did not have to lock me up when their friends and relatives came to their place for dinner. I was not a person who brought death to people anymore: instead I could bring nourishment and joy to people. What could be better proof of this than being asked to make their food and eat together? Who could be a better person than my grandmother to authorize me to do all of that—she who was a doctor's wife and who loved all her grandchildren, who would never risk their lives in any way?

13   At the beach, we rented a *tatami* room on a tower made of bamboo for the day: we could see the whole ocean from that tower. In the middle of the horizon, in one particular place, white smoke stood like a pillar. My grandmother told me, "That is the mouth of the bay. From that mouth all the waves of the ocean try to rush into this bay. That is the reason the smoke stands there like spray: it is a dangerous spot. But we are all staying inside of the quiet bay, so you don't have to be scared." My mother and two sisters and my cousin rushed out to the water. Grandmother stayed with me in that room. I lay down on the *tatami*, and she folded a towel and placed it under my head as a pillow and covered me with a bigger towel she had brought from home. "You are tired after making all forty-three rice cakes," she smiled. "There was a red bridge in the garden, wasn't there?" I wanted to ask her, but I was too tired to talk. I was watching her with my head on the towel pillow on the *tatami*. She was sitting with her knees folded tightly in the simple white summer kimono with the narrow gray *obi*, looking at the faraway horizon. She would tell me there was a red bridge on the pond. She would reassure all of my memories and I would embrace them tenderly in order for them not to drift away too far. Whatever happened to it, as long as these memories lived in my mind, the mansion would be alive. I would not be like the Shining Princess in the story: I would embrace these memories for a long time. The voices of children on the beach, and the sound of the ocean, came close to me and went far away. I dozed off.

14 The opportunity to deepen and sum up my thoughts about the meaning of my sickness—something I had thought about for a few years—came rather unexpectedly. One day my home room teacher who taught us Japanese literature suggested that I edit and send one of my writings to a contest for schoolchildren for which some famous writer was a judge. He was known in that time as a writer who expressed the most delicate Japanese sensibility. My literature teacher was new in the school, different from the other teachers who had a very strict traditional style of education which placed more emphasis on memorizing than on expression. He encouraged us to write about our thoughts, and wrote us back his comments on everything we handed in. I had written many essays to him just as if I were writing him letters. The essay that he recommended I edit and submit was about my sickness. In the essay for the contest, I described how much I had thought about and prayed for understanding of the meaning of my sickness rather than wishing or praying for recovery from it, and how gradually I started realizing that if I did not have the experience of this sickness I would never have thought about things like death and life. Now I had become a person who loved to think because of my long sickness. Probably part of the answer to what I had been questioning was that I had become a person of thinking, and that is what I wrote about in the essay. When I reflect on it now, I realize that I was taking one small, modest step towards my much bigger, more distant goal of understanding my life. It seems I had two things to figure out and one of them was the meaning of my sickness—a sickness which felt like an intense message to me, so intense that it never even occurred to me to pray to God for a recovery; instead I wanted to hear the message. And anyway, I never viewed my sickness as something I could get out of. But I started to feel then that the message would never come to me as a series of words: I began to feel that to understand the message would be something like understanding the architecture of a huge cathedral in which I was standing, or rather it was almost like I had to understand the whole meaning of the Ninth Symphony which I listened to with muffled sound in a dark room during the war, a memory that was still with me.

15 And then the other thing I had to figure out was the mysterious world that I experienced. I did not know how to start even to describe it or how to think about it. It was so overwhelming and probably forbidden and yet it seemed somehow related to the meaning of my sickness. My inner world—the seed that was planted in me during my sickness and which was connected to the realm of some sacred Presence, was growing bigger and stronger throughout my sickness and afterwards. And in order to understand that world I was trying to start from the one solid step I knew how to take, which was thinking rather than letting myself go deeper into that world without thinking and losing myself in it.

16 One of those days, during the long summer vacation, a memorable incident happened. When a little bush in our yard moved, and something came out of it, I could not believe what I saw. The first thing I saw was a pair of small eyes, wild and tormented. Next, the body covered with blood, and then next, a wound itself opened, slashed by something like a hatchet. It was a cat that had been the victim of some harsh violence. I was afraid to hold him, to carry him inside of my house: he looked too frightened to be held. I was watching and leading him to the open terrace of the house by changing my own position. He walked or rather slid himself towards the house. I rushed into the kitchen and grabbed the butter, which was a present from someone for me because I still needed special nourishment to help me recover from tuberculosis. I pinched off some butter, softened by the summer's heat, and lay it on the ground on the path leading to the house. He did not quite eat it— he was probably too sick—but he certainly smelled it and followed it.

17 I helped him pass over the threshold to the house. The moment he passed it, he collapsed. I called my parents in a loud voice and they rushed into the room. I sat behind the blood-covered cat, who was stretched out on the floor, just like the samurai sat when they entreated their lord: "Please help this cat," I said. I put my hands on the floor in front of my folded knees in that certain way and bowed. My mother screamed and ran away to the kitchen, saying, "That cat makes me sick! Put it away—he will die anyway." But my father's doctor's conscience seemed to be moved. I did not think he had ever treated a cat—he was a doctor for humans, not a veterinarian. But he examined the cat, and brought some instruments and medicines from his office, and began treatment. In front of the cat, now bundled up by white bandages, father groaned, "He might survive."

18 The cat recovered day by day, beyond anyone's expectation; it was a quick recovery. He turned out to be a beautiful black-and-white cat. I decided to call him Q. It was just after I learned the alphabet in school, and how to use the alphabet as Roman characters to write and pronounce in Japanese: it was part of Japanese language study, and we learned the whole alphabet. I was fascinated by the letter Q, the shape of which looks exactly like a sitting cat from behind.

19 He was extremely quick and wild: when a mouse or rat appeared in the house, which after the war was not too uncommon, wherever he was he jumped out and changed direction, in midair if necessary, and in one flash, he caught him. One day he came in from outside holding a big grilled fish in his mouth: the fish was in perfect shape with its head and tail and all its fins "as if he were jumping out of the water"—the way that grilled fish was prepared for special occasions like weddings. We were all astonished: he had swiped it from the formal table of some wedding! We almost felt we had to return this fish to its owner: it was such an incredibly fancy delicacy. But we had no idea where he stole it from. And we could not take it out of the cat's mouth and put it back on the formal dinner plate for a guest to eat, could we? He proudly ate the whole thing by himself, leaving the clean skeleton in perfect shape. He was independent and quiet: sitting on top of the 5 x 5-inch gate pole in front of my father's office, always on the same side—the side from which he could see the ruin of an old warehouse where the kidnappers of children lived. Those kidnappers stretched out their arms and if the children walked by too close to the windows, they grabbed them and pulled them inside and then sold them to the circus, everybody knew. And he could see the graveyard on top of the hill. And over those he could see the sky where the light of Pure Land was reflected at sunset. He sat with his four legs close together and his tail coiled tightly to fit completely in that small, square space: he looked exactly like the Egyptian statue of a cat which I saw in the special teachers' section of the school library. *He wants to go far away, he will go away beyond this scene, far beyond this graveyard and ruined warehouse,* I always thought. *I know how you're feeling because I too am going away—very, very far away beyond this scene, when my time comes.* I put my arms around the pole on top of which he was sitting, and looking up, I talked to him in my mind.

20 One day I heard the news on the radio that dogs and cats in a certain district of the town were getting a strange disease: they became crazy, violently agonized, and died. And their death toll was climbing higher. The city investigated to see if it was an epidemic and whether it was contagious to humans. They recommended to not let pets, or any small animals, outside for a while. I remembered that district of town: I had visited its Shinto shrine and its garden with someone I don't remember, a long time before I got tuberculosis. It was very far away from my house but I knew my Q went very far away when he went out at night. He might go into that part of town, and being bitten by other cats as often he was, he could easily get that disease and be agonized to death. That idea panicked me. I thought about how I could restrict Q from going to that district, and yet allow him to move freely in and around the house. Because a Japanese house is always accessible to outside nature, we could not completely seal it. Was there any leash long enough and not too oppressive that I could use it for Q only for a short time? Then suddenly the idea came to me that I might use a roll of gauze bandages, soft enough, not too oppressive like a chain, and one roll would be long enough. That will do! The only thing I had to know was whether it was too expensive. I asked my father if he could give me a roll and he said he was just going to discard an old roll of bandage that was produced during the war because the new product was so much better for medical purposes. "Take the old one," he said.

21 Everything was set. I tied one edge of the bandage to Q's neck and held the rest of the whole coil of it in my hand. But Q crouched down and did not move. 10 minutes and 20 minutes passed but he did not move. I decided to put the coil of bandage near my desk on the *tatami*, the straw floor, and start doing my summer vacation homework. It was just a second later that I saw Q rush out of the room to the outside—to the yard and then to the street in front of our house. The whole coil was already gone. I rushed out and saw that he was running towards the graveyard.

22 I saw the long white straight line moving upward along the slope as if it were a string by itself automatically running at full speed. I followed it as best I could but there was no way to catch up with him. I was gripped by fear. "He will be in danger, this long string will get tangled up with everything. A car will be on the string and he will get tangled up under its wheels." I had to do something to prevent that but I felt totally helpless. I walked through the ruins of the kidnappers' warehouse to the graveyard, but nothing was there. On the way back I knocked on several houses' doors and begged people I knew or vaguely knew, "If you see my black-and-white cat anywhere, please tell me or my family." That was the only thing I thought I could do. I came back home and told everything to my father. I sat without moving, overwhelmed by worry. I had done something—the most terrifying thing—to Q: if it were me, it would be just as if I had been pulled into the torture chamber at the Fascists' headquarters. He was surely panicked just as I would certainly be in that situation. His terror, his boiling anger at being betrayed—I felt as if I were Q.

23 In the early evening a man visited my father. He was one of the neighbors I had talked to. He said he saw a black-and-white cat in the burnt field. That field was located in the opposite direction from where Q had run. In fact you have to cross a big street, which had rather heavy traffic all the time, in order to reach that place. *Did Q cross that heavily trafficked street with his long string attached?* I was agitated. The neighbor could not answer whether the cat had a long string on his neck—he could not see it because it was already too dark or because the cat disappeared under the tall grasses so quickly. Or maybe that cat was simply not Q, maybe it was a completely different cat who did not have any leash, or what he thought was a cat was not a cat at all, just wind moving through the grass. The more my father asked him questions, the less he was sure about what he saw.

24 We appreciated his kindness. My father certainly did not want his questions to sound like an interrogation, but the man's answers did not offer a clear view of what had really happened. And it was already too dark to look for Q. My father told me, "We will find Q and I will cut the string from his neck: that is absolutely crucial. Be prepared for that task, at dawn tomorrow. Sleep well." I prayed more than any time in my life—almost all night, at least in my child's mind I did not sleep at all because of my prayer. My most urgent prayer was that we might cut his string as short as possible, so that he wouldn't be caught by a car on the street, or tangled up in the burnt bicycles or in any broken machine in the burnt field. Another prayer was that I might have a chance to convey to him that I blessed his journey wholeheartedly, because I had always sincerely loved his freedom, and that tying him with the bandage (which I now I regretted bitterly) seemed to be a very short temporary solution for him to avoid a traumatic death from the diabolical disease. I wanted him to know this, in order for him to start his journey which I was so sure he already decided to make, without dark terrifying agony.

25 When my father woke me up at dawn, he was already fully dressed and he was holding a pair of shining surgical scissors in his hand. With these scissors he would cut the bandages off; I knew how his scissors behaved. I had never seen these scissors used for any other purpose outside his surgery. I felt his commitment was deep and serious. I dressed myself quickly and went to the kitchen and got some tiny dried fish my mother used for soup stock: I grabbed it in my left hand, thinking that in any emergency, my right hand should be free. And I put on leather shoes, which were only for going to school, because the wooden sandals I usually wore might not function well in the burnt field with so much debris. All those things were decided while I lay awake during the long night.

26 The burnt field was full of debris. Concrete ruins were everywhere, broken old machines were rusted and sharp-edged. And yet tall green grass grew vigorously, in some places almost to my height, in other places just at my knees' height. It was like an ocean or rather a swamp where you cannot see the ground on which you are standing. Dangerous sharp objects and lots of human skeletons of people who died in the bomb attacks, must be there—insects and worms made their nests in them and snakes might be coiled over them. We were calling Q and cautiously looking around. When I approached a big chunk of concrete ruins, suddenly I saw that Q jumped up out of the grass and stood on top of that chunk of concrete as if it were a pedestal. He stared at me. Our eyes met. He looked exactly like my Q that I visualized over and over all night long, and yet he looked different. His eyes recognized me, of course, and yet he was not exactly like before: he was wild, his eyes had a certain light that only a wild animal's eyes had. *He became half wild!* I exclaimed in my mind. Neither of us moved. For the next several seconds, deep acknowledgement and deep understanding filled our minds—both Q's and mine. And we knew those feelings were mutual between us. In the corner of my eyes I saw my father approaching in the quietest way like a *ninja*, his surgery scissors open, the two blades almost six inches away from Q's neck, and the next moment the two blades touched each other with a solid sound and Q jumped and dived into the ocean of grass. Everything succeeded.

27 My father and I stood there for while, without words. The white bandage was left on the concrete pedestal after father cut it off. It was not white at all any more: with morning dew and oil and whatever else, it was heavy and narrow. With mud and rust, that string almost became a black rope, and it had become only a few feet long. Then I opened my left hand: some fish that was crushed and wet with my sweat in my hand I scraped off with my right hand. "I forgot to give this to him," I murmured. "Don't worry about his food, he is on the way to some kitchen now to get the biggest grilled cod for his breakfast." Father's joke reminded me of how proudly Q had showed us his victory spoils—how beautiful he looked, how his black-and-white fur waved, shining. I cried for the first time since he had run away the day before. "He came to us when he needed help most urgently, and we were able to provide exactly what he needed, and now he is a strong young man," my father said. He needs to go to the world, so he left. Everything went as it was supposed to be. There is nothing to be worried about, nothing to be sad about." He looked at his watch and took my hand to cross the big street. *He goes to his office to provide help that sick people need,* I repeated in my mind. *That is what work means, that is what he does every day, this is what he said is the way it is supposed to be.*

28 I have been able to repeat what my father told me about this whole episode in my own words. But when I try to focus on what happened between Q and me while our eyes met for several seconds, it is difficult to verbalize. After I met Q in the burnt field, for several seconds of silent meeting my mind was completely resolved. I felt deeply that he understood and accepted my love towards him—that the love was not meant to confine him or possess him, but to release him with my blessing. He understood not only that my father and I were there to cut his leash, not to trick him and chain him in order to bring him home; but he also trusted my love in a much deeper sense. We were so sure that we both acknowledged this mutual understanding, and that understanding released our anxiety. It was mutual. It was a communication directly soul-to-soul, completed in a few seconds.

29 For some period of time afterwards, I still had thoughts about why Q showed up so intentionally that last morning. If he believed severely that he was betrayed by me and angry at being chained, he would have gone away by that time and would have never showed up by jumping on the pedestal in front of me. If he wanted simply to be with me, he would have showed up at our house any time before dawn. He too had some anxiety that he had to resolve before he went on his way, I thought. That was exactly my prayer. I asked God for Q to understand my love, that I would release him to the world with my blessing. I knew if he realized that, he could have a joyful, powerful journey. God accepted my prayer: so many pieces had started moving on the path towards that resolution. One of the pieces was our neighbor: even though he may not have been the greatest witness, without his testimony we would have never even been there in that burnt field. In that place life and death were piled in layers: decay and growth were intertwined. Those things finally found their place in the map of my consciousness. My inner world, the realm of some sacred Presence, expanded, became bigger and even stronger, by including this map inside of it.

30 The essay I submitted to the contest on my teacher's recommendation received a prize. I must have been somewhat pleased but I don't remember except that it felt strange to find my name mentioned in the nationwide newspaper among some other names. But I experienced great pleasure when I opened the notebook in which I had been writing my essays and where my teacher's comments were, and found his words, "I am always looking forward to reading your essays to find what you are thinking. I am moved by your realization how much your sickness helped you to think. Though your body may still be fragile, you are a person of strong soul because you love to think. I am proud of you." Other students were still standing in line to receive their notebooks from the teacher. I walked to the corner of the classroom quietly and covered my face with the notebook like a fence, and read it again slowly, and read it over and over. It was only many years later when I found the news that the judge of this contest, Yasunari Kawabata, had received the first Nobel Prize for Literature in Japan, and that his suicide followed soon after, that I thought about his encouragement for me—his choosing my childhood essay for a prize—with deeper feeling and gratitude.

31 Another opportunity to express myself was also given to me quite unexpectedly. America invited Japanese young student artists to submit their artwork to a contest for young artists. The winners' works would be exhibited and travel to some American cities. I was chosen by our art teacher to be the student artist of our school to submit an artwork to this competition. That was the time when the peace treaty had finally been signed between Japan and 48 Allied nations in San Francisco, acknowledging that the war between Japan and the Allied nations was officially ended, and that Japan's independence was recovered. Some of the nations—Russia, India and China—had still not signed, and there was still a lot of unfinished business. But MacArthur and his troops left Japan after celebrating six years of successful occupation: big friendly crowds waving small flags of America and Japan saw him off cheerfully. It was clearly a new phase of history. Nothing called "international" had ever invited Japan to participate in anything before the treaty: Japan had been deeply ashamed and we knew that the whole world accused and despised us for what we had done to them. But finally the curtain was lifted. This art contest was co-supported by UNESCO and it offered the most exciting opportunity for any school to submit its student work. Especially for our school, nationalistic as we were, everybody thought this was our chance to shake off our nation's humiliation. I wanted to paint a figure of some sort, because in those days that seemed the most natural way to express my feelings, and my confidence had been built in this area by the art teacher's constant encouragement. I started thinking about what sort of painting I wanted to create for the contest.

32　One day when I came home from school I was astonished to find a table covered with a white lace tablecloth and some pink flowers placed on it in a pot, which was unlike anything I had ever seen in those miserable after-the-war towns. And my young sister, wearing her best bright-red sweater, was sitting at the table as proudly as a model. Two big sheets of good quality art paper and a box of twelve colored Cray-Pas (oil pastel markers) —all of those things which could not have been found in those towns—were on the table, prepared for me. I instantly knew that the whole set was for my painting so I could apply to the competition. My father and my mother and even my elder sister were all there waiting for me to start painting this scene. I was horrified. This whole set struck me as a phony, hideous lie. I felt it was something dark and evil. "I don't want to paint this, this is a lie! Let me paint in my own way!" I cried. But "my own way" was the very thing they had already determined not to let happen. The whole point of making this set was to avoid my doing it "my own way." I knew what my parents were talking about before they prepared this horrible set: "We cannot allow her to do something she wants to do. You never know what she will come up with. Remember the time she wrote about insects' tombs." My father, my mother, and my elder sister stood around me, and bent over to examine every stroke I made on the paper. Every line and color upset them: too strong, too wide, and too sloppy. "Can't you do it more carefully?" "Look, her eyes are not equal." But finally I finished the painting.

33 I had one extra paper left. I begged them to leave me alone: "I finished my obligation to you, now let me do my own thing," I said. The last person who left the room was my elder sister wearing a yellow sweater; she twisted her body to look back at me in the doorway. Suddenly that movement of her twisted pose gave me a whole image for my new painting. I quickly sketched her body on the new piece of paper: grasping body movement in a few seconds was what I had been trained to do. That figure of a girl started growing on the paper into a woman in yellow whom I had never seen. She twisted her body with pain and agony but her head looked up towards the sky, still seeking something, longing for something, her whole body elongated with the sorrow of mourning for the dead who cried out to her to express their deep remorse and indignation: their cries had never been heard, they had never been comforted, since peace came to the land which they loved and died for.

34 My hand moved quickly before I knew what to do. Enormous pain filled my heart. A crying voice almost gushed through my throat, but it didn't. Instead all the voices rushed onto the painting and splashed themselves on the paper. The background rapidly turned red, flaming, just like the painting in the church I had seen long ago, just like the night sky beyond the rice field under the carpet bombing. Something very important started to happen in the painting. I realized it with awe and I just followed my fingers, which moved so fast I didn't know where they would take me. It was something beyond agony, beyond pain and remorse, something extremely tense and beautiful that welled up from behind the painting and arose and filled the entire painting. And suddenly the whole tone of the painting changed towards something lighter, higher. It was a surprise, but it happened. The next day, I brought both drawings I had made to the teacher.

35 A few months later, I received notification in the morning ceremony in front of all the students that my work, "A Woman in Yellow," was chosen as one of the Japanese young artists' works. And now it was going to be exhibited and the show would travel to many cities in America. America was so far away! I had never seen any photographs of America, except once when a friend of my mother's— whose husband was sent to America on a special diplomatic mission involving preparations for the peace treaty which Japan and America would sign—brought back a viewer into which you looked through special glasses attached to the box and saw a three-dimensional picture inside. It was one of those souvenir gifts but it was still very costly by Japanese standards. "This is so expensive, I will allow everyone to look at it for just a few minutes," she said. I remember three of the pictures, now that I look back: one was a magnificent landscape of the Grand Canyon, another was a big house with white columns in one of the Southern states with two women in big skirts, and the last was a highway with flowers on both sides. I was fascinated. I wished so much to own those pictures. But my memories of those pictures did not help me to visualize the kinds of places where my art would travel. I was not so excited at having won the prize: my mind was filled with too many thoughts. I kept asking myself, *Why did American judges not discard my work? Did they like it even though it still might be seen as dark and frightening? Is it possible to like such "unpretty" work? Could they possibly have found it beautiful? I kept thinking. Did they feel it expressed my honest feeling? Does honesty matter in America?*

36   The fear that I might not be allowed to be honest was deep. I fought bravely against the huge darkness that prevented me from doing the honest thing, and I won just barely in the end: *I might not be able to fight again, or win next time*, I thought. My mind became extremely heavy. *Why can't I appreciate my parents, who are so excited about my being chosen for the contest and tried to help me like magicians, getting me all the best materials and things that no one else could get so I could do the best job? As everyone always said, my parents were the most enthusiastic, supportive educators of their children. I should be grateful to them.* But I felt I was violated, I felt I was tricked into a conspiracy designed to trap me into dishonesty.

37   I knew for a long time that my parents were ashamed of me: when they talked about me their voices got lower and I heard a hidden tone in their voice when they told people that I was doing well, as if they were saying, "She is okay so far—considering, you know." I did not know what it was, but I always felt something was deeply wrong with me. It was not only my tuberculosis: the sickness seemed only to give them official validation of their shame. My good grades, my winning contests, did not only fail to change their view of me, but also made them worry more, for the more I got honor, the more difficult it would be for me to conceal my shame. A time would come that all my problems and shame would explode in the middle of the most honorable moment, and it would be disastrous, like a huge explosion, they seemed to think. I did not know what my problem was—or problems were.

38 The question of what really happened while I was painting stayed in my mind. Strong emotions which flooded into me were forming various layers and they had overwhelming power. If I had to choose only one word for those emotions, *it was death:* the dead came to me and spoke to me of their violent deaths and their mortification. I had to let their cries, their regret, their agony out onto the paper. They had not resolved the violent death—either that they were killed or that they were forced to kill others. They had not recovered from it. It was so harsh and frightening. I felt my body was torn and thrown up into the sky. But then what was the thing I saw in the painting later, only just before the painting was completed—something like a light, so intense, so vivid, so beautiful, shining through behind all the agony and remorse? What was it: was it a light only I could barely see or could others see it too? Every time I tried to think about it, a strong crying voice welled up high in my chest. I could not think it through.

39 I fulfilled the minimum attendance requirement and graduated from the elementary school division of the Emperor's school with academic honors. I even played Mozart's Violin Sonatina at the farewell ceremony, held so that all the graduating students could express their gratitude towards their teachers. Finally, my long sick period was over and a new life started.

40 General MacArthur's order of coeducation of our school was up to the sixth grade. When we finished elementary school, the junior high division of our same school received us—after going through six years of a historical experiment of mandated coeducation at a different campus. We had come through very well, with boys and girls friendly to each other and doing many projects together without any incident so far. But now we were going to be separated by gender according to the tradition which this school had maintained for nearly 75 years. Boys and girls were separated in different buildings, which were located at opposite edges of the campus, after entering through the big iron gate at the front of the campus. We were told that the original rule was that boys and girls were in different campuses in different districts, so that boys and girls did not have to share the same big iron gate, nor see each other. This campus was a temporary solution because the boys' campus had been damaged by the bombing and it was now under construction. We greeted our old male classmates at the gate if we happened to see them and then we walked to our separate buildings. It was natural for us to say "Hi"—we used a slightly more elegant word in that school—after six years of being together in the same class. But it was a shock to the rest of the school's students to see us greeting each other so freely and openly. We were ordered neither to greet boys nor to acknowledge them, because that had been the rule there according to long tradition.

41 I became president of the class. I focused attention on this rule and opened up a discussion about it in our class. It did not take much time for us to come to the conclusion that this rule had to be lifted. Teachers did not know how friendly we were, both boys and girls, or how we did everything together, and how unnatural it was for us not to smile at each other and say "Hi" and to instead look the other way when we saw each other at the gate. The older students here never had that experience, so of course they don't say "Hi" to strangers. "We should tell them," I said. I was aware this was not as innocent an issue as other students tended to think; I was aware of the discomfort over this at the school.

42 I sensed there were two points I could make against the school's policy. One was the incoherence of the school's educational direction: we had been encouraged to be friendly and now we were being told to ignore friends—a lack of integrity of the rules themselves. The second was that despite the school administrators knowing of their own incoherence and lack of integrity, their imposing old rules in a new situation as if nothing had happened in this huge revolutionary change after the war was dishonest and an irrational abuse of authority. Receiving unanimous support from my classmates, I arranged a gathering of a few hundred students in the big hall after classes so that all the girls in the junior high could attend, and the principal and all the teachers were invited. I carefully visited all the teachers one by one in their offices ahead of time and explained the purpose of the meeting with respect. Everything went well. Our class was expressive and well-mannered. The big meeting was extremely successful. The principal and all the teachers agreed that reason was on our side. The Rule was lifted. Girls and boys no longer had to look away when they saw each other. Our classmates congratulated each other on our success.

43 The first day in school after the meeting, after the weekend, I found a different world. No one greeted me, no one smiled at me nor talked to me, and everybody avoided my eyes. Teachers also did not meet my eyes: they turned cold and distant. No one was greeting the boys at the gate either: they all acted as if they never knew their old classmates, as if they had never gone through coeducation. The school turned back 100 years over the weekend: I was invisible as if I were lost in the group, from a different dimension of time. Fear ran through my whole body: I instantly knew what it was. It was a typical form of excommunication in Japan which targeted people who stood out in the community—"the different." It was a tactic used over and over by the neighbors' spy groups, and I had heard tons of stories about this from the people in town, the village, and various groups during the war. It was one of the cruelest things people could do to others.

44 Because close attachment to the group forms one's identity in Japanese culture, excommunication is often followed by the victim's suicide. The death toll was especially high among children and teenagers. No one ever warned the victim nor told him the reason. Often the offenders would not know the reason clearly enough to verbalize it to themselves either. Everything would be carried from the darkness of the unconscious of the community to the darkness of the unconscious of each individual in the community. It happened as if it arose naturally. No one knew who was responsible. Therefore there was no one to fight against.

45   This phenomenon looked as if it happened naturally, so it is different from the political form of fascism that was imposed on the masses by clear commands emanating from a strong dictatorship. And yet in the hostility towards the "different" individual and in the irrational authoritative expression of that hostility by the masses, and in the justification by the deceptive idealism that covers their fear, it was unmistakably the same mentality as the political form of fascism. The only difference between this kind of fascism and the usual one was that the unconscious fear and hostility in them were so widely shared in the community that they didn't need a clear theory or order: fear and hostility were so innate in them that they didn't need any leader to command them. They could carry the unconscious message like a disciplined army would without a leader and without being told what to do. Consequently no one checked who was leading this phenomenon—secretly or not. No one took responsibility for this phenomenon: how does it go from here, how does it end if it ends, what is the goal they want to reach? No one asks, and no one answers. I knew all about this phenomenon and I was afraid of it all through the war. I was afraid of this being done by my own people more than I was afraid of being caught by the enemy and falling into their hands. And yet I just had never thought that organizing a student meeting like that—openly, rationally, checking every step, getting consent from everyone involved—would provoke this phenomenon in this new age of democracy, after so many years had already passed since the war was over.

46   I remember that three classmates got together and came close to me when I was standing against the fence outside of the tennis court on the edge of the campus and said that this was not their own intention: their parents told them not to talk to me and the same thing was happening to all the others and they all felt terribly sorry. Faint smiles were on their faces, innocent smiles. Even though they were expressing their hostility with the severest, cruelest action, they still expected my appreciation for reporting this to me. I walked away. *I should not allow them to come close to me,* I thought. They had no concept of integrity, no respect for the integrity of education or the integrity of coeducation. That is what we started fighting for in the first place. Now they wanted to get approval from every direction—from teachers, parents, classmates, and even from me: they threw away their own integrity.

47 I did not want all my classmates to think that their weakness of character—throwing away their integrity and trying to get approval from every direction instead—was my rescue. I wanted to know what exactly had happened: just a weakness of character, as I suspected, or something else, something still hidden from me, something crucial to solving this whole thing? If I could only understand, I would be able to fight against it. *I have to understand, I have to think.* Thinking was crucial and urgent. I had been mourning over injustice, dishonesty, deception, abuse of power and lack of integrity, but I did not have anyone to talk to about it. I could still smell the old books which had a suggestion of those words in their titles on the spines: I pulled them out from the bookshelves in the old school library, which was built 100 years ago and had escaped the bombing. It was used as a military stable during the war: the books had been put back yet the strong smell of the stables remained. But there seemed to be none which dealt with any of those terms. I was walking along the bookshelves as through a forest in the cold dark stone rooms, thinking to myself, *I have to understand those words and fight.* But I still did not know what I was really fighting against. It was around that time that Hannah Arendt published her book, *The Origins of Totalitarianism,* in New York: a book born out of her deep reflections on World War II. That kind of knowledge and information were beyond my imagination at that time, totally beyond my reach. It took many years for a Japanese translation to become available. If I could have read that book in those days, I could have understood my experience of excommunication—which I took to be a uniquely Japanese phenomenon—in the larger light of totalitarianism. I would have been deeply stricken by the discovery that the essence of totalitarianism is the eradication of one's own free will and one's own creativity. Even though I could not have reaped any practical help from that knowledge, I would have been deeply stricken by the solemnness of my own experience. But at that time, these things were all completely beyond me.

48 I was fighting against tradition—, that much I knew: the tradition of more than 75 years of that school—more precisely thousands and thousands of years of history starting from the unknown periods of time—against the monster which had lived in the deep black hole for all those years. Tradition by its nature belongs to the unconscious world of the human psyche. If it did not sink into the unconscious world then no matter how long a period certain actions were repeated, they would still be called habit, custom, rules, or teaching. Only when it sinks deep enough into the unconscious world will it be called tradition, and as soon as that happens, it gains unfathomable power and that power functions as an irrational authority. Because it is unconscious, it has a tremendous power to transform people and heal people. Religion, art, and various kinds of human relationships and education have known that power all through history and have used it effectively through the community. But this tradition is a double-edged sword. The unconscious hates rational, clear thinking. At the surface level, people can think and deal with tradition rationally and sometimes try to change it, ban it, or get out of it if the rational mind is convinced this is needed. But at a deeper level, they all feel guilty, frightened, like a primitive people who are forced to break the taboos of their tribe, angry and resistant to change at any cost. And because it is unconscious, their resistance takes the form of irrational, childish, dark, destructive, and cruel behavior. When people form a community based on tradition, that community can instantly kill thousands of people under the name of tradition.

49 The fear and detestation of the teachers and the parents—especially the former aristocratic parents—were huge when they saw what six years of education about democracy did to students. In their view, the human behavior experiment established under MacArthur had failed. This is what America had done to Japanese children: now children think, they talk, and they organize meetings. They used to obey whatever the teacher said, now they question the rule and they fight against it—something that had never happened in that school or in the whole history of Japan. Parents and all the authorities of the school did not know what to do. Democracy was the last thing they knew. And yet it was an absolute demand of America and Japan's survival depended on it—just as this used to be true of fascism. The old teachers there were the ones who taught the biography of Adolf Hitler to the students during the war, under the government's instruction, as the biography of a great man—just as they were now teaching democracy. Neither of those ideas came from them, nor from the people: both were commanded from above, from the higher authorities. They had no ideas of their own, only their fear was enormous.

50 There is another reason that their fear was so intense: this issue was related directly to the issue of sexuality, to the deepest part of the unconscious. When the demand of cultural change comes to this point, resistance becomes irrational and aggressive. I had been aware of the sexual flavor of this issue all through the transaction with the school authorities as much as a 13-year-old could possibly be. But this discussion was not about whether coeducation should continue; we never assumed that we had the right to make that kind of decision. It was just about greetings—about saying "Hi" or not. I also intended to keep the sexual issue irrelevant. A somewhat monastic feeling towards sexuality was deeply seated in the authorities and had never been challenged and never required to be verbalized in their history: it was still at an unconscious level. If they were clear enough to be able to talk to me about it, I would definitely have given serious thought to it. Now when I look back, I have some suspicion that I might have even been fascinated with the whole idea of sexuality behind the issue at that time.

51 It turned out that I was witnessing the secret process of a tradition turning into the most hideous monstrosity of irrational authority. I wanted to grasp this monster's tail with my bare hand at the moment of the horrible transformation, but I failed and became a victim instead. The monster was gigantic and the process of transformation was unfathomably complex. No one in Japanese history ever caught this monster and stopped it before it transformed itself into irrational authority and formed a community which fed the monster instead. The Emperor is the biggest sacrifice that has been thrown into this black hole to feed the monster, over generations and generations for thousands and thousands of years in order to keep this monster alive and powerful. As far as my life was concerned, I was pressed under a big rock; I was crushed day by day. Sleepless nights continued and the excommunication continued longer. It worked to destroy the victim's core of human dignity: that is why so many victims committed suicide. My grades drastically went down in spite of my strong intention to hold myself high. The shame that my parents had tried so hard to hide from the world seemed finally to have erupted. The Explosion: that finally happened when I was most eager to be honest, and committed to express myself publicly. This was exactly as they had feared and predicted for a long time. Now I was the shame of the school as well as of the family.

52 I listened to my grandmother's stories when she managed to come and stay with us in our new house, in a suburb of Tokyo. My father had made a detailed plan for the house and let a contractor build it. It was a big westernized residence, but mainly built for music activities: there were practice rooms for many pianos and other instruments and a little hall for concerts. My grandmother put straw mats and Japanese-style cushions on the hardwood floor of the house, and sat on them folding her knees, in the living room. She sometimes put a mortar in front of her and mashed up yams—my father's favorite dish—with a pestle as preparation for dinner. I held the mortar with both my hands for her, to prevent it from slipping. Always there was the sound of the piano, often of two pianos as both my sisters were practicing, and of other instruments which visiting young musicians played, coming out of the music rooms and filling the living room.

53 Grandmother talked vividly about the mansion of the Motoyasu and about the richness of the traditions, tangible or intangible, which the family kept. And she talked about the fight against tradition which she had fought fiercely: tradition that included family oppression and persecution, and love, marriage, death, and religion—and how much she asked God for help, and always received the strength to fight. She was sweet and cheerful when she talked in spite of the gloomy subjects. I could not say anything, nor even formulate questions to ask her. I was listening quietly but I was terrified that the narrative of my own life might be destined to be the one of a revolutionary like hers. The real fights might still be ahead of me—lots of fights just like the one I had lost bitterly in the school which I would do anything to avoid if it came up again, even if I had to bury myself deep in lies for the rest of my life and never utter a word against authority or community. How could I travel the road that my grandmother traveled? I was frightened of my own weakness and at the same time I was frightened by my own suspicion that there was something deeply wrong with me, so that even if I believed I was doing right, I might be completely wrong. In either case, I would not be able to live as a good, honest person ever. This fear made me feel sick. My childhood was gone. The memory of the summer day when we made forty-three rice cakes on that persimmon-colored table in the dining room of the Mansion of Motoyasu had been placed into my childhood memories and sealed. My grandmother's calm and cheerful mannerisms, which had not changed at all since then, seemed suddenly too far away for me to reach.

CHAPTER 8

1 The mansion of the Motoyasu was still like a secret well even after having afforded my grandmother a means of living all through the war by bartering its treasures for food. I remember that she took out all the old kimonos hanging in the room and spread them on the *tatami* floor, opening the windows wide to make the air go through them. Splendid, dazzling colors with mysterious hues and tones, exciting patterns of living things, were like waves of the ocean in the room. Who could have imagined that little insects behind the summer grass, or silver fish caught by the fisherman's net, or even rats with trembling whiskers, could be so delicate and humorous before some genius designer drew them into the exquisite patterns? The smooth, sensuous textures of silk, the strong hard masculine texture of the *obi* (the sash) and the deep sadness at the memory of the women who once owned these—it was all overwhelming.

2 Those kimonos were sewn by extremely skilled hands in such a way that even from the reverse side no stitches were ever shown, as if they were put together by magic. When they were washed all the parts were unsewed, so that even the dust hidden inside of those invisible seams would be cleaned too. They washed those long pieces of fabric after they were unsewed and stretched horizontally like a long hammock between two poles. They stuck hundreds of delicate bamboo needles along the length of the silk from one side to the other at intervals of a few inches so that the fabric stretched by tension. Those bamboo needles made hundreds of semicircular curves all along the fabric. They looked like a dragon's belly. I remembered many colorful dragons rolling and swimming in the wind in the sunny garden.

3   My grandmother taught me how gently, how respectfully the kimono has to be folded in a particular order: you lift part of the seam with both your hands and hold it against the other seam, curving your fingers in a certain way, one section at a time, which itself was a ceremony, so that such a thing as ironing would never be needed even years later when you opened it. And it could be handed down to women for generations in perfect shape. Among these refined, subtly colored, gentle nature-motif kimonos, I saw a few that exhibited bold abstract patterns with flamboyant colors that stood out from the rest. Those belonged to my late uncle's bride, who left the mansion long ago, leaving them behind. Not knowing where she was or how to return them to her, my grandmother had been taking care of them all through the years with the gentlest hands.

4   Wearing a cherry blossom-pattern kimono in the autumn is of course out of the question, she said. Cherry blossom should be worn early in spring just before the real flower opens, so you can participate with nature and share the anticipation of the celebration of the coming season with others, which was a good way to show respect towards them. You celebrate nature with them. She was talking about one aspect of the essence of Japanese culture: this sense of oneness with nature—not a oneness with chaotic nature, but a oneness with the essence of nature which one can reach only by refining it. Celebrating the season is participating in the rhythm of the universe. If you omit the *kigo* —the word symbolizing the season which all *haiku* must have inside their short space of seventeen syllables—how much can *haiku* mean to Japanese? It would be like a photograph without focus. I understood her talk completely. "I think you are just about coming to the age that you can wear some of these beautiful kimonos," she sometimes said, smiling, when I visited there alone.

5   But how far away my mind was while I was listening to those words! My mind was in a totally different place. I was seeing the desert in my mind's eye where people have to wage a severe battle against nature without seeing any sweet thing like a cherry blossom: the only thing they embrace in nature is the constellation of the night sky above them. Would they be moved by this beauty, by oneness with nature? Would their sorrow, their remorse, their agony and fear be comforted by this beauty? How about the little statue of the half-naked man hanging now in her room? How did it, which had nothing to do with this beauty, reach her soul? My mind was closer to the people in the desert than to the people who lived in this garden of kimonos. It must have been the desert of the burnt-out field where dead bodies lay piled underneath. *I have to get out of this exquisite garden: I cannot be honest here,* I thought.

6   I was thinking about my art, which had been my secret since the experience of painting for the competition under my parents' manipulation. I kept my painting secret, but how could I explain that to anyone? For I found that in order to keep my painting secret, the works didn't have to be concealed from people's eyes: they could even be hanging on my wall and yet they were still secret and the secrecy of my art was safer than the secrecy of my diary, which I hid in a special place in my room with utmost care. Even if my art were spread in front of their eyes, they could not see anything in it: it would still be kept as the deepest secret.

7 My art was my baby, still pale and gentle: I did not know exactly where he came from; he came from somewhere and was born in me, as an illegitimate child. He was with me in my small room upstairs in the home in Tokyo—the very small room with almost no space left to walk after accounting for my narrow bed, although a big window sill stretched out that I used as a desk to do my painting, writing, and reading. The windows opened to the east where the sky turned red at dawn behind the big pine tree, which stood straight in front of my window. I had to raise my baby—but how? How could I know what to do? I was just a frightened child myself. I looked at the kimonos spread out in front of me. *No!* I suddenly screamed in my mind. *I don't want to raise him in a beautiful garden like this! I have to raise him on the ground, in the burnt field, in the place where there was nothing left, nothing to assume, nothing to rely on.* I had to raise my baby with my honesty; I somehow knew deeply that only with my honesty could he gently breathe.

8 Japan was just starting to open up to the world's art, from which it had been kept away by the long war. Picasso's "impossible to understand" art was introduced through reproductions for the first time, and people were shocked by it, detested it; some pretended to understand it, some laughed at it as crazy Western nonsense. But I was preoccupied by the movement of European modern art itself, which included Picasso. Information was very limited and, of course, seeing the originals was out of the question. I was reading thin, very poorly printed art magazines which had just started to be published, and books of art criticism which were just being translated, over and over again until I memorized them, or until the books and magazines finally fell apart and their letters disappeared from the pages. I was struck by the honesty of the artists of the modern art movement: their almost abnormal degree of intensity and their determination to create honest images by going down deeper and deeper into their inner world. This was the place that no one talked about before in Japan but it was the place I had been in since I was sick, to which I had traveled every day and night. Their passion to bring images from that world, their determination to make the invisible visible, was exactly congruent with my own determination to raise my illegitimate baby.

9 I thought of the small reproduction of one of Paul Klee's works, which I had seen in a poorly printed magazine. It was the first time that his painting was introduced to Japan. It was titled "Dance of the Red Skirts". It was a painting with figures of women wearing red skirts spinning as if seen through a kaleidoscope. The images were fragmented and behind the fragments was a big dark circle that looked like an empty vacuum—a black hole. It was a frightening, dark, sinister painting. But I instantly identified with it and the pain found in it. Sharp pain came back to me: the pain of the dignity of individuality being violated, the pain of realizing that although I lived in a perfectly orderly and peaceful society now, underneath that surface lay pervasive corruption and a hatred of individuality. That pain, which I had never seen expressed in my own culture, I saw expressed in Klee's work. Because I had never seen anyone express that pain, I did not know whether my own pain was legitimate. I even thought something was deeply wrong with me to feel such pain. Klee's words were there on the same page of the magazine: "To note experiences that can turn themselves into linear composition even in the blackest night." Reading his words, I realized there was a place somewhere outside these small islands where honesty mattered, where the inner world and human dignity mattered, and where the threat of losing that dignity caused this urgent, intense fear—fear of being fragmented and spinning into the black hole. If once my little child put his roots deep enough into the ground, the blackest ground, no one could ever replant him in this little garden—this exquisite, meticulous, magnificent garden. Until then, I had to protect him from this, this most overwhelming temptation of beauty.

10   My mother's desire to give a perfect music education to her two daughters escalated and found and connected the first-class young musicians and educators in Japan. Together they built the most ambitious, high-level music school, first for children and then a high school and finally they built a university. This school raised and sent a star conductor to a prestigious orchestra in America: he was the first example of a Japanese conductor on the international music scene. And violinists trained at that university would occupy many concertmaster positions in major orchestras all over the world. My two sisters grew at exactly the same pace as the school; in fact, in my mother's mind, the whole school was built for her two daughters.

11   She never had any ambition that I should be a first-class musician like her other two daughters. "You have already missed the last age to start lessons on any instrument with an opportunity to become a great musician." Although she pronounced this sentence on me, the truth was that from the beginning, such an audacious desire about me never entered her mind. But she had a clinging hope that I might be able to be a second- or third-class professional musician, and she was determined to make that come true. She began to take me to one of the most prominent violin teachers in addition to requiring me to practice strictly with her every day. Soon, she took me to the music school that she was involved in and made me study music theory, harmony, and dictation after attending my regular elementary school.

12   It was during my recovery period from tuberculosis. By the time my mother and I reached the teacher's house, I was exhausted and sick. During the lessons, I often fainted. Standing for one hour and holding up both of my arms was a torturous task for me. My mother and my teacher, instead of realizing that they were forcing me to do too much hard work, decided together to spread a *futon* in the next room and to keep the door of that room open. Whenever I started feeling faint, without missing a beat, they carried me to the *futon* and the lesson continued as soon as I woke up. The teacher kept encouraging my mother, saying that her daughter was talented and musical and that I should continue working hard. I listened to those words like a prisoner receiving a capital sentence. And one day, responding to my mother's nagging questions, the teacher replied that her daughter would be able to be a professional musician, and if she wanted, could easily play for a first-class orchestra as long as she continued practicing with discipline as she had been doing.

13 My teacher was a violinist educated by the first violinist in Japan who was directly trained by a famous European violinist who had come to Japan to teach Western music in the Meiji period. My teacher herself produced many professional musicians and set up music institutions before the war in Japan, so her words had great validity for my mother. On the way back home my mother said, "So, after all, you will be a last-position violinist in the second violin section—you know, the one sitting at the edge of the stage, almost behind the curtain, probably in some third-class orchestra somewhere in the outskirts. I am so relieved." I noticed fully that this was not what my teacher had said about me, but when it came to my life, my mother pulled everything down to paint the worst, most dreadful picture. But even if she had not done so, I knew very well that my mother believed that unless you were a superb, first-class musician it was not worth playing music—it would be a blasphemy of the music. I couldn't possibly escape being accused of that sin. A strange thing I must add: even now I cannot stop noticing the violinists who sit at the edge of the second violin section on the stage. I feel special respect and affection for them and secretly I send cheers every time I go to an orchestra concert, as if I were saying, "I am on your side."

14 It was during those days of violin lessons that a crisis arose. One day when I was playing some piece, I don't remember what piece, I made some mistakes. It was a complicated section in the sheet music; I had to figure out the music while I also had to handle the physical coordination of my fingers and the movement of the bow. I could not do it. The more the teacher asked me to do it again, the more I became confused, and after many trials, it became impossible for me to play even the simplest passages. She kept telling me to play, but my bow moved on the string with just squeaky sounds. A question struck the teacher and my mother at the same time. What is making this little girl behave like this: some serious brain problem? Is she retarded? Or is it her rebellious stubbornness against the teacher? The teacher ended the lesson after a silence which had lasted for a while.

15 On the way back, it was a total disaster. All through the dark quiet road in the fancy residential area where the teacher lived to the lighted area of the station, from which we would take a train, I cried and begged my mother to believe that I was not rebellious against the teacher, that I was trying my best, but the more I did the more I became confused. But this remark did not relieve her, because believing what I was saying would have confirmed her darkest suspicions about her daughter—that something was wrong with my brain, a possibility that had frightened her for a long, long time. Now finally she had to confront the truth. She was convinced. She said, "You are retarded!"

16 All the memories rushed back to her and to me. When I finished the first grade at the public school I temporarily entered when we moved to Tokyo, I was chosen as the best first-grade student of the year. According to the Japanese tradition, the best student from each grade received an honor certificate from the principal. There was a rehearsal for that ceremony. You were supposed to stand up and walk, starting with the right foot first, step up the stairs for five steps, then proceed to the principal, bow to him 45 degrees, and step backwards— you should not show your back to the principal—and turn around pulling your left foot back first. The instructions for this ceremony were practiced over and over. Every time I made mistakes, the principal's harsh voice shouting at me echoed in the big empty hall, which was the only part of the building left on the school grounds after the bombing. Finally, I was completely confused: now I could not tell which was my right foot or my left foot—a distinction that had been hardest for me to memorize to begin with. The gentle teacher of my class tried to help me, but the principal shouted at her, "Couldn't you choose a little smarter one for heaven's sake? She is supposed to be an honor student, isn't she?" When it was over, I rushed to my elder sister who was there in rehearsal as a third-grade honor student and performed brilliantly on her first try. I begged her not to tell what happened there to my parents. "I will promise to do perfectly on the real stage after a lot of practice at home. You can probably teach me how." She shook me off and started running away from me, saying, "You made me embarrassed!" I ran after her, begging, "Please, I promise I will not do it again!" We ran all the way home.

17 The moment she opened the front door, she burst out shouting to our parents how terribly she was humiliated by my stupidity. "She should resign the honor, she should not be there, and she is not entitled to be there in the first place. I will never have anything to do with her anymore!" I have no memory of how everything went afterward in the home, nor of whether I went through the ceremony without incident after all or whether that honor was taken away from me. But I do remember that I could not write simple letters which any infant knew, that I could not answer my age—suddenly I forgot, that I made mistakes writing my own name, and that the teachers were aghast. "How can it be possible for a good student like her to make mistakes on her own name?" Memory after memory of being shouted at, accused as a rebel, beaten up, ridiculed, came back. Pain froze me.

18 It was after I came to America more than two decades later that I found out there is a syndrome of such learning difficulties which exactly fit the symptoms I have suffered all my life: difficulties in learning letters and numbers and in following instructions; confusion of right and left; handling body coordination. But in those days in Japan, those symptoms were all considered defiance or simply insanity, a sign of being retarded. All those difficulties came back with amazing sharpness once again in America. Learning a new language all over again, the difficulty and pain felt sharper than they were in my own language.

19 Quitting violin lessons was easier after that incident. My mother accepted my desire to quit—something which I had been begging her to let me do from the beginning. I quit the music school, too, and dropped the whole music scene from my life. "Anyway she was not talented; she has no patience, no will power to try hard. She is lazy." Those became my official labels in addition to "retarded." All my parents' hopes that I would someday get better and become normal someday were dashed.

20 Life in my family had been taking a strange direction for a long time before that. Something was wrong, something went terribly wrong, but for a long time I could not figure out what it was. My two sisters were robbed of the freedom of going to school regularly, of eating dinner together with the family, or of going out to do anything with friends. Even doing their school homework was not quite encouraged. Having intimate conversations, having any fun with my sisters, was getting harder. My younger sister loved to listen to my storytelling. She seldom read books and I was a walking treasure box of stories: The *Arabian Nights*, Hans Christian Andersen—I had read the complete collection, stories of the dark forest in Germany, and Japanese tales—ghosts, monsters, and weird animals who deceived people—and even Greek myths, the *Divine Comedy*, and Hamlet. It did not matter if I did not remember the whole thing: I would make things up and endlessly change the stories as I went along. Sometimes I put a simple chair in front of her and part of the seat of that chair became an instant stage. I picked up some old toy blocks: here is the king, a fat one, and here she is—this tall skinny one—a queen. A magician is there too: I picked up a sly looking block hiding behind— I quickly added a flat block—which became the partition in their bedroom. He is coming out quietly—I moved the sly one slowly with no footsteps. Suddenly the chair became a whole Arabian court and the little blocks all started moving around, making sounds, talking to each other aloud. I added a pile of books on the seat of the chair. "In the meantime, on top of the roof of the court, a beautiful princess"— a little slender rectangular piece of wood swaying her body—"is desperately calling for a big bird to pick her up. 'Help!'" Endless! My little sister stared at the blocks and did not even move.

21   One quiet evening, I was telling one of my stories to her, and she was listening with complete concentration, and screamed when it came to the scary part, and then we laughed at her frightening scream itself. My mother came in. "What is going on?" My sister replied, "Sister is telling me a really scary story." My mother said quietly, "Listen, you have important things to do. Practice if you have time; otherwise take a rest, save your energy for practice. Don't let her take your precious time. She will pull you down, she has nothing to do in her life." Then to me she added, "Your little sister has to have a quiet mind for practice, she is sensitive, don't make her mind crowded with your stupid stories." The practice, lessons, concerts, tours, broadcasting, and all the promotional activities filled her and my elder sister's lives. And they became my mother's goddesses.

22 I prepared my clothes over the weekend for the whole week ahead: I washed them, ironed them—in those days there were no wrinkle-free fabrics—and hung them in my closet, so that during the whole week, without paying attention to those things, I could concentrate on study, painting, and reading. It was sometime after my horrible experience in the aristocratic school. On Monday when I had come back from school, I saw that my closet had been thrown open and all my clothes had been tried on and thrown in an astonishing mess, all over the floor. My favorite pure white blouse, with delicate lace, which I had spent a long time ironing, and a pair of white socks that I washed specially by hand to make them bright white, were missing. My elder sister who played hooky from school in order to practice piano, which was always encouraged by my mother, put on my blouse and socks and went out. When she came back in my blouse, I protested to her and demanded that she return them to me in the same condition. But things took a very strange turn. She ignored my request and made fun of it, laughing, and saying, "Sorry like this?" as she played a melody of the ending of a comedy while still laughing, and then started practicing.

23 When I realized that she considered the case closed by her "apology", I was upset and repeated my demand to her. My younger sister came to me, saying that my demand was too much and too outrageous for her, since she wouldn't even know how to use the washing machine and could not handle the iron. "You know she has no time for such things." So she cried out, "Let me do the washing and ironing for you on her behalf. I know you are upset but please forgive her for the sake of our family's peace." I went to my mother and asked her to help me enforce my demand on the older sister. Surprisingly, she scolded me bitterly, saying, "Stop saying such nonsense. The most important thing is to give her more time to practice piano, nothing else matters. You should be happy that your blouse was ready for her when she needed it. You should throw away your selfishness and make yourself more useful." I went to my father. He did not listen to my appeal all the way to the end, but when he came back home the next day, he had a box with a new blouse for me. I was totally devastated.

24 I thought about this incident over and over for years to come. The most important thing in the family was the two sisters' music, music itself, and their career promotion. And for that, I should not only contribute my time and energy to doing good things for them, and willingly sacrifice what was important to me, but I should also let them violate my fundamental rights and my personal boundaries, and let them abuse me. Our parents were thinking of me now only in terms of the other two sisters: is she an obstacle to their glorious lives or can she add anything beneficial to them? Their answer to that question became more and more definitively negative. Those were the obvious things I realized immediately. But deeper thoughts started growing in me.

25 I did not take my father's act of buying me a blouse as simply intending to silence my nagging request. I thought that he saw me upset over a little thing like a blouse in a sibling power struggle and felt some sympathy for me for my over-sensitiveness about it, and he wanted to show his sweetness towards me. In fact, it was a very unusual thing for him to buy a young girl's blouse all by himself—a blouse which, incidentally, was quite elegant. But that kind of solution was the furthest thing from what I was seeking from my father. I remember that I was wondering why people emphasized love in the family. Some would take him as a loving father for his act. I knew that in his mind at that time, his sympathy and affection towards me were genuine. But love is different. I wanted to get a *judgment* affirming that I was right to insist on my boundary against my sister or against anyone. I was *entitled* to have her put the things back, and my anger towards my sister's bad faith had a perfect legitimacy. I considered my father as the authority over me and my sister as an equal, and he had an obligation to acknowledge that my sister's act was wrong and to make her carry out the action of putting the blouse back in the same condition as she found it. That is the love that I would understand. To me, love should not have been something extra between people, adding a sweet gesture of affection: that had nothing to do with love, and in fact, created some confusion and made my appeal more difficult. My father was the final court to which I could appeal.

26 But he destroyed all my hope by showing his personal sweetness towards me and by not taking responsibility as an authority for his children. He destroyed my hope of acknowledging the legitimacy of my claim to me and to the whole world, and he killed any further chance I might have had of carrying my appeal further. And he succeeded in degrading my appeal into a little fuss over a girlish matter, and assured my opponent of a complete triumph. What I needed was nothing but the strong sense of justice: the proof that in this world, however chaotic and cruel it may seem—an aspect of the world to which I had been exposed all through the war—at least I had a system that I could rely on and through which I could find and establish something rational, a coherent order in the universe. Not because that system would always bring justice but because it would be rational enough for me to work in, to think and talk through. I would not have minded working hard for it. I was even ready to accept the result, the judgment which might not be what I anticipated, as long as it upheld the commitment to the fairness of the whole process. I would have not even cared if my sister did not obey the judgment: I had no interest in her, nor in the blouse—washing it and ironing it was literally nothing as long as the judgment stood and her disobedience was considered "contempt of court". The whole affair made me see that I was seeking a court system at home: what I was desperately seeking was nothing but an imaginary, ideal, perfect, complete judicial system on earth, in my home.

27　　We don't have a tradition in Japanese culture of setting up universal moral values outside of the system and trying to follow them. There never was any tradition of respecting the person who followed moral values against the pressures of society. The only value that Japanese think ultimately has to be followed is *wa*, harmony of the group you are in. This *wa* they do call a universal value. But it is not. *Wa* is usually translated as "harmony" in English, but in Japan it means oneness with the group without different forces or impulses— unanimity rather than the state in which different forces are in good balance, which is the way "harmony" is used often in English. This wa is the state which is supposed to exist from the beginning—the normal, natural state, it is in the mother's womb in Japan and is considered to be ideal. If any conflicting forces appear, that is considered abnormal, a situation which has to be repaired and returned to oneness, which is the normal state in the mother's womb. In the West it is considered normal for many different forces to appear: we have to lift ourselves up from the mother's womb, from tribal unity, from that paradise, to a higher level, where we are awakened and individuated—and this we can achieve only through dialogue.

28 This concept of *wa* is traced to the first constitution established in Japan by Shotoku Taishiin the sixth century, which was based on Confucianism, and people still bring in his name as an authority every time they feel they have to emphasize wa in order to create pressure to reach a unanimous decision, to silence the minority who have a different opinion. And then there was the law that parties in conflict or dispute were equally punished regardless of the reason or cause of their conflict because conflict itself is wrong. That was established in the 16th century. In spite of the fact that this old law was repealed about 100 years ago, the judicial sensitivity of Japanese courts is still not completely free of its influence—to say nothing of what goes on outside of court.

29 In that kind of society, the language of dialogue, discussion, or debate never developed. People felt uncomfortable talking. They manipulated people and situations to move things their way, rather than expressing what they wanted: one word starts taking on a thousand hidden meanings in that environment. The sophistication of discussion skill was never developed either and people felt free to bring everything into the discussion if they dared to converse at all. The concept of relevancy, the concept of personal versus public, was never defined; the attention to "meta thinking" did not exist. It was the most frightening thing to go into a situation where you had to talk. It was just like walking into a swamp: at every step you had no idea if your foot actually touched the floor of the swamp, unknown plants tangled your feet, unknown creatures might pull at you and drag you down without a sound. You had no idea when your opposing party might say, "You are breaking harmony!" wherever you are in the discussion, and in that one moment you had go desperately on the defensive. I must have known that very well by the time I was 13 years old. When my three classmates came to me and talked to me at the fence of the tennis court at my school, I remember clearly that I was saying to myself, "Don't let them pull you into the swamp, you will never get out of it." So I walked out.

30   The belief that we are all one, and that if things go normally as they should there would be no words necessary, is strong. Uttering words is a betrayal of that belief. The more you talk, the more eloquently you talk, the more people are hurt: all words seek the original silence, the silence that you had in the mother's womb. The only words that are loved are the exclamations, almost sighs, that became short-syllable poetry. Language was never allowed to be Logos in Japan.

31   In the silence of misunderstanding, people died, and in the silence of injustice, people were executed. Those people would bring storms and lightning and earthquakes and floods, and all other diabolical natural disasters to the living after their deaths, for their vengeful minds would not be settled and would want to take revenge. In order to avoid the harm they would bring, people built Shinto shrines for them and promoted them to the status of Deities: over hundreds of years they all became generous sweet gods who helped the people who worshipped them. If I died before the injustice was acknowledged and corrected, I would certainly become a storm and blow in the whole sky and earth and destroy everything in between; I would be lightning, flashing a blue light over the entire sky and I would never cease. I would do all those things, not because I wanted to take revenge on people who put me into that situation, but because my cry of desperation that the universe is a complete chaos with no coherence, with no meaning in it, would never cease. If the universe has no meaning at all, how can my cry take any form of expression? If the universe does not hold the other edge of this huge tent, pulling tightly with reliable hands while I am pulling the other edge so hard, all my suffering will just hang down powerlessly and the tent will never take a form, nor take any place in the universe. Human creation requires and relies on the whole force of order in the universe: there would be no language and no images could grow into art if the universe did not hold the other end. My cry would never become a song; instead it would simply blow through the forest making the wind, and my tears would just flow onto earth and become a flood, unless I received one piece of justice, of order. Being feared, being worshipped, by people for hundreds of years could never give me the power to cease my crying.

32 My silence was demanded now, without my being allowed to give an explanation against any wrongful accusations my two sisters raised. I had to cover up the truth for them, and allow them to take any of my personal possessions at any time without my consent while their possessions had to be respected and protected.

33 The clear-cut distinction between being talented and not being talented, parallel to a simplified version of good and evil, was applied, which was one step away from the idea of pure race and non-pure race in Nazism. My mother's absolute manipulation and control of their lives was camouflaged by the illusion that it was their own will, that they were doing it all, combined with a severe isolation from anything outside her values—those were the same elements which form the base of a religious cult. What she created here was exactly like a cult: my mother became the founder of the cult of this new religion of special talent worship. The talented one should grow his or her talent at any cost and the untalented one would be saved by serving the talented person: this was the bottom line of the dogma. Showing all the symptoms of a religion which had a substitute for God instead of the real God—deception, corruption of morality, malignant narcissism— it was sick and destructive. Young musicians who shared this dogma occupied our house. Some stayed there for a long time. I had no way to escape from my mind swaying like a big tree in a storm, listening to one most passionate piece of classic music after another—music from the European Romantic period—every night. All of the musicians played quartets, trios, and ensembles using fully the four pianos in the music rooms in our big house in a suburb of Tokyo.

34 While all this was happening, my mother tried once more to save me from the sin of not developing my talent. She made a tremendous offer: she would hire any famous artist as a teacher if I just gave his name to my mother. She would persuade him—whoever he was and wherever he lived—that there was nothing she would not do for them and that whatever it took to develop my talent she was ready to give, just like she was giving my two sisters. The only alternative way to be saved would be to become a helper for the talented, which I had been doing to some extent. That was the final expression of her love for me. She would treat me like she treated my two sisters, she would be proud of me, she would take me everywhere with her, she would not leave me alone to cook for my sisters, she would defend me from the mean world of people who were ashamed of me.

35   This is what I had been longing for: love, acknowledgement, protection, acceptance by her. But I had already seen what would happen if I accepted her offer. I saw it in my art competition, when she forced me to be dishonest with myself, and I saw it in my two sisters' lives taken away from them inch by inch every day. I saw how I would be trapped inside this cult and would lose the ground where I stood and where all my strength came from, where I prayed to God. How could I raise my baby without being myself? But by saying "no" to her I was taking a real risk, not only of losing her approval, which I had already lost, but of the humiliation in the family and in society which I had to continue to endure—and the biggest risk was that the art education she was offering might be the best education I could receive. Her offer forced me to choose between the two, between the love of my mother along with the possibility of an excellent art education and refusing to sell out my soul to get those things.

36   I had one more concern about my own art education. My extreme fascination with modern art did not seem to be shared with any of the artists in Japan yet. I came to know it only through advanced art magazines and through a classmate who took private art lessons from a prestigious artist. Modern art was new to every artist in Japan, as

well as to me. The horrifying old-fashioned form of traditional art education was everywhere, including my school's junior high division. Modern art was a revolution against that traditional art, and I did not want to let myself fall into the enemy's hands. My baby, though he was fragile now, would grow and flourish in the revolution; I did not want an old musty, dusty teacher who had nothing but ignorance and hostility towards modern art try to crush my baby.

37 I said "no" to my mother's offer, saying that Paul Klee was the only artist I really would have wanted to study under. He died the year after I was born and left great works—I had seen reproductions—and he also left the greatest bible of the secret of art, *The Thinking Eye*, which he had written as a textbook when he was teaching at Bauhaus. No Japanese translation was available yet, but I knew some of its contents from people who could read German and I knew a few sentences here and there by heart. He was the only teacher I really wanted to study with. Instantly my mother gave me her last word, using the Buddhist expression, "You have to live under the bad *karma* from now on. Whatever calamity befalls you, it is your fault, you chose it." She made it clear that it was me, not her, who would destroy my life. Her remark gave the family official permission to now ignore my needs and my rights. "She herself wants to destroy her own life. She chose it."

38 Is it too much to suspect that she knew I would say no at that time? She wanted to get rid of her perpetual guilt by making it clear that it was not her fault if I failed in life, but my own. And she wanted everyone including herself to know that she had tried her best to rescue me from the sin of not developing my own talent, and remaining in laziness, once and for all. My label changed from "lazy" to "self-destructive." But I was beginning to realize that saying no to my mother's offer was the first time I had seriously stood up against the force that would have made me lose my integrity. The meaning of my sickness was finally being revealed. My inner world seemed to have grown stronger since the seed was planted during my time with tuberculosis. It was now much more than just "thinking."

39   Both of my sisters were regarded as goddesses in this cult, but in our mother's mind, only the younger one was. She was made by talent but the elder one was made by effort, as my mother saw it. When the older one was young she was expected to become a doctor, following in our father's steps, because she showed exceptional brilliance in school. But now she had fallen into her mother's whirlpool in order to tear off the "made by effort" label my mother put on her. She started having physical pains and troubles. The only difference between her and me was that she thought she was a star; she did not know how deeply, how dangerously, she had fallen into the swamp. My mother's secret belief that she had only one goddess, my younger sister, was never stated openly, and that made the whole cult system even more complex, sinister, and cruel than it already was.

40   Even after all my emotional preparation for the consequences of saying no to my mother, my mother's words had a tremendous power on me as a curse on my life. The curse came with dark sorcery power; it was the kind of spell that only a religious cult can cast over another human being. I did everything to break this curse, but everything I did turned out to be just more proof that the curse was working. Only very late at night was I safe from music. I painted only through the night until dawn: piano practice would start after dawn and swayed my will power to keep my mind quiet by the torturous repetition of the passionate music of German Romanticism in which I started to hear some signs of grandiosity, which reminded me of the grandiosity of fascism.

41 How did that pure longing towards the highest beauty and passion to transcend her suffering through music come to turn my mother into a monster almost to the point of the fascism we experienced during the war and which she hated more than anybody else? I remember very well that my mother played Beethoven's Ninth Symphony on the phonograph for us during the war, wanting us to experience the most beautiful thing before we might end our short life. *What happened to you? I thought. The experience you gave me is still vividly alive in me; I am working hard to build a cathedral of my own by creating my own paintings every night since then. Can't you see it?*

42 One day, a young teenage boy, tagging along with his mother, stood in front of the front door of our residence. He wore pants that were somehow too big for him: you could not tell whether they were supposed to be shorts or long trousers. He was clutching a black violin case to the left side of his body as if he were clinging to it and his mother had an expression of being at a complete loss. They were from the town where the mansion of the Motoyasu stood. They came to see my mother in order to find out if the boy was talented enough to be a professional violinist. In our music room, his mother told my mother that her boy played the violin all day every day: he did not go to school, he had no friends, there was nothing else he was interested in except playing the violin by himself. The violin teacher who taught him when he was a child did not have anything to teach him anymore. "He will never become a man who can make a living!" his mother said with that at-a-loss expression on her face. He played Mendelssohn's violin concerto for my mother. It was fantastic. A tormenting tone filled the entire music room and even outside that room, where I was spying on what was going on, and I trembled.

43 My mother decided to take him under her wing but with severe conditions. "You have to get a middle school diploma in order to get into high school," she told him. "Once you get that, you will take the entrance exam for the highest level of music education in high school, which I have been involved in establishing. In order to prepare for the exam you have to study music dictation, sound detection, harmony, reading music, and the history of music. But most important among all these things: you need a first-class violin teacher, and under his instruction, several hours a day of serious practice has to be maintained. You have to study before going to school in the morning and there will be no time for going out for fun. If you are ready to do all those things with the most strict discipline, you can stay with us. "Yes," they both replied with their at-a-loss voices. They stayed in our house overnight. Then his mother left her son in our house and went to catch the train back to her town. I had no idea what kind of arrangements were made between the two mothers but I saw his mother saying, "Thank you very much for all your kindness," and she bowed and left. I have never seen her since then nor heard from her. It might be simply that I had not followed the situation thoroughly because my own situation would become so traumatic after that.

44 My mother let the young man move into the room next to mine upstairs. Then the true hell started. He played Mendelssohn's violin concerto every single night until midnight: after all his hours and hours of mandated practice of boring textbook violin pieces, finally he allowed himself to play Mendelssohn in order to keep his dream in sight. He never stopped playing Mendelssohn. We called him "Mendel." He was tormented, just like all the other cult members in our house. The music had risen and threatened my little upstairs room like a flood of water for a long time, and now the next room upstairs was finally flooded. My mind was deteriorating even faster than the water could reach my room.

CHAPTER 9

1 My mother was like a foreigner without knowing it. I can identify now after spending many years in a foreign country how deeply my mother was isolated from her own culture in her own country. She had to find out little by little, only through painful experience, that she was a foreigner there. She married a man whom she met only once, with her eyes cast down, believing he loved music. She had no idea what loving music meant in Japanese culture, nor did her parents. How naïve they all were! That happens when you are one of a very small minority and seldom see your own kind. How many Christians did they have contact with? No one can make his identity clear without seeing himself in interaction with others—like using a mirror. The percentage of Christians in Japan is still now less than one percent even after the great influence and support of the period of American Occupation. In those days, I wonder how they kept their identity as Christians. The Secret Christians who formed a very isolated special culture had moved to Nagasaki in the Meiji period and formed an isolated community by themselves, and kept their faith intact. But my grandparents, who were more open as Episcopalians, lived among people who had no idea what Christianity was. It is terribly dangerous to be naïve about your own identity like that: one might become just like me when I was thirteen years old. After six years of being in that school, I did not realize that I was a complete foreigner there, and I was excommunicated without anticipating it and without knowing why I became a target.

2   My mother's piano playing was her father's delight. But her father was an extraordinary man who was converted to Christianity, not only philosophically but also thoroughly in his heart to the point that Western music became his natural expression. He was transformed by his faith and he was expressing his faith straight from his core through helping people in the community. It was honest; it was a joy that renewed him every day. Although the people in the community were not Christian, they became "neighbors" to him. The accusations and isolation from his relatives only intensified his faith. But for my mother Christianity was never a matter of faith, it was just a matter of tradition, a tradition imposed upon her without her conscious commitment. Religion without believing in God becomes just tradition and culture. It is a dangerous thing even though it looks harmless. Without God, the presence of God becomes a mere theory and mystery becomes false, and the joy of being with God is replaced by morality and makes people rigid and hypocritical. It becomes an empty shell in which only authority dwells. Only the image of the Christian—not the real Christian—remains in that dwelling. Mission school was a foreign land in Japan. Christian missionaries, who very often had neither knowledge nor respect for Japanese culture, tried to train and mold Japanese girls to this image of the Christians. Religion died, and only the anger at being violated at the core of life remained in the people it touched.

3   My mother did not know that people in Japan had lived completely inside the restrictions of tradition—especially in a family like my

father's. They were leaders and models in their community. They represented tradition. They took responsibility for caring for all the ancestors and worshipping them in order to assure the community that as long as they respected the ancestors we would all be safe and prosperous—a responsibility my mother's family would have taken if they had not converted to Christianity. I wonder sometimes if my father's parents were alive whether a *miai* with a Christian family would have occurred at all—even though her being a princess had some benefit to them. One cannot connect things outside of his frame-of-reference when one's whole sensitivity is already highly trained and integrated into his system. My father was not like those young men in the village who came to love Chopin's Nocturnes: their sensitivity was not cultivated until my grandfather educated them. But my father's sensitivity was already fully formed. My mother did not know that it takes a painstakingly long time to get out of one's own cultural framework, even if one ever wants to do it, without risking the destruction of the integrity of one's self.

4 When you do something naturally, the way you usually do, you believe it is a good thing to do. You believe that everyone will accept you because this is human nature, until suddenly you are crushed by the other's totally unexpected response. Sharp pain runs through your body, blood gushes out from your skin, and you don't understand what happened, what went wrong. Then gradually you start seeing the complicated map of patterns of communication—you see that you were following the pattern of communication that your culture expected you to follow—but until then you did not know you were following the script of your culture, or you did not even realize yet that there was such a script in your culture. To discover your own culture's script, which is so deeply innate in you that you never thought it was a script, is a shock. It is also a shock to the other side. Only an analytical intellectual process will tell you where each script came from and how they were different from each other and what the essence of them is.

5 You can assume that everyone has a different culture and that all cultures are equally worthy of respect. It is possible and probably important to have this attitude. By accepting this kind of cultural relativity you can probably go along smoothly for a short distance. But in any serious relationship you will inevitably come to the point that the relativity of cultural differences arouses nothing but anger and hatred between the parties. Sooner or later something comes up that you don't compromise, something so crucial to your center that you would feel it as a serious threat to your personality to compromise it. Only from that level can a serious relationship possibly begin. Reexamination, reconstructing your structure, commences at the risk of destroying your personality. The boundaries of personal, individual orientation and cultural orientation are complicated. But blood has already been shed and the pain will not go away so fast. It is extremely hard and dangerous work. All through the process of the frightening struggle, both parties reveal their own depth of commitment to their own lives, to their own growth, and to the integrity of their own personalities. Being struck by the beauty of those qualities in each other, and moved by the other's serious effort to change and accept, it is possible that love and respect deepens and leads them both to a higher level of relationship, if they can survive in the meanwhile. At the one-step-higher levels, reconstruction and growth will continue.

And painful moments continue coming. They always come when you are off guard, when you are vulnerable, when you were taking off the armor of culture just for the intimate moment.

6   Western music, which my father never truly heard in his life, was nothing but a violent chaotic storm to him. It was like that statue of a half-naked man on the wall; it did not fit into the rest of the culture of the world he knew. He was a man who kept his father's final moment deeply in his heart since he was six years old. He watched his father sit up from his deathbed and assume the pose of Zen meditation to receive the moment. He wished for a death like his father's, and wished for a life that would lead him to it. His sensitivity was extremely refined and disciplined: that is the way he controlled his tormented mind and the pain of the childhood in which he lost his parents so early in his life. He was afraid of the loud, disordered, undisciplined indulgence of emotion which Western music seemed to be to him. It was immoral, it was too vulgar, he detested it, and he was afraid of the power of this music which seemed to transform right under his nose—this flower-like princess whom he fell in love with at first sight—into an unknown monstrous being.

7   He told her not to play the piano anymore immediately after he first heard her play, which she did in response to his innocent request to play in the little hall attached to the fancy Western-style hotel where they stayed for their honeymoon. He had expected traditional Japanese music, but instead she played one of Chopin's Ballades—a good choice that her father would have certainly praised. But how sharply my father's words penetrated her heart and made her realize that she was a complete "foreigner" to her husband, in the midst of the most vulnerable time for a woman. Her loneliness must have flamed up through her whole body.

8   I saw my mother's *miai* photograph a long time ago. Because the hospital where we lived during the war was bombed with many of our possessions in it, that photograph was a precious thing that remained and let me see how my mother looked when she was young. This was the picture that was sent to my father and ultimately led to their marriage: my father must have kept this close, otherwise it would not have been there. It was a photograph taken by a professional in his studio. She was sitting on a simple sofa, not leaning back on it, but rather leaning forward to come closer to the camera. Her hair was pulled back straight in an amazingly simple manner and tied in a chignon lower on her neck. Her face, without striking or characteristic features, had a certain Japanese classic beauty: small eyes and small lips, not expressive by our modern Western standard but delicate, gentle, elegant, and matched to her slender body. Everybody would classify her as a beautiful woman at first sight. She looked more alert and alive than the women in any of the other pictures I have seen from that period, but still she shared an incredible degree of innocence with those of that time. She is smiling a harmless smile, in such a way as to hide all her strength and tremendous capability and aggressiveness so as not to make a man feel in the least threatened—in the exact way that we, women of my generation, were trained to our bones.

9   The most surprising thing in this picture is the kimono she was wearing. It was simple, the simplest it could be, probably too simple for an occasion like this, the *miai*. Its sleeves were the modest length of an everyday kimono, and on the soft sage-colored silk, probably subtle beige, were drawn the flowers of bush cloves, the flower which grew in the garden of the mansion of the Motoyasu, in the wild field of the family quarter, the place once used for falconry. The kimono's small delicate flowers were white, embracing passionate red purple cores in the center. They appeared on the kimono only under her knees; they would have been entirely hidden under her knees if she sat on the *tatami*, so to avoid that, a few branches with flowers were scattered on her left shoulder. It was the most modest kimono design I had ever seen, though artistically it was the least modest; rather I would say that it was an ambitious attempt at the expression of a perfect combination of delicate beauty and strength expressed through unnoticeable flowers of the wilderness.

10   My mother told me that this photo was the second one she had taken just to have an extra. After she went through the formal process of taking the *miai* picture, in the most gorgeous kimono with the help of a professional kimono assistant, her hair piled up with pasted oil, and with heavy makeup on, she insisted on having her picture taken in her own way. She washed the pasted oil from her hair and put on the kimono she was wearing when she came into the studio, which was her favorite. She said to me, "I wanted to show the real me, honestly, to my future husband, whoever he was. If he did not like this, he should not take me." Then she gave two pictures to the respected family friend of Motoyasu, who had offered a "good case" to her parents. She let them decide which would reach whoever was the candidate to be her husband; she would put her destiny in the hands of the universe. I was astonished to find out that she did exactly what I had done in the painting competition. She did not fight vigorously enough to destroy her parents' plan. Instead, with a little fight, she got a chance to add her own expression. She did not plan this beforehand; rather she acted spontaneously on the spot. But it was not capricious: she did this driven by a strong desire to show her real self and by her anger at having been forced to be dishonest. And how perfectly it turned out to satisfy her purpose: no compromise was needed in spite of her decision on the spot to control every detail of her expression. Everything went well and now she could trust her husband, who saw the real her and accepted her.

11 At her wedding, according to the samurai tradition, she inserted a dagger in her bridal kimono between the two collars folded on her chest. Only a bright red tassel hung from there, so only those who knew what it was would notice. This dagger was meant to be used in case any man approached her: if such a thing happens, you draw it and point it to stab—not the man who approached you but yourself, to protect not yourself but your husband's honor. She was ready to kill herself for her husband's honor. But she had never prepared, never thought, that she could be killed by one word—not one sword, but one word—from her husband.

12 One word of a man is the fate of a woman in Japan. Her pain, her separation, her resentment against her husband, the stranger, was enormous. She sought her father in her mind, who had always been there any time she needed him, and then she was stricken suddenly by the realization that her father was the one who had not only not warned her about the world that she had to live in from now on but also had put her into the peculiar culture of that half-naked man which made her isolated from her own culture and made her such an outlandish woman. All that had spread deep into her body and it turned into a dragon that lived deep underground and shook the entire earth from there, rumbling around in the dark.

13 I looked to my father for help once more from the darkness of the cult. I thought I could reach him because I had special access: I made dinner for him often when my mother and sisters went to concerts or to other performance activities—unless they joined him after the event was over and went to a restaurant together near his office. So I was alone all evening at home with him. Usually when he was alone, he came back from his office at 10 p.m. and we sat together at the table, and I always knew that we shared a certain amount of loneliness being alone in the family as those who were not musicians. I thought: *He likes me; he is like me; he is suffering from not expressing his own creativity and feels isolated from the family because of it.* I knew that he kept writing something in his office while waiting for his patients, and the pile of his papers must have reached his own height by now. My mother would laugh and said to her children, "No one will be able to read his handwriting; it's all a waste." I would read what he wrote with tears if he ever allowed me to read it.

14 But I could not reach him when I brought my sadness up to him: it was as if he did not belong to this world. I thought if I made a greater effort, if I climbed the stone steps of the castle high enough, just like Hamlet did to contact his father's ghost in the castle in Denmark, I could reach him. Didn't Hamlet learn the secret of the family and learn what his father wanted him to do in order to straighten out the family by listening to his ghost? And didn't he make an enormous effort to pursue the necessary action the way his father wanted him to do—even pretending to be insane, and letting his loved ones die? I would do the same.

15 *Hamlet* was one of the books I read over and over in translation, slightly modified for younger readers, when I was in bed with tuberculosis. Many evenings, when my mother and my sisters were out at concerts, my father, who kept his office open until very late at night, came into the living room during the intervals between the patients where I was lying down alone under the piano. He sat a little away from me, for very brief moments to write, with a sharp pointed pencil, letters of the Japanese phonetic alphabet onto the pages of a book next to the many difficult Chinese characters which that book included, so that I could read the words the same way I pronounced them, and in this way I came to be able to read practically any book in the whole world. Although I did not know all the meanings of those words, I would know them by continual reading, and soon the difficult Chinese characters became familiar to me. He was sitting and doing this task quietly, seriously, and methodically. It was a great idea of his and I loved it. He was wearing his white doctor's gown, and when he was wearing it, we were prohibited to come close to him or touch him because he was full of germs, which I knew were powerful enough to make grownup men look so desperate and which led to death. The faint smell of creosol reached me. I waited quietly, until he gave me a copy of the book and left the room for the next patient, and I read the passage he had just completed. If I finished that part before he came back, I started memorizing the whole story word for word. Now that I knew how to pronounce it, memorizing it was nothing but pleasure. Sometimes, when I felt weak from my sickness, he finished so far ahead that many books were piled near my pillows waiting for me to become strong and read them again. Sometimes I was ahead: I memorized everything I had read, so that I did not have to pressure him, knowing that he was so busy taking care of other sufferers. It was a secret conversation between my father and me without words.

16 I painted the scene of the communication between the ghost and Hamlet every night in my room upstairs as if believing in some mysterious way that my art could reach his soul. But the artworks only piled up in my room, and soon I could not paint either the ghost or Hamlet; the cold endless stone steps became the only things I could paint.

17 When I came back from school, I saw a pair of black leather men's shoes—I could not recognize who they belonged to—on the shoe platform inside our front door. Because everyone takes off their shoes inside a home in Japan, you could usually tell who was visiting by looking at the shoe platform in the hall. From the living room, the sounds of voices and loud laughter overflowed. It was Saturday and school ended before noon, and it sounded like they were having a little lunch party. Then I suddenly realized that this was the day that an 18-year-old man would be visiting us from a faraway old city in the snow country. He had traveled for ten hours by steam engine in order to take an entrance examination for the highest university in Tokyo. He was one of the children of the professor of medicine with whom my father had studied and for whom he had always expressed the greatest admiration and towards whom he felt the greatest loyalty. After the professor died, shortly after the war, my father had been helping and financially supporting his widow and his four children. In the beginning he tried to establish long-term funding for the sons' education because there was almost no scholarship system in Japan in those days. He tried to raise funds from former students of the professor, his former classmates, all of them doctors now. The first round of money came, but then stopped because no one was able to continue. It was the most severe period of inflation and for my father personally it was also the most severe time—during my tuberculosis period too. But my father continued to help them all by himself. The first son became a medical student and finally the second son would now start university life. The widow had kept my parents regularly informed of her children's accomplishments, so we all knew that this second son was "brilliant." He had not only won the top medal of his district's academic competition, but there were rumors (as the widow put it) that he secretly studied and read Shakespeare in the original Elizabethan English, and even that he memorized many lines in those plays and could recite them like an English actor of the theater! My parents knew him for a long time without having seen each other often: he called my parents "uncle" and "aunt", and my parents called him "the guest of honor" for the day.

18 They were in the middle of a lively conversation about music when I came into the living room. The young man stood up and we exchanged greetings. I sensed a lot of self-confidence. He was outgoing, cheerful, and friendly. He showed no awkwardness as many boys of his age did in Japan. But his hands and their movements were very delicate and sensitive: even though he was a man, they looked almost more delicate than my own. My mother told me to bring an extra chair from the music room, so I could sit there at the table. I couldn't open the closet of folding chairs in the music room, so I brought a heavy piano chair with dark red velvet and fringes. In the living room they went back to talking. Many classical composers' pieces were flying across the table, sometimes they were humming short passages of melodies to make sure they were talking about same pieces. But when I tried to listen to the conversation, I found they were not talking about music, they were talking about my two sisters' careers: their solo recitals, their tours, their broadcasts, their trios, their quartet performances were endlessly mentioned. My two sisters added some funny episodes here and there and they all laughed. The bright young man, our guest of honor, seemed to know every piece they mentioned, every collaborator. Every violinist, cellist, and conductor he seemed to know. My mother was sky high with joy when she realized it.

19   The moment the conversation halted, he unexpectedly asked if anyone had seen the movie *Casablanca*. There was silence. "Didn't anyone see it? I cannot believe it, I thought everyone in the whole country had seen it and cried!" he said in a joking tone. "I did see it but I didn't cry," I said, the first time I opened my mouth. "Didn't you find it great? Please tell me." My mother interrupted before he finished the sentence, and turned to me directly and asked me out loud, "Did you say that you saw that movie? How can you do such a thing to go to a movie secretly, how could you? Why didn't you tell me? Who did you go with, if you have anyone to take you to such a faraway movie theater?" I answered: "By myself, mother. I did not know you wanted to know." She looked at our guest. "You see how she reacted. I am so embarrassed by my own daughter. I am so sorry, but everything she does is a secret, we can never know what terrible thing will happen next." Then our guest responded to her rather cheerfully, "I too went to see that movie secretly. The examination day was already close. My mother and sisters went out to see that movie, saying to me, 'You study hard, okay? We won't bother you.' After they left, waiting for a while until the time the movie was almost about to start, I jumped on my bicycle, pedaled with the highest speed, and just as the previews and the news were ending, I slid into the back seat of the theater, and when it was over, when the credits had started, I jumped on the bicycle again and rode back home. It had started snowing heavily in the middle of the movie, so bicycling at high speed was a little bit of an adventure, but I made it. When my family came back, they saw me at my desk studying in exactly the same posture as they saw me when they left home—a perfect crime!" My mother was upset: she thought the conversation took a wrong direction as soon as I responded to the young man's question. All the glorious talk was over. He addressed me again: "So, tell me what you thought, I really would like to..." But his words were again interrupted by mother's words. "It is not worth listening to her, she thinks only weird things, she never sleeps at night— don't ask me why. We don't know what she is doing at midnight, but anyway, because of that, she cannot think straight. We are always worried about her, you know. You should forget about asking her such a question." But I noticed his questioning eyes were still on me, so I decided to reply to him as quickly as possible and as briefly as possible.

20 "I did not think the woman, the main character, the beautiful woman, was described well at all. What was her life about? What was she serious about? What was she longing for in life? None of these answers were there. The love between her and the cafe owner was not written well either. I feel that in order to arouse the power of tragedy in us, a writer has to convince us that their love has some profound meaning to them. The more the writer emphasized that their attraction was intense and that they could not forget about their beautiful memories] together, the more I felt the emptiness of their love. As soon as the lovers met the second time, their conversation revealed their suspicion and anger towards each other. There was no genuine respect and trust in each other, so they don't communicate well. How their conversation quickly brought them down to such a low level is amazing: real love was not built at all, so how could the writer expect the viewer to feel this separation was a tragedy? Her husband was an underground activist helping refugees. I liked him the best among this movie's characters—he was the only one who was not an infant—but he had not built a strong or profound relationship with her. We know that he loves her, but we never had any feeling that she understood what his mission means to him or that she herself participates in it in any deep way. She is loved, she is beautiful, but both are very passive qualities, as if the writer is saying that is all she has and all she needs. There was lots of preparation for the final rescue and self-sacrifices were prepared. I was astonished there were so many practical and emotional manipulations. Under the name of love, and under the name of self-sacrifice, so many assumptions were made and there were so many manipulations that affected the feelings and thinking of the person in question. It gave me a chill when I realized that serious manipulations were possible among people we live with, and that such manipulations must actually be performed every day in our lives, without the person in question ever realizing it."

21   "Hmm, I have never thought about such a thing. This is such a new view for me. I want to think it through. Hmm. But you thought it was romantic. It is beautiful, didn't you find it that way?" I answered:

"Yes, it is beautiful, but rather superficial. It is romantic but rather sentimental. But I wonder if it manifests real Romanticism. If it does, then I don't think I like Romanticism." Our guest was a little puzzled and yet he was thoughtfully watching me. As soon as my talk finished I went deeply into my own thoughts, thinking about romanticism in music: The music of romanticism has an element that is very dangerous, seemingly to make people lose their mind or make them intoxicated, swaying them into grandiosity. It can be used to propagandize, or it can be destructive to individuals and groups of people who otherwise have a good, solid base of thinking. That is what I realized and I was afraid of being soaked in the flood of music every single day. I must indeed be deteriorated.

22   If anyone at this table caught a glimpse of what I was thinking about for even one second, he or she would find a victorious proof of my mother's words spoken to today's guest of honor: "She thinks only weird things...She cannot think straight." My mother changed gears and lifted up the tone of the conversation: she started talking about new events and new concert tours. She succeeded in regaining the power in the conversation. After a while, laughing and talking came to life again. "You will have a new life here in Tokyo," my mother said to our guest. "You will be invited not only to every concert and every event my two daughters are involved in, of course, but also, when we have great musicians come from America and Europe, I will do my best to get extra tickets to invite you. Let's do everything together. Oh, how exciting!" She spoke as if he had already passed his exams. "Then you have to watch out very carefully," my father added. "If you follow my wife's whole schedule, you will not have one minute left for your own

study, I assure you." Everyone laughed, the glorious lunch was safely ended, and everyone stood up.

23 "Put the chair back in the music room," my mother said. I put my hands on the velvet seat of the chair. "Let me!" the young man offered, flying to my side from the other side of the table and putting his hands on the chair. The moment I withdrew my hands from the chair, my father's voice suddenly pierced me as if he were shooting an arrow at me: "You don't let our guest of honor carry your chair for you, do you? For heaven's sake, can't you do anything right?" Our guest of honor immediately cut in: "Oh, uncle, please let me play the role of a knight here." The rumors about Shakespeare's plays crossed my mind. Clever, I thought, that he sensed the generation gap involved here. Before the war, asking a man to perform such a humble task was considered an insult. But rather than pointing out the generation gap to my father, he made a swift move as if he were asking him a special favor. "Oh, you may, indeed, you have my permission." My father, without stumbling, replied with a smile.

24 I guided our guest, who was lifting the piano chair with both hands, and opened the door to the corridor that led to the music room. It was cold and darkened with thick curtains for soundproofing, obscuring the sunny winter afternoon . He placed the piano chair in front of the piano. But he kept his back bent over the chair with both hands still holding the chair. I was wondering what was happening. I bent over towards him and looked up at his face. His eyes were filled with tears. "It was too painful for me to see that you were treated so cruelly by your parents like that," he said. "What is going on? You are so beautiful and obviously brilliant, why do they treat you as if you were a shame of the family? Whatever reason they think they have, it is wrong, it is injustice, I wanted to stop them. But obviously I failed." Tears fell from his eyes onto the red velvet. I was completely out of it. I did not understand what was happening right in front of my eyes. I did not say one word, with only murmurs repeated in my mind: *Can a man cry too? I have never seen a man cry. If so, why is he crying?* He straightened his back and stood tall. "Probably I shouldn't have said such a thing to you about your parents. If those words hurt you, I am sorry." He wiped his tears with the back of his hand, and with a gentle and thoughtful voice he said, "Shall we go back to the living room?"

25   Only after midnight that day did the meaning of what he had said come to me. As if the huge sounds of bells, of many bells, started ringing at once over my head, the sound pierced my ears and made them bleed, and made my body tremble. Each bell sounded loudly and said, "He saw the truth. He saw what really is happening. It was reality, not illusion as I thought. Something is terribly wrong with my parents, not with me. Injustice was done to me, not the other way around."

26   It was a cold day, sometime while my shunning was still continuing at school. When I came back from school, the house was freezing as always. I started putting coals on the fire in the stove: in those days this stove was the only heater we had to make our home warm. There was only one stove in the house, in the living room. But on that particular day, the coals seemed to be wet for some reason, and I could not light the fire. I cleaned the inside of the stove and started from the beginning with twisted old newspapers. I repeated the process many times but only white smoke kept coming out. Finally the whole house was completely filled with smoke. I opened all the windows, darkness fell, the temperature seemed to drop down to the freezing point, and the house became unbearably cold. I went upstairs and sat on my bed, wrapping myself with a blanket over the school uniform I was wearing. I sat against the wall away from the opened window, and was overcome by fear of what would happen next at school. *I don't think I have enough strength left in me,* I thought, and my desperation over my own powerlessness froze me to the point of paralyzing my mind.

27 On that particular evening, my parents and two sisters came back home without going to dinner at a restaurant as they usually did after a concert. They were carrying bouquets from the concert, which the performer that evening had given away: the extra ones he could not carry. The bouquets were so big that their faces were almost buried in them. As soon as they came into the living room, they were furious to find that the stove was not on and dinner was not ready It was my responsibility to handle those things for them according to our cult rules. Accusations started, the dogma was repeated: the talented ones had to do their best to develop their talent and the untalented one had to help them; what else can you do that is worthwhile? How can you be so selfish and egotistic while your sisters were working so hard for important things? How can you be so undisciplined that you have not even changed out of your school uniform? I was the only one in the family who was supposed to put on an apron over the everyday dress whenever I was at home.

28 My mother allowed my two sisters to join aggressively in these accusations against me. "Her whole problem is that she does not even know what her goal is," my elder sister said. "It does not matter, she would not accomplish anything," the young one said. Then my mother picked up on the tirade. "What was your problem that you could not make the house warm, or make dinner for them, such simple things that any idiot can do? Why are you so dishonest, saying you could not make a fire?" As she said those things, she made a fire and quickly made dinner. She thus proved how lazy, how impotent, how dishonest, rebellious, and malicious I was. By the time I was released after the recitation of my long list of my crimes to my room, the east window of the room was showing the first light of dawn.

29 How these accusations took so many hours, it is hard to recall now. I sometimes felt a faint tone of envy in my sisters' accusations towards me; it came like a flash to me, but then it seemed too odd, too outrageous a thought for me to ponder further at that time. But now when I look back I am stricken to see the clear picture of their envy. How accurately their accusations towards me were targeted exactly to those things that they struggled with. They saw the freedom in my actions, even though it breathed in me in the most miserable form. Freedom was exactly the thing they had lost. They saw the strength of fighting in my action, however powerless it looked: that fighting was another thing they were not allowed to do against mother. They ridiculed me for not knowing my goal, and that was the area in which they had lost their freedom most because they didn't own their lives anymore. They were not sure if they had chosen their goals: if they had freedom, would they choose the same goals? They could not afford to doubt the dogma they were given or fight at all against their parents, and they could not afford to think about, doubt, or create their own lives. They would lose all approval from our mother if they did any of those things and her approval was an absolute necessity for them. When they accused me of dishonesty, deep down in their minds they knew that their own lives were founded on a huge deception.

30 Their envy towards the person who had the very thing that they wanted, and yet could not have, was enormous. And their desire for the total destruction of the one whom they envied secretly was fierce. This very mechanism is something I started to see in both the act of excommunication at school where I became a bitter victim and in the act of accusations towards me in my home cult. Both my aristocratic school and my home cult succeeded in maintaining their sanctity and grandiosity: the more intense their persecution of the despised one became, the more sanctified and aggrandized the school and home became. But those ideas were just a flash, just a momentary hallucination for me then. I was crushed by the overwhelming notion that injustice had been done to me again, not only at school, but at home. This realization became drastically clearer and strengthened after that brilliant young man shed tears for me when he witnessed the injustice being done to me in front of his own eyes. And yet I still had some suspicions about myself that something very deep in me might be causing them to be so angry: this suspicion was still hovering over my head and those doubts pulled my mind into a deep abyss of darkness.

31 One thing became unmistakably clear though: My father could not save me. He asked me if I had at least studied while not performing my duties. I sensed instantly that he was throwing a lifeboat to me, since I felt I was thrown into the cold stormy ocean and struggled alone. Saying yes to him meant grabbing the lifeboat. He could convince my mother, "At least she did something constructive, she is not bad as she looks." Then he could pull the rope of the lifeboat to the shore. He need justification to help me, he needed my mother's permission to "forgive" me. I said "No!" His big hand flew to my cheek with the speed of lightning, and my cheek started swelling immediately. He was betrayed by me, he was hurt by me, and he knew exactly why I said "No!" I had been wrong for such a long time to have thought that he and I were victims of the cult. But now I knew that he was an insider in the cult. He was a respectable member of my mother's cult. He was afraid of losing her approval as much as my sisters were. And just like those three classmates at the aristocratic school, he wanted to have approval from both sides. I had been alone for many years. I had done all my drawings of Hamlet based on a foolish illusion.

CHAPTER 10

1 The doctor who cured my tuberculosis told me bluntly that I was having a nervous breakdown. My mother took me to his office because I often would not get up to go to school. It finally came to the point that I was not able to move myself from the bed and I became an officially branded "insane girl". All the shame of sickness that I suffered many years before when I had tuberculosis came back to me once again. After taking one semester off from the aristocratic school, after a life of hell at home, I took the transfer examination and was accepted into a new school.

2 But behind this simple description of how I ended up in this new school, there is a story. One day, one of those hellish days, the young man who had come to our lunch party as a guest of honor visited our house and told me a story. He was walking around the campus of a school near our house when he walked under a fantastically powerful oak tree. Suddenly a girl who was wearing a beautiful light-colored skirt flew down from the branch of the tree to the ground, her skirt inflated like a parachute, right in front of him. She smiled at him—he was totally surprised—and asked him who he was. He told her that he wanted to explore this beautiful campus, and added that he did not have to ask her who she was because he knew that she must be one of the fairies who lived in the big tree. Before he could finish his sentence, half a dozen other girls, who were hiding in the thick leafy branches of that oak tree, one after another flew down to the ground. They guided him all around the junior high school division of their school. On his slender student uniform was a new silver insignia of the university which he now attended. Everyone in Japan knew that insignia: it must have been shining, and it made those girls feel safe and excited and happy to guide him. I could visualize it well. When he told me this story, he added: "They have an atelier, a music hall, and even real woods and a river where they can camp out overnight. All through my explorations, I was thinking about you, Junko, that this kind of school—full of freedom and new experiments—is what you would like and what you deserve. What do you think? Would you like to drop out of that musty old aristocratic school and go to this new one? I could talk to your mother, if you like." The truth is that unless he did talk to my mother, there was a strong possibility I would become a junior high dropout (though we never heard such a phrase in those days in Japan) and I would probably end up being committed to some kind of institution, or very possibly committing suicide.

3 The new school was in the affluent suburb of Tokyo where we lived, within walking distance of our home. It was a private school, known for its liberal and creative philosophy of education. It was coeducational: boys wore a suit and tie, and girls could wear basically anything they liked. It was recognized not only for its high level of academic accomplishment, but also for its innovative projects, such as an internationally famous movie director (Akira Kurosawa) teaching young students how to make movies even in those days before computers existed. I dropped all my aristocratic language and started to use the usual Japanese which everyone spoke, such as "Good morning" and "Thank you," and I dropped the militaristic, monastic uniform I had been wearing for seven years.

4 I encountered a striking young man in that new junior high school. This man opened up a whole new world for me: with him my adventurous journey to my inner world began. This young man was a math teacher there, a beautiful, strongly built man in his mid-twenties with a slightly eccentric manner. During math class he would sometimes suddenly start reading poems or short stories to us. In spite of his unusually vigorous, outgoing manner, and his rough language, his choice of those poems and short stories was extremely sensitive. And the class immediately became quiet to listen to him. Reading such things during math class was in itself an enormously rebellious act against the school authority. He had a country accent from the Northern districts, a place where they grow a lot of good rice. People said he was the son of a rice farmer. The memory of the rice fields where young green rice plants stood with their sharp translucent blades pointing to the sky came back to me immediately when I heard of his homeland. Boys loved him for his freedom and his masculinity, and girls hated him hysterically for the same reasons that boys loved him— a hatred I thought very well might be the reverse expression of interest in him as a man. I was elected to a book-reading committee of students whose work involved making a list, as student body representatives, of book acquisition requests to be submitted to the library and managing other tedious library work after classes. And this math teacher was in charge of the committee.

5 The school library was located a little away from the main building where all our classes were held. Descending long stone stairways with trees grown around them that formed an arch over them, stepping into the cedar forest at the bottom of the stairs, and walking through the forest for a while led you to the library. When you stepped into the building it was always surprising to see, through the library's tall glass window, the wide field, which was at the rear of the campus and spread to the far end of another forest. The library was never crowded, and after closing time, the quietness of the forest loomed and filled the whole building. I read the books the teacher recommended to me, and he listened to me attentively as I told him what I felt about each book. He then openly told me what he thought about it. All this happened in that quiet room after everybody left.

6 A whole new world rushed into me like a flood. The math teacher brought Rainer Maria Rilke into my world for the first time. We read the Duino Elegies aloud together, in Japanese translation of course. The moment I touched Rilke's words, all my chaos, all my boiling, confused emotions, all my pain and agony instantly aligned themselves in one certain direction in a lightning flash and flowed in that direction like a violent wave. It all happened in one second: there was no need to think or to study for it.

7 It was the world I had been aware of when I was painting, and yet I could not define it until I read these poems of Rilke's. It was the world of my art that had not yet been realized. Those days I was painting every night. I was pouring my stormy emotions into painting in my little room, sitting towards the window facing the eastern sky. I sensed that beyond those stormy emotions was another world—a world of nihilism. It had an urgent sense of reality to me, sense of aloneness, of not belonging to anyone or anything, of there being nothing to rely on. But when I went further, I felt an absolute quietness, a profound solitude which is different from the feeling of nihilistic isolation. And then, only very rarely, I felt a completely different space standing in the midst of this solitude. This space was visible like a transparent form of architecture. It was slightly similar to the architecture that I found myself in when I heard the Ninth Symphony in the dark room of the hospital where we escaped from the bombing. But it was much less material, much less tangible. It was an unexplainable, indescribable space. I called this space the secret cathedral. Rilke suddenly talked to me from that cathedral:

> Who, if I cried, would hear me among the angelic
>
> orders? And even if one of them suddenly
>
> pressed me against his heart, I should fade in the strength of his
>
> stronger existence. For Beauty's nothing
>
> but the beginning of Terror we're still just able to bear,
>
> And why we adore it so is because it serenely
>
> disdains to destroy us. Every angel is terrible.

These words shook me. Even beyond this secret cathedral, there would be another space I could only foresee. And this is what Rilke called "terror!" If you see it with your naked eyes, you will be destroyed and you will be made to vanish. There is no other word for it than "terror". And yet this is a dazzling, brilliant space, so bright that we can recognize it only as darkness. One cannot bear it. Rilke was pointing out this brilliant space to me.

8 It was ten years later that I learned about the "divine darkness" of medieval mysticism, the idea that the unapproachable light in which God dwells is so brilliant that humans can experience it only as darkness. This idea moved me deeply, not because it was new to me, but because it had been so familiar to me since I encountered Rilke when I was fifteen years old. This is the darkness I wanted to paint— the darkness that forced me to paint. What I really wanted to see in my painting was this "terrifying" light shining through this darkness. I wanted to paint only this and nothing else. *No wonder* that I could not paint the way other people did, nor the way other people expected me to paint. In a second, the mystery had been solved. Encountering this poetry was an awareness of the solitude of my life to come, and it was the terror of seeing my own destiny in a flash. Those things became more clear and verbalized as the years had gone by. But at that time, when the math teacher and I saw the depth of our own inner experience, evoked by Rilke's poetry in each other's eyes, we were both trembling with astonishment and joy.

9   I started reading other works of Rilke, The Notebooks of Malte Laurids Brigge and other poems. The idea that the seed of death grows in each of our lives was almost identical to my own thinking, born during my long days of tuberculosis, and I had been aware of that growth of death almost every day since then. And about love, the idea that love is to release the one whom you love to the space of freedom sunk into me deeply, and Rilke's intense words that one has to become a person who loves, not a person who is loved, made profound sense to me. I was suffocated, chained inside a cage by strong manipulations, controls, and deceptions all in the name of love. I felt that Rilke's

228

words supported me to go forward in the direction that I had struggled towards and towards which I had been already half awakened. I started painting with more passion and more conviction almost every night. My math teacher started writing small poems, guided by inspiration from those Rilke poems. Our lives seemed to be moving towards becoming richer and fuller.

10 One day the teacher in my home room class gave us a survey about the books we had read during the semester in our private time. Among both parents and students, he was trusted and popular as a man of good character and as a passionate educator. He was a man in his thirties, a Christian, who held his head straight up and walked with dignity, with determination, as if he wished to put the definite mark of his righteousness on the earth with every step. His suit was right, his shoes were shined, his black thick hair—just like that of many Japanese men—was styled with pomade and never moved on his head. I heard that his brother was the minister of a church. We heard that his elderly father was known as a significant Meiji period scholar and religious figure, and that his mother was one of the first women to receive a college education in Japan in the Meiji period.

11 Around this teacher there was always an atmosphere of Stoicism and scholarship. He was teaching us English, but his real ambition was to be a minister of a church, a writer, or both. Students talked a lot about him because he was a Christian, different from us. His survey of the books we had read was to further his educational purpose, not for censorship. I responded to the survey very seriously and gave him a thorough report, and as a member of the book committee I felt a responsibility to be honest.

12   My mother came back from a PTA meeting and told me that my reading list was a target of concern for him. He did not reveal my name at the meeting, but my mother knew immediately that it was me by recognizing some of the books she knew I was reading. He pointed out Rilke from my list as an example of a book inappropriate and too early for a 15-year-old. And the parents who had never even heard of Rilke all joined in his concern. Immediately I felt a dark black cloud hovering over my head. Why does this always happen to me? Why is it such a problem for me to read a book in which I found my life? The memory of the shunning I had experienced was still very vivid. I thought, "I have no strength left to fight against that sort of thing now. I might have to simply leave this school too."

13   The next day, after waiting for everybody else to leave, I told my math teacher about my mother's report of the PTA meeting without telling him about the shunning I had experienced in the previous school. He burst out laughing the moment I told him. And the moment he started laughing, an uncontrollable sense of funniness came over me, too, and we laughed hard together. "Sure, Rilke is too early for him, this teacher of yours, it is inappropriate for him to read it!" We laughed at his small-mindedness, at his effort to control a world which he might not be able to handle, at his search for some standard outside himself—good book, bad book, too young, too old—and his apparent effort to apply those standards to his inner world. And we laughed at his deception: by abusing his power to evoke the same fear in the parents, he was trying to control his own unfathomably frightening inner world and to confine the most terrifying thing of all—our unknowable unconscious. After that, once in a while he would ask me how my home room teacher was doing, to make sure that nothing horrible had developed. It was a great relief for me. I felt that although the world was still terrible, I didn't necessarily have to be a victim every time I evoked fear in others. I could laugh; I was strong enough to laugh, so far, at the size of this problem, if it stayed this size.

14   It was the first time I experienced emotional freedom since the incident at the school. My math teacher's laugh showed his strength; it was different from any other man's laugh I had ever heard in the aristocratic environment and different from the laugh of the neurotic young music geniuses who filled my home all the time. It was a hearty and good-natured sound. And yet it made me feel that he himself must have had many experiences of being "persecuted" along the way as an eccentric man. I sensed his compassion in it. And that struck me as an extremely masculine and attractive quality.

15   Suddenly every day turned into a most pleasurable day. I felt my body become suddenly light, I felt like floating: it was as if I became a thin silver antenna, standing on a small gentle boat, floating over rivers and oceans for the first time since my tuberculosis period long ago. I was in an embrace with the universe, and the world seemed to cease being hostile and frightening. My mind became light and my mouth became light: words just came out of my mouth without my preparing what to say beforehand. I said, "It will rain tomorrow!" He said, "It is most likely so: it is the rainy season!" "No, I mean, exactly at midnight it will start raining!" Then it happened: I heard the first drop of rain hit the roof of my upstairs room exactly at midnight. "Is he awake? Is he thinking about me right now as he hears the sound of the rain in his bed as I think about him?"

16 Then I thought: You will feel the first drop of rain when you come down the stone stairs to the library tomorrow. The next day he came into the library: "It is weird: it just starting raining on such a sunny day!" Some students lifted their faces from their books and saw pouring rain at the window but no one really paid attention. He shook his head—his hair moved as he shook his head—and how wonderful his hair looked. It was like a bamboo forest when the wind goes through, the whole forest swaying and trembling, never just one part of it, each movement triggering another movement; or rather it was like a jellyfish that moves in the water, its whole head moving in such a joyous way, in so sensuous a way! He was shaking his head at me jokingly, teasingly, but a little puzzled. He remembered what I said! My heart filled with warmth. It went further. I said, "We will have an earthquake tomorrow!" This time he did not yield; he was a seismologist before he became a math teacher. "Now you are being scientific, you are absolutely right; we have an earthquake every day in this volcanic land of ours, only we don't necessarily feel them." "But you will feel it tomorrow." At dawn a palpable quake shook our district. We enjoyed this little game in a very lighthearted way. Sometimes when I talked about these things like a little girl, I had a vision that his arms were stretched from his shoulders towards me, and I felt as if they hugged me gently as a loving grownup does to a little one. I turned around quickly, so as not to show the tears of joy that filled my eyes.

17 Everybody in the whole school knew he had a fiancée, a sweet-looking gym teacher. I saw them often walking together towards the station to go to their homes when I left school very late for some reason. For a male teacher and a female teacher to walk alone together was considered eccentric. The gym teacher had changed from her gymnasium uniform into an elegant skirt and high heels and smiled cheerfully as they walked. They looked like a beautiful exciting couple and the students loved to see them. But one day he and I were the last people to leave the school and walk together to the front of the train station. I bowed goodbye to him and walked from there; he took the train alone. But our innocence could not last forever.

18 There was none of the legal sensitivity that exists in America now: the thought that a sexual relationship between an adult and a minor was a crime, or that the minor's consent could not be valid. It was not that idea that prevented us from expressing our feelings in any act of intimacy or sexuality rather than words and silence. It was because of the traditional and strict sense of the difference in our positions. The distance of teacher and student, of the upper status and the lower status, was clear and absolute. We used to say, "Walk three steps behind the teacher in order not to step on his shadow." It was an old saying, of course, and after American culture rushed into Japan people laughed at this kind of saying. But when it came to real life it was still alive, very strongly, and it functioned as one of the strongest taboos in society. We were using different levels of language: he used rather casual, friendly words, and I was using the politest expression which only a person in the lower position was supposed to use while talking to a higher person—even during the playful conversation about the rain premonition. The degree of the language difference between higher and lower was less significant in this new school than in the aristocratic school I used to attend. And yet the hierarchy of position is deeply innate in the Japanese language and determined our consciousness and behavior.

19 When we recognized in each other's eyes that our emotions had already traversed the line of that distance, the fear and the guilt of one who had already broken the taboo overwhelmed us. At the same time, an excitement and sense of unity as accomplices filled both of us with a sensuous intoxication whose power was beyond imagination.

20 We were in the midst of the clash of sexual cultures in Japan in those days. America brought drastic change in sexual consciousness to Japan: coarseness, vulgarity, and the use of sex as a commodity were everywhere in town, and made decent people cover their eyes. But the natural warm expression of love and affection between man and woman were never seen at home or in town; none of us ever saw our parents holding hands or even walking together—because the woman would always walk a few steps behind the man. It was only a decade or so after the time that talking with the opposite sex on the street attracted the attention of the police. That is why the math teacher and his fiancée walking together was such a sensational, refreshing thing for their students to see. Serious men and women were afraid of their own power of sexuality, and wondered how it could be integrated into the culture in the midst of the confusing clash of the cultures of America and Japan—and the clash between tradition and the new Japanese culture. It was a difficult problem.

21 Treating a woman's virginity as something that had value as a commodity was characteristic of pre-war Japanese culture: if you kept it you could sell yourself in the normal part of your social range in marriage, but if you lost it, you would have to set your sights quite low, to the point of ruining your life. Therefore a man who was responsible for a woman's loss of virginity was obligated to marry her unless he wanted to be the scum of society. I trusted my math teacher to take absolute responsibility for his fiancée, if he was responsible—and somehow I thought he was.

22 He told me that he saw something unbelievably beautiful and unique in me and that he found it so precious and attractive, and that was exactly the reason he should not tie me up with his feelings. "I should not wait until you become grown," he said, adding that if he were to do such a thing, he would limit my freedom. "You need limitless freedom to grow; you should never grow up waiting for me at the other end. I should go my own way; I should marry my fiancée as I planned. And our relationship should end." And then he said that sometime we probably could cultivate and elevate this relationship together into something very unusual and beautiful: we would read the same books together and exchange our thoughts, and we would write regularly and steadily so we could learn and study many things and express ourselves together, however unusual it might sound. We could do it, we could grow together, and it would grow beyond his marriage. His thoughts went back and forth. Though it was painful and confusing, his respect for my future, my potentiality and need for limitless freedom to grow, was always strong.

23 How extraordinary it was for me to hear those words. I had been told over and over all my life that I had nothing good in me. There was my parents' fixation on my future as a second violinist and now as the companion of my sisters—both occupations there were far from my aptitude—and after the endless discussion of my lack of talent, my laziness, my being "retarded" and my "insanity", I should have been ecstatic to hear such remarks. And yet now, hearing him say those words, my mind was filled with thoughts of suicide. Gradually I was focusing all my thoughts on suicide: just like a Renaissance masterpiece painted with perfect perspective, all my other thoughts were lining up and diminishing into that one vanishing point.

24   One day, one of those urgent days when summer vacation was coming close so we would not be able to see each other every day as we had been doing, we finally chose his apartment as a meeting place during the vacation because it was the only place that would be safe from the eyes of all students and their parents. We agreed to it knowing that very likely it would change the nature of our relationship. A few days later, at the library, after everybody left, he told me that my mother had visited him at his apartment, the evening before. She had read my diary. "I cannot destroy you, this has to end," he groaned. He stood up and stepped towards me. He will hug me, I thought. And then he stepped back. My chest, the whole front part of my body, was torn and ripped off from the rest as he moved back, like a tree hit by thunder, torn and split vertically from the top. The flesh of the tree, the pale pink, pure and shiny, vulnerable flesh of the tree, in the din of sharp ripping sounds, with a splash of fragrance, was revealed.

25   And suddenly, he stormed out of the library to the field at the rear of the campus. No one else was there. He walked across, and continued walking on the grass far away, the edge of his jacket flowing in the wind, with the long grass beneath him waving—was it a windy early evening? —and passed in front of the gymnasium and walked towards the swimming pool. I watched his shoulders, his legs, and his beautiful hair—the wind going through it. The desperate scream of a person who had been kicked off the cliff to the abyss below loudly echoed in me.

Suddenly I saw a grille made of stone in the style of a European medieval dungeon. It loomed in front of me. The space inside each grille gradually filled up and finally it became one huge stone wall. It stood right in front of my face and no matter how hard I tried, I could not see him anymore: only the surface of gray rough stone. I could not tell whether it was a real wall or a hallucination.

26 I don't remember how I came home. I saw my mother and my elder sister in the living room together. Suddenly I grabbed something hard in my hand from the table nearby. I raised my arm, the thought running through my mind in a flash that this is the kind of moment when one could commit murder. Then I don't know what happened. When I awoke I was in bed and my mother was sitting and watching me. She said that my math teacher loved me; he saw something special in me, and he was suffering and he was in tears; he is an honest, sensitive young man. I told her that she did the right thing, and so did he, and I was going to do the right thing, too, so she did not have to worry about me anymore. That was it. Everything was done very quietly and rationally.

27 Everything was over but I seemed to have lost everything. It was as if I had cut my own artery. My painting stopped coming to mind; all that came was suffering, most passionate suffering, all through nights and nights. My smile, my laugh, wouldn't come back. And changing dresses—even into nightgowns from daytime dresses—never happened anymore. No baths, no combing my long hair, it all stopped. I went to school every day in the same clothes and with the same school bag without ever opening it. He did not teach our class anymore at that time, and I was trying to hear his voice in case it came from some other classroom where he might be teaching. But his voice would never reach me, and the pain and ecstasy came over me alternately, repeatedly, so that I fainted and was carried to the infirmary room many times.

28   Passages from Rilke's poem were still with me: "If anything is wrong it is not to enlarge the freedom of a love with all the inner freedom one can summon. We need, in love, to practice only this: letting each other go. For holding on comes easily—we do not need to learn it." My math teacher had done this: enlarged the freedom of a love: with all the inner freedom he could summon, he released me into the sky, into the future. He did this for me. And I decided to do the exact same thing: release him to his space of freedom.

29   I imposed a strict discipline on myself not to put him in my sight, not to turn around when I knew he was behind me by recognizing his footsteps among hundreds of students' footsteps. The summer had gone, and fall and winter passed that way. One spring day the gym teacher stood at the microphone to say goodbye to all the students, shyly smiling, a beautiful woman. Everyone knew that it was so she could marry the math teacher. Without allowing myself the joy of looking at him once, even if he came into my sight, I graduated from junior high and moved to the high school campus in the same school, a few blocks away.

30   Questions still remained. My diary was full of thoughts of suicide: after my mother read it, why did she not do anything about it except prevent me from seeing him anymore, at which she did succeed? And why did she not notice or do anything about my sudden change of lifestyle after that? Our whole house was like a candidate's election campaign headquarters, filled with excitement and anguish, and strategy and calculation: in preparation for my sisters' concerts my mother memorized 2,000 ticket buyers' names and matched them with the seat numbers on the charts: no one in the cult paid attention to anything else but "winning", which was defined in this case as my sisters' success. I would have vehemently denied it if anyone had suggested at that time that I wanted my parents to see my diary. But it is true that even after having read my diary my mother still did not hear my desperate cry. Even after she learned that the math teacher saw something special in me, she did not change her view of me. These things made my isolation from my family definite: it was not that she had violated my privacy.

31 The only person who noticed my drastic change and was concerned about me was my homeroom teacher. He unsuccessfully tried to contact my mother several times. Then he invited me to the church at which his brother presided. I washed my hair and combed it, put on a white long-sleeve blouse and black velvet flare skirt, and went to the church. He was waiting for me with his bicycle as his side at the small suburban train station. He showed me the long way to the church from the station. Walking through the crowded market street and residential area, we took a winding little path between wooden high fences. He was there at the station, waiting for me with his bicycle at his side every single Sunday after that until the end of the school term.

32 The church was rather small but very special. It was founded by my home room teacher's father in the Meiji period, and he kept its complete independence by risking his own life and persecution by the fascistic government during the war. The building was burned down by the bombing and this building was just recently rebuilt. Because he had become quite old, one of his sons—my teacher's brother who had studied in America—presided over the church. When his father founded the church, Christianity was still considered revolutionary, especially his church, which viewed Jesus as a human being. This was the only church that practiced humanistic liberal Christianity in Japan. They even invited Buddhist and Shinto priests to conduct services once in a while. The church had often become the target of various kinds of persecution. His contemporary friends, who were all passionate revolutionaries in the Meiji period, seldom attended services anymore because of their age. The younger generation, mainly the minister's colleagues and his students in the religious department of the two universities where he was teaching, comprised most of the congregation. But those scholarly members were still imbued strongly with the spirit of revolution. I was by far the youngest and least educated among them, but they received me warmly and invited me to many activities, such as lectures given by them or by religious scholars and representatives from the Shinto, Buddhist, or other faiths and other denominations—the entire treasure box of religions practiced in Japan. I was intrigued, and full of respect for those people. I was grateful that I was invited to the church by my teacher. I found those people most comfortable to be with—not at all like the crowd I knew at home or at school.

33   Outside this simple modest church was a small residence where the father, who was the founder, and his wife and my homeroom teacher lived. When he attended the services at which his son presided, the father always wore a formal kimono, kimono skirt, and kimono jacket on which his family crest was dyed beautifully. When he saw me he stopped walking, put his cane in front of him, and bowed to me very deeply—the kind of bow that the person of a lower position makes to pay respect to the higher one. I was always astonished at his bowing that way towards me, and I bowed towards him in the way that I learned in the aristocratic school in my childhood, the way reserved only for the person whom you respect the most—usually meant only for the Emperor in that school.

34 My teacher was taking care of his elderly parents and undertaking all the tasks of the church single-handedly. Their residence was covered with breathtaking flowers. Every inch of the yard was covered with flowers every season so that, all year long, the old parents were surrounded with flowers. Especially when the peaches and plum trees were blooming, the members of the church and anyone who came to that house just stood there and uttered a cry of pleasure. Their voices were for the flowers and trees, but also for my teacher, who maintained the garden in this dreamlike beauty. Everybody praised him for being so devoted to his parents and to the church.

35 One Sunday morning, at the small station where he always waited for me, he asked me if I would not mind riding on the rear seat of the bicycle to church, instead of walking, because he was in a hurry to do some work left before the service started: it was some special day on which many activities would be held in the church. "You have plenty of time to walk to church alone if you would rather do that," he said. He was polite and considerate. He came all the way to tell me this; I would have to hold my arm around him if I accepted the offer, I knew. I folded my big flare skirt under my knees and sat sideways on the rear seat just like the aristocratic ladies in the movies do when they ride horses. When his bicycle started rolling through the market street, with me on the back with my arms around his waist, his hair was right in front of my eyes; the comb's teeth left their trace on his pomaded hair, which never moved even in the wind on the bicycle. An unexpectedly strong sadness pushed my chest as a pain; tears fell like a waterfall. They were dried by the wind and fell again and again on my cheek. It was the first time I ever touched a man, and I wished acutely it had been my math teacher instead.

36 In the evening that Sunday, after the activities were over, my home room teacher invited me to his study. It was a little one-room house detached from his parents' residence in the same yard, connected to the churchyard without any fence. Two walls of the study were filled with glass-covered bookshelves from floor to ceiling. Through the perfectly clean, shining glass I saw many books of philosophy, religion, and literature from the West and the East, orderly arranged. On the other wall was a very good quality reproduction of one of the Barbizon school paintings, a landscape of the forest of Fontainebleau, where the artists who sought nature as the expression of their spiritual quest lived and painted in the 19th century; it was hung in a modest frame of good taste. On his big old wooden desk was an iron pen plate; several fountain pens were neatly placed on it. The room, illuminated by a standing light in the corner, was filled with meditative quietness, simplicity, and modesty. I suddenly felt that I had sought those qualities all my life and had never found them.

37 In this quietness, the contrast to the clamor of my house suddenly overcame me. I felt that I could not bear it anymore: it represented exactly the madness of my whole family. Unlike this one, my whole house was filled with the sounds of two or three or more different pieces of music played by different instruments at once, and they were all the students were all in the severe process of practicing, repeating every passage over and over, correcting endless mistakes until things finally made sense to them, and experimenting with various interpretations of phrases tried over and over. In the living room, the dressmakers holding satin dresses for my sisters' stage appearances were always walking around, shouting and laughing. Young people with big cello cases in their arms walked into the house without knocking, some of whom I didn't even know, and they talked and laughed. The 14-year-old boy whose mother had brought him from her hometown near the mansion of the Motoyasu, who we called MENDEL, was now occupying the room next to mine. Now the only space for which I had fought for quietness, my little room, my precious inner world, where I received mysterious images of art in the faint light of the east window before dawn, where I wrote and read, where I saw the soaring transparent cathedral, and where I saw Rilke, had finally been invaded by the flood of violin sounds—the sounds just like tearing cloth up—finally coming down to destroy me. Meanwhile, in the refrigerator in the kitchen, the food decomposed quietly and milk turned and molded rapidly until it was green. No one noticed, no one cared.

38   When I sat down on the couch in the teacher's study, when he gently placed the tea that he made himself for me on the table—which was so unusual for a man to do in Japan for a woman or a student— I thought that this was the time for me to express to him my gratitude that he invited me to this church. No one noticed that I urgently needed nurturing. I had not seen my math teacher since I saw him through the library window walking toward the swimming pool at the edge of the school grounds the day he told me that my mother visited him at his apartment. I left the library when my hallucinatory image, the stone grid, prevented me from seeing him; I left alone before he might have come back to the library that evening. That was the last time I saw him and already four seasons had passed since then. It felt to me like it was many years ago and I had not wept and wailed for a long time, except when some time tears fell like they had this morning on his bicycle behind his seat. If my home room teacher had never invited me to the church, what would have happened to me? I wanted to express my gratitude in a way that good grownups do, with good manners in this quiet room. I started doing that. But then a sharp pain formed a lump in my throat and globs of pain leaked out one after another, flowing over as sadness in a succession of groan. Chaos and desperation thrust up in me like magma trying to find its crater. Totally unplanned and unexpected, I opened my mouth to say the things I thought I would never say: I let the whole story out about the math teacher and me. It spilled out around me like lava from a volcano. I cried and could not stop crying. The moment I was done, I was crushed with fear. I had done the most terrible thing; I had done something I could never correct.

39   It was true that I was planning to express to him how grateful I felt that he invited me to this church. But suddenly I had fallen apart in the worst way. It was the most seriously destructive way I could have acted in front of this teacher. Worst of all, the most unexpected thing I did was to talk about my math teacher, betraying my most precious person. I had broken his trust in me. He would never imagine that I would talk about our secret to his colleague. I was totally panicked.

40 After listening to my chaotic fragmented outburst, the home room teacher's response, repressing all his rage underneath, was quiet but firm. "He is a servile, sordid creature, a shameful man. His affair with the gym teacher has been a heinous scandal among the teachers, and yet as if it was not enough for him, he put his hand on a student, too." He groaned: "You had been immaculate, and yet now you are contaminated, stained by his evil temptation. You have lost your purity." Then he added: "But from now on, I will protect you from the hands of evil—not only his hands but from all others, so you don't have to worry about anything."

41 His words were dark and had an enormous spellbinding power to pull me down into an abyss. He made the whole thing into a drama of evil. Did I talk about it in the terms he was using, as a drama of good versus evil? My math teacher was evil, and I who was immaculate was tempted by him and lost my purity and sank into shame? Now this man feels he is a saint and hero who will forgive the stained woman and protect her from evil and slash the bad guy? Did I portray my experience like that? It was a complete shock to see the plot unfold like that; this plot never even once crossed my mind. His talk also had the tone of the police hearing the criminal's confession: a minor who is in deep regret is confessing what she has done in conspiracy with another. He is telling her that he forgives her because she is a minor, therefore she is a victim instead of an accomplice. The other one tempted her; he is the only real villain. I found these plots applying to my own special experience bizarre and frightening.

42 Is this the way all people viewed what I have done? Good decent people like him? Do all adults think this way? Is this the way I am supposed to see the whole thing? Have I been so completely out of it all through those times that these things never came to my mind? Or does he think this way because he is a Christian, and for him everything has to be part of the drama of good and evil? I did not have answers to any of these questions. But certain things were clear to me: he does not try to reach my mind and he does not know what I saw in my math teacher or in my whole experience. He is not interested in what I feel or think at all, or in what I am longing for in life. He does not think I have feelings, and passions for thinking and seeking. He seems to think of me only in terms of being victimized, being tempted, or being stained—words meant to be used only for those who have no will of their own, nor the power to think, being incapable of having thoughts, or those who are forced to be in a powerless situation. Am I automatically to be considered in that category because I am fifteen years old, a minor? Suddenly I realized like a streak of lightning that he did not care what I saw in Rilke when he had expressed his concern to the PTA of his class. The only reason he believed Rilke was not appropriate for me was that I was fifteen years old. I would be ready to write a serious essay about what Rilke meant to me—right then, if he cared that much.

43 His intense anger sounded almost like pain at the fact that his image of me, of an immaculate pure maiden, was shattered. But what is the purity of a human being if one can lose it by falling in love? I had noticed long before that people projected their own fantasy images on me, and they used the images they created like a weapon to put me in their own prison. This home room teacher had created his own purity image of me; he never thought this girl might have her own feelings and passion for thinking and seeking, and the will power to decide about her own life. And another thing that stayed as a puzzle in my mind was that all through his talking, he used expressions such as "he put his hands on you...you were immaculate but were contaminated, stained...you lost your purity." Were those expressions that suggested that sexual acts had occurred, that something sexual was done to a young woman against her will? Didn't he hear that there was no physical contact between us whatsoever, not even shaking hands? Only through silence and talk had we expressed our most profound feelings towards each other.

44   I did not want to examine him to find out if he misunderstood this point. Even if he had been under a false impression about it, I did not want to correct him. If he found out that there was no sexual contact between us, would everything be okay with him? I did not use this fact that no sexual act took place as my defense of my innocence. "We did not do anything, so everything is okay" was the last thing I wanted to say. My shock came from two sources. The first source was that he ignored the fact that I have my own autonomy: I chose the math teacher as much as he chose me, and I chose to develop this relationship so it could grow into something beautiful just as he did. Our relationship did not start and grow because I was deceived by him or tricked by him or manipulated by him. Even though we stumbled a lot, we stumbled together. But for this home room teacher, my autonomy was one thing he never thought about, and it is true that if you have no autonomy then surely you will be a victim. The second source was that he did not know that I have my own inner life, nor did he have any respect for it. He had no idea I could share my inner world with someone. The math teacher brought Rilke to me and we stepped into our own inner world with his poems. More precisely, I had already come to know this adventure of the inner world all by myself, alone in perfect solitude by that time, and the math teacher only helped me to verbalize it in this world by bringing Rilke to me— so we could share this deepest personal experience together. The core of our relationship was the awe for our mysterious inner world. This home room teacher says he will protect me from evil without knowing my inner world at all. What does he want to protect?

45 I felt enormous guilt. It was not the guilt he wanted me to feel, but the guilt that rose up from exactly the opposite place where he expected my guilt should come from. I had revealed my deepest secret, the most sacred thing in my life, to this person whom I had considered to be "an authority"—but what authority? He was my home room teacher, and when I was "drowning" in the darkest hole, he was the only one who tried to make contact with my parents—and when he failed, he brought me to this fantastic place, this church, where finally I could breathe between my thoughts of suicide. He never asked me what happened during those darkest times. Why was I so unhappy? Did I feel responsible and obligated to confess what happened? Yes, I wanted to express my gratitude, and I wanted him to know that what he did had a great effect on me. Yes, I considered him not only as the teacher of my class, but as a caring person, and found out he was an important member and teacher in the church. I assumed that he must have felt a certain kind of responsibility towards me. Saying thank you was a way of expressing respect for that responsibility. But what did I expect this man to hear? I knew from the beginning, from the time he made remarks about me reading Rilke, since the time that my math teacher and I laughed at his small-mindedness, that he was not interested in what I was seeing in Rilke's poems at all. The fact that I was fifteen years old was all that made him decide that Rilke was not appropriate for me. He had never been interested in me as a human being; my inner world did not count for him. My weakness, my unfathomable weakness, made me forget all that, and I submitted myself before him, I cried and let everything out to him, as if he had the power to pull me out from this incredible darkness of the abyss I was still in.

46   Not only did I betray my math teacher by revealing our sacred secret, but I also betrayed Rilke, who never ceased talking to me through the secret cathedral which stood so high, and I betrayed all my paintings which I had created through many long nights. I betrayed them because I could not hold on to my honesty, my integrity; I submitted myself to an authority whom I did not trust even for a second.

47   Suddenly I saw a translucent structure—not the cathedral itself, but enveloping the cathedral, standing higher than the cathedral in the night sky. I had never seen it clearly like this, but now I saw it. It was slanting, huge, and crumpling down from its root with a frightening sound, and crashed to the ground. Under the enormous cloud of dust, I saw my illegitimate little baby buried alive, he who could live only by being embraced with my honesty and integrity. Pain penetrated my whole body, I could not hold myself, and I slid down from the couch and covered my face with both hands.

48   Into my ears unbelievable words reached. "I have been deeply attracted to you since you were transferred to our school. I found your purity precious. I have disciplined myself all my life, for thirty years. I have never had an affair with any woman. You are the only woman in my life. I had decided to keep my feeling towards you to myself until you graduated from high school, and I was going to propose to you. But now things seem to be different. I have to fight against evil, which is the only reason I am confessing my feelings to you. Please trust me, I had already shared these feelings with my brother and my parents some time ago. They found you a perfect woman to be a church bride; they were celebrating us, if you allow me to say that."

49 Things changed precipitately. I was visualizing myself still squatting on the floor of a dark hole in the bottom of the abyss. It was as if a huge bundle was thrown from the sky onto the floor on which I was squatting. I was alarmed. I realized that this bundle was not part of the response to my confession. He was not talking out of the sense of responsibility, nor from any kind of authority, nor as a home room teacher, nor as a church member or religious teacher. He was talking as a man, a man who was in love with me and wanted to propose marriage. But he had to wait for a marriage proposal for three years because he had to wait for me to finish high school. Meanwhile, he believed that he had to fight against evil to protect me. Who were the evil ones? A man like my math teacher and the like—a fraud, a swindler? Or just a love rival whom he had to win me over from? Who gave him permission to check all of my friends and surroundings and identify the evil ones and fight against them? Did he prefer three years of semi-engagement before making a formal marriage proposal so that he would have three years to control and clean up my life to the point of immaculate purity before marriage? I thought I should remove myself; I had to be alert. I told him that I was going home by myself without his escort.

50 I made a long walk through the residential area, along the narrow path winding between tall fences, where only the lights on the closed gates of each house showed my way. Near the station the stores rolled down their metal shutters and only a few stores had lights on top of those closed shutters. Through the window of the brightly lit-up train, small yellow lights spread into the darkness of the suburbs' quiet towns. I did not want to go home; it was another hell. I lost everything today, I said to myself. I will never be able to create art again; I have buried my baby alive. I deserve to lose everything that I worked hard for. The preview of the marriage proposal seemed to me to be seriously wrong. *If I am too young to be proposed for marriage*, I thought, *then giving me a preview of a proposal is wrong too, because it gives me no opening to say no.* It made my life even darker.

51 My parents did not say one word, did not open their bedroom door. They did not ask any questions of their 15-year-old daughter who had come back very late at night without an escort. I figured that my homeroom teacher called my parents after I left his home. Neither the church nor his residence had a telephone in those days, so he must have gone to the booth, which stood on the street ten minutes away by bicycle. I had no idea what he had told my parents, or in this kind of situation what on earth grownups would say to each other. It was a small relief—I had no energy left to deal with my parents. But it was strange, as if I was handed from the hands of one protector to the hands of another. Something had happened. It felt like the custody of the criminal was transferred silently between authorities—from my parents to him. I was frightened.

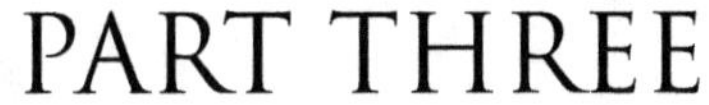

PART THREE

CHAPTER 11

1 I have been wandering in the dark forest, sometimes stumbling over the intricate roots of big trees, sometimes halting when I hear an animal growling, sometimes being drenched with showers, and on some occasions, being led by a mysterious light. I have been writing these passages following her, my own youth's, steps deeper and deeper into that forest, wondering what all those experiences meant to her. Did she believe that life had some meaning, that there is a reason for certain things to exist and to be presented in this particular way? Did she believe that life had a purpose, a profound purpose we have to fulfill for ourselves, for others, and for the world? Did she believe that life is connected to eternity, something beyond this scene that we see every day, something vividly alive in her inner world, and that without strengthening the connection to that eternal part of her, she would have lost all meaning and lost the purpose of her life? I think she did. Now that I think about it, I think of her experiences of listening to Beethoven's Ninth Symphony, during the nights of the bombings, and her constant questioning during her tuberculosis period, asking the meaning of her getting that disease, and finally, in her early teens, of the solemn, transparent cathedral which appeared in the east window of her upstairs room, night after night. I think that she had always lived with a strong connection to the eternal, mystical part of herself. These images were at the center of her inner world and gave her tremendous energy and strength to go through the difficult situations she encountered. At the same time, I must say that these are the things that brought her an acute sense of isolation and solitude. Because people around her did not share those things with her, talking about them might have even brought some danger to her. She always stood and saw into the center of her inner world as if she had already crossed over the boundary of death, and was looking back at this world from the land of eternity. Then she came to the darkest part of the forest, even darker than what came before: from the evening when things happened in her teacher's serene, modest study in the exquisite little churchyard, from her confession about her math teacher to her home room teacher and his precipitate confession of his love towards her, to the following three years or so, it is difficult to follow the steps she took and to trace the path that she wanted to take. Let us hear her talk.

2 I had been aware of two deep sources of the despair that overcame me during that evening when I confessed my relationship with my math teacher to my home room teacher—and when his own confession, totally unexpected, came out. That despair came first from the acute realization that I had betrayed my most precious person by telling an outsider about our relationship. The promise to keep it secret was never discussed between the math teacher and me. Still, talking about the relationship to his colleague was beyond any conceivable expectation I had of myself. I realized that by outside people's standard, the relationship was probably so minor that it might be considered just a silly girl's crush, and therefore, he would not lose his job, nor would any problems of that kind arise. But I was shocked by my own betrayal in this matter. And yet my real guilt came from a deeper place, which seemed far beyond this level of betrayal. He was the only person who shared the transparent cathedral with me, the world of Rilke, but it had started even further back than Rilke. Before my encounter of Rilke, almost every night I had received a mysterious light from that world and that was my source of power, the only source of the strength that enabled me to continue to live this dismal life. My math teacher showed me the meaning and powerful dimensions of this space by introducing Rilke's poems to me. With Rilke's poetic language, this space became something I could verbally grasp. Looking up at this whole world he stood with me—shuddering, with terror. It was not a secret in any ordinary sense—we never decided to keep this secret from others—nor was it a shared confidence. But I knew that it was sacred and secret, and I had blurted out this secret revealing my math teacher's name with it, to a person who I was so sure was incapable of sharing this sacred vision—a hostile complete stranger. Ever since I betrayed this secret, my whole vision came to an end and the night sky remained dark. I destroyed my own integrity, my self. My sense of guilt and despair was deep.

3 The second source of my despair had to do with my baby: my baby was buried alive when I betrayed my own integrity. From that time on my art halted abruptly. Often at night I was awakened by my baby's cry: I looked around, I concentrated on listening to the faint sound, but everything had gone. I could hear only my own cry being squeezed out of my chest, towards the empty space. It was my baby, my illegitimate baby; he was born from me, from my own flesh, father unknown. I don't know exactly when he arrived here but he had come to me, through whom his life was to be fulfilled.

And I knew very well that he was dependent on me. He was able to breathe and grow only under my protection, under the protection of my honesty and integrity. This baby was the only reason that I was able to fight so bravely against my parents: I had to be strong in order to protect him, and I was the only one in this world who could protect him from the dishonesty and delusion that spread all around me. Someday he would grow big and strong, and go out into the world to make his contribution to society. Until then I had to fight in spite of all the humiliation and insults, all the laughing and spite thrown at me. And yet, it was I who had let the cathedral fall and crash on the ground, and let my baby be buried alive underneath. What meaning could I find in life now? How could I continue living if I could not live the life I believed in? I could visualize it ahead of me: a straight road stretching to suicide.

4 My family finally deteriorated. My two sisters were taking on the challenge of the most serious piano competition yet, sponsored by one of the biggest nationwide newspapers. After that, the possibilities included the biggest international competitions—American, French, Russian—all listed in their strategy notebooks. Everything they did had to be concentrated and focused on those targets. Nothing else ever bothered them anymore. I don't know if they even had any meals at home, as it had been a long time since I was expected to prepare my father's dinner at ten o'clock every evening. Was my family gathering at some fancy restaurant, sitting at a table without me? I was given some small change from my mother each night because in the morning no one got up, or they were already gone when I left for school. Every lunchtime I would run to a guy who came from a bakery to the school gate to sell the students some bread that was in the basket on the back seat of his bicycle. Almost all of his customers were boys who needed extra food for their sporting activities. I ate the bread standing right there: that was my lunch and sometimes it was the biggest meal or my only meal for the day. My health finally started to deteriorate too: in the annual health examination at school, I was told that my general nutrition level was too low. "We are so sure that your father must be very worried about it as a doctor when he receives this note, and we are so sure that he will pay serious attention to this situation," the school nurse said. My family still looked perfect to the casual observer; they dressed perfectly elegantly and attended all the concerts and cultural events. Even if people suspected something might be wrong, they would say that the middle daughter was the problem, that she was going to the most expensive high school in Japan but that she is just terribly spoiled.

5 I always thought that if my parents ever sought help for their "shameful difficult-problem-child", I am the one who would end up being in the iron cage, in the juvenile delinquent institution for whatever reason they could find. If I were the one who sought help, I would be the one ending up in the iron-caged ward of a psychiatric institution as a serious patient, in one of the notoriously formidable, dungeon-like treatment wards which were standard in those days in Japan. I would be treated as a patient who pleaded to the doctor to protect herself against parents based on delusional accusations that were all caused by her own illusions and hallucinations, by her believing herself to be a victim of parents who were in reality perfect and ideal. This thought itself might have sounded like a childish exaggeration, but when I recall the experience of the violin lessons, it seems reasonable. My mother, and the intelligent, high-minded teacher both considered what I was doing as a rebellion against my teacher. They thought I was a hostile, angry, rebellious child who wanted to trick and make a fool of my teacher. No one thought I was suffering from a learning difficulty, mild dyslexia. Of course, in those days that term was not known to anyone, nor was the concept of parental abuse. In the land of the absolute authority of parents, no one would listen to the child.

6 Escape from my home and my family became an urgent prospect. I needed a quiet place to sit alone and I needed regular decent meals. Those two things were most important and urgent for my soul and my health. Again, just as he had rescued me before by inviting me to his church, when no one noticed my crisis, my home room teacher offered to let me use his study to sit: I could read, write and do some school homework there. One day I went after school was over. I went to his study directly without any greeting or small talk with his elderly parents: it was arranged beautifully. When he came back from school from a long bicycle ride, he checked to see if everything was okay and if there was anything I needed, then he walked to the church where some students were waiting for private tutoring, and after that a group of ambitious students who were aiming for prestigious universities were waiting for him to give them private English lessons. After everything was over, my teacher went to his parents' quarters and then brought a small tray with dinner for both of us into the study. Everything was so perfectly arranged. I had hours of quiet time alone there, no sharp violent sounds of instruments, no shouting nervous voices around. The quietness was the most precious gift for me.

7 I was there receiving quietness every second, with pleasure and gratitude. Although my mind was still deeply tormented—and desperation was still rolling like a wave in my chest, so I cannot say that I spent a peaceful time—I was fully aware that the silence in a place like this for hours made me strong on the inside. The word 'meditation' belonged to the strictly religious category in those days. Usually people did not use that word—not like nowadays, when many use it to mean something that's good for you like physical exercise or eating well. But for me, sitting alone in this serene place for hours was real, powerful meditation. The meals on the tray were simple, modest and very small: a bowl of rice, a tiny piece of grilled dried fish and boiled spinach with soy sauce. The spinach was not just leaves; it had small red roots attached to the stems. I knew you had to wash each root very carefully with cold water for a long time, until your hands became numb, because that was the spot where all the soil of the winter ground was caked, but this part of the spinach had a faint sweetness and was believed to have some medicinal power. The memory of the old woman in the country who told me this during the war when she was washing spinach at the well rushed back to me. It was a food cooked with care and love for the people who would eat it, but also I sensed that it was filled with a deep respect and gratitude for nature. My teacher seemed to have decided that the plan of inviting me to his study was successful. He scheduled my visits to continue once a week.

8 My intuition after that evening of confession turned out to be quite accurate. My thoughts: *As if I was being transferred from the hands of one protector to the hands of another"* and *It felt like the custody of the criminal was transferred silently between authorities— from my parents to him.* I concluded that the transferring I suspected was exactly what was happening. The scale of the system he built for my well-being and my education was far beyond what I could imagine. I started to vaguely see its scale, and the layers and steps of the system, but always it had a next step and another layer, and as I stood up on that step, the vague scale turned out to be much bigger than I thought I saw and it made me realize that what I saw was only a very small fragment of the whole system. Once a week visiting his study soon became twice a week, and he prepared some little goodies, such as some small cans of foreign gourmet food, to add to the tray: obviously he was preparing a perfect plan of nutrition for my health. On evenings when he did not have to tutor students in the church, he spent his time teaching me in his study. He helped me thoroughly with all my homework—not only English, literature and history, which were his fields, but also mathematics, analytical geometry and chemistry. He wanted me to do everything right and to pay attention to every detail. He had to confront the overwhelming despair which came over me and pulled me down to the point of dropping everything: I did not care if I dropped out of high school or dropped dead. He spent so many hours encouraging me, comforting me, his patience and tenaciousness were amazing. His passion for educating me was not targeted only for school projects: he took me to theaters, especially *kabuki, Noh* plays and *bunraku*—all traditional Japanese cultural forms that were rather new to me, and which without his guidance would have remained unfamiliar. The books he gave me, the movies he took me to see, all drastically expanded my interest and activities. All those activities cost very much: I noticed that he excessively exceeded the boundaries of his normal budget.

9 I was acutely aware that I was being incorporated into the elaborate system which my teacher built with the most calculated carefulness. It worked fantastically well: I was getting healthier and stronger. Some academic areas that had been neglected because of my depression and frequent rushing to the infirmary were recovered. The more I became better and stronger, the more clearly I realized the trap I was in. This whole system was not one of charitable love nor of the parental sort of love because both of those are supposed to be selfless without any personal agenda behind them. But the love I had been receiving every day now was nothing but a particular man's strong personal desire: to grab me, this young woman, aggressively for his own as his future wife, the bride of the church. And his system of educating me was nothing but a means of molding me into his ideal future wife, to become the bride of that particular church.

10 I realized that I did not know anything about the transaction which might have happened between my teacher and my parents late in the evening after our confessions. In my home, all conversation between me and my parents had almost ended around that time; I just suspected that my parents had dumped me on that teacher's lap. I thought over and over about what he said when he confessed his feelings towards me, trying to understand what he really meant— that he had planned to keep his feeling towards me to himself until I graduated from high school, and that then he was going to propose to me, but that now things seemed to be different, and he had to fight against evil, which was the only reason he was confessing his feelings toward me now. I had neither accepted nor refused his marriage proposal because I had never been asked directly in the present tense. I was told that he intended to propose to me three years later, when I was going to graduate high school. Perhaps I had three years' time to decide. But my fear was that I was certainly encouraging his wish by accepting meals twice a week and all the other tremendous benefits he had arranged. He might be taking it as a positive sign towards a "yes" to his proposal of marriage. He might have been adding up all the points. Was I taking advantage of him, of his feeling towards me by accepting everything he offered, which in the first place were my parents' responsibility? Or was he taking advantage of me, the situation that I was in, of the dysfunction of my parents, and letting me fall into a place where I could not say "no" to his marriage proposal anymore?

11   Suddenly some clarity came to me when I thought about what really happened that evening of confession. When he confessed his feelings toward me, I stood up and left his house, refusing his escort. Even though I was in the bottom of the abyss, even though my head was occupied with my own drama—betraying my math teacher, crying over him, crying over the dysfunction of my family, and crying over the deterioration of my sacred transparent cathedral—I had a clear enough mind to walk out. I had a clear enough mind not to respond at all to what he had just said. I realized that his confession should not be poured into any part of my drama because it had nothing to do with the drama and mourning in which I was still deeply immersed. Only one remark made him think he could justify making his confession right in that moment rather than three years later: it was when he uttered, "I realized that I have to fight against evil now"—and he continued—"That is the only reason I am confessing my feelings to you now." But what on earth was the evil that he had to fight against so urgently?

12 I enjoyed attending church every Sunday. That was the only place where I could be myself and that made me feel comfortable. Many of the young members were serious about their lives and had already accomplished a lot in their fields. There was a 25-year-old physicist who was known to have received a PhD as the youngest recipient in Japan: in those days a PhD in any field was considered to be something you could earn only after you were 40 years old or so. And a lawyer with the reputation of being a genius who passed the bar examination before he graduated university. There were also some interns and doctors who were involved in many new, advanced medical fields, and some students and professors of philosophy and religion who were students and colleagues of the minister, my teacher's brother, who was teaching in the most prestigious university divinity school in Japan.

13 Those excellent young members were people who came to this church to seek the truth, to seek how to think about their lives, in more serious, more profound ways than most people. These were people who were challenged by something, some destiny you might call it, that made them realize that they could not solve these problems by the ordinary ethics and values that schools and society tried to provide to young people. That something, that destiny, might have been a mother's sudden death, a sibling's serious mental handicap, or a patient's spiritual struggles with his own imminent death. Whatever they were, these things confronted them, challenged them and forced them to awaken to the ultimate existential questions of life: For what purpose do we live in this world? And what meaning does that destiny have for our lives? Those questions were the reasons why they were in that church. They sought answers, they wanted to learn and they wanted to think and have friends who could listen and to their talk in a deep way. No one came to that church just because they happened to go to church ever since they were children, or because their parents were Christians. In Japan, the Christian population never reached even one percent of the whole population, despite years of occupation by America and despite the fact that Japanese believed that Christianizing Japan was one of America's big agendas. Young people came alone to the church, probably with no other members of their families knowing it—not to keep it a secret from them, but for the same reason they would not necessarily tell their parents what book they were reading—there was no need to share it with them. Some had come to this church after trying other religions, other institutions. In short, no one came to that church unconsciously, or I might say, everyone who visited that church was standing in front of the gate of religion, if you can say that asking ultimate questions is the entrance to religion.

14 That made me very comfortable, because I was one of them. I was invited to come to this church by my teacher, during my crisis, in my last year of junior high. I came here in despair, with ultimate questions weighing on my mind: "Why do I have to live?" That question was very heavy, a deep temptation for death was lying just behind it. I did not get the answer in this church but I got some strength here to keep questioning, and I began thinking more deeply and broadly than before. Our minister was a man educated in America who received a PhD from the University of Chicago Divinity School. For four years, during the war, learning English had been strictly prohibited under penalty of imprisonment and torture. Yet after the war he was accepted and earned a degree from that prestigious university. That was a great surprise: how and when had he studied English and Western Christianity? After he returned to Japan, he co-translated with the Emperor's brother, himself a famous historian, a book of Biblical study by an American scholar, to manifest his father's belief that we needed objective Biblical scholarship. And he started teaching in the religion department of a prestigious university in Tokyo. He was a national hero in the defeated nation of Japan: brilliant, outgoing, he strongly grabbed people's minds, both young and old. But for me, always, the presence of this man, my teacher's father, the founder of this church, was most significant. I felt the warmth emanating from him, and by just sitting near him, or even just bowing to him, often in silence, I received it, I became calm and uplifted.

15 Young people in church were not always dead serious with grave faces: when they sat around the minister, laughter often surrounded them. Someone said, "I listened to a new type of music called jazz, it was just awesome! They have a jazz band at the teahouse at the back of the station." And at the next moment everyone stood up and rushed to the back door of church to the teahouse like a swarm of bees. I started noticing very faintly that walking a long way to the station together with those young people, after the service or after the discussion, became scarce. More and more often, my teacher had scheduled me to go with him to theaters and other events: somehow it seemed that there was no time left to go to teahouses and talk with young friends anymore.

16 Some great exhibition of Western art came to the land of Japan from France: selected works from the Louvre Museum were exhibited. It was a big media event; people were excited about the fantastic opportunity that we could finally see the greatest works of art in the world. News was reported about this exhibition every day. Introductions and comments by critics and art historians were everywhere. One day my school sent the high school students to that museum, as part of the art curriculum, on a day when it was also open to the general public. The museum was in a quiet park. It was a very authoritative old building, built in the Meiji period, suitable to showing Japan's appreciation and gratefulness towards the French government for sending us their national treasures. We gathered in front of the building, and after going through the show individually, the rest of the day was free. All the students rushed through the show, and after some time, the museum became relatively quiet. I walked through very carefully.

17 Disappointment came over me and overwhelmed me. No matter how I tried to shake off my dark feeling by telling myself that I had to be open-minded, that this was the first time I was exposed to original Western masterpieces, that I should be humble and should learn as much as possible, disappointment grew in my mind and finally turned into detestation. This strong feeling of detestation reminded me immediately of the reaction I had to the Western classical music that filled my house—the music of ego power, I called it. Almost all these paintings were filled with an enormous feeling of glory: even the paintings of the battlefield showed some hero riding a horse waving the flag of his king, along with the family crest. There was no empathy with the soldiers dying in cruelty and misery. Here is a man dying, but no one asks what is the meaning of his death. The art was all about glorifying kings and aristocracy, glorifying violence and victory, glorifying church and God.

18 It was after some years had passed before I realized that there was a strong stream in Western art history—you might call it the dark side of art—in which artists concentrated on penetrating the dark side of life: people possessed by Demons, exploited by society, left alone with poverty and disease, labeled criminals and blasphemers. This sort of art was dark and dangerous: one art historian called it "chaos unleashed". This stream we can trace back even to Bosch in the 15th century and then to many modern artists of the 19th century: Goya, Daumier, Ensor, Munch, Kokoschka—artists who made us see what is the real danger for humanity, the real threat, and what is it that we really have to be afraid of and fight against. From those artists, the 20th-century's modern art revolution was born, a revolution I deeply identified with.

19 I don't think this exhibition of the Louvre in Japan included works which presented this dark side of art history, nor did it bring the revolution of modern art to Japan. Because the Louvre was primarily a place to display the royal collection, the major part of the collection consisted of Napoleon's spoils of war; the museum had originally been called La Musee Napoleon. And its new works were accumulated up through Louis XVIII and Charles X and the second French Empire. So it was only natural that they did not include those 'dark side' artists. Even now in the 21st century, Western art history is often spoken of in relationship to the glory of political, national, military and Imperial power.[For some people art is nothing but glorious treasure confiscated from all over the world.

20 Without having any knowledge of those things, I said to myself, "If these artworks should be called the greatest in history, I would not want to have anything to do with art." Then I was thinking again of Klee's painting, "Danceplay of the Red Skirts," the painting that made me realize that I wanted to become an artist myself. For many nights in my small room upstairs, I had studied the history of the modern art revolution by myself. But I had never known that the tradition those artists fought against, and turned upside down, had this stupendous structure to it. I was frightened, oppressed, by the gigantic power of Western culture. Where on earth did those modern artists who were so sensitive and introspective get the strength to fight against that tradition? What is it that we have to fight for and fight against now? I stepped out of the museum into the crisp air of the autumn noon, and I started walking slowly along the path in the park.

21 "Forgive me but I have been watching you looking at the artworks in the exhibition. I have never seen anyone looking at art with such concentration and seriousness. I was moved by your way of looking at works. If you don't mind, I would like to have tea with you, at the teahouse nearby. I would very much like to listen to you talk about art." A young man, well mannered, unassuming, serious but cheerful, was talking to me. I looked at him and instantly had a good impression of him. He was a refreshing young man in his twenties, perhaps a university or graduate school student, or even a little older. He was wearing casual clothes—not a student's uniform, nor a suit which in Japan most of the men working at companies wore, so I could not tell his circumstances. I was surprised by his tone and it was far from usual to talk to a high school kid. After a moment, I said to him, "I am sorry, I have someplace to go, I am in hurry, I have to go," and walked briskly toward the station. Why did I say no to him? Why didn't I say yes and have tea with him? My first answer to myself was, *Because I carried heavy thoughts about art in my mind all through that huge exhibition. Those thoughts themselves were a shock to me, and I had to figure them out by myself: they were not the kind of thoughts I could pour out to a stranger, especially to one who was most likely an art lover, and yet I did not want to discuss some polite noncommittal subject about art with him or anyone else.* Those were my honest feelings. But then the second answer came to me: *Because I thought about my home room teacher, he appeared in my mind as soon as this young man started talking to me, and I instantly knew that my teacher would not like me to say yes to this man at all.*

22 By the word "evil," my teacher meant these people: people who wanted to talk with me and have tea with me, who were attracted to me in one way or another. I finally understood. These were the people he insisted on fighting against, protecting me from, and he thought that was an urgent project for him. He clung to the old- fashioned Japanese tradition that without proper introduction, a young man approaching a girl is a delinquent. *Did he have to eliminate them before that young man could become his rival? Is he trying to do the same thing in our church?* This realization frightened me. I should have known it. I knew I had been in a trap. Suddenly the voice of my math teacher was once again ringing loud in my head: "You cannot grow with anyone waiting for you at the other end. You need complete freedom to be honest, to be yourself; don't let anyone interfere with your process of growing. Don't make decisions about your life based on someone's expectations for you."[Oh! This is the situation that I am in, exactly what he meant and warned me to avoid. "That was the reason why I decided not to wait for you to become a certain age," he said to me at that time. He knew me so deeply, he knew that if I were prevented from being honest with myself, I could not live. I would find my own honest way to live and grow, under any circumstances. *In spite of your trust in me,* I replied to him intensely in my mind, *I am already deeply in a trap.*

23   This was not the first time I was spoken to by young men on the street. Especially on the way home from school going through the little woods when I was walking near the university division of my high school, university students tried to talk to me and invited me for coffee or tea. But a most strange incident had happened more than twice: it happened that my teacher suddenly showed up on his bicycle out of the blue and spoke to the young men who were talking to me, just casual talk as a teacher of that school. And the young men sort of faded away from an awkward situation. I did not feel that I had missed a great deal: I did not feel like going out with any of them to have a good time in the teahouse anyway. But suddenly the image of a bamboo cage appeared to me, the kind of little crafted box you can buy anywhere on the street when summer approaches. It is very small so that you can hold it in your hand: its four walls are made of delicate, needle-like bamboo bars, and a tiny door also made of bamboo needles will open and close with a little handle. It is for crickets: some people put a small cricket into this box. A cricket's life lasts only for one summer, so all his life he must stay in this cage by himself, without seeing any other insects, without feeling the wind blow on the fields of grass in the mountains, without participating in the great orchestra with all the other insects, whose music goes up to Heaven, to the star-studded night sky of the summer. People insert a sliced cucumber into the cage every day and listen to his sounds every night because they "love" him so much. Was my teacher going to do that to me?

24 But this time, with this man who started talking to me in front of the museum, it seemed a little different. My teacher did not show up in the real world, he showed up only in my mind; I was the one who let him interfere. I had lost my independence. I might have missed an opportunity to develop a friendship with a man with whom I could talk about art for the first time in my life. But was it realistic to think about such a possibility? Was it even conceivable to express my "detestation" for those authoritative masterpieces? Would it be okay to talk about the modern art revolution? So many serious people still felt uneasy and angry about modern art itself: it touched their fear and pride very sharply, the fear that after all, they didn't understand what those Western artists were doing. And if I ever mentioned "my buried alive illegitimate baby", it would be the end, I would have to be put away in the insane asylum—even though it was the concept of my illegitimate baby that created the nexus between the inner world of the human mind and the inner revolution of the world, between the integrity of the human being and the integrity of art itself, and the integrity of the world. The loss of my buried-alive baby overwhelmed me again; I had lost my independence, my integrity, everything with him. Between this world and my inner world, there seemed to exist an unfathomable abyss, probably too big for anyone to cross over. I could not cross over and reach another person's heart, and neither could others reach me. Where was I standing? What did I want to do in this complicated landscape?

25 Since the time when I started going to the church, almost more than three years before, every time my train approached the small suburban station where the church was located, I checked through the train window to see if my teacher was waiting for me at the little station. And every Sunday morning, without exception, he was there, waiting for me, with his bicycle leaning against him. I asked myself, *If he was not there, what would I do?* The answer was always certain: I would continue riding in that train and keep going to the end of that line, a big terminal. At that terminal I would have two choices: one would be to go up and down the stairs to the opposite side of the platform and take the express train that runs back in the direction I just came from That express train would run straight through, passing the little stations of the church, my home and my school at full speed, and it would take me directly to the beach in two hours. I knew that beach: I had gone to that beach alone some time before, to make sure it was deserted. No one was there out of season. The black waves surged and swelled from the shore to the dark horizon. It would be easy to walk into that black surge. No one would find my body, at least for a long time, I thought. And the other choice at the terminal was to leave the terminal and walk to the amusement quarter of downtown. I would walk around and find a way to become a prostitute there, in order for my life continue. To become a prostitute was the trap that many girls fell into when they ran away from home. But in fact it was a part of a dark, prohibited fantasy of my childhood. Those places where I could go were where the young women who came from to my father's office to become his patients were found: they too had no place to live, no other way to make a living. My heart went out to them when I saw them through the crack of the window of my father's office in my childhood. But it was perfectly clear to me, like approaching a waterfall when you are in the river: at the next moment you know that you would certainly fall into final destruction. The whole idea had to be dropped. Although I had a fantasy, a story I heard: a man, a soldier who came back to Japan from a faraway battlefield on an Asian island, found his wife and children and his entire extended family had been killed in the war. He tried to hang himself on the burnt branch of a black tree. A prostitute appeared and took him to her hut. He stayed all night inside, wrapped in the warm arms of her body, and she shed tears for him. He gained strength, and the next morning he left her hut and went to town to live. This story was told in relationship to Kannon Bosatsu, a Deity who has been known to give the deepest mercy to people when they are in crisis. I wanted to be like her, like that prostitute. That was the deepest secret desire of my childhood. But everything has to go now. I had to drop the whole fantasy.

26 This map I had in my mind consisted of one straight railroad line: one endpoint was my childhood fantasy that ended up in the waterfall and the other endpoint was the faraway deserted beach ending up at the black horizon. And in the middle, much closer to the first endpoint, was marked a church. On this map, roughly corresponding to the geographical scale, only three points were marked. I could go to only three places. This was the reality I grasped. My parents' home where I was still living was not marked on the map, because the whole reason I made a map was that I could not stay in that house. The situation of my house had become worse since the time when my teacher rescued me more than three years before. It was urgent that I leave home now. I had become much stronger and more capable since then, and yet the map of the places that I marked had not changed since three years earlier. Finally some clarity, just like a vivid flash of lightning, had reached me through the intricate tangles: I have only one crucial problem that was causing all my questions and problems: my parents' dysfunction. I was sure that if my parents were functioning decently, and fulfilling their basic obligation as parents, I would now be working hard to prepare for some prestigious university. I would be concentrating on what I wanted to do, what made me grow and develop, without being desperate over where to live or where I could even survive. I would stay in my parents' home during my college years until I married someone, just as women in Japan in those days were strictly expected to do. But my clarity told me that I had lost the fundamental thing—the base, the safe and healthy environment in which minors can live and grow. Without those needs being fulfilled, integrity, independence and assertiveness—none could be realized. The biggest thing my parents did wrong was that they gave up their custody and threw me on my teacher's lap. "Thank you for your all kindness!"

Did my mother say that to him just as the mother of that 14-year-old violin genius had said to my mother, at the moment that she dropped the heavy burden, her son, on my mother's lap?

27 If I were not a "rescued girl", so many problems I had been facing now would not even exist. I would have handled his marriage proposal in a stricter and much more straightforward way: I would have simply said "no" to the proposal. I believed even in those early days that marriages should become a topic only as a consequence of a spontaneous, mutual, deepening love, and only after both parties' natural spiritual growth had developed from that love. All lives in the universe naturally grow and change, and love is one of those agents of change: when two sides are involved, its growth and change creates intricate patterns in the process. You cannot simply make a proposal of marriage as if you were making a reservation, or buying a ticket far in advance, and then insist on your right when the time comes. So, under different circumstances, I would have refused to think about a proposal to marry three years later.

28 My way of thinking about marriage was unusual in those days. Arranged marriage was still overwhelmingly common in the society, and what they called love marriage was still a target of scandal and envy. But I would have had no hesitation to express it to my teacher more clearly than I thought I did—if I were not "rescued." My relationship with the church would have developed in some way, but there must be many ways for me to have been involved in the activities of the church, and I would have had a natural, spontaneous friendship with the young and not-so-young members. Perhaps my teacher could have been included, if he wanted to be, and if he still wanted to have a special relationship with me, he might have had to compete with young people, the ones he called evil. But the little bamboo cage box problem would not have happened. He would not have had any opportunity to try that on me. If he ever did try, he would have failed. But thinking about all these "ifs" was meaningless, unless I used them to confront the severe reality in order to see where I really stood. The reality that I reached showed me two facts with merciless clarity. One was that I had only one place to live—his home, and with it, the church, where I had to live if I wanted to survive. And the second fact was that I had no way to go to college, neither from my parents' home nor from my teacher's home and the church. Marriage and college life would never combine for many reasons. No university would accept a student like that in those days. I had to give up the entire idea of going to college.

29 These two facts were quite grim. But the truth beneath these two facts was much harder to see, and much harder to accept. One of these truths was the realization that integrity, independence, assertiveness— the qualities I admired most—could not be realized in a situation in which the basic need for safety was unfulfilled. I blamed myself bitterly on this point: my incapability of integrity, my lack of independence and assertiveness. I saw the lack of those qualities in my life every day and I blamed myself, and for three years I saw them as my character flaws—but they were not. The other truth was the realization that a rescuer was absolutely needed, and here too, I was blaming myself constantly: *Why am I accepting this help?* But when I saw the severity of my reality with merciless eyes, I made a decision to admit what I saw was true. The truth was that I had been fighting for my own survival. My real fight was not how I would conquer my character flaw: it was a fight for my survival. I saw for the first time with cool-headed clarity the total powerlessness and helplessness of being a young girl in this situation. If I had not received my teacher's help, I would have been literally dead—either by relapsing into tuberculosis from undernourishment or by reaching whichever of the alternative endpoints of my map that I would choose. Things could have been much worse, in many conceivable ways. But before falling into the unfathomable abyss, or should I say before falling too far down the abyss, my home room teacher scooped me up and saved me. I was rescued, and continuously, steadily rescued for three years by his incredible will and capacity and—in their very hidden, reserved way—by his family who kept giving warm spiritual support to him me all the way through.

30   Finally I looked around to see if I could find any pieces I could pick up to build my new life with, and the first thing that caught my eye was his room. From the moment I started coming to this place, the first thing that drew me in was his study. It was a room of serenity, a room in which a reproduction—an excellent print—of a 19th-century painting of the Barbizon school, "The Forest of Fontainebleau," was hung. It was a room filled with a meditative quietness, simplicity and modesty; a room where I had received strength from the beginning, so many days continuously for three years. It was still intensively alive. Here I sat alone, quietly, with myself, and I was aware that my strength was filling my inner world. I was always grateful that my teacher let me sit here for hours. I wished I was not an intruder: if I were, I wanted to be a quiet intruder filled with admiration for that space. I used to have a small room like that upstairs in my parents' home where every little thing—a small Klee reproduction, and seashells and stones I picked up—were shining like jewels, but that space was invaded by the violent flood of the music of the cult people who overran the whole house. But here, in my teacher's room, I could study: even though the possibility of going to university was completely gone, I could still study here surrounded with great books, which emitted a strong vibration of the deep longing for truth.

31 The second thing that caught my heart was the church. I thought I might help the church, in a very small way of course, but for three years I had seen the many problems it faced. Since the church had almost no way to raise money, everything had to be paid for from the family's personal income, and that forced everybody in the family to overwork. The minister had two university jobs and wrote books, even with a sick wife and two children. And my teacher struggled: besides teaching at school every day, he took on private tutoring, took care of his old parents and attended to the social and office work of the church, fulfilling the old congregation's special needs even though they had a good enthusiastic group of church members. All of these were enormously demanding. Perhaps, I thought, I could help in some way.

32 And the third thing that caught my heart was the possibility of changing the character of my relationship with my teacher, from an upper-and-lower, vertical relationship, to a much more equal, 'horizontal' one. The relationship between me and my teacher had always been between a teacher and student, between a grownup and a minor, between a custodian and his ward, between rescuer and rescued. And inside of that framework, his desire—his demand for my love—

made the whole thing complicated and sinister. Focusing on this issue was the biggest insight of all that I had picked up. By being married to him, I could make this relationship equal, independent, and make it possible for us to both contribute to each other and to the family and to the community. And even before this, the position expected of me in my family was that of a helper to my sisters. But marriage would be different: under Japan's new constitution I was entitled to an equal position. We were entitled to an equal relationship and reaching that stage would depend on our effort. I learned thoroughly that unless you build your own strength in your life, you allow others to destroy your life. I had to start from the small bamboo cage box I was in now, but even there, inside of the box, I could start. I would do my best to grow and develop my life here and I wanted my teacher to do the same thing in his own life, and I knew he would. So we could contribute to each other, and together we could contribute to the community. When I committed to accepting my reality with all its harshness, severity, and misery, a Copernican revolution seemed to have quietly begun. I finally decided to accept his marriage proposal, which had been ongoing for three years. I chose the last alternative on the map: survival.

33 In my high school's Japanese literature class, a teacher who was known as an accomplished traditional *tanka* poet told us that she decided to hold a competition in our class for a lecture on a work by a Japanese writer. Each applicant would choose one Japanese writer's work from among the historical writers, at least one whose works were in the textbook our class was using. The applicant would have to choose the passages of the work he or she would read aloud to the class and would identify the themes in that writing clearly, and trace how the writer developed those themes in his or her main work. And in the final hours a winner would lead a discussion of those themes involving all the students in class. All of us were expected to participate in this competition. Each applicant had to submit a table of contents including the things the teacher had discussed in class. But it also had to clearly state what the applicant wanted to say: his or her real opinion should be there, not just academic facts, not just a theoretical framework. Instantly I decided to apply to this competition and immediately I decided that the work would be *The Broken Commandment* by Shimazaki Toson. The main theme was 'live with honesty'. While the teacher was explaining the project, I had already created the table of contents in my notebook. *This is the time that I will establish my confidence,* I said to myself. I wanted to do the whole thing myself without the help of my teacher—my fiancé now—who had been offering all along to support and help me with any project of mine. But I wanted to know how far I could go myself. Probably this would be the last school project I would be involved in, I thought, for my whole life.

34 *The Broken Commandment* was published in 1906 during the Meiji period, in the middle of the war between Russia and Japan, in a time when militarism was at its peak. The writer quit his job as a teacher, his only source of income, in order to write this novel. During the two years while he was writing, his two children died and his wife became sick due to undernourishment. It was one of the earliest novels in Japan to deal with how awakened modern individuals could deal with the old pre-modern society and solve the serious psychological and sociological conflicts which constantly arise when individuality becomes part of their thinking. Before the beginning of the Meiji period, literature had been considered more craft or entertainment, like a beautiful or humorous artifact. This work became the leading novel of the Naturalism movement in Japanese literature. The main character is a young man, a teacher of a high school in the snow country. He came from a certain social group, called the *Eta*, a word of reproach and insult in those days. They were the people who handled dead animals, horses and cows, and dealt in leather goods from generation to generation, and lived in isolated places. They were prohibited to mingle with other social classes in the Edo period. But in the Meiji period, all feudal systems were gone and the new, modern government established a new constitution under which all people were equal except for the Emperor and his relatives, the aristocratic classes. So the Eta was not legally discriminated against anymore.

35   But strong prejudice still continued among people, and the *Eta* still observed the strict command to hide their background: this was essential if someone from this group ever wanted to make it in the outside world. This young teacher was raised being told by his father, "If a priest breaks the rule of religion, he is only an apostate priest, but if you confess who we are, you will be completely ruined." *The Broken Commandment* is the story of the inner conflict of this young man who was educated and went out into the world, and the desire arose within him to be honest with his closest friend and the woman he loved and a student he was teaching about honesty. The desire became stronger and stronger, pushing against the command which had been imprisoning him since he was born. Finally he confessed who he was. As a result, enraged crowds of parents accused him of cheating his students and he lost his teaching job, ruining all of the accomplishment he had ever achieved in his hard life—even though the parents were opposed to the law. He was relieved from the internal conflict in his mind, however, and that gave him a certain peace. But he had to leave, and the reader is left not knowing how he would live after that. His only temporary destination was Tokyo, where he might contact someone who might help him, and there was another vague suggestion that he was thinking he could emigrate to America, to Texas. In the last scene of the novel, he leaves the snow mountain alone by sled: only a few friends and some students who took the risk of being punished by the school authorities, came to see him off.

36   I won the competition. I was given plenty of time to talk about what I had studied and what I thought and how I had developed my thoughts. The discussion period which followed immediately after my lecture was extended substantially by our literature teacher because the students were excited and enthusiastic; every one of them wanted to participate. Many themes were discussed. 'Is it so important to be honest and confess who you are and where you come from to the people you live with every day? If it is, why is it so important?' And: 'Why do people have to be equal? If everyone accepts his given position, without being contaminated by the ambition of jumping out of it and lives inside, does it not make him happier?' And: 'Where does the idea of the equality of people come from to begin with? What kind of basis does this idea have in the history of thought in the world and in Japan?' 'Don't we all have to fight against prejudice? Against any group of people who are discriminated against? Then why didn't this young teacher fight against that prejudice more aggressively rather than simply 'confessing'?' And: 'Does literature require all of us to fight and change the world into a better place? If the writer describes a main character who could not fight, and who would not stay there to fight to change the world, isn't this a serious limitation of this work?' And: 'What would be the role of literature in this social conflict?' And: 'Wasn't it just a dream of escape to think about going to America, to a place where other prejudices might be waiting for this helpless immigrant?' (In fact, many years later, I learned that in 1906, the year this book was published, there were major race riots in Texas. Twelve black people were killed and many of the rights of Japanese legal immigrants were taken away. But in those days, Japanese were not really aware of what was going on inside America, and the author of the book thought of America as an ideally free society.) And last: 'What would you do if you were in the position this main character was in?' The students' hands shot up like trees in the woods. The themes developed in many directions. Finally the five hours given to me over a period of two weeks for this project was over. Our literature teacher told me that my talk and my way of leading the discussion was powerful, and that I had reached the soul of every one of the students in the class. And she added that she had never seen them concentrate so deeply on such serious themes, and never seen them so vividly animated. And she added more: that she wanted me to seriously develop my talent in this direction. I knew she was thinking about this direction based on her assumption that I would study in college, and I did not say anything to correct her. The realization that I would never have the opportunity to do things like this again in my life saddened me deeply.

37   I had reached the souls of others, the literature teacher told me, but I noticed that I had reached my own soul, too, by doing this project. I too had a secret just like the main character of this book. And I made a confession to a person, just like this main character did. What was my secret? I had believed for a long time that my secret was my feelings towards the math teacher. And what was my confession? I let my feelings out. It led me to the images of a falling transparent cathedral, under which my illegitimate baby was buried alive. Why did I confess my secret to this person, my home room teacher? After doing this project of *The Broken Commandment*, I was clearly able to say that my desire to confess came from a longing to be close to others without having a secret, because a childlike unity between two persons, which stemmed from my desire to be honest and to be accepted as I was—that was my weakness, my unfathomable weakness. Without even thinking what I was going to do, without even questioning what and how I was going to say it, without thinking if my confession had any relevance to this person, as if I were a child, I just blurted it out to my teacher—pushing it out, rolling on a wave of loneliness. Now after this project was over I could say clearly that my secret that I had to keep was not about the math teacher. My real, deepest secret was the transparent structure itself, which I called a cathedral, solemnly soaring in the night sky, in the east window of my room. I didn't know what it was or where it came from, only an enormous feeling of awe, and an awareness that something incredibly solemn and beautiful was happening. And I knew it was related to the core of who I am: it was the space from which Rilke said to me, "For Beauty's nothing but the beginning of Terror which we are still just able to bear..." This was the space from which my art came. This was my core, and that is why I felt I should keep it a secret. I mentioned this cathedral in only a very small part of my confession in relation to my math teacher and Rilke. When I come to think of it, my teacher did not even pay attention to the secret cathedral, which was often the case when my secret was open—no one noticed. It offered a little relief. But still the harm had already been done, my illegitimate baby was still buried alive.

38 When I thought about the secret of the young main character in *The Broken Commandment*, I clearly knew that his secret and mine were fundamentally different. In his case, one word, *Eta*, was enough to be a confession. The moment that one word was uttered, he was in danger in the society, he would be kicked out. He had to be prepared for that kind of reaction and many, many other things to come. Confession is just the gate to a huge fight or to the end of the fight. He had not prepared for it. His confession was prompted by his craving for warm honest friendship, his weakness, the same as mine. If he had done it with determination, with the strong intent to influence or change the consciousness of the society, and had plotted strategy for a long difficult fight, we would have to call it a declaration instead of a confession, but the writer of this novel never used that word in the book. Confession is shame-based, often followed by an apology; a declaration has affirmation or pride and righteousness in it. My secret was very different from this young man' secret. My secret had not yet revealed its whole meaning to me, nor its whole depth. A big part of this secret was still hidden from my own eyes. Would the time come when its whole meaning would be revealed to me? If that happened, I wanted to bring this open secret to the society, I don't know in what shape, I don't know how small and humble, but it must have some meaning for society. I wanted to call it my declaration, not my confession. That is the way I could be connected to the society with honesty and responsibility.

39 When I told my parents of my decision to accept the proposal, a storm unexpectedly blew through our living room. The idea that I would not go to any university, which inevitably came with the decision of marriage in those days in Japan, especially upset them. My parents knew very well that no university would take a married applicant and that no decent company would hire a woman living alone, away from her parents' home, even an educated professional woman, no matter what the reason. That was a normal restriction in those days. But the storm raged quite high. It was another shame I had bestowed on my family; they could not accept the idea that they would have a daughter who would not graduate from university. But finally my mother said that she would yield to my decision, saying, "No man would ever want to marry a girl like you, a horrendous, frightening monster-like girl, in the future. So after all it might be best to accept one who wants you now." I felt she really meant it. But to my great astonishment, they provided a good dignified wedding for me and even offered money for some remodeling, adding a little room and a kitchen to his study. "So she can build her own household there, not like an old-fashioned bride being incorporated into their old family hierarchy, in which the new bride holds the lowest position, just above the servants—if they have any servants. Instead the new bride will have freedom to make decisions, to run her household in her own way, and she will be respected as the mistress of the new household." It turned out that my parents seemed to be afraid that the whole thing might look like the worst sort of scandal scenario, that their juvenile delinquent daughter had run away from home and rushed to her schoolteacher and married him. Instead, they wanted to create the impression that their daughter had been admired and desired so highly that she was sent out from her respectful household and would be welcomed with honor into another respectable household. So they wanted to do everything in a dignified way.

40   My family had undergone many changes by that time. My two sisters had won the competition sponsored by the authoritative newspaper. The elder one won the third prize and the younger one got the first prize the following year. Now they were recognized throughout Japan as the young, brilliant sister pianists rather than as child prodigies. Offers of concert tours, interviews and photo sessions were rushed to them, their house becoming like a newspaper press itself. There was not even one second of silence; no personal concern had any place in the house.

41   When I told the teachers in my high school that I was not going to apply to any universities, they were all stunned. In Japan in those days, which university accepted you was the most serious matter in every young life. Everyone talked about 'the entrance examination war'. Because Japanese society had no flexibility to change the ladder you had to climb, if you failed in this war and could not get into the highest university you could qualify for, usually you were considered to be right on the way to failure. I was one of the students of the special class assembled with the most ambitious students who were applying to prestigious universities. My teachers could not believe that I was going to throw away all those precious possibilities. "You are the only student in our high school who is not going to college," they said. They showed me the list of names of the excellent universities where I had good possibilities of being accepted. When I told them I was going to marry, without telling them to whom, they were again stunned. In silence they gave up and withdrew everything.

42 "It was a ritual of human sacrifice. I had never seen such a thing before, of course. But today, I finally saw it for the first time in my life. It was a wedding I was supposed to be invited to, but it was not a wedding, it was a ritual of human sacrifice." A woman my mother invited to my wedding, one of a very few among her friends, called up all her friends after coming back from my wedding and said this. This remark of hers became legendary in their social circle. There were an extraordinary number of white-haired elders at my wedding. My parents-in-law were both over 80, so it looked like a daughter-in-law's good nursing would be needed at any moment, for in Japan in those days that was strictly a daughter-in-law's obligation. Besides them, there was a group of elders standing up with canes in their hands, some wearing old silk kimono jackets and skirts, some wearing old Victorian-style three-piece suits that made us guess they must have been tailored, literally, in the Meiji period. All of them were far over 80 years old and had a hoary appearance. All were prominent figures who studied the Western culture of many fields; every one of them had published significant books on Western culture, dictionaries, trans- lations of Western literature and philosophy; and some had founded educational institutions. They had planted the seeds of Western culture deep in Japanese soil. They were all men of strong influence, and they had taken on the roles of intellectual, spiritual leaders with my father-in- law in the Meiji period in Japan. But they looked totally out of the world of Today. This was the kind of scene where, if you were a comedian, you might say, "Where did they dig them up?"

43   All those people came to the wedding to celebrate our marriage, but there was one thing that they particularly wanted to celebrate: one of the new small schools of divinity in America had accepted my teacher, now my husband, as a graduate student for the ministry on full scholarship. The only condition was that he had to submit his university diploma on time. This was big news for my husband and for the other people who knew him well. He had just graduated high school in the old educational system when he was drafted into the army. His military work was to practice throwing himself under the enemy's tanks with bombs tied to his body. He dug holes to hide himself until the tank approached close enough. He was forced to be a human bomb and he trained for that every single day for four years of his youth. When he came back from the war, he had to face the problem of how he would support himself and his old parents. His father had suffered a stroke and his mother suffered from cancer at that time. This was a period in Japan when inflation shot astronomically high. The story of his brutal struggle for survival was hidden behind the glorious success of his brother's brilliant career. He could not afford meals every day, and he exchanged for food every skill he had—including his skill of hole digging, which happened to be all he learned in his youth. He could not afford to go to college, but in spite of all his disadvantages he got a job teaching at the prestigious junior high school where we met. He had started correspondence college some time ago; now he would finish that college and go to America. Finally the long abominable war would end for him. War changed everyone's life drastically: how it changed it was largely dependent on where he happened to be in the passage of his life when the war started.

44 This news had a different significance for those elders: it was more than just a happy ending for a young, unfortunate man who was victimized by the war and who was now recovering by being given the opportunity to study in America. Those elders were among the people who had struggled severely with Western Christianity when missionaries landed in Japan during the Meiji period. The missionaries' view of Japanese religion was that it was theologically wrong and corrupt, that Japanese should immediately drop their primitive idolatry and animism, and accept all the Christian doctrines that they taught. The missionaries wanted to create a duplicate, miniature version of their own church system on Japanese soil, and they wanted to westernize the Japanese mind. Those missionaries could not separate Christianity from their own Western cultural identity.

45 My father-in-law, who was already deeply devoted to Christianity, took a completely new attitude. He and his followers had created a conceptual system to encourage people to see Christianity from a critical, rational, modern, humanistic point of view based on the systematic, historical study of the Bible. And with the empathy which only one who had a deep, personal experience ofa connection with God himself, he respected other religions. He and his followers called it 'liberal Christianity', and finally established a church based on this concept of religious study. His church influenced the Japanese religious educational system in the university and that influence is still continuing in Japan today. It challenged traditional Christianity in Japan. Many Christians in Japan viewed Liberal Christianity as heresy. But this attitude towards religion influenced many, especially among Japan's intellectuals. My father-in-law's first son, now my brother-in-law, continued and re-established the new church. And now, his younger brother, my husband, was supporting him. As if proving that his father's respect for other religions was working, there were many religious leaders from other religions who were at our wedding celebrating us. And the dean of the School of Religion at a prestigious university married us. The elders of antique appearance saw that what they had worked hard for all their lives was bearing fruit. They believed it was good for Japan, and probably good for the new generation all over the world too. It was worth it for them to have gotten up from their 'deathbeds' to come out to celebrate this young couple.

46 We had guests from Motoyasu at the wedding: my uncle who came back from Manchuria after a long adventure of youth, and his wife and their small daughter. "Who would come to Tokyo was a big discussion over there," my uncle said, "because someone had to remain at home and take care of their baby and our young cousin." Grandmother yielded and delegated her son's family to come to attend my wedding. They were so excited to come to Tokyo, and to see Tokyo's astonishing revival from burnt fields and the miraculous strength of the Japanese people that the city revealed. They were very sweet, repeating that I was the most beautiful bride they had ever seen. They repeated that as if there was nothing else to say. It was true, we had nothing to say to each other except exchanging those sweet words. How could they know what this wedding meant to me? We had been too far apart from each other. Their young daughter was almost the same age as I was when I attended the wedding of the first son of Motoyasu. In fact, she was wearing almost the identical dress I was wearing at that wedding: a white one-piece dress. The only difference was that her dress was cotton instead of silk, and instead of the blue embroidery on the chest of my dress, her dress had pink little flowers embroidered. Her face had very different features from the Motoyasu I was used to. She had big expressive eyes. She stared at me with those eyes. Even when I smiled at her she did not smile back at me. I could not break her concentration, but then slowly she stretched her arm and touched the silk flare of my wedding dress, and when she realized I did not mind that, she carefully slid her finger on the silk. I was moved: she observed everything. Just like I gazed at the bride that time long ago and saw the shadow of the funeral cast over her, just like I saw all the ancestors of Motoyasu standing up from the ground, and saw that they were celebrating the union of the alive and the dead. Was she seeing something through me? Was she seeing a funeral overlapping this wedding? She might have been, for this wedding was the funeral celebrating the death of the old me.

47 It was a bizarre wedding, as it did truly look like a ritual of human sacrifice in a way. But if the friend of my mother thought that a young beautiful maiden in white was offered on the pedestal to her parents-in-law in order for her to take care of them, to become a nurse for them for the rest of their lives, then she was wrong. If she thought that a maiden was laid on the pedestal as an offering to the elders of antique appearance, in order to satisfy their nostalgia and complacency about what they have done in history, she was wrong. Certainly a sacrifice was offered on the pedestal. But the difference was that the god to whom the sacrifice was offered was not my parents-in-law nor the elders of antique appearance as my mother's friends thought. It was to the god my mother worshipped, the god of glorious talent. My mother offered her second daughter, a maiden, to her god, as a sacrifice. And he, the god of glory, gave her glory, unlimited glory more than she could handle. She dragged everyone around her into her god's temple: her other daughters, her husband, and other young musicians who were talented and sought glory through her. But they had not yet noticed what was happening to them. Yet the most extraordinary thing had happened: the maiden who was offered to the god came back, without being killed. Was not her body ripped apart? Was not her blood sucked? She was injured and bleeding, skinny and fragile, but she came back. She was standing, not lying down on the sacrificial pedestal; she was standing up in church at her own wedding. There was a human sacrifice and its ritual was still going on. But now she was away from it. We don't know how she survived, how she came back after a dark, frightening journey. It was all over for her. She could now build her new life from her inner world, grow herself towards the outside—and perhaps thrust her way out of the small bamboo cage box entirely.

CHAPTER 12

1   The garden in the back of the church changed its expression from the mysterious beauty which many people called *Togenkyo*, a mythological garden believed to have existed in ancient China, to a somewhat modern beauty. In the center of that traditional garden, two hundred bulbs of tulips were buried and now they all burst out blooming, and roses which had big petals surrounded them. The change was made in the most sensitive way so that the balance of traditional and modern was perfectly harmonized. It was dazzling, yet still a quietness remained. This had been done by my newly wedded husband: he did the whole thing by himself to welcome his teenage bride who expressed her love for Western-style flowers. And to his small study where I sat many, many evenings alone or with him, holding dark torment in my chest, a new small sunroom was added, and from the windows of that sunroom and patio door, people could view this whole garden.

2   From that patio door my father-in-law and mother-in-law visited me every day at 10 o'clock in the morning. I prepared tea and some sweets and for an hour or so we talked. Often, our talk started out being about how beautiful the garden was. They noticed which plants had sprouted, which flower buds had bloomed that morning. And our conversation often developed into the subject of our church, the current situation we were in, the long history of the church, the lives of various old and new friends of the congregation. It was fascinating to listen to those stories: they were always entangled with huge currents of history—not only of Japanese history but also of world history. Once they told me that my father-in-law was the man who introduced "Greek mythology" to the Japanese intellectual community for the first time in history. He translated it into Japanese from an English translation that was published long ago in Boston. Vivid memories of a book flashed in my mind: the book my Motoyasu grandmother sent to us, which she had bought for my mother when she was a child. My father decided to bring that book into the cave, as one of the precious books which would save all of us from falling into a caveman mentality. There was no way of knowing if this father-in-law's name was in the book since it had been lost long ago, and anyway it was a book that was rewritten specially for younger readers. But I felt a mysterious connection between myself and my parents-in-law: without that book I would never have known Medusa, my favorite figure. That information was mentioned only as one of many side stories of my parents-in-law's journey.

3 Their journey was like rowing a little boat in a huge river, a stormy perilous journey. It was a journey of spreading liberal Christianity (that was the way they defined their beliefs) in order to open up the consciousness of the Japanese intellectuals towards Christianity while viewing Jesus as a human being—totally the opposite of what Christian missionaries were teaching, and what put so many Japanese intellectuals off. Liberal Christianity was spreading in the land of

Japan, along with the Western philosophy of religion, and respecting Japanese religions and comparative religious studies. And it was also a journey of loss: my father-in-law lost 12 children of his own, grown-up sons and little girls, and he lost his first wife to tuberculosis. He lost them one by one. It was not uncommon in Japan in those days to lose family members to tuberculosis or other diseases, but it was not too common, either. And then he suffered persecution, imprisonment, and the destruction of the church he built by bombing. I heard from some of the old members of his congregation that in those days, his sermons included extensive quotations from the Book of Job. And yet I kept hearing my parents-in-law's overwhelming passion still flaming to fulfill their mission. There was a story that when my father-in-law was over eighty years old, one of the American judges who came to Japan for the Tokyo Trials found him, and reported to Boston, his hometown, that there was one Unitarian church existing in Japan—and through support from Unitarians in America, this little church we were in was rebuilt and my parents-in-law's long prayers in the shelter were finally realized. They told me that they were happy to find me in this late time of their lives. It was a big surprise for me to hear that: how could they be happy for accepting me as a daughter-in-law, a young teenager who was so immature, so insecure, so incompetent, even to the level of being retarded, and with so many, many weird problems. And yet, they embraced me with deep love and respect, which I had never experienced from my own parents. They called me a God-given bride and introduced me with those words to their doctors and nurses, who visited our household regularly. And all the other people, the neighborhood wives who had nothing to do with the church, called me a 'bride of the church'. That became my name.

4 Busy life started. In order to share 10 o'clock tea with my parents-in-law peacefully, I had to spend five hours of uninterrupted work beforehand. At 4:45 a.m. I got up and dressed for the day, and at 5:00 a.m. my husband got up. I opened all the windows of our little house, even in the middle of winter. At the very next moment, all the *futons* comforters, sheets, pillows and blankets were neatly folded and I put all of them into an upper closet. Any mistake of folding or placing them would result in disaster: you would be underneath a huge bundle. It required concentration and physical strength. Then I had to sweep the floor and unfold the breakfast table on the floor. Now the bedroom became the breakfast room. Meanwhile, before any activity started in the kitchen, my husband had to use the water facilities in the kitchen for brushing his teeth and shaving, and as soon as he finished those things, I slid into the kitchen and started cooking breakfast. It was the typical traditional morning meal: miso soup, boiled vegetables, and tofu. When he finished putting his suit on in what was now the breakfast room and sat at the table, I served him breakfast. While he was eating I made up his lunch box, which required quite a lot of cooking: rice, fish, vegetables, even deep fried tofu. Usually it was three kinds of dishes besides rice. When everything was done he grabbed the lunch box and put it into his briefcase and pulled out the bicycle at 7:30 sharp, and I would see him off at the church gate. He would be on the train from there, and would reach the school in one hour.

5 During those morning hours we had almost no talk: talk would break our intense concentration and slow down the whole process. From 7:30 when he left to 10 a.m. teatime with my parents-in-law, I would eat my own breakfast, clean up the kitchen and breakfast table, and wash the clothes, then hang them in the backyard—and other clothes, including my husband's dress shirts, had to be ironed for the next day. Only after a nice teatime with my parents-in-law did my real work for the church begin. There was visiting old church supporters in their houses for greeting, or sick old ladies in the hospital, or attending funerals. Because we did not have a telephone in our household, unexpected sudden visitors were frequent occurrences. Our little rooms were used for those occasions. Once I got up and got dressed, I had to be ready at any moment for any social activities.

6 My husband came back at 6 p.m. and immediately started teaching a student or group of students preparing for their university entrance examinations. At 9:30 p.m., after having dinner with me, finally his own time came. That was when he studied through a correspondence course in order to get a university diploma so he could attend graduate school in America. On weekends, he had to devote himself to all the activities of the church: he had to prepare to play the organ for services every Sunday. And I greeted the members of church, chatting and trying to follow the things happening in their lives.

7 One day, I met a tall, skinny, middle-aged woman who wore her humble kimono very neatly. Since all kimonos are made for the same size, traditionally everyone can wear any of them, skinny or fat, even throughout pregnancy. Because of the kimono's flexibility, it was often handed down generation to generation. Therefore the kimono itself does not necessarily express the taste or character of the person who is wearing it. But the way she wears it—tightly or loosely, how loose the neck area is, how long or how short she wears it—expresses that woman in the most distinctive way. Under my grandmother's influence, I became sensitive towards those things, even though I seldom wore a kimono myself. This lady looked cautious and methodical. She greeted me politely, with a smile, and she opened her purse saying she would like to give me a present. It was something small, simply wrapped in white paper, which she was going to put into my hand. Noticing my momentary hesitation to take it, she said, "Oh, this is a very humble thing which I made by myself. It does not cost anything." She opened the wrapping herself and showed me what it was.

8 It was a beautiful small wallet. "I kept all the postcards I received in my life, I cut those postcards into narrow threads and dyed them red, and I wove them into this wallet with my own hands. It is for you." I received her gift with gratitude and complimented her on her amazing craftsmanship. But my slight apprehension about accepting a present from her had not disappeared. After all the church activities were over, I asked my mother-in-law about the lady. She did not know her well either; she was a friend of an old member of the congregation, but that member had been dead for a long time and this lady had shown up only when people had just about forgotten her. When I told her that she gave me a present, she smiled at me. "I am sure she likes you and your gratitude and compliments made her happy." But she added, "You can always say 'No thank you' if you feel uncomfortable for any reason. I have a feeling that she is making those wallets to try to get petty cash."

9 On Sundays our private house was not private: people jammed into our tiny kitchen to make tea, like a scene from some comedy. Many were standing in our tiny hallway in front of the bathroom, waiting for it to become vacant. There was no water system in the church, only a very primitive toilet behind the church. As evening fell, sometimes an elderly lady could be seen resting on our sunroom sofa: she was exhausted after her long trip to church, which involved transferring from many trains. She needed to gain the energy to go home, so a nice warm dinner was required. Neither my husband nor his brother received any money from the church. They used their income which came from teaching school—my husband at junior high, my brother-in-law at two universities—to keep the church going and to take care of their elderly parents. Only what was left after that went into their own pockets, and that was all the money we had to live on. My husband also had a certain amount of debt because he had rescued a girl (me!) for three years from undernourishment and provided her an education with the highest cultural opportunities. We all were in a severe situation all the time. I discovered a revolutionary bookkeeping system, after research and study, and I decided to use it. It worked, miraculously, and every month a very small extra sum of money was saved up. Paying back the debts was a long way off but it started to get under control.

10   We were not the only ones who were working hard. Before I got married and came to my husband's household, a young girl from a faraway northern part of Japan, a small village in the snow-covered mountains, came to his household and stayed with them. She was sent to our house by her family: they were in brutal poverty, and her parents could not feed her. If she stayed with her own family any longer, all her younger siblings would starve. Her parents made it very clear that she would do any work that was necessary but had no need to be paid. Being fed was all they wanted for her. In those days the government encouraged all of us to engage in that kind of arrangement. She was 14 years old, and had just finished mandatory junior high in her village.

She was short and plump, her long straight shining black hair pulled to the back and tied tightly with a rubber band. She had strong will power and was a hard worker. She started doing housekeeping work for my elderly parents and taking care of their old-age problems. They made this arrangement in order to separate their household from my household, to save me from that work and allow me to concentrate on my new home and on the church. Neither my parents-in-law nor my husband could afford an extra room for her to sleep in: she came to our household with a tiny bundle and that was all her possessions. She wrapped herself with some old blankets and lay in the wood-floor hallway and slept. But by the time I came to live in that place, she already knew which fish store carried the freshest fish, which vegetable store was good and inexpensive, and which days were particular stores' discount days. She cheerfully and proudly told me all that information.

11 My mother in-law was preparing to teach her the skill of sewing kimonos. That was one of her areas of expertise, and she believed that that skill would help her financially for all of her life if she mastered it. My husband and I started making a plan that she should be able to visit her family in the faraway mountains once a year and we had to start accumulating money for that: buying a two-way train ticket, and her clothes and shoes for the trip (she came to Tokyo wearing old wooden sandals on her bare feet), and some gifts for her parents and her siblings. And for ourselves we needed to hire a nurse or a housekeeper while she was away for two weeks. We decided to let her have one day a month off in case she wanted to see other places in Tokyo—places that were more active, more fun; places that young people would love to go and see in Tokyo. I was ready to take her. But

I was wrong. Tokyo's air was unbearable to her: the smell of gasoline and all other kinds of pollution bothered her bitterly. And any simple dish in a restaurant bothered her too: she sensed some chemical in almost every course and it made her throw up. She was safe in our house in the suburbs and the foods that my mother-in-law taught her how to cook were all old-fashioned, directly from nature. It made me realize that she came from a completely different place. We made a different plan. We found a small, rather humble movie theater in a quiet district, walking distance from our house, where old comedies were always playing. She laughed all through it in the theater. When it was over she still could not stop talking about the comedy we had just seen, and we laughed together. Then she said, "Let's go home." I explained that this was her day off so she did not have to work, but she looked really sad and said she wanted to go home and cook dinner for my parents-in-law, just like any other day.

12   Long after, only after I came to America in order to live, not just to see it as a visitor, I started to understand how much difficulty she had trying to cope with life in Tokyo. She spoke standard Japanese well. Standard Japanese was established in the Meiji period to spread the unified education system all over Japan. The Tokyo dialect was chosen as the standard at that time. Tokyo people speaking standard Japanese had no problem, but in all the other districts that form of Japanese was taught only in schools and used on the radio. Just as Americans take it for granted that their language is the common language so that they can go to many places in the world and speak English, we in Tokyo expected others to speak standard Japanese and took that for granted. When I think back, I was one of them: I am afraid that I forgot, however good her standard Japanese was, that this was a language she never spoke to her family and friends. She had to be tense and alert all the time, living with weird smells and eating weird foods, just like the first time I had Coca-Cola in America: I literally thought this must be some kind of chemical poison. I was urgently forced to decide whether to drink it or spit it out. In the same way, she was frightened. When everything around you is new and unfamiliar, or uncomfortable, you don't welcome one more unknown thing as a way to have fun. She wanted to stick to the everyday trivialities with which she just started to feel comfortable. Now I know that her research into the markets was her first conquest in Tokyo, which she showed me with all her cheerfulness and pride, and now I wanted to embrace her.

13 Though everything was difficult, even chaotic, I found a way to handle things somehow. It was completely different from the difficulty and chaos that I experienced, and could not continue handling, in my parents' house. Here I experienced every day's trivialities one after another, and yet I found that they were beautiful and moving. There were many trivial things which had to be improved or just dropped, but many had to be respected. Polishing one window glass is trivial work. No one was impressed that a little window was spotless, but without respecting that work, life starts deteriorating from the bottom, from the inside. And working on this little task, the life of the person who does it gradually changes and grows in a constructive direction. Behind one good meal, how many good intentions, how much effort and actual work was done by people—I kept seeing that every day. I thought I would never take that trivial everyday work done by me or others for granted. And this was the difference between the experience of my parents' home and the experience of this place. In my parents' home, trivial everyday work was despised. Cooking, washing, cleaning, or even going to school every day, they were all despised—even though my mother was a fantastic cook, and impressed guests at every party she hosted. But everyday work is different. Those things were tasks for ordinary people which, in my mother's mind, meant for untalented people, or talented but lazy people who did not develop their talent. Those people should be working on trivial things, usually material, physical tasks, in order to help talented people. That was the dogma of my mother's cult. And she went even further than that: those trivial tasks usually categorized as material or physical work were seen as punishment for people who were not talented or who did not develop their talent. I was the one who should be punished.

14   Suddenly everything became clear. *No wonder* that no one ever said "thank you" to me for preparing dinners for them so many evenings while they were away for concerts, or for whatever housework I had done for them. I was atoning for my sins, and paying my punishment in their eyes. *No wonder* that neither my father nor my mother ever told my elder sister to return my blouse to me, which I had ironed after she took it from me without getting my permission. In my family, the distinction between talented and untalented was just like the distinction between wardens and inmates: it was absolute dogma, it was so deeply rooted in my mother's cult that it was unthinkable to break it. Then what was a talented person in my mother's mind? A talented person meant a person who brought her absolute glory, a person who dazzled her mind so she did not have to confront her own darkness, sorrow, fear, emptiness and powerlessness; who could insulate her from her own repressed rage and instead give her an absolutely glorious image of herself. Everything was done in the dark depth of the unconscious, so no one could confront it. Suddenly things became more clear to me, by living with people who lived by completely different norms. I detested this huge whirlpool of glory in that cult in my home. I was frightened of it, and so I was happy that I left home.

5 My young sister won first prize in the most prestigious piano contest in Japan. And then, she applied for Fulbright grants. She was the first in Japan chosen to receive a full scholarship, and she was accepted at The Julliard School in New York, based on the tape she sent. Filling out all the necessary information on the application in English and recording an excellent tape—these were tasks that the son of my father's professor who came to our house often as a guest of honor, and who now had a job at the most prestigious press in Japan, thoroughly helped my mother and sister with. My husband and I were invited to see her off at the airport. When she left for New York from the airport in Tokyo, there was a forest of big banners which people were holding with my sister's name written on them. The media's cameras flashed everywhere. So many media swarmed around her at the airport that they had to open some extra rooms for them. Many stories circulated, such as that she was reading and writing music notations before she started reading Japanese in picture books; composing on paper while she was still in the bomb shelter; and could dictate the score of a whole orchestra just by hearing it—all of these stories were told. "The Motoyasus' talent for music flourished: it always takes three generations to flourish," they said.

16 Eighteen years old, separating from her parents for the first time, going to an unknown country where she knew no one, with very limited language skills and very little idea of what kind of place America might be, she looked like a lamb ascending the sacrificial altar rather than a glorious goddess as my mother believed. She was pale and stiffened with fear (her head drooped) as she walked up the steps into the airplane. And my elder sister followed a similar path. She won the same contest and went to Julliard the following year.

17 I have been wondering how it was possible that such a beautiful garden could be created by a man like my husband who had no time— not a single minute—to do anything. How could he accomplish such a time-consuming project like this garden? *Was there any magic involved?* I jokingly asked myself, because of its magical beauty. My question was answered. One night I awoke in my *futon*, at 2 o'clock in the morning, and I realized that my husband was not in the next *futon*. His *futon* was empty. I heard a faint sound, and after listening to it for a while, I got up and opened the rather thick doors that we closed only at night—the doors between the bedroom and the sunroom. Suddenly I saw through the windows of the sunroom a strong electric light shining in part of the garden. And under that light, a black figure was moving. I stared at the figure: it was my husband. I went out to the garden. He was digging a hole, a rather big one, so big he could almost bury a dead body in it, I thought. But instead a big garbage bucket of food was next to it, and he was about to pour it into the hole. "I am making compost," he said," in order to have the soil fertilized." It was cold, and yet he was sweating. I saw the whole thing.

18 He had a certain recurring dream that often caused him to scream and jump out of his *futon*. That night he probably did not scream, or he did but I did not awaken. All through the war he had been trained to dig holes, hiding in the hole until the right moment and rushing towards an enemy tank wearing a bomb on his back. He was trained as a suicide bomber. Being forced to commit suicide, being forced to train yourself for that, the detestation, and rage, anger, and desperation, were deeply repressed. Only at night when he was sleeping did it splash up like a volcano. That was when he went out and started digging a hole. I could not figure out why he had to dig a hole, as if it were a ritual. I could not understand if this repetitious act helped him to heal his anger or intensified it. In Japan in those days, I remember that no one had knowledge of those things, and there was no place to seek help. Was he digging holes to bury his own dead body? During the four years of the war, he must have buried hundreds of his own young bodies in his mind. He might, after all, finally commit suicide sometime in reality, I thought. Once when I asked him why he did not marry until he was 33 years old, he replied, "I always wanted to preserve the right to end my own life as an autonomous right of my own. Having a wife and children, which requires heavy responsibility, would make it difficult for me to preserve this right." It is not unusual to think that to commit suicide is the final right. "My life belongs to me" had been regarded as a high-minded notion in the past in Japan. It was allowed only to a certain group of people in society who were allowed to carry swords: commoners were not allowed this right. Because of this right, the integrity of one's life, honor, honesty, and dignity could be saved, people believed. Because of my husband's dark night ritual, the trees in this garden grew extremely fast, and the flowers shone dazzlingly. Does extreme beauty demand dark torment for its nourishment? After witnessing the ritual, I could not see the garden as innocent as I had previously seen it.

19   I, too, was experiencing my own dark torment as he was experiencing his. Mine might have been even darker than his. In spite of leading a diligent, constructive daily life in this new place, whenever I closed my eyes two images rushed back at me. One was the image of the collapsing translucent cathedral high in the sky: the sound of a baby's cry came with it, and then, the silence followed. The image that I saw was in the same place in his study where I was now living, on the evening of my confession when the teacher's (now my husband's) confession followed. It was the destruction of my connection to God, and the killing of my art, my own illegitimate baby by my own hands. The other image was the image of a horseshoe crab that I saw on our honeymoon in the aquarium we visited. I saw a horseshoe crab for the first time in my life in the dark underground aquarium tank. It appeared suddenly in front of my eyes as I proceeded to the next display window. It was motionlessly sitting on the floor of sand, covered with its own heavy hard armor. I was struck with emotion, and tears fell from my eyes. I was 18 years old and I saw this horseshoe crab over my newly wedded husband's firm shoulder: by those shoulders my own vulnerability was guarded, and my vitality and freedom were repressed tightly, just like this horseshoe crab that was barely breathing underneath its amber armor. This horseshoe crab cannot keep his life inside of this armor forever. A vision of it exploding followed. I thought I foresaw something—the most frightening thing in my future.

20   These images pulled me into an overwhelmingly powerful quest *to find who I really was*, a quest that never gave me rest. The quest raced around my mind at full force all the time: every single second, every single day. The quest was deeply related to my religious aspiration, and my art. One certain clear realization was with me all the time: that at this period of time—living at the church, living with passionate prayers every day, ministering busily to the church community, and performing as a church representative to the public— these particular years of my life were when I felt furthest removed from God. I could not go into the center of myself anymore to encounter the images for my art, or to see God there. God, towards whom I felt very close throughout my childhood and early teens, was lost to me. I was an empty shell, moving around busily. I was very much suffering over it.

21   I volunteered to become a teacher at the Sunday school. There were only four or five students in the Sunday school when I came to this church. All were children of the young professors of the university where the minister, my brother-in-law, was teaching. They came with their fathers on the early morning train, but only on some Sundays, and somehow the Sunday school was almost fading away. Our church was located right on the border between a middle-class residential district and a very poor district where most of the families were receiving welfare. I had the idea of mixing the children from both districts. My brother-in-law, the minister, assured me that I would have complete freedom to design the Sunday school programs, but there was no budget so all the activities in that church had to be run 'out of pocket.' I convinced a young church member, who was older than I was, a university student, to work with me for free: he was so busy with his studies he could not come regularly, but he was excited about many of my ideas. Everything was set.

22   The only time I could talk to the parents of the children in the poor district was early in the morning, before they went out to their jobs performing physical labor, when it was still dark. I visited them and saw how they lived. I invited them to church and the children started coming to Sunday school. We did singing and painting and I told stories, just like when I had told stories to my younger sister. Stories started springing up in me, and I wrote a script for a play. The only conditions the university student and I put on the script writing were that every one of the children had to have some part in the play any time he or she attended the church, and that every part be a "speaking part" with at least one word to be spoken, even if it was only "hello" or "yes" in unison. This made it clear that every part had to be considered equally important and that every child had responsibility for the success of the play. The children practiced and performed in the tiny theater that we set up in church. They did astonishingly well. Enrollment at the Sunday school increased dramatically as students came from both of the districts. Four years later, there were forty-six students: no one stopped attending, they all just brought their new friends. At six o'clock every Sunday morning, the children gathered in the churchyard: they could not wait for eight o'clock, which they knew was the time I would open the church door for them. One mother visited the church and asked me if her son was telling the truth when he said that he was playing a very important part in the play in church. She could not believe such a thing was happening. She told me her son had always been a troublemaker in school. But her son and all the other boys and girls, in spite of big age differences and lifestyle differences, brought off the whole thing remarkably well.

23   I saw many dark things in the children, too. Some had purple swollen hands or had their skin broken so it looked like a rotten tomato, because of frostbite due to the lack of electricity or logs to make a fire and because they had no gloves. I had frostbite too: I almost wanted to say it to the children, as my feet were still purple and swollen. I could have shown them by taking off my shoes. But I hesitated to do so, and decided against it. During the war everyone had frostbite: it hurt physically, but psychologically it was nothing because everyone was suffering in some way. But those children's frostbite was different: in a time of peace, in a time of Japan's recovery from the war, only they were left out of society and their frostbite was a stigma of the shame—even the children knew it. I wanted to respect their pain by keeping my silence. Poverty did not play a major part in my own life—except for the brutal poverty during the war and just after, the poverty which everyone had to go through. But I was struggling with my own, different shame. "Junko is the shame of the family," the words I heard throughout my childhood, were still ringing in my head even then. This Sunday school experience gave me a most serious opportunity for healing.

24 One day my mother-in-law came to my quarters and asked me to visit a lady in the hospital. She was a young bride recently married to the Dean of the Religion Department at the prestigious university, the one who had married me and my husband. "She just tripped on the street. Her high heel got stuck in the bad road. It was a very simple fall, but an ambulance was called, and now she has been in hospital already for two weeks." My mother-in-law looked puzzled and worried. That lady was a remarkable person who was educated in America and earned a graduate degree from an excellent university. As soon as she came back to Japan, she married the Dean and got a teaching position at some fancy Christian university in Tokyo. I liked her immediately when I first met her when she attended our church accompanying the Dean, her newly wedded husband. She was a bright young woman with a sweet smile, full of humor and life. We became friendly.

25   I was taken aback when I opened the door of her private ward in the hospital to see that every table and chair in the room and even part of the floor was covered with stuffed toy animals. And as if that was not enough, those stuffed animals were stretching their territory even to part of the ceiling: they were hanging as wild animals do in the jungle. "You are surprised, aren't you?" The young strong voice came to me from my friend in the bed. "They are all presents from my students. They are so sweet, they thought the animals would cheer me up, and they do. But I told them to stop it, it's enough. I have to find some way to give all these to some orphanage or children's hospital when I leave this place in a couple of days. Otherwise my husband and I will have to start a new life in a crowded zoo!" *Oh, how Americanized she is!* I thought. In America charitable institutions have good systems for encouraging outsiders to join in and support them, I had heard. But in Japan, even arranging for a car to carry these toys would be an overwhelming task. I did not know a single person who owned a private car. Orphanages and children's hospitals in those days had not one inch of extra space left to put this kind of thing in their rooms, and if they did, it had to be used for an extra bed. And there was an extreme shortage of working hands: the staff was all overworked, cutting their own sleeping hours in order to catch up with their work. To hand these things out to each child was beyond their capacity. We discussed this a little bit, but I did not want my negativity to overwhelm her. She seemed not to find it a problem. She said she would handle it somehow and I trusted her. The short visit went cheerfully and the time passed full of smiles and laughter. She said she had gone through medical test after test, but that they had found nothing wrong. "I am really tired of lying in bed for no reason! I will leave this place in a couple of days."

26 A couple of weeks after that visit, we received notice of her funeral. The Dean's wife had died in the hospital. We were told she had injured her liver badly when she fell. I was stunned. And my mother-in-law told me that the Dean lost his first wife to tuberculosis after a long marriage. Since then he had two wives but both died after the honeymoon period was over. My mother-in-law was worried about the new bride when she heard that she was hospitalized, but since she was such a full-of-life person, a different kind of person from any of his former wives who were all very repressed, quiet women, she thought things would be all right. "I thought it would be better if you were not told the story of the past," she said to me. The funeral was not held in our church but in a big, dark, stone, almost Gothic-style church where I had never been before. I don't remember much about the funeral. My husband must have been there with me, and most likely my brother-in-law too, and some other members from our church. The only thing I remember was the Dean: a tall, beautiful, dignified man with a deeply sorrowful expression on his face, standing straight and returning bows for condolences from the attendees who formed a long, long line.

27 At one point I walked to the restroom in the dark basement of that stone church. When I came out, a skinny, tall woman was standing in front of me. She was wearing a black funeral kimono in a very proper manner, in spite of the fact that her silk looked rather worn out. It did not take me long to remember who she was. She was the woman who gave me a red paper woven wallet. Now she almost grabbed me by my arm, and pulled me into an even darker spot, right under the stone stairs where they reached to the floor, into that small triangle-shaped space. She whispered to me, "The Dean's first wife has still not realized that she is dead. She has not accepted her own death: after all these years she is still screaming and crying with sorrow, anger, and resentment, which she has not resolved. How can her husband, the Dean, not hear that cry? If he ever once listens to what she is saying, understands what she is saying, and cries for her and with her, this will all stop at once. The young new bride did not have to die. No matter how deep the sorrow is, if a person cries with her from the bottom of their heart, it will be resolved. Just one person is enough; only one cry is enough if it is real. Okay, suppose he cannot hear, then at least he can ask a translator (she used this word instead of "medium") to hear what she is conveying to him. You know that there are many people who can do this for him, who can communicate with the dead, you know of them, don't you?" She gazed at me. Her eyes were sharp and frightening. I slowly nodded. I had heard enough stories about it. In Japan, it is part of a long tradition. "The Dean knows them too. But he is arrogant. He thinks all those things are superstition so he does not want to become involved."

28   She looked around and she pitched her voice even lower. "Christianity is not a religion. If you cannot save the dead, this world will never be a better place. We live amongst the dead, you know. It won't help even if they have a special mass and prayers and music and all sorts of rituals for the dead. All those things are for the living, *they* need comfort. Unless someone who really loves the dead, cries for her, even if that someone happens to be a complete stranger to her, if the cry is real, then the dead can be saved. I can spot people who have that ability to communicate with the dead and to cry with the dead. I can tell who is real and who is phony, but I cannot save the dead directly myself because my love is not big enough, strong enough, deep enough. It is dangerous for me to try to really communicate, to become really involved with the dead. I will be pulled into their world. I know many people who died in the middle of communication with the dead." The memory of my mother- in-law's words suddenly came back to me: "She used to come to church with her friend, but her friend died." *She must have been her lover, and she died during the translation-with-the-dead episode!* I thought. She continued: "Religious institutions have to support those translators, and train them, and educate them, and strengthen their love. Some of them are doing enormous work without any support from any institution."

29   I don't remember how my husband and I went back to our home. But I remember that all through the trip I clearly visualized once again how the dead ancestors rose up from the ground in the wedding room of the mansion of the Motoyasu. That room became the space where the living and dead meet. Just like the stage of a Noh play, the dead were intense, quiet, and yet their stormy emotion reached out to the living. Oh! I saw them all in their gorgeous clothes and armor.

30   And now gradually I began to realize what was really happening when I was painting "The Woman in Yellow", the painting which received the UNESCO prize, when I was 11 years old. I was angry to have found that my parents had arranged a beautiful stage set for me to sketch. Artists have to paint something pretty—did they still believe that? And the first thing they thought of was pretty flowers. So flowers on the white lace-covered table were there. *I don't want to paint this phony hideous lie,* my mind screamed from inside me. *Underneath this whole stage set there were still dead bodies piled up underground. Don't you see them? Don't you hear their growling? No, of course not. Their voices are never heard, they have never been comforted since peace came to the land which they loved and died for. Let me create what I really want.* Then suddenly my eyes caught the movement of my sister in her yellow sweater twisting her body in order to look back as she was leaving the room. I caught that movement of her with Cray-Pas. Instantly her body elongated and it turned into an expression of despair on the surface of the art paper.

31 I heard the cries of the people who died in the burnt field, while I was drawing the woman. And a group of the dead soldiers appeared to me and spoke to me of their violent death, their unresolved mortification, their indignation at having been sent to the field of blood and fire to be forced to kill others and to be killed. Acute sadness filled my chest: it was almost impossible for me not to burst out crying. But I did not. Instead I let their cries splash out onto the art paper through my body and fingers holding the Cray-Pas. Like an enormous flood, their cries spread, and instantly filled the entire pictorial space with violent darkness. My chest was burning, my arms were cramped, I could not really move them well. But my paper gradually showed something like an intense light. It solemnly moved far away, into the sky. I did not cry for them but the art itself did something incredible. Even after taking both my hands off the painting, my hands were still trembling. What really happened? Did they burst to cry through me into the pictorial space? Was I 'possessed' as some people call it? Or was I entrusted by the dead? Did I complete the work they entrusted to me if they did? Have they finally reached the world of the dead after wandering around the world which floats between the living and the dead? Did my art transcend their darkest mortification? Can I call it transcending? I could not answer any of those questions.

32 Why did that skinny tall woman talk to me like she did under the staircase? What did she expect from me? Yes, I had these experiences and others on different occasions and she might have even sensed that at first sight when we met, perhaps because of her psychic sensitivity. When she wanted to give me a present, I felt as if someone who is a member of some secret society was offering her hand with a secret handshake, inviting me to join the secret society, as if whispering, "I know you are one of us"—and at the same time testing if I were sensitive enough to understand the meaning of the handshake and if I were ready to share my mystical area with them. That was even before the subject of communicating with the dead came up. Did she want to have a romantic relationship with me? I remember my mother-in-law said to me when I told her that woman gave me a wallet as a present, "If you felt uncomfortable, for any reason, you can say just 'no thank you' to her any time." Is that what she was thinking? I had not had a romantic experience with a woman, and I was not interested in that with her now. I did have some experiences communicating with death, but I considered all my experiences to be subtle and fragile compared to many psychic people's experiences. I might just call myself 'sensitive' or say that I have 'a certain tendency'. And yet this is the area where my secrets are darkest.

33 This area of communication with the dead, and all other mysterious areas, in fact, used to include my transparent cathedral. Though it has been halted for many years, dreams and intuition, as images, as a vision, still invade my life and my personality like a flood fills a room. I have to fight against that flood taking over my life. I have to struggle with this fierce invasion. I have to strengthen my so-called 'normal' consciousness in my life steadily and methodically in order to get through everyday life. It seems to require miraculous strength from me.

34 And yet, at the same time I want to embrace and cherish this flood. The truth is that is only place I really wished to live in. The force of this flood is the force that moves me towards the Divine, and moves me into the creating of art. In those days I had already come to the vague realization that the lives of others are not quite like that. They don't care about, or they even ignore, the mystical side of their lives. For them, each thing like religion and art, the living and the dead, sleeping and waking, are placed into certain appropriate drawers and categorized and labeled as if life were a big cabinet with many drawers. But in my case it is completely different. Even though things are separated from each other, which I had never been confused about, still they work together, they tangle together, they create a gigantic chaos together. Only from that chaos was something new born in me.

35 What is this unfathomable chaos, really? How much further do I have to keep going into this huge chaotic flood? How much more miraculous energy do I have to squeeze out from myself to make a seemingly normal life? I was wondering all the time. *But the time might come that I will understand what it is all about, what I am, and what I am doing—if it ever comes, I said to myself. Then I will* *acknowledge my secret, and reveal it if necessary. But until then, I do not want others to touch it nor to become entangled with it. Until then, however urgently she wants to talk about this subject of the dead with me, I will not become involved in this talk with her, probably not for quite some time.*

36   My husband finished his university diploma, six years after the end of the war. The day of his going to America was set. He would be at a divinity school in California for two years. He wanted me to join him for the second year, in America. It was an extraordinary idea. In those days in Japan, the prohibition against Japanese citizens going abroad was lifted, but there were still many governmental restrictions. One was that every Japanese traveler had to have a sponsor with American citizenship who would swear that he or she would take the whole financial responsibility for that particular Japanese visitor during the time he or she stayed in America. To find such a person almost required a miracle. But surprisingly my father offered money for me to visit America and stay there for one year. If we could find a sponsor who trusted my father to actually pay all the money out of his own pocket for his daughter, so that the sponsor would not carry any financial burden, I could go. My mother found such a man through the Motoyasu connection and the problem was solved.

37   Suddenly, everything around me had drastically changed. Many guests started visiting our church from the East Coast of America, from the Midwest, and from the West Coast: Deans of divinity schools, ministers of churches, scholars and writers known all over the world. Around the same time that my husband left for the divinity school, which had just been established under a new consciousness of the relationship between religion and scholarship, some academic, international religious conferences were held in Japan. In those days there were few homes and facilities that could accept guests from foreign countries, and among those were very few people who could speak English. My brother-in-law's fluent English helped him communicate with the foreign guests. And my father-in-law, over 90 years old and speaking only Meiji-period English, also communicated well with Americans. Sometimes it took them several minutes to figure out that what he was speaking was indeed real English, but then they saw that it was the perfect literary form of English. He had never forgotten English after he published an English-Japanese dictionary more than a half a century before. So the tiny room and sunroom were filled with guests. The most serious topics—religion, education, and world issues—were discussed. In the little kitchen, cooking tempura dinner for them, I tried hard to catch even fragments of every English sentence they spoke. The big world was out there and I wanted to know it.

38 One winter evening on one of those busy days, I was walking out the door of my parents-in-law's quarters on the narrow path that led into the little yard where the private hut occupied by me and my husband stood. I had just taken a warm bath in the parents-in-law's quarters, bowing good night to them while holding my little toilet kit under my arm, and stepped out into the cold air. Suddenly I saw the transparent sacred cathedral which used to be so familiar to me rising up in the night sky. It soared up in the narrow rift which was open between two eaves that almost overlapped. This transparent cathedral, so refined and yet so powerful, used to appear to me in the eastern sky from the window in my little room in my parents' house only when I had completely gone into the inner world and reached the center of my self, usually when I was deeply concentrating on painting. I had lost sight of it for many years. I could not see it no matter how desperately I longed for it. But after many years of absence, there it was now. I stood on my wooden sandals with bare feet on the narrow path and looked up at it slowly beyond the eaves. Enormous joy and a sense of gratitude filled me. And yet feelings of awe and serious questions rose up in my mind.

39 "You will leave this place, you will pursue your aspiration towards God in your own way." I received these words from a voice without sound. It was almost like I was being given permission to pursue my own self-determination. And in the most subtle way I received a warm feeling, so faint, but I could almost say it was an 'assurance' that my baby, my art, was not destroyed: he had been protected. I did not know how on earth I could reach him, how I could pursue my path, where I should go. Furthermore, how could I ever reveal this new frightening determination to my husband and his family who loved me and trusted me so deeply? How great a destruction would I bring to their lives? I had no idea how my journey would turn out. And yet I was already so certain that the church—however much it emphasized the freedom from denomination and however freely all the excellent scholars discussed religion—was not the place where I should pursue my aspiration in my own way. That is not because I found anything negative in their faith: on the contrary, I found their devotion truthful and respected them deeply for it. I was aware only that their experiences were not my experiences, that their faith was not my expression of my own aspiration, and that I would be dishonest to myself and to them to present myself as a church person.

40   I told my husband of this incredible experience, with deep hesitation and utmost carefulness, stumbling and yet with some conviction. Instantly he made a serious offer and gave me advice about how I should compromise and find a way that everything could be smoothed out. "I have been noticing that the church takes too much time and energy from you," he said. "I know you want to create art; it is important for you." And he made the most generous offer: that he would make every effort to drastically reduce my church work in order to provide me the space and time I needed so I could start to create art as I used to do. I knew that would require enormous sacrifice from him because his life was already filled with difficulties and enormous self-sacrifice. But it became very clear to me that no matter how he and I changed the situation in which we lived, I would cause total disaster to myself and to others as long as I stayed there. I knew I could create art only if I had the inner freedom to be honest to myself. That was the issue that was causing me to suffer. Even though my appreciation of his offer was genuine, I realized that we were in a different terrain in this discussion.

41   That was the first time I said the word "divorce" to my husband. I wanted him to know the possibility of "divorce" had in fact been planted in the long-term map of my thinking. I wanted both of us to face the reality: pursuing my aspiration towards God, my aspiration towards art, was not being fulfilled. The freedom to be honest to myself had been repressed. These were my own problems. I could not imagine how anyone could help me with those things. To fulfill those goals, a lifelong journey would be required. But I wanted him to know that I had allowed "divorce" to be one of possibilities to start this unknown journey. I did not want to surprise him, or frighten him, or take it as decided, especially at a time when his going to America was coming closer. But I did not want either of us to cheat ourselves with the dream of a glorious marriage or glorious lives. My hope was that just like when death grows in our center our lives would become more constructive and more fulfilled. I was hoping that putting the word "divorce" on the table in front of us would help our lives become stronger and more serious, and help make our marriage healthier. But to my surprise, I found that he could not pronounce the word "divorce" without lowering his voice, just like when people have to mention venereal disease, sexual perversity, or worse. He said that I came from an abnormal home surrounded by crazy musicians who divorce and marry all the time, and otherwise such a diseased ugly idea would not have gotten into the head of a dignified lady like me. Yet come to think of it, I had never known anyone who divorced in my personal life. I had never heard anyone talk about it, except for some gossip I read in a translated Hollywood magazine. We were still living in a repressed society. Again I had to: accept how utterly far away I was from the world of common sense. The possibility of divorce was in our future: that is one thing. Whether he is ready to think about it, that is another. But we had to deal with America first.

42 Life in America would be extremely difficult for both of us. I sensed it by watching American guests gathering and talking in our little rooms. Without a high level of English fluency, which neither of us had reached, we would not be able to have social relationships or be able to be a part of their conversations. It was a severe challenge, especially for him, because he was the one who had to fulfill their requirements. Difficult lives were ahead of us. Another thing I sensed from the conversations of those American guests was that something completely new to us was out there: in order to understand and learn from it, we probably needed to have wide open, flexible minds which probably could come only from a deep understanding of our reality. My husband and I would help each other, we would support each other, spiritually and practically, all the time we were there. We would never waste this unfathomably fortunate opportunity which had been given to us. Let us use this opportunity for our spiritual growth and for constructing the firm structure of our life missions, we thought— however those missions might alter their direction, and however mine might separate from my husband's mission.

43 He left to America by boat: we could not afford a plane ticket. It appeared that the long unknown journey that lay ahead of me would be extremely severe, with or without a marriage. After he left, I spent an even busier time than before taking care of my parents-in-law. I gave our helper time off for the second time, for her to visit her home village, and took care of my parents-in-law myself. Often I stayed with them in their bedroom to watch over them all night: there were times when that was required.

44 A church friend, a Japanese Buddhist priest who established his temple in California, and his wife brought my husband to pick me up at the international airport in San Francisco in their car. Then they dropped me and my husband off at my husband's apartment in Berkeley. At four o'clock in the afternoon, the strong California sun was still up, and when we walked in, the light, refracted through the hanging shade of the window, was making a striped pattern on the cheap green carpet. I glanced at the folding sofa, which probably occupied almost the entire room when it was unfolded to make a bed at night, and at a small green card table and folding metal chair in the corner of the room. This was where my husband must have done all his study and written all his correspondence to me and to his parents.

45   There was a knock at the door and a smiling American woman was standing there, half her face hidden behind a pot of dazzling pink azaleas which she held out towards me. The petals were huge, and it was a variety I had never seen in Japan. She was the secretary of the president of the graduate school where my husband was studying. The card on the pot said "Welcome, Junko"' and the President had signed his first name. "Welcome, Junko"? Do they call me *Junko* here? Am I *Junko* here? The thought was rushing around my head. Some years had passed since people stopped calling me "'Junko" in Japan. I was called *Okusama*, which is the respectful way of addressing someone's wife, or "bride of the Church", or "God-given bride", but my given name was seldom pronounced. So here I was not a role, nor a status: I was Junko! That was the first freedom I felt in America. That did not mean that I was just an isolated person without a role, without a status. On the contrary, I knew my husband was invited as a student, and at the same time as a representative of Japanese Unitarians, and of the only Unitarian church in Japan, which had been discovered by an American. We had an official obligation and capacity. But in spite of those things, the fact that to them I was "Junko" here gave me deep pleasure.

46   I received the greatest news just after my husband and I went to visit his school, a school for the ministry, to greet the school's president. It was the news that I was encouraged to audit the classes that my husband was taking. It was a decision based on the idea that in order to support the work of the church, the minister's wife needed to be educated about many things in the same ways her spouse was. The basic idea was that ministers' spouses were expected to be an important force for both the church and its community. I could not believe this tremendous prestige that was being given to me. Giving up my chance to go to university in order to leave my parents' house had been the saddest thing in my life. I had been encouraging myself all the time, telling myself that even if I would never get a university education, I could still continue studying, educating myself. With my husband's permission I picked up his books from his bookshelf and made covers to prevent stains, and I read them. I had been reading them one after another: if I had 2 minutes free, even while cooking, I read. If I had to go out for church business, I read sitting on the bench of the subway station and I read while I was standing up in the train. Now I was not only allowed to study: I was *encouraged* to study. Why did God give a miserable high school graduate such an opportunity of learning in a graduate school? And all the classes were taught, of course, in English! "What does it mean to my life?" I kept asking myself. I attended all the classes that my husband attended with the utmost enthusiasm.

47 One of the classes I attended was a mock psychotherapy session. For some reason, that class was always held in the big stone church in a town thirty minutes away from school. The stage was dark except for a spotlight shone on one chair, in front of which was a desk, and somewhat away from there was a chair for clients. The psychologist, a professor, came out and sat in the chair. He was a man with a beard. He sat down at the table, took a pipe out of the pocket of his tweed jacket, and start cleaning his pipe. He never smoked it, or at least we never saw him smoking there. He cleaned it for a while, in silence. That was his introduction to his class, which had been repeated every week, and it got us ready to be pulled into the unconscious world. Clients were played by volunteers from among the students in the class. I could not tell whether they were supposed to be talking about the problems they were facing in their real lives, possibly having been allowed to camouflage those problems with different details in order to protect their privacy, or even allowed to present totally made-up fiction? Because of my language limitations, many things remained as questions to me. Many of the exchanges between the psychologist and the clients I could not follow. Sometimes significant words were uttered and the secret was revealed to the audience unintentionally, and the audience roared. On such a dramatic moment, I failed to catch that particular key word. And yet, near the end of every session, I understood that everything became genuine, no matter how well it might have been camouflaged: everyone revealed what he or she really wanted in life, what they were really scared to death of, and what they had tried to push away into the darkness.

48 I had read some books by Freud by that time. When his complete volumes were translated into Japanese for the first time, I was fourteen or fifteen years old. I was in deep torment at that time: I felt I was falling into the crater of a volcano headfirst. Reading the books by Freud, I had found that there was some help available in this faraway land—help that would assist me to find out what I had been tormented about. What was the real identity of the dragons who were tumbling around in my dark interior? In order to go through the process of grabbing the dragon, they used the power of talking, the power of language, the power of Logos. That was the most surprising aspect about therapy for me. In those days in Japan, whenever people had any psychological problems, they were recommended to empty their minds by meditating or by going into nature. Sitting under the waterfall in the splashing water had been the symbolic image of Buddhist self-discipline. Language has a different place in Japanese culture from what it has in the West. Eloquence, clarity, the logical use of language—all these things were despised. All language seeks *silence* in Japanese. We did not have a tradition of speech, confession, declaration, dialogue, or discussion. We have a huge tradition of silence. To go to the realm where language is not needed had always been considered the eternal goal.

49 I was also moved by the desires American people seemed to have: the desire to know themselves more deeply, far beyond the ordinary sense, and the desire to change their lives by breaking their own complacency, even if that involved unfathomable difficulties and the determination and courage that went with it. It seemed to me that underneath all these admirable qualities, I saw that there were deep assumptions that your life had to be owned by you, and the assumption that everyone has or should have his own aspiration for life. Those were the qualities I thought I saw in the guests from America when they came and gathered in our little house. And I identified those qualities as something completely new: as part of the new world I might encounter in America. It was all so completely different from the desire to play your expected role in society well, which is what everybody is expected to do in Japan. Even if that desire is expressed with utter passion, still it is different from aspiration. The expected role is the only one for you, and you cannot change it or create a new one. Only one ladder is prepared for you to climb. If you fall off, you are a second-class citizen. If you step off deliberately, you are not only a second-class citizen or a failure: you will be categorized as something much darker. Without aspiration and the other positive qualities that come with it, which are rooted deeply in Western culture, psychotherapy could not have been born, could not have grown or spread. It could not have happened without these great qualities being deeply rooted among people, I thought.

50 How would this psychologist respond if I ever said to him that I am thinking about divorcing my husband right at this moment? Where did the idea of divorce fit into my structure of psychological growth? I kept asking these questions in my mind, but talking to him in English was out of the question. I started reading the book by this professor, which was recommended to the class for supplemental reading. My husband was under the stress of other classes in the curriculum, so I decided to read that book myself and translate it for him, and tell him as much as I understood. This became the first book I ever read in English from cover to cover. Would the day come when my English would become good enough to sit in that client chair, and articulate the identity of the huge dragons that lived in my inner darkness and tumbled around there? And would the time come when my aspiration which had been growing for a long time would finally find the crater and erupt?

51 As the wife of the representative from the Japanese church—my husband, a minister-to-be—I was invited along with him to many churches and gatherings of congregations. My husband spoke proudly at those churches and gatherings about how his father fought against Japan's fascistic government, even going to jail in order to keep the independence of his church. We were also regularly invited to weekend stays at the Northern California homes of many of the school's and church's supporters. In this way, we were exposed to some of the best aspects of American life: a highly intellectual group of people, highly cultured and highly humanistic. We were so poor that we could barely afford to buy groceries, but we were invited to visit divinity schools throughout the United States and we attended commencement ceremonies at prestigious universities in the Midwest and on the East Coast as guests of honor. In order to fulfill those official functions, we made a long cross-country trip from the West Coast to the East Coast by car. We traveled part of the way with a friend in our class who wanted to visit his parents' home, in his car, because he was willing to share the cost with us. And for the rest of the trip, we took a Greyhound bus. It was a big privilege for us to experience America in this way. Although we experienced some hostility, coming from the defeated nation that was until recently America's enemy, we mostly experienced overwhelming friendliness. My sense of the world has changed drastically since then: now whenever someone mentions "people", images of black people sitting in the back of our Greyhound bus come to my mind, along with images of houses made out of cardboard boxes that I saw from the freeway, lining the faraway agricultural fields, in which Native Americans lived. But whenever someone mentions America, there are also images of the soaring towers of redwood trees in the California mountains.

52   The students in our class were rather older than average graduate students. Some of them already had two PhDs and wanted to change their careers from being professors to the ministry. Some had already been ministers of a church of a different denomination. There were many women who were in the middle of changes in their lives: getting a divorce, or completing their role of raising their children and starting a challenging new career. Some were white-haired and had grandchildren. As for me, I was the youngest and least accomplished academically, just a high school graduate. I wanted to know how they were building their lives, how they expressed their own religious spiritual aspiration. Just watching them—their way of walking, their way of talking—was all that I had been doing. One day one of my class friends said something to me and I could not understand her English. She slowed down and repeated what she had said two or three times. I still did not get it. "I am so sorry to cause you such trouble," I said. She looked at me with a serious and very sweet face and said, "I am the one who should say 'I am sorry,' not you, Junko," she said. "This whole conversation you have carried as your burden. You carried the whole burden by yourself single-handedly." I replied: "But I always feel so bad about it. I came here to your country to learn from you, the American people, and your school is helping us. I am supposed to understand English well enough to learn." She replied: "In a class, I suppose, but this is equal friendship. I am not taking my share of the responsibility of friendship. I have not learned one word of Japanese yet." I had developed many thoughts around my experience of language since I had come to America. There were many sensitive, complicated issues here around foreign languages I had started to notice. But her sensitivity and sweetness hit me deeply.

53 When my husband and I were together at our apartment later that evening, I told him what my friend in our class had sweetly said about my difficulty of speaking English. "Didn't you know that woman is a divorced woman?" He lowered his voice when he pronounced "divorced woman." He continued: "I overheard her talking with another woman; that is the way I found out. Don't be close to her. I don't want you to be contaminated by her." I was expected to not talk to him about divorce at all. I wanted to share the sweetness of the brief conversation I had with my friend. Or if I could go further with him, I might want to talk to him about the aspiration of the people here in this school: how coming to this school itself was an expression of their aspiration to God. Was that her aspiration? Did she achieve it? Of course we could only guess the answer, but that was what was in my mind. Yet unexpectedly he revealed to me his detestation for the whole idea of divorce and for her, and for me to have a friendship with her. He revealed that he had stayed exactly the same as he was before he left Japan. He still wanted to push the word "divorce" away, as if it were a germ or something harmful outside of him, as if controlling that germ was the only way to guard his safety. He had no idea that my friend and I had our own minds, and desired to grow, that we wanted to pursue our own aspirations and take responsibility for our lives. He had no interest in those things. In fact, he had not changed since that evening of confessions in his study many years ago, when he swore that he would fight against the evil of other men who might have been interested in me. He thought he should and could make my friend go away by disparaging her. Did he believe that by doing that he could kick the word divorce out of his life? When actual divorce happened to him, what would he do? His rage and disgust might totally crush him. By displaying his detestation towards her, he was actually strengthening and preparing his self-detestation in the future. If this gigantic America, which gave me such profound thoughts and conferred such radical changes, could not make him awaken, how could I ever expect him to change?

54 When we arrived at the pier at the San Francisco port, among big shining boats from many countries one very small boat was anchored: on a short pole sticking out of its edge a flag was hanging. It was a Japanese flag that looked like a piece of rug. It was barely recognizable as a Japanese flag, and because of the long hard trip it had just made across the Pacific Ocean, it almost looked like a symbol of the defeated Japan in the war. This was the boat we chose because it was the cheapest way to cross the Pacific Ocean to go back to Japan. The minute we stepped onto that boat, the strong smell of fertilizer hit my nose: it was a cargo boat carrying fertilizer, and only six passengers, including the two of us, were allowed passage on the boat. All six were Japanese. They seemed happy that they could now finally speak Japanese openly after many months or probably years of using only a foreign language. I went down to the kitchen area, asked them for an apple, dug into it with my fingernail, and held it under my nose: the smell of the fresh fruit shut out the smell of fertilizer. All through the trip, I kept doing that, only sometimes I had to replace an old apple with a new one.

55 The first few days, the boat proceeded like a knife cutting the ocean into right and left, steadily, calmly. But one evening a sudden strong shock hit our boat and made it sway violently. Life jackets were swiftly handed to each of us: the captain announced with a loud voice that a huge ship from Yugoslavia had crashed into our little boat. Through the small round window in our room, I saw the massive black wall of a large ship standing just next to our boat, so close that it made you believe you could touch it, and the wall prevented our view of the ocean and the sky completely. After a few days of emergency repairs, finally our small boat started moving again. And then the storm came, the huge waves knocking on the bottom of the boat and monstrous waves standing up in front of us reaching to the sky. We could not stand or walk, as the floor slanted sharply and kept moving up and down. Nothing stayed vertical, nothing stayed horizontal. Nothing was static. There was nothing we could hold or rely on. In the small bed, tightly attached to the wall, I laid myself down; and in the other bed also tightly attached to the other wall in the other corner of the room, my husband laid himself down. The apple I was holding fell out of my hand, and rolling on the floor, it hit my husband's bed and rolled over to the other wall and then hit my bed, rolling down and rolling up with enormous speed all night. I could not catch it because of the severe dizziness that overcame me.

56 Hearing the squeaky, crushing, banging sounds of the boat and the growling voice of the wind—like an animal's voice—and even with the dizziness and overwhelming sense of powerlessness, I was experiencing a very strange exaltation. I was certainly not a victim of this storm: I was running into flashes of lightning and climbing up the entire mast of the little boat. I became a storm myself. I could identify with the raging storm and I felt a oneness with the universe. I had already decided to divorce my husband the moment I set foot on

Japanese soil: this fury of the ocean was the landscape of my own inner world at the very starting point of my new spiritual journey. But it went further than that. I started having the notion that this might be the real identity of the universe: underneath the everyday movements in the world, this violent dynamism is hidden; until your consciousness reaches a certain level to resonate with that dynamism, you will never see the true universe.

57 When I looked back at the boat after stepping off it after 17 days, at Yokohama harbor, I was aghast. As if a serious operation was underway, the inside of the boat was open. Some mechanical parts were visible and looked just like a rib cage, and because of rust they were all shockingly red. Keeping its wound open, this boat went through a violent storm and we were all relying on it for our survival. In Yokohama we heard that our boat had been banned, and the practice of carrying passengers on this kind of boat had been banned altogether. It was considered too dangerous. We were the last passengers on that line.

58 Another inner world landscape appeared and challenged me when we finally got home. A welcome dinner was waiting for us. I saw the table on which soup was boiling in an iron soup pot. Raw materials were piled on a big plate and each had to be picked up with chopsticks, dipped into the boiling soup in the pot, and eaten. There was a bird on that big plate. My body almost went numb with fear. Since the faraway past, during the war, when I confronted a bird hanging upside down and blood dripping from the head that had been chopped off in my uncle's living room, I had developed a strong phobia of birds. Birds became a symbol of being a victim of fascism, a symbol of being the victim of any irrational authority. Chopping off the head was a symbol of controlling, punishing, torturing, and executing the individual who wanted to be himself. I had avoided every situation that might have reminded me of that scene as much as possible. But here it was and any attempt to cover it up would be useless. I saw a sliced up and chopped up dead bird on the plate.

59   A strange man was introduced to us by my parents-in-law a long time ago as a member of the congregation. He told us that he was the mayor now in some town in the faraway mountainside, and he added: "I just wanted to celebrate your coming back from America, it is such a glorious occasion! I thought about how to express how honored I feel at getting know you, so I captured a wild bird in our mountain, a big white feathered one with a long neck. And by my own hands, I twisted her neck. And I jumped on the train and rode carrying this bird for several hours in order to be on time for this glorious dinner. Here I am. I did everything only for you!" He laughed. My husband knew that it was legally prohibited to hunt this bird in that district. His face stiffened. My eyes drifted to the corner of the room and caught something white and soft there. *Oh, that man plucked all her feathers right here in this room!* I exclaimed in my mind. "I don't feel well; I would like to be excused," I said. My mother-in law immediately told our young helper to come help me. I heard my husband apologetically saying to everyone at the table that Junko had not taken food for almost 17 days on the terrible boat. My drastic, extreme weight loss since I had left Japan one year ago convinced everyone that I should be excused.

60   Even now, I identified myself as a bird, as a victim of fascism, and a victim of many irrational authorities who prevent me from being myself. My fear is still so deep: I felt myself so vulnerable, to the degree that I was frightened just looking at the soft white feathers, which reminded me of my own vulnerability in life and the cruelty of irrational authority. Am I not projecting irrational authority on my own husband, to his controlling of me, and to his prohibition of many things? That tendency he displayed was one reason I thought about divorce. But was I not too critical or abnormal? I was critical of his rage and his control of me even though he had never been violent with me or with anyone, not ever, which was very unusual for Japanese husbands in those days. In fact I was never afraid of him: every time I confronted his rage and his control of me, I felt deeply sorry for him. Because I came to know that he spent his entire youth practicing to kill others and kill himself, and he was prohibited from expressing any horror or rage against that cruel authority. What else could he do in order to stand up in the world? If he was not allowed to control his own actions and others' on every step of his way now, where will his enormous rage be expressed? This is what he expected to do now after being completely controlled and having his own right to live completely taken away. He tried to heal himself from this horrendous experience by taking care of the beautiful garden, by digging holes in the garden to nourish the soil to keep the plants alive. He needed to keep life alive and grow, instead of killing them. Did I not understand that and try to help him? I kept repeating these questions.

61 I had one other reason why I believe I had to leave this place, which was more difficult to articulate. This issue was purely between God and me, so to speak. The only thing I can say clearly is that I could not express my aspiration towards God here through someone else's religious spiritual experience. No matter how much my parents-in-law's experience was genuine and no matter how deeply I respected it, it was not mine. I had no person to talk to about this. I was longing for my own experience.

62   The helper who my mother-in-law asked to assist me in my little detached house spread a *futon* on the floor and put fresh sheets on it for me. She did everything so efficiently and tenderly. She had grown into a mature young woman even though she was still in her late teens. After one year of hard work taking care of my old parents-in-law, and doing all the other work so brilliantly while I was away, when I expressed my deep appreciation for her with a joyful smile, she expressed how happy she was to receive me home again. After she left the room I kept thinking, *Why can't I live like her, with appreciation for what she received and by doing her best inside of that situation?* I was so extremely fortunate; I had received so much more than I could have ever imagined. I noticed that young and not-so-young members in my church here who already had excellent credentials were envious of our going to America. I was just a high-school graduate—a young, innocent, and ignorant girl. And yet they had been so supportive: I saw that when I read the newsletters of the church which they mimeographed and sent to us.

63   I was allowed to attend many classes offered by the graduate school, which was affiliated with many services and communities in various churches from the Bay Area in California to the East Coast— both as part of the curriculum and outside of the curriculum. I was given so much more than anyone could have expected in this situation. The helper who was so happy about my coming home had no idea what I was going to do next; in fact no one did. People were expecting me to continue and develop, and do somewhat revolutionary good works in the community of the church as a "coming back from America" success story, and at the same time, somehow settle down and have babies and be happy. That is what was in their mind, especially in my husband's mind, who had just received news of a great promotion in his school: from teaching middle school to high school in the same big school system. But the two images from my inner landscape that I received during this long day remained powerfully in my mind: the boat with open wounds pursuing its destination in the violent storm, which had been banned from its own function, and the white bird with the long neck who loved to fly powerfully that had been killed. Those things—the functioning of the boat, the flight of the bird—had to be fulfilled through my own life. Bring function to dysfunction, bring life to death, bring light to darkness: I had to work. Isn't it the whole meaning of my life? Hadn't I been preparing to do this work all my life? I wanted to do this work through art, by creating my own art. I had to start now.

CHAPTER 13

1 Divorce was a traumatic experience. From the filing of my petition for divorce to the final signing, it took two years. My husband's signature was a legal requirement and he did everything he possibly could to change my mind: his behavior was more aggressive and often more destructive than anyone could have imagined. After a violent avalanche of his anger, he attempted suicide, though he recovered after being rescued. Finally he signed the papers. Divorce was traumatic for everyone involved. Divorce was the end of my seven years of church activities which included the years I had been involved in the church before marriage. It was the end of all my obligations to the church and my participation in its mission. Divorce was also the end of my relationship with the Sunday school children who had now bonded to me with a strong tie. Divorce was the end of all the friends and all the networks in the congregation. At home, it was the end of my relationship with the young helper, a relationship of strong affection and mutual respect. And besides all of these, it was the end of my relationship with my parents-in-law, who were like foster parents to me. They had always treated me with warmth and respect, and because of them the wounds I had suffered all through my childhood and my teenage years had healed. Every morning, at my mother-in-law's request because her eyes were no longer clear, I read the newspaper aloud to her. I read the editorial pages, the political news, and all the coverage of international affairs as she requested. It was only after many years—in fact, it was during this divorce process that I realized that this was a most considerate gift to me from my mother- in-law. She was one of the first women in Japan to graduate from university. She gave me this gift because she knew I had given up higher education after high school in order to marry her son. She wanted to support my self-education and keep my eyes open to the world. My parents-in-law were the most understanding of this divorce: in spite of their difficult position, I felt deeply their strong warm silent prayer for me throughout the whole process of the divorce.

2 I walked out of the little hut in which my husband (now my former husband) and I had lived for four years after our wedding, and I returned to my parents' home by myself. I was not sure that my illegitimate baby was still alive after I buried him alive almost seven years before at the night of confession. I trusted that he was protected from my destructive action. I trusted my vision, or rather I should say that I trusted my own feelings, which came to me through the vision that I saw in the winter sky before going to America. I would wait until I became strong—strong enough to be able to embrace him again.

3 Bamboo trees formed a soft forest, scattered here and there near an unpaved road at the foot of green hills beneath the faraway mountains. This scene surrounded the village that was the hometown of my mysterious priest 'friend' who had visited me when I was in bed with tuberculosis long ago. His house—rather I should say his hut— maintained the same temperature as the outdoors because of the drafts that came in from everywhere. In winter, water in a jar in the kitchen turned into ice overnight. His books were piled to the ceiling, which made the *tatami* floor slant under their weight. Village people visited him with bunches of green onions tied with a rope which they twisted with straw, and sat there to talk to him. This place was a sanctuary for many people who needed spiritual recuperation. He was there for me, too.

4   I heard the legends about him there, such as that he wrote an enormous number of letters with incredible speed: a man would come back from visiting the priest and he would find a long letter from the priest already waiting for him at home. He did that even though he traveled to prisons all over Japan, with a heavy black overcoat thrown over his tall skinny body and wearing heavy black shoes, both of which were made by the inmates. He must have spent all the money that he received from the church for postage stamps, they said. The letters were always written on the reverse side of all kinds of wrapping paper or fliers to save money, with brush and *sumi* ink. His calligraphy struck people's soul with its intense vitality and its passionate masculine speedy stroke, which caused you to feel the movement of his breath pouring into the powerful black lines with his firm commitment. It was disciplined, dignified, and yet the most delicate and complicated emotion was breathing subtly between those strong lines. There was a long training and tradition of calligraphy behind it. He was in fact a 'master of the sword', just as I thought when I saw him for the first time at the mansion of the Motoyasu when I was so little—not of the sword, though, but of the brush in calligraphy, a master of line in art.

5   Another legend was that he was the son of a geisha. Whenever this legend was told it was always with an affectionate and respectful tone; it said without words that because he was the son of a geisha he knew the dark sensuous passion like we do, yet at the same time people instantly knew that he must have experienced a lot of exploitation as he was growing up. People knew that the social status of the geisha was quite low in spite of all the romanticized notions about it. He had gone through it. He was not like other priests who just translated the Western teachings. The abstract theory, dogma, and structure of the church did not mean anything to those village people. When they said, "He understood us," they were expressing their solemn joy of being with him: encountering someone like him on this earthly plane was itself a profoundly religious experience.

6 When I returned to my parents' home, my two sisters were already in America and the house had suddenly become quiet and empty: the atmosphere was quite different from what it was when I left. My parents were absolutely supportive of my divorce and they were ready to help me in any way I needed. Divorce at the woman's request was legal but still viewed as something diabolical and formidable. A woman who was divorced by her husband was considered to have brought shame and disgrace upon her family and his. But a woman who initiated a divorce was something beyond all conception, something unthinkable. Her actions brought shame on the family similar to the shame the family of a sex offender might suffer in society today. I heard many reproaches: She ruined the best opportunities for the good marriages of her two sisters, so now there could be no buyers for them anymore, they said. What could she hope to gain by destroying her own sisters' happiness? One day when I came home from some errands, my parents told me that a policeman had visited them saying, "We understand that one of your daughters divorced and is staying with you in your house now, which is located in my police district.

I have to keep my eye on this." We had no idea how he found out about my divorce or why he thought he had to keep his eye on me. I realized more than ever that the community did not allow for lives of individuality: in fact, the effort to become an individual invited suspicion and persecution.

7   I applied to one of Japan's foremost private universities: Waseda. A woman applying to university after divorce was another unthinkable thing in Japan in those days—and it was nearly impossible, too, because the growing number of young, ambitious students from all over Japan made the entrance examinations brutally competitive. In that particular year, as if it was not enough, one of Waseda's professors wrote a book which became a national bestseller. The title: *The Theory of Female Students: Accepting Women to University is the Way to Ruin the Country.*" But I was accepted to the university without having to reveal my past. After passing the written examination, and before the interview, everyone strongly suggested to me that I should not say anything about my past since it was one of the most competitive universities and they would never accept me if they knew what kind of woman I really was. Being older than most students was already scandalous enough. I was twenty-three years old and divorced. Everyone had to do certain things at a certain age. Don't ever be "different" was an absolute demand in Japanese society. Either going behind others or even sometimes ahead of them, one had to prepare for persecution." But I was accepted. It was a considerable accomplishment in itself and especially under those sociological conditions. I majored in art history and the Western and Eastern philosophy of art. I graduated from Waseda University with a B.A. at the age of twenty-seven.

8 It was the university which had been founded by a great statesman in the Meiji period who worked hard to revise the unfair treaties with Western nations so that Japan could have equal relationships with them. Many statesmen and prime ministers have come out of that university since then. It was known to young people that this university was the scene of political demonstrations and that it was most active and radical. And for people of an older generation, this university was known as the place where the complete works of Shakespeare were single-handedly translated into Japanese by a novelist and Waseda professor of literature for the first time in Japan, and as the place where the new culture of Western theater and literature started. This university had always been the central force of new culture in Japanese history and the pioneering spirit of new culture was still alive in the university when I was there. I encountered high-minded, idealistic professors and students there. It provided me plenty of room for adventurous exploration and life experiments. Finally I was able to take a small step towards bringing art, philosophy, and religion to a place where I could examine and study them, all of which had been the source of my passion and turmoil in my little secret world for a long time.

9 I pursued extracurricular studies at an institute of *dessin*. The French word *dessin* has a different connotation from the word "drawing" in English or Japanese. I learned a whole system of *dessin*: drawing plaster replicas of Greek and Roman sculptures in that institute. An excellent young sculptor who was active in the art world, and who also taught in a prestigious art university, was my instructor. He was a student of the student who studied and later on became assistant to the great

19th-century sculptor in France, Maillol. It was a classic old-fashioned European course of training in *dessin*. It was a tradition that all masters from the Renaissance to modern art had respected and disciplined themselves to learn and master. It was very strict: it involved hours of standing in front of the easel every day, sometimes continuing very late into the evening, and my fingernails were worn away from scraping against paper over and over for hours. This tradition continued until later modern art scorned it and threw it away. But I sensed that the tradition of *dessin* was not about how to draw, as modern artists might have thought: it was about how to *see* things, where the force of things was hidden, how the power moves in the sculpture. The process of drawing is the process of searching until you see the power moving in the object; then the process of destruction starts: your new discovery destroys the result you have just reached on the paper and a constant going back and forth between destruction and construction continues. "Here is something very precious," I thought. I enjoyed it.

10 This Renaissance way of training was the first professional formal art training I ever took, and I learned enormously from it and I was excellent. My second professional training was in oil painting: I went three days a week to an artist in his studio for private lessons—and he was also a professor in one of Japan's best universities. And yet this was the time those serious questions and doubts arose again in me— about what I was doing and how it really connected to what I wanted to do in art. I realized even more clearly than ever that what I wanted to do in art was utterly foreign to those professors, even though they were young and excellent artists themselves. It caused deep philosophical turmoil in me. But this turmoil was not unfamiliar to me at all. I was taught basic skills of art as part of the curriculum by professional artists since elementary school, because the schools I attended (starting with the Imperial school) were very special private schools where it was believed that art training was an important part of high aspiration. But perhaps the artwork for the UNESCO competition, where I won the prize when I was 11 years old, might have been the last honest work that I showed my teachers. At both my middle and high schools, which were both private schools with a good art education, I did not show anyone the works I created in private. I could not show them to my teachers because my own art had become too far out for those teachers. It would have been taken as a most aggressive, hostile, personal, and rebellious action against their authority.

11 Since my teens, every time my schoolteachers found that I was talented in the traditional ways I had to go through turmoil. The teachers were so sure that they were right about everything, always without exception—hundreds of years of tradition supported them. They kindly offered me private lessons; they suggested staging shows. They gave me model drawings they drew themselves which were often images of cherry blossoms, well executed but dead. Some of them even wanted me to imitate those images, copy them over and over, until all the life force died out from all my strokes on paper and everything was utterly dead. How could I trust that they knew anything about how to raise my illegitimate baby who was relying only on me and demanding so much of me? How could I know they wouldn't kill him—he who was still so fragile, breathing softly in my arms? The time passed; how much longer should I keep thrusting my feet into the swamp? Am I already dead and performing an autopsy on myself in order to find out what really caused my death once and for all?

12   After many years of wandering around in a dark forest of art in solitude, encountering brilliant art philosophers through their books about the subjects I had been struggling with was a striking experience. It was with deep pleasure that I finally met the people whom I was destined to meet. One of them was Herbert Read, a great English art philosopher, still a contemporary at that time. In his book *Icon and Idea*, he expressed his basic idea about art: that art is a primary act of dealing with reality and a way of forming consciousness. The moment I read his idea I felt a beam of light penetrated me. He said that in spite of what many earlier theorists had supposed—that art was a playful activity, an expenditure of surplus energy at the dawn of human culture—art was in fact the essential instrument of forming consciousness, and because of that, an essential key to human survival. And he advanced the idea further: that religion, philosophy, and science followed as consequent modes of thought from that first conscious-forming experience. Because the development of the human mind is always expanding the area of consciousness, art still remains an essential key to human mental survival. He also made it clear that art started out as images of Vitality, which is different from Beauty. Later art, which seeks Beauty, developed through notions of harmony and proportion, but both of these two currents continued throughout art history, twisting around and over each like in a rope.

13   When I read *The Principles of Art* by R. G. Collingwood, I realized that the writer was describing the concept of the honesty of the artist—just what we saw in Read's book but discussed in an even more severe and stricter sense. To create art becomes a matter of being completely truthful towards oneself. Honesty does not belong to anything outside of the artist. Rather it is honesty towards himself, his feeling, and his emotion. The artist explores and reaches his inner truth using his honesty as a compass. Once he embarks on the first step to transform his desire into visual, physical reality, it is only then that his next step becomes clear. The artist must submit himself to a force larger than himself, moving step by step, letting his own creative process lead him. If the artist knew beforehand where he had to go—what conclusion he was supposed to reach—the art would lose its searching quality. Even if he seeks to express his own thoughts and his faith, to create art from any preconceived idea will bring corruption to his art. According to Collingwood's strict definition, craft, most representational art, much religious art, and art created for entertainment—all of them have to go. He warned that the artist's life is constant warfare against the corruption of consciousness, which involves the ever-present possibility of defeat.

14 Those writers' words reached right into the huge tangle in my mind that I had struggled with for many years—and they straightened it out. The idea that art has been a primary act for dealing with reality I understood instantly. Every single line, when I put it on the paper, I was saying, "This is the reality I grabbed." This was so since I was very young. If a drawing was another person's reality which he experienced, and if that experience was authentic, I would be moved. But if it never once had reached his heart, or if it was already conceptualized and already had become a lifeless formula—in other words, if it did not start from his direct honest experience of forming consciousness—I could immediately tell, and would detest those images. That was it.

That is why my furious reaction sprung up against those dishonest drawings some authorities had produced and which they forced me to imitate for an "educational purpose". I saw now that my anger was deeply justified. I was not wrong. This was the same kind of realization that was brought home to me by the young 18-year-old guest of honor of my family many years ago, when he told me that it was my parents who were wrong—not me. It was a big eye-opener. And to know that the origin of art was the quest for Vitality was another eye-opening realization about my own inner sense of art. The catchphrase that art seeks beauty had never satisfied me.

15   Hans Sedlmayr, a German scholar, had written a book—quite a big volume *Art in Crisis: The Lost Center*. The English translation became available to me while I was at Waseda. The book is about the crisis art had been facing in the 19th and 20th centuries. Sedlmayr presents art history as something like a medical record of how human symptoms of sickness start and develop. The sickness he talks about is that we humans are ignoring, losing, and destroying the center, the ineffable center of our inner life—the center of our being. He established a new image of the artist in the 20th century, an image of how the artist becomes an artist in the crisis of history, in the time of losing the center. He said: "Since the 19th and 20th centuries, artists have been moving along a narrow ridge. On the one side there is the danger of falling into the seduction of the unusual, the forced and the merely interesting; and none of that is art. On the other side there looms a beauty that is false, hollow, and mere seeming; and that is not art either." It is given only to powerful spirits to travel this narrow ridge: lesser ones lack the requisite inner certainty. That is why in the 19th and 20th century, the word "genius" takes on a meaning quite different from that of previous centuries. Only genius can bear the ever-increasing weight: the word "genius" defines that essential thing without which no one can reach his inner certainty to be an artist through the dangers of the time.

16 To see Art as a crucial force of moving history—that deeply inspired me. At the same time the intensity of the battle which inevitably comes with the artist's life overwhelmed me. Those books were all published in America, England, and Germany in the 1950s, and were translated and published in Japan in the early 1960s. These books were not in the university's curriculum: in the art department of the university, we studied more classical, musty-dusty theory. I found these books by myself. But still, I am very sure that if I did not come to the university, I would never have read these books. I was surrounded by highly educated and cultured people in general. And yet they were all full of narrow prejudices about art, and I was a victim of those prejudices to the point of being almost crushed to pieces. I was so grateful that I had the chance to encounter these books. And besides these books, I encountered the classic Chinese book on the philosophy of art, the *Kogahinroku*, which was translated into Japanese in the 15th century. I learned from that book that art is considered one of the most serious ways to contribute to the development of human spiritual flow and to strengthen one's life force. I saw that the time had come when terms like 'talented', 'self-expression', and 'seeking beauty'—words often used to justify ego-glorification—were a deception I did not have to live with anymore. There is a world beyond those ego-oriented words: a world where deep, truthful visual experience makes its strong impact on human consciousness. Art reflects the spirit of the age, but the deeper truth is that art has the power to create the new age, and we artists, and viewers too, are responsible to create the new world. Reading these great books, "What can art do for mankind in the course of human history?" is a question that rose up strongly in my mind for the first time in my life.

17   I took a class taught by a professor who was known for his study of mysticism as well as other accomplishments. Many of his books were published as a scholar and as a *tanka* poet. He published a periodical, *Tanka* magazine, which consisted of his own works and those of a small group of poets he invited to contribute. He was a man who was handling two different sides of himself: his scholarly side as an academic and his creative side as a poet. He did it mostly successfully but not without some grief. Mysticism was not known to people as much as what we see now in society as part of the New Age movement. It was long before the New Age: in normal conversations, no one spoke about near-death experiences, meditation, or visions. Those topics were considered to belong to superstitious people or to people with mental problems. So to include the study of mysticism as part of the university curriculum required an extremely broad-minded academic attitude. It was considered a musty-dusty, old-fashioned study which should be part of medieval studies.

18   But I learned that mysticism is not a denomination of any particular religion, nor is it a dogma or a theory, and that instead we must see it as the essence of all the great religions of the world. In fact we find it in Eastern and Western religions and in all eras of history. I learned that essential qualities of mysticism evoked my own mystical experiences which had caused me so much suffering because I could not explain them to people. I was deeply stricken by the dark painful passionate struggle of the mystics throughout history to seek direct unity with the Absolute and their refusal to be satisfied with anything less than that. I was reading the autobiography of a mystic written in the 16th century, *The Interior Castle* by St. Teresa of Avila, over and over, in the university library. As I read it, I thought about the mystics whose passion for direct union with the Divine never faded away throughout the darkest nights. I was keenly aware at that time that I was in a tiny boat in a perilous ocean far from the shore where the secure and respected religious life was assured and that I had deliberately thrown all that away by divorcing my husband and cutting any relationship with his church. I probably paid the highest price I ever paid for anything in order to have a direct relationship with the Divine. I secretly identified with those mystics.

19 Among many mystic ideas, one attracted me particularly: the idea of the divine darkness. There is a divine light so dazzling, so brilliant, that we humans, not awakened, see it only as darkness. This medieval Christian mystical thought immediately reconnected me to Rilke's 'terror' and synthesized many fragmentary experiences in my early life and the experience I sometimes had during the process of creating art: darkness is light as it is. I thought these experiences might have a deeper meaning than I had originally suspected. Would the time ever come to me that this darkness which I was in could be viewed as a dazzling moment when I look back?

20 At the time that I studied with him, the professor was translating the works of Martin Buber into Japanese. I read his translation of *I and Thou* as each section was completed, and I became immersed in Buber's thought at the same time that I was studying art history and art philosophy. Under my professor's guidance while he was a visiting professor at the University of Bonn in what was then West Germany,

I completed my graduation thesis, "Spirituality in Line: The Inter-relationship of Art and Religiosity". It was about the significance of line in artworks: how line reveals the most essential spiritual flow. During the year he spent abroad, countless letters, draft translations, and manuscripts passed between us. The association of mystical, existentialist religious ideas with art, which I learned about during my five-year relationship with that professor, remains an important aspect of the philosophical base of my art. But my own psychic, mystic tendency, which had become noticeable and caused me so much suffering, still remained unresolved, and it still had to remain secret.

21   During this same five-year period, the time when I was deeply involved in the study of mysticism with the professor and the group of people who surrounded him, I became involved with a young man who was completely outside of this circle. He was a serious, active Marxist, a fiery young leader who organized labor unions in factories and at construction sites. Although I did not believe in any politically established form of Marxism and had never been interested in any of the Communist movement's activities, I was attracted to Marx's disclosure of the falsehood and conspiracy built into our society's power structure. I felt drawn towards his uncompromising sense of ethics and towards his compassion for the victims of that power structure: the poor. And my young man also shared this passion and profound empathy for the poor and exploited. Through this young man, I met people who had fought and survived extreme torture during World War II, including his father, the main editor of a major newspaper in Japan, who was caught up in the Red Purge. These people were tortured and jailed because they had worked to bring about the ideal world they believed in so wholeheartedly, a world in which the exploitation of the poor would end. It was a complicated, even weird life that I led then—going back and forth between my religious mystic surroundings and the world of Marxism. When I visited the Communist Party headquarters, the receptionist at the front desk took one look at me, lifted the telephone receiver to her ear, andturned around to tell my young man, "Your capitalist woman friend is here." The atmosphere among these people here was very different; I would never be considered one of them in spite of my young man's remark, "You would be a great wife of a Communist leader." But I saw clearly that Judeo-Christianity and Marxism are the two heads of a double-headed eagle—the spiritual and the material—atop the eagle of Western idealism. I also saw the passion to seek absolute truth in people on both sides. And I received the message from both sides that they were ready to sacrifice themselves in order to fulfill that highest truth. They were, after all, quite alike. I see now that I had to walk a tightrope between those two huge ideas and between two circles of people in order to keep my integrity and search for my own truth.

22 That tightrope aside, all the human relationships that I was involved in during that period, especially with men, seemed to have one thing in common. They sent a distinct message to me that was exactly the same message that I observed everywhere in Japanese society: "Don't dare to be yourself. If you want to be yourself you will be persecuted." It was surprising, however, to find that my divorce never became a direct obstacle to men to propose marriage to me and it was never even directly discussed in a negative way. Still, the 'Don't dare to be yourself' message was always underlying the relationship. This message was so deeply rooted in society that most people seemed to be completely unconscious of it. When a romantic feeling towards a particular woman was aroused in men this message entangled with the women in a peculiar way. The desire to understand that particular individual woman would be completely gone. Instead the man became busy manifesting his own idea of a perfect woman's image, whatever it may be, and he wanted the woman with whom he became involved to play that role. He wouldn't realize that he was persecuting the real individual by doing so. A real individual is not able to live in that relationship anymore because the woman has to keep playing the image of the man's ideal woman. It affects the women, too. Instead of being themselves as they really are, they are extremely keen to play the roles that everyone agreed they were supposed to play. The relationships built on those messages and those roles take on a peculiar form of false relationship, which I call "romanticism". The people in these relationships never see that this whole mechanism inhibits the spiritual growth of both men and women. I wanted to be myself and be individuated; that is the bas of my ethical being and of the creating of my art. It was the exact reason I had to divorce and it became a more urgent issue as I grew older. I wanted to study the about this phenomenon: was it a cultural issue unique to Japan or was it universal? Every day was extremely busy and intense. I was transported to the hospital by ambulance several times during my university days.

23   Earning money and becoming an independent woman had been on my agenda since I was a teenager. In Japan in those days, until you entered university, earning money was strictly prohibited for students, except in very unusual circumstances. If society considered you to be a special professional who could make a contribution, and wanted to pay you for your for special talent or accomplishment, that could be an exception. My two sisters, both active pianists, were considered to be exceptions. Their activities in concert and radio broadcasting and teaching were well paid—perhaps much more than a young businessman's salary. But the sums they had to spend for career building were astronomical so their compensation disappeared. My mother's teaching income was quite high, and my father had always been a superior supporter of our family. In this financial field too, I was alone, far at the bottom, without any income and totally dependent on my family—a failure. Since I had been wondering in my teens if I should become a prostitute or commit suicide, now I wanted to be a financially independent person, and that became one of my important projects. It was rather exceptional for a woman in Japan in those days to think about such a thing. After divorce, I started earning for the first time in my life. As a person returning from America, I started teaching children very elementary English, making English cards with lots of drawings and full of color, with the names of things, animals, and other English words woven into stories. This little class became a joy for the children. Some high school student preparing for the university entrance examination enrolled too: university students were encouraged to study English as part of their preparation. It was still far from financial independence, but for the first time in my life I earned a little allowance money of my own. With that little money, I started going on short trips alone, away from Tokyo: that became my precious resting time.

24 Riding on a slow train between mountains, to a little village or town surrounded by forests or rice fields, or to a quiet beach, I wandered. A woman traveling alone was another very unusual practice that arose many suspicions. But using the small travel agencies close to the stations, talking to the staff, and becoming friendly with them, I always found some very inexpensive, clean quiet inns where my safety and privacy were guaranteed. I would take public baths together with local women who worked on the farms, and visited little bars where they served drinks with noodles. I would talk with the locals in their dialects, and every time I made mistakes in their dialects, it made them burst out laughing with pleasure. Or suddenly I would get on a big boat to Hokkaido to visit the Trappist monastery, and sitting in the chapel I would converse with the young priest. Once I found a black dog leashed on the street, and when I walked close to him he stared at me and I saw that he was a little bear cub. "Hokkaido is the land of the Bear God!" I exclaimed. I had forgotten all about that. Some encounters, small romances, and plenty of good deep solitude, I enjoyed it all very much. Six years had already passed since I began my stormy spiritual journey across the perilous ocean. It was a success: divorce and entering university were things I had done right. But still I stuck my feet in the swamp of creating art. And issues of religion and philosophy were still in turmoil in my mind. My financial independence was still far, far away. Creating a really honest mature relationship with a man or a woman was something I still had not reached.

25 Posters for my younger sister's Comeback Home Recital were everywhere in Tokyo. On the poster was a photograph of her playing the piano with the orchestra in Carnegie Hall, in the most splendid kimono with sleeves that reached to the floor like heavy, creamy flower petals reflecting the light. After graduating from Julliard at the top of her class, she was welcomed in the university that our mother had worked hard to build, now considered to be the best music school in Japan. And she was its youngest ever professor. It was expected of her that she would enter the serious international contests in Europe as a representative of Japan and win.

26 The recital was successful. The next day, from early in the morning, the telephone kept ringing. In order to give my sister a decent rest, my mother kept answering all the calls herself. The committee that would choose the representative of Japan to be interviewed and give a new concert in Europe, and people from broadcasting networks, kept coming in. Finally my mother had to wake up my sister. She went into her bedroom and saw that her room was empty, and her bed had not been slept in. Little holes in the ground made by her high-heeled shoes were visible in the flowerbed under the window of her bedroom. She had eloped. It was the most devastating blow to the cult. She quit being a goddess; how could all the members of the cult who sacrificed so many things and bore so much pain be justified, now that we all knew that what she wanted was the ordinary happiness of being the wife of a man she loved?

27 My father did not have room to embrace a fallen goddess who had betrayed his trust, his devotion, and all his sacrifices for her. She broke all the promises, rejected his sacrifices, and ran away from the pedestal, after supporting his dreams of abundance and glory for such a long period time. It had taken him a long time to open up to Western music, he had gone through many inner steps to support his daughter, and later, he supported her full-heartedly. He went to his office at 7:00 in the morning and came back at 10:00 at night, seven days a week, except on New Year's Day, the biggest holiday in Japan, when no one would come to his office. He supported my younger sister's extraordinarily high-cost career, in addition to our whole family's extravagance, and the whole cult, all by himself, all the way through. He had become a big part of the force that sent her to America, and ironically it was America that gave her the courage to leave the cult. He took it as a personal betrayal by his goddess, but he also took it as his beloved daughter's rebellion against him, against his love and pride as a traditional Japanese father. But the truth was that he would never have found the ideal candidate for her to do *miai*, and he would never have given any man his permission to marry her if she had found one, since no man in the whole world could ever be good enough for his goddess. So after all, eloping was the only way she could ever be able to marry. She knew it and she did it. The deterioration of the cult was horrible. But the "religion" seemed to be able to continue without a goddess for a while because the dogma of a cult functions in the minds of the people who are involved and lasts for a long time after the cult collapses.

28 In 1968, I was twenty-eight years old. After graduating from university, I left Japan for the second time in my life. It was six years since the first time I had gone to America. I departed from the airport with a sightseeing visa and told everyone around me that I would be away for just a short period of time and would be back in a few months or so. After a few months I enrolled as an art student at the State University of New York at Buffalo on a full scholarship: part of the reason was that I wanted to extend my stay in America by changing from a travel visa to a student visa. My academic training in studio art skills could not be transferred to this university, so I decided to enroll as a freshman. Without knowing how some of my trauma might be resolved there, when I walked into the first art class at the university, I instantly realized that I could throw away my double life once and for all. I could create my work honestly in front of this professor whatever his canons were, and whatever his expectations or his guidance of his students. Showing my honest work to him would not offend him, but even if he would be offended, personally, nothing terrible would befall me, such as being kicked out of school or deported back to Japan. From the very first project, the professor started explaining that the work had to satisfy many conditions, such as that the three-dimensional image had to exist in two-dimensional space, and that the form had to be composed with smaller forms, and each line had to be used as part of the composition and at the same time united to the bigger composition. Everyone wrote down what he was saying, but my English was not good enough to play two roles at once, listening and writing, so I decided to just listen.

29 In my inner eye, an image clearly appeared. It was a strange planet-like image, but when I concentrated on the image I realized it was composed of small images and that each line in it functioned to support the overall image. When he finished his description, my image was already completed in my head. He added that this was a very complicated project and that anyone who had questions should come to him, but otherwise we could go to the school art store and get anything we needed and get on with it. I rushed to the store, but when I came back more than half the students in the class were surrounding the professor. His requirements were far from Collingwoods' theory— just the opposite—and yet instantly I understood, and found perfect rationality in it. It was about the function of *dessin*, the base of forming shapes. He gave us plenty of freedom inside of that framework. I approved of what the teacher was asking us to do. I finished the planet-like image rather quickly, and the image on my drawing board floated in the dark universe. I was the first student to finish the assignment. The teacher was surprised. He said this image not only satisfied all the conditions he had given us: it was a striking astronomical image. "Exciting!" he exclaimed. That work was sent to be hung in the university's "The best work of this week" gallery. This incident made it clear to me that I could show my honest work to people here.

30   A few months later, one woman student in the class when I was present asked the professor about my works. "Every week Junko's different works are hanging in 'The best work of this week' gallery. Other students' works get chosen only occasionally. Why are only her works always picked up? Is she a genius or something?" The professor replied, "I don't know if she is a genius or not. But one thing is very noticeable: everyone who walks into that room stops in front of her work. I don't know if it is because they like it or because they really dislike it. But her work always makes people stop and think. Something is there, some strong power is in her work, don't you agree with me?" The Professor asked and everyone agreed. This was a small incident in a freshman class at the university. But it was very much America, I thought. No professor, nor any students, ever claimed the power of manipulating someone's inner world under the name of authority— whatever authority it might be. Everything happened naturally. Whether real acceptance of my work in the real art world would come, I could not tell. But that would be decided by the work itself—not by how obediently the artist followed the canon or failed to follow it. I was grateful that my trauma that had lasted for so many years was resolved this way. I did not have to live like a split personality who had to have both—the artwork to show and the artwork to hide—anymore. Neither my professor nor my fellow students could have imagined the darkness that I had carried for a long, long time.

31 Whenever I think about Buffalo, I hear the sound of a strong wind blowing in the sky above me. Under that sky, I was walking to the school with a big canvas tied to my back, my body almost being lifted up as if the canvas were a sail, my feet barely touching the ground as I walked on the iced snow to the first class of the day. It was dark; I could see even stars in the sky at seven o'clock in the morning. Later, Japanese men, PhD students, took turns coming to pick me up in their cars to take me to class, and helping me by taking me to the lumberyard and hardware store to make frames on which I could stretch the big canvases. They were all lonely, isolated, and missed Japan terribly: reading Japanese, writing Japanese, having conversations in Japanese—they missed these things and were starved for everything about Japan. Ragged weekly magazines, several years old, were still circulated among them. They read them and talked about actors' gossip in the magazines that no one in Japan remembered anymore, and they all laughed together and continued talking on and on as if it were current news. To make people laugh is the best way to make you feel powerful. It is the best way to recover from the miserable foreigner's position; the relation between yourself and others could be turned upside down, even if it might be only for a few seconds. But that is the worst thing to try for a not-so-eloquent foreigner. Some tried bravely and failed; every one of us there had sour experiences or nightmares in that department in the school, or at some gathering in

America. Here, we all had something to say about the miserable actor in the Japanese weekly magazines, and we all had a need to make others laugh and to recover from the nightmare. "I can still make people laugh, I am not so bad," you could then say to yourself. But there was always someone who wanted to be the last person to make others really laugh. He would stand up and say, "Even though all the situations were discussed and we all agreed what this idiotic actor should have done with that miserable woman, I still have one more little suggestion to add to our discussion, if I may." We all burst out laughing again—some even sliding down from the big ugly stained sofa left as garbage in the street, which they had carried together into the 2nd-floor apartment, losing their balance by laughing too much. All the Japanese there were extremely ambitious. They knew that they were going to be elites who would contribute something to the glory of Japan. Some of them already had contracts to teach in prestigious universities in Japan, avoiding the slowdown in their careers which would have been involved in climbing up the career ladder in foreign universities. To make themselves stand out from the pack, they all had to work extra hard in many ways. Some of their parents had already prepared piles of marriage candidate papers and photos, and the women were waiting for interviews with them so these men could choose their wives from among them. The blueprint of their lives was there in front of them; all they had to do was fill in the blanks as they were expected to do. Until that day of going home, they could undergo any hardships that were required; the idea of "until that day" was where their strength came from. After that, all they would have to do was follow a clear blueprint. They had no worry about it.

32 As far as my own life was concerned, the idea of going back to Japan became more and more remote for me. It seemed impossible to push myself back into that little place—into Japanese society—as Ruth Benedict, a scholar of Japanese culture called it, which I had already anticipated when I left Japan. "If the bonsai tree is once planted in the ground, no one can replant it back in the bonsai tray, its roots will have grown too deep and strong," the saying went. My roots did not look like they were too big to be replanted in the bonsai tray, at least not to the eyes of many people around me, such as those Japanese graduate students. They often said, "Junko always looks like a perfect Japanese lady." But my roots had grown too deep underground; the truth was that they were too big already and sticking out from the tray to begin with. In fact that was why I came here. I never wanted to become a beautiful bonsai in a tray: I always wanted to be a real tree standing on the ground. But do I really have the strength to grow deep roots in this foreign land? How can I ever support myself in this land? How can I ever support my illegitimate baby, my art? Can I really throw away the idea of "till that day of going home"?

33 A few months later I was proposed marriage by a brilliant American young man. He was twenty-six years old, four years younger than me. He was doing some exotic computer programming, and had founded an advanced computer software company on a fancy street in Boston, hiring some employees but doing the computer work independently. It was exotic because his idea was far advanced, but also because the computer itself was completely new and the whole idea of computer skill was still surrounded by mist. It was before the personal computer age, so few people had even seen a computer. The machine he used was in huge, air-conditioned hidden room in a building in the forest of an

Ivy League university campus. Just like Frankenstein's monster, it had to be heavily air-conditioned 24 hours a day even on below-zero winter days or it would not survive. People talked about what the computer could do then and what it would do in the future, talking about it as if it were a golem. "Will it be able to play chess with humans some day? If it did, which would win: the computer or the human being?" Now, in the 21st century, these questions sound so primitive. But in those days, they were shockingly advanced, adventurous questions, and this young man was an expert in the field of artificial intelligence. He participated in endless discussions of future technology and philosophy, and of how those things would affect future society, with excellent young professors at the technology university and with other members of Boston's intellectual community. What could new technology do to make this world a better place? He thought about it constantly and passionately. He developed and marketed "expert systems" used to design very large-scale communications networks for fifty of the largest companies in America.

34 He asked me when we met for the first time if, many years before, I had ever sat in front of the fountain at the university campus in Berkeley. "Yes," I replied, "that was the place I sat whenever I had time alone." That was when I was trying to collect all my energy to prepare for manifesting the frightening thought of divorcing my husband. Now this young man told me that he, too, sat on the other side of the fountain, as a student of philosophy in Berkeley. He earned his way through college teaching Hebrew, Latin, and Greek, and working as a cantor and assistant rabbi in various synagogues. Those were skills he learned from his father, who was a noted rabbi, and he was expected to be a rabbi just like his father. During times of extreme busyness and hardship, whenever he had time alone he sat at the fountain with his deep thoughts. He too was in torment, thinking about divorcing his young wife. The image of the Asian woman he saw at that moment was engraved in his mind. Because in those days Asians were so scarce at the university, it very likely was me who he remembered so vividly. He talked about a certain coffee shop in Berkeley. "The entrance was on the street level and several steps down is where I sat," he said. "Every time someone opened the door, I would recite in my mind, "I will lift up mine eyes unto the hills, from whence cometh my help." I remembered that coffee shop, though I seldom had enough money to buy a coffee there. But we were sharing our youth, our hopes, and our existential fear of those times even as complete strangers to each other.

35 His apartment building was on a Boston street almost facing the River Charles. The original building must have been built in the late 19th or early 20th century as an elegant residence. Clearly now the interior of the building was all chopped up into small sections with simple facilities added to each section in order to rent to many different tenants. He took the section that included the beautiful library. In order to get to the library, one had to climb up a big, rich front staircase. Deep-brown, wood-sculptured bookshelves reached to the high ceiling and the big fireplace was old and black but still very dignified. These bookshelves were now packed with his own books, written in English, French, Greek, and Latin, and some in Hebrew: the Talmud, the Kabala, philosophy, mathematics, and law, and lots of sheet music. There were none written in any Asian language I could find. In the middle of the room sat his big desk: he lived like a 19th-century philosopher or scientist, or a magician or even a detective like Sherlock Holmes. On the floor, on the deep-colored red carpet, many papers were scattered. Picking some up, I saw they were all in algebraic notation, with mysterious marks all over them. Something terribly important must be going on in his head: that was the only conclusion I was able to come up with.

36 As the night advanced, his friends one by one or in small groups climbed the staircase. Many were mathematicians, scientists, lawyers, computer technologists, psychologists, or architects. Some had PhDs, some were in the process of getting their degrees, and some were already teaching in universities or active in business. The women were all beautiful and had the identity of feminists, one way or another. Every one of them wanted to listen to his story of the day or the week. He talked about how his business was going well for selling big new communication systems to major companies in America. People listened with rapt attention as he talked about the breathtaking developments of the business.

37 "I cannot understand what he is talking about, I cannot follow his English," I whispered with desperation to the woman who sat near me on the sofa. "Neither can I," she rather cheerfully replied. She was working as his secretary in his office every day, and that evening with her architect husband she was attending this gathering. She was embracing her knees with her arms on the sofa, adopting a pose common among hippies on the street. "To tell the truth I suspect that no one in this room understands what he is saying or doing." She continued: "He invented some system of artificial intelligence in which the language of animals is involved. It is a big thing in the computer world; many people have talked about it. And then they said, 'The time will come, if cats say meow in front of the computer, the computer will start translating to us exactly what the cat meant. I am telling you, Junko, because in his office I read many, many things he writes, or at least the ones I can somehow cling to. This language thing is very, very difficult. It is about the development, history, and functions of language. He has written the most difficult essays about language. It is philosophy he is writing. You know he talks about philosophy." As if the word philosophy were a magic word, she lowered her voice. "There is no way to follow for a person like me. But everyone is excited that the time may come when we can talk to animals through computers. It is so exciting being with him. Everyone follows him around. In a way I would say everyone wants to fill their own inner vacuum: conquer their fear, or the difficulty of their life, by filling it with this excitement he provides us. We all ask, 'What's next?' and follow him around."

38   As the night advanced, people began leaving and finally he and his best friend, a young professor at MIT, got together and started scribbling on sheets of paper, showed their scribbles to each other, and dropped the papers on the floor. Hours passed and the papers covered the floor. It seemed this kind of night continued to the morning almost every day. The next day I asked him about what was on the white paper. He explained to me that he and his mathematician friend were trying to solve the mathematical problem called the Poincare Conjecture, which had never been solved. I wrote the name down in my notebook without knowing what on the earth it meant.

39   I found him deeply attractive. But not for the reasons why all his friends gathered around him found him attractive. I saw beyond this visible surface of his brilliance something extremely beautiful and precious to the level of being almost frightening—something deep and strong which you could call his core—a huge love towards life. That core emanated in him and one beam radiated towards the outside of him as a beam of enormous curiosity towards so many things in countless fields, and there was a desire to do something good that would lead mankind towards eternal values. He had a strong belief in human effort and growth. But this huge love towards life did not have an authoritative tone. This light did not come from the obedient acceptance of some teaching or command. His love had nothing to do with obedience to any authoritative agency's command to love mankind—like God's or like the commands of many religious institutions. It came directly from himself, as naturally shining pleasure. And his curiosity was just like that of a child who starts to run towards a sandbox the moment he sees it in a park. This beam of light belonged to his natural positive, productive framework towards life. In spite of the lifelong religious training he received in his father's home and in the synagogue, throughout all of his life this shining quality did not have an authoritative tone at all. Because of my first marriage to a church person and my mingling with religious people in the congregation as a member of the church family, and attending religious school in America with my first husband, I knew that this quality of his was quite unusual. To see this natural shining light come through from him gave me great pleasure. "This man will never compromise," I thought. "Money, fame, success, victories in all kinds of competition in life—which so many people in America believe in and take for granted as their goals in life—were not the goals of his life." He wanted to become a successful man, but not by betraying himself to get there. I felt awe towards him for that. But, at the same time, I also saw a deep whirlpool in his inner world, like a storm in the ocean. I also saw his deep enormous Self rising in the storm, and in order to reach his goal, he still had go a long way. He would still have to do a lot of digging and cultivating to bring many things to be integrated. "He will carry out an enormously difficult task," I thought. "He might become a very successful man, or end up as a 'voice in the wilderness' doing good things for mankind but not necessarily rewarded. But whatever he does, he will never compromise his true destiny. Can I be strong enough to go through the crazy life he is carrying on? Can I go through the many revolutions he will undergo on his way, cherish him and participate with him in that life task, while carrying the difficult task of living my own life? Can I raise my own illegitimate child with this man, make my baby grow and flourish through my art? Can this man and I both grow together, interact, mingle and tangle and influence and support each other to create each of our lives—he, this most eloquent man I had ever met and I, having the poorest language skill and poorest life skill in this vast foreign land?

40 Many letters were exchanged between Boston and Buffalo. Demonstrations against the Vietnam War became fierce. Many classes were canceled, and using those non-class days cleverly, many visits were made to Boston by plane and sometimes by long train rides through the snowstorms. I often came back exhausted, almost destroyed by following the crazy life he was leading. But I finally agreed to marry him and moved to Boston where he lived. Our wedding was a civil ceremony performed with a stranger as witness in a room upstairs in an old tilted house in a Boston slum. This was in order to avoid the Jewish ceremony and conversion of any kind, and to avoid any flavor of any religion altogether, including Unitarianism. His mother, a widow of the rabbi who expected his son would carry her husband's honor by also becoming a great rabbi, and all other family members and friends were shut out. Marriage has a strong social component, but religion was simply a relationship between God and me—probably the deepest mystery of my life—and I did not want to make a mess of it. The time would come that I could build a special and meaningful relationship with his family. He shared my feeling and felt exactly the same. It was the most solemn, dignified wedding I had ever attended. With his strong arms, this man, my new husband, embraced me, a woman still sailing through the storm on a tiny boat with a huge surgical wound showing the red inside of its iron body—and as a white bird, her feathered wings still powerless and unable to fly—finally holding her illegitimate baby in her arms again. The baby was alive, still pale but breathing. I embraced my new husband for his great passion to make this world a better place, and for all his difficulties and traumas that were still to come in the process of becoming himself. The long dragged-out Vietnam War had cast a dark shadow over America. Many news stories, many images of the war, brought me back right to the war I went through as a child. In 1971, by marriage, I became a permanent resident of the United States.

CHAPTER 14

1 We moved into a big white house in a suburb of Boston. My desire for a house with windows through which I could see a big tree standing was satisfied at first sight: a tall maple tree spread its branches and cast a clear shadow in the front yard. In order to get extra space for my art studio, we rented the whole upstairs. We were told that the house was built during the Civil War by a general. It was a big wooden house, beautifully painted entirely in white, and though it was more than 100 years old, it was well-functioning. It had plenty of sun and cheerful wallpaper throughout. The front stairs were wide enough for ladies dressed in long, full skirts with big petticoats and their escorts to stand on. I put my clothes into a big closet, which was covered on the inside with wallpaper in quiet old colors of a repeating pattern of small women in long dresses standing under trees—an elegant and rather humorous design. In the corner of the closet close to the floor, I noticed a small torn patch of the wallpaper. I brought a little knife and I opened up as small a part of the wall as possible. Underneath was wallpaper of a strong design in black, red, and gold. I proceeded further and gradually many different wallpapers appeared. I could not keep going without doing permanent damage to the wall, so I stopped. I realized that many generations must have lived in this house. The biggest and most beautiful room had a big fireplace, and it was meant to be a living room for throwing big parties. But my husband had a different idea: he insisted that I use that room for my studio and I accepted his idea. That room faced the huge maple tree in the front yard, and in the fall, when the leaves turned almost gold, casting their colors even inside of the room, the reflection was dazzling. We called this room 'Junko's studio' and I spread all my tools and materials for creating art on the big working table, and got ready to start my work.

2   One day, our young landlady who lived on the first floor knocked on our front door. She apologized, but explained that without going through our living quarters she could not get to the attic where she had to go to pick something up. I invited her in. The closed and locked heavy wooden door at the end of corridor was the entrance to the staircase to the attic. She started talking about the attic. "When my husband and I bought this house some years ago, we found the attic was packed with old things—antique furniture, old clothes, and chests full of things. Some we sold, some we threw away. But we did not know what to do with the piles of papers and notebooks that were with filled with handwritten letters—nothing like business documents, just handwritten letters. What were they? What kind of people wrote them? They must have spent so much time doing this it seemed that it must have occupied a big place in their life. We were just overwhelmed. Finally we hired a big bin truck—you must have seen those, the huge ones, you know—and let it park under a tiny attic window and we threw out all the papers and notebooks and dropped everything into the bin. We failed many times, papers flew up and spread to the sky and fell around the bin, or sometimes they scattered and fell quite far away, and in the middle of our process it started snowing. It was a big mess, but we finally became better at throwing things out, and in the end everything was handled. But after everything was done, I noticed a leather-covered notebook that looked like an old diary. I was holding it in my hand without noticing it. I must have just kept it without throwing it away. I opened the first page, and it said, 'Today, I came to this summer house from Boston by coach, today is the first day here, and I started writing this diary.' This house was a summer house!" she cheerfully exclaimed. I asked if she kept the book, what year it was written, and if she knew the writer's name. She said she probably donated it to charity or to some library with other bundles of things. "I thought it might interest a local historian or something," she added. It was a woman's name, but she did not remember the name and did not check when it was written. "Somehow it was very difficult to read the handwriting of people in the past—something is different about their way of writing." And she added that was the reason she did not continue reading after the first few lines. "Would you like to come with me?" Looking up at the ceiling, she smiled at me with her ring of jiggling keys. The attic was rather clean and organized, and nothing interesting was visible.

3 My imagination about that diary in the attic, and the woman who wrote it, was stimulated more and more in my mind every day. This woman writer took on the shape of a life. When I was looking down at the front yard from my studio window, where the landlady's family barbecue party was being held, and looked at the people wearing shorts and T-shirts and holding paper plates while the children ran around, this woman appeared to me in a light-colored long dress standing quietly next to me. She, too, looked down at this summer party, just like she used to watch the beautiful summer garden parties with the ladies in long, big skirts and the gentlemen in high-collared, blousy-sleeved shirts. She was often standing near the fireplace, too, in her light-colored dress, staring at the fire in silence while I was working. People write when they feel a profound gap between their outside and their inside: they start writing to fill that gap. Serious writing starts from there. I felt that woman and I were sharing that particular moment with each other. She wrote a great amount, every day, and perhaps many hours a day. Did she go back to her house in Boston at the end of the summer, or perhaps something happened and she stayed in this summer house until the end? That would explain the huge volume of writing in the attic. Or maybe even from the beginning she was sent to the summer house to live alone with her servants for some serious reason—and that is why she determined to write from the first day of her arrival here, in order to grasp what really happened in her own life, day by day, to understand her life and commit to manifesting the meaning of her life here. We have no way of knowing.

4   But another image of the attic, the image of handwritten papers flying up into the sky and falling down into the huge bin, was a sharp and compelling image for me. When I was listening to the landlady describe what they did with those writing piles, I saw clearly that my own drawings and sketches, now placed in a big portfolio case, were opened up and were flying up in the sky and falling down into the bin. It was a clear message I received: I thought that people would throw things out eventually, especially if those things did not confer any practical benefit. People like our landlady, as kind as she was, had no idea about writing, just like they had no idea of what creating art is. I came to realize that what I should do with my works was a question I had to take seriously. Otherwise the same destiny that befell those writings would befall my works: they would simply be demolished. This topic brought up further, more serious questions: Why should my artworks be kept after my death? Why should my works be seen by other people to begin with? What meaning does my work have for the world—if it has any? If it has no meaning for the world, is it better for it to be destroyed with my death? I started thinking about the two words that represented two concepts I created and used when I talked in my high school class: confession and declaration. My art had been greatly meaningful for my personal healing and spiritual growth. It had been working as a confession very well. But was it a declaration? I had no idea yet.

5 Our new life started. I dived into my creative work: drawing with a very fine pen. My husband's project, his telecommunications design business, suddenly flourished. Many of the Fortune 50 companies decided to use his system and his work often required him to work all through the night. Having guests over for dinner and being invited out to dinner became frequent activities for us. And we traveled together to many states, all over the East Coast and to Canada. In Washington, D.C., we stayed for many weeks in a suite in a suburban hotel in order for him to attend meetings, conferences, and parties (where I would join him) involving his new technology company. Often my husband rushed out to solve and deal with computer emergencies, which took all-night work. I often brought my work along, which happened to be a series of pen drawings. I carried Arches paper and ink and a special pen to the hotel, and I remember that I often worked all day in the 23rd-floor suite in the towering hotel: it stood in the middle of a field of undeveloped land surrounded only by the horizon. It looked like a symbol of the computer industry itself in those days, in that science fiction-like environment. I worked while my husband went out to see business people all day, and often, in the evening, I changed into a long dress and attended business parties talking with the wives of the executive businessmen. To be able to bring myself into the intense and deep concentration required for my art, no matter what was happening around me and no matter what I was required to do, that became crucially important.

6 Living in a foreign country required one most severe condition from me: using English in social, public environments—English, my second language, which I had studied throughout my school life for more than a decade with diligence, in the Japanese school system back home. I earned first place in my English class at Waseda University after coming back from my one-year stay in America with my former husband. And here in America, I was a scholarship student on the Dean's list at the State University of New York at Buffalo, and earned a diploma confirming that my English was at a professional level. But that was not at all enough: you had to go far, far beyond that if you wanted to present yourself honestly, not as an ethnic role-player but as a serious career person by international standards, or as the wife of an intellectual, ambitious professional. In this extremely aggressive, competitive society, a much higher and more sophisticated level of English was an absolute requirement.

7 Language difficulty not only isolates you from society, it also makes you invisible. My eyes, directed towards each English speaker with the utmost intensity and desire to understand them every time they spoke in academic or business settings, seldom met their eyes—sometimes never even once in an entire evening. America is a very verbal country and language is the weapon you need to assert your right to exist here. The strength of your existence is defined by your level of language. To keep my identity in society at the same level I had in Japan was far beyond my English-language capacity. In Japan, when I looked back as an adult, I realized that I was treated as a smart, well-educated, and strong person, but here I felt myself always being treated as a member of a disadvantaged minority. To English speakers, I often seemed unsure of myself and shy, not well-educated, and certainly not a capable or strong person.

8 I started noticing the groups of people in America who are minorities for one reason or another—because of language, ethnicity, age, or some physical difficulty. All of them were living with the pain of not being accepted or respected in this society. I heard their unspoken cry of aspiration like the howling of a wolf everywhere I saw them. I identified with them and with their cries. I looked back at myself in Japan—at how much I had taken my own language ability for granted. I had been a member of the proud side of society. How proud I was of being expert in Japanese! I used to believe that with this language, I could go through any difficulties in life, and that language was and is still intensely in my mind like a secret. But if I let that secret out it spreads and takes over all my heart and flows over the rim of my heart as tears. I had to accept my new reality, just like a former athlete in a wheelchair has to accept reality and spend all his effort now on physical rehabilitation.

9 The difficulties of language I had to overcome are deeply rooted in cultural, historical, and sociological differences, and struggling with them required me to step out of that whole social matrix. First, I was required to step out of monologue and into dialogue. Japanese is a language where the subject of the sentence is suppressed, or only implied. The use of the pronoun "I" is very rare. This promotes a self-effacing attitude. And there is no tradition anywhere in Japanese history of dialogue—of debate or public speaking. In order to live in America, I had to learn how to confront difficulties directly, how to stand up, how to explain, how to persuade and convince. All these are things which, in Japan, we women especially learned *not* to do—never to directly confront, nor express. Instead, only in a very delicate way, by reading the "air" of the situation, did we learn how to manipulate matters and handle them. But in America, a more direct and yet sophisticated language had to be used, and for that, a radical transformation was required of me. It was like performing surgery on myself with my own hand.

10 I had been working ten hours a day in my studio, and my creative urge was so strong, so overwhelming, so out of proportion to everything else in my life, that it brought me to a certain state of consciousness that was familiar to me throughout my childhood and my entire youth: the awareness of a mystical unity, a deep insight into the nature of being and into self and its relationship with the universe. And yet this consciousness often manifested itself as various kinds of undiagnosable sickness, and pulled me into deep desperation. I started using the phrase 'altered state of consciousness' to describe this state of consciousness, particularly after reading many books of transpersonal psychology. Abraham Maslow, one of the major pioneers of humanistic psychology, offered a theoretical understanding of the new higher transcendent consciousness, which is associated more with the Eastern than the Western religious tradition. I saw myself hanging from the cliff of America by both hands, craving for Japan like a drowning person gasping for air. And yet I knew that to go back to Japan would be destroying myself. I was frightened that any day, any moment, I would release my hands and just let myself go, from desperation and exhaustion.

11   During this most critical period, my strongest support came from the least expected place: a spiritual teacher in Japan, whom I had never met nor heard of. One morning in the fall of 1972, I was in bed in the upstairs bedroom in Boston, eyes wide open. Desperation and exhaustion had finally overwhelmed me. I knew that the time had finally come that I should take my hands off, the hands which had been gripping the cliff of America, leaving me hanging, gasping for air. I had failed living in America, I cannot grow myself here, I felt. And yet I did not want to go back to Japan: I knew so well that I could not be myself there. The telephone rang. I had not answered the phone for many days: I would ignore it this time too, I thought. Then I thought it might be my husband, who left for his office early in the morning, leaving me to sleep, and I wanted to hear his voice—it may be the last time to hear his voice, I was thinking. I picked up the phone. "*Moshi moshi.*" An unfamiliar woman's voice was saying 'hello' in Japanese. She identified herself: she was a woman we had met and spoken to at some parties in New Hampshire. She was an accomplished and active *haiku* writer, and her husband was a scientist for a Dartmouth-related institution in New Hampshire. She told me that she and her husband had a very long acquaintance with a spiritual teacher in Japan, and he had just visited

America on a short trip. The day before he left, the last day he was staying in America, they were talking about American life with him. She mentioned my name to him as one of the Japanese she had met in America. Suddenly that teacher told her that the woman who she called Junko is an artist and that "God is painting through her." He saw my painting through psychic eyes. He said certain things about me and my art and my future, things my friend had never known. In those days, of course, there were no computer networks, no way of receiving any information about me. It all came as a complete surprise. My friend and her husband talked to each other about this all night, asking each other whether they should tell this to Junko. Finally they concluded that they should tell me because it might give me some encouragement. That is why she called and said, "If in any way you feel intruded upon or offended, please forgive us." It was serious and warm, straight and dignified talk. God made a telephone call at the last moment to detain me in life, I thought.

12   I decided to visit New Hampshire to see this couple and to listen to them talk about this spiritual teacher some more. I went to New Hampshire by Greyhound bus. At the dawn of the day of visiting the couple, in the hotel in New Hampshire by myself, I had a dream. This Japanese spiritual teacher appeared in my dream. "Is there anything you want to ask me?" he said, and questions rushed out of me like a flood. I asked them one by one. He answered them one by one but soon his figure started to fade away, and instead, white light appeared and surrounded me. Because of the dazzling light, I could not see anything. I was there in the light for a while. Then I woke up. I could not tell whether it was a dream or something else. A strong feeling that something extraordinary had happened came over me and the realization that I was not the same person I had been before this experience became clear to me. It was a far stronger experience than I had had many times in my life with the transparent cathedral.

13   In the meeting with my friends, I found out that this spiritual teacher was known to a certain circle of people in Japan for his extraordinary psychic and healing ability. He was a student and assistant of a well-known religious teacher whose religion was one of the many new postwar religions which sprung up like bamboo shoots after a storm in a bamboo forest. But the assistant had become extremely psychic after he went through severe disciplines and many miraculous phenomena occurred in his life. People whose family members were sick and dying invited him into their house, and that house would immediately be surrounded by a crowd. So many people who suffered with all kind of problems in life were cured and started new lives after they saw him. He was followed and surrounded day and night on the street by people who wanted to touch him in order to be cured from various sicknesses and sufferings. It became impossible for him to continue to stay in the religious institution as an assistant. Because he refused to accept any money for his work, he lost a place to live. Finally people who were saved by him stood up and made arrangements to form a corporate organization so he could survive. He had written more than a dozen books presenting his original thoughts and teachings of love, influenced by a mixture of Pure Land Buddhism, Shinto, and a touch of Christianity. But to my friends, the New Hampshire couple who had known him since he was young, he was more than anything a man of most profound love.

14   The strong feeling I had after the dream, that something extraordinary had happened, continued after the meeting with my friends. In a few days I started to realize that my psychic energy had become directed and confined to the activity of creating art as a constructive power instead of being scattered in dark and light areas of my life as before. That had been my lifelong complex problem. Now it was resolved in the way I supposed it should be. It was like adding to a house windows and doors that you can open and close for certain purposes and at certain times. Just a few weeks later I saw my art starting to change. Through the changes I realized the depth of my own art and the significance of the direction that my art was taking. I finally came to a thorough acceptance of my creativity as my destiny much more deeply than I ever had before. That led me to a deeper commitment to my art. And my doubts and desperation over my English writing and speaking ability were replaced with a commitment to do my best—as part of my deep commitment to my art.

15   I wrote a letter to this spiritual teacher in Japan. This was the first letter I wrote to express my deep gratitude that he appeared in my dream. I also thanked him for all he had done to help me clean up and rearrange my spiritual house while I was sleeping. His letter in response arrived exactly ten days after I sent my letter. It took five days by airmail one way, so his reply was awfully quick. It said that he was seeing light radiating from my art and added other strongly encouraging remarks.

16   My husband had committed to help me to be an active artist and to bring my work to the world, and he was assured and encouraged by this spiritual teacher's words. He approached a professional gallery with my work and the gallery agreed to arrange my first solo show for me. It was a gallery on Newbury Street, in Boston's fancy "arty" district. The show opened a few months after that spiritual teacher made contact with me.

17 After many years of hiding my art from other people's eyes, I saw people's reaction to my art for the first time. A young black man with lots of snow on his fur hat and his shoulders stood in front of one of my drawings titled "How much longer should I wait?" It was a drawing of a man in agony, standing in flames but with his feet rooted on the ground. That young man whispered to me, "How can you possibly know this feeling? I have lived all my life exactly in the feeling of this drawing." And one of my other drawings, of people holding onto a cliff and falling one by one into the abyss, a drawing titled (a horrendously long title) "How much farther should I keep falling down to the boundary that I will not be myself any more?" was sold to an Italian man who owned a barber shop in Boston. He told me, "I am a Barber in Siviglia!" humming Rossini's tune cheerfully and sweetly, when he talked to me at the opening. A few weeks later he came back and bought this drawing. "This is my drawing: it was created for me and I need to see it every day," he said. Now it was my turn to whisper in my mind, *How can you possibly know this feeling that I have had?* I had been stunned all through the show at seeing the deep mystery in people. And I felt that the viewers and I were connected to each other in a deep mysterious place. The show was very favorably reviewed in the *Boston Herald* and it opened the door to another show in New York the following year.

18   A few months later, my friend, the *haiku* writer who had introduced me to the spiritual teacher, told me a story about an old woman who happened to meet the teacher on the day before he was leaving America, the very same day my friend talked about me to the teacher. She was the wife of a successful retired businessman in Tokyo. When she and her husband got older, they decided to live with their son following the Japanese tradition. Their son and his family had been working for a respected institution in New Hampshire. She and her husband came to America to live with their son and his family in one house, located in very small Japanese community in New Hampshire. It literally created a hell. The old woman could not speak any English nor eat any American food. She had to live without any TV programs in the Japanese language and without any Japanese food store or restaurant, and learning to drive was out of the question. The daughter-in-law was overwhelmed by the enormous demands this woman created every single day, and those demands leaked out of their house to the whole small Japanese community and caused all kinds of troubles. Even her grandchildren, who could not communicate with her in English, called her "witch". When the people in the community found out that the spiritual teacher was visiting from Japan, they decided to bring this lady to him in order to ask him to shape her up.

19   My friend described the following scene: The old lady opened the door of the hotel room where the teacher was staying. The moment she came in, the teacher looked at her and his eyes filled with tears and he said, "You have suffered a lot!" The moment she saw his tears, she burst out crying. He knew all the turmoil she had gone through, he knew all her husband's betrayals and infidelities, he knew all the abortions she and the other women had to go through. He shed tears for her and with her for quite a while. And then when her crying subsided, he told her that a few days after he left to return to Japan she would have a little incident: "People might say that it is the beginning of the end of your life, but don't let them persuade you. It is the beginning of a new life that you will finally start and in which you will accomplish the particular mission that you came to America for. I will be with you in your mind and I will keep helping you." And it actually happened: a few days later she fell down the stairs in the house and broke her bones. After surgery she was taken to an old age home. Her "new life" began in a wheelchair in the old age home covered in the deep snow.

20 There she met so many old people who had unresolved problems. She did not understand one word of English and yet she deeply understood their sorrow, their anger, their desperation. As she sat in the wheelchair, she carried a big notepad on her lap on which phrases written in English with a big magic marker were on one side and on the reverse side were phrases written in Japanese by her son at her request. She managed all practical communication with that minimal number of words. But her understanding of their sufferings was so deep that she did not need English phrases for that. People started talking to her about their own lives, and she often cried with them as she was holding their hands. She started realizing that her own suffering in the past made her reach a special level of sensitivity and understanding of other people's sufferings and that the tremendous sufferings she had experienced worked, without wasting a single drop, as the biggest treasure for her to fulfill her mission. It did not only work as a tool:

unless her own despair had been this deep, her commitment to fulfilling her mission would not have been possible to begin with. Her son once asked her if she wanted to talk to the spiritual teacher in Japan once more—he was ready to arrange a telephone appointment. She seemed surprised to hear that and answered, "I see him here in my mind every single day and he talks to me all the time. That is why I can talk to anybody and understand everything. I am having pleasure here every day. Please don't take his time with such a thing as a telephone date. He needs all his time to save so many other people who are desperate like I used to be." Soon it was not only the old people: young nurses and even doctors wanted to talk with her about their lifelong unresolved problems. The people in the old age home became sweeter to each other, more cheerful, and even laughter filled the rooms more often. Soon people started saying, "An angel came down to our home." Much later, my friend, the *haiku* writer, told me that this lasted for two years until the old lady died peacefully.

21   "No matter how deep the sorrow is, if a person cries with her from the bottom of their heart, it will be resolved. Just one person is enough, even if he is a stranger; only one cry is enough if it is real." Suddenly those words that the skinny tall woman said to me many years before in Japan about the dead—when we were talking in the dark corner underneath the stairs of the stone church on the day of the funeral for a young bright bride of the dean—vividly came back to me. Those words were about the dead people who still clung to their own suffering and to the living people who seem to have caused it. Since then, thirteen years had passed. Now I realized that it did not matter if that person was dead or alive because we all do the same thing: we all stick to the suffering. And crying for them and with them works in the same way. When the suffering is finally resolved, the dead and the living both start to notice the sense of mission in their own lives, and quietly they flow into their own missions and start to accomplish the purposes for which they originally come to this earthly plane. And they gradually realize that the dark, harsh, painful sufferings they held onto for decades turn into precious treasures without which they would never be able to fulfill their missions—just as the old lady in New Hampshire realized. If she had never experienced those sufferings, how could she ever understand the suffering of the old residents and comfort them without any language skills? If the first wife of the dean who died in desperation and indignation, I murmured to myself as I became tangled up in the old memory, had encountered a person like this spiritual teacher, even long after her own death she would have resolved her dark, harsh sufferings and released her hands clinging to the young fourth bride of the dean, and that bride would not have died a tragic death. Furthermore, if the first wife was able to shift her attention to her own mission after having resolved her suffering, even long after her own death she might choose to celebrate and even from the different plane, to help the dean and his fourth wife have a good life together as part of her mission.

22   It was almost fourteen years since that woman tried to convince me of the empathy between the dead and the living, and I had finally come to the point of understanding and acceptance without any feeling of conflict. Probably there is empathy in people before they are born as well as after they die, and perhaps at a different level of consciousness there is empathy in us for trees and animals and rocks and water. This is not an 'expansion' of consciousness. It is more like lifting the heavy fence which has been placed between us and other lives in order to confine our attention only to the people who happen to exist within the short span of our lives on this little planet.

23　I thought about this story of the lady in New Hampshire over and over. We had all heard many stories about someone who was in a wheelchair who encountered a miracle healer, and after meeting the healer, walked back to his home leaving his wheelchair behind. In Japan, too, those stories were told throughout the land. But this story of the lady in New Hampshire was completely different—the opposite of those other stories, you might say. Before she met the teacher, she was in her late seventies. In those days she was considered old but not sick, in fact she was living in the room upstairs in her son's house, using the staircase every day. A few days after meeting this teacher, she became confined to a wheelchair. She hated to be in the English-speaking world, nor could she stand American food. Even though her family and community talked to her in Japanese, and cooked Japanese food for her as often as possible, her anger and hatred against the people around her became intolerable. After she met this teacher, she had to go and live in an institution where not only no one cared about her need for Japanese language and Japanese food—those issues did not even exist in people's minds there. Some people might say that you create the world around you as an exact duplicate of what you are thinking in your mind: if you hate something strongly you create a life full of the things you hate. But the truth was that when she came to the institution, she had already changed herself completely. She was happy and grateful there, and enthusiastically gave her love to everyone in that institution. A miracle had already happened. This is a different kind of miracle from the miracles I had heard of before. The spiritual teacher saw her sadness, her wounds, her rage, and her desperation, and he empathized deeply. But he did something more than that: he looked straight at her divine self, behind all the dark clouds. His belief that all people are divine at their core was so powerful that he did not have to preach about that to her. Instead, her divine self was pulled out in front, responding and resonating with his love. All the dark clouds that wrapped the radiating core melted away. That is love: to see the divine self in a person, and in yourself. Nothing could stop her divine self from doing its work anymore. When you are deeply loved, you start loving others. And that is the thing that looks upside-down to our eyes, as if all virtues in life are turned around: the most cruel suffering you experience turns into the most precious tool you use to help others. The most hideous person becomes a saint. In many religions we see this upside-down phenomenon. And that is what happened to the old lady in New Hampshire. That is the same kind of upside-down phenomenon that Shinran, the Pure Land Buddhist priest in 13th-century Japan, was talking about when he said: "Even the good can be saved, so needless to say, the evil will surely be saved."

24 My own encounter with this spiritual teacher was not as clear-cut as in the case of the old lady in New Hampshire. The teacher and I did not see each other in person, nor did we ever cry together. But the remarks he wrote to me—especially that he saw the light radiating from my artwork—had a deeper effect on me than anything else he could have done. My art had been a dark secret, buried under complicated layers of secrecy piled on top of each other. The images I had been creating on paper were dark and grotesque, harsh and destructive: I was afraid that some of those images might even be harmful to the viewer. Almost all the people who saw my art expressed some uneasiness, and some refused to glance at it a second time. But underneath the deep layers of secrecy, I believe that I was drawn into the light, which is described by a medieval mystic as "so brilliant that human beings would see it only as darkness." To reach this "dazzling divine darkness" was my unceasing craving. At the same time, this craving had been held inside me as the deepest secret—a secret even from myself. The spiritual teacher's comment about light radiating from my art was the last thing I expected to hear from anyone. If he had said such a thing to me on a less serious occasion, I would have said immediately that he was wrong. But when it was stated with such undoubted sincerity and as serious encouragement, I realized that this teacher was standing right on top of the pile of my secrets and intended to turn my deep self-doubt totally upside-down. I made a solemn decision to believe his remarks and I made a commitment to myself to live accordingly. From this commitment, I started to show my artworks to the world. Unless my art had something positive to give to society, why should I send it out into the world? Art can awaken people, art can warn people, art can be a remedy for society: how about light radiating through art? I had to send it out to the society. All my childhood nightmares came back: seeing the glorious, inflated egos of those talented musicians, seeing how they rushed into the quicksand and lost themselves, how they turned out to be empty shells or even evil. Once more my childhood fear of not being allowed to be honest came back and haunted me. But finally the shift was made: from having a suspicion that my work might be meaningless or even harmful to society to believing that it might have some positive meaning. It happened the same as with the old lady in New Hampshire: I, too, started a new life from that point on.

25 My anxiety around the secret was resolved after the positive communication I had with my art viewers, and with the newspaper art critic who wrote at some length about my darkness—and whose headline was, "It's the way of the Devil." But I can clearly say that even though the anxiety around the secrets was resolved, the mystery of art remains. The artist should not try to work to convince or comfort the viewer: even though the artist's intention is intense love for other human beings, the artist's first loyalty is to the Divine—not to the viewer. That is the biggest difference between art and all the different kinds of therapy, including spiritual religious guidance. The therapist goes with each stage of the client's growth process and takes responsibility for him at each step. But the artist should not. The secret can be explained and analyzed for the viewer without compromising his or her integrity of the experience. But the mystery should not be explained away. Otherwise we will receive only the shell of the mystery. The artist and the viewers both stand humbly—the viewers in front of the work and the artist behind it—and if the work is successful, both participate in the mystery together.

26 The spiritual teacher died in 1981. When I received the news of the teacher's death, I thought about what he once said in response to one of his young students who asked him when he was going to die: "Don't worry. I won't die until everyone who is in contact with me becomes strong and solid enough to fulfill their own mission without my help." When I heard that, I felt his love towards his student. He wanted to prepare even his own death to be a positive impetus for students to grow, and that was consistent with another remark he made: "Don't become my follower: surpass me, every day surpass me, otherwise this world will never become better." And those words of his worked on me, too. I found myself feeling stronger and more solid, and knew that I was on my way to fulfilling my own mission without him. Suddenly an image of the imaginary flower in an Indian fable, a white delicate flower called *udonge*, which opens only once every three-thousand years, appeared in my mind. Legend says that if you ever see this flower, your life changes forever; how it changes, it does not say. No one knows where to look for that flower; no one knows when it opens. I realized that I had seen the flower of *udonge*, a beautiful white flower in the dark valley when I lost my way in the faraway land for a long period of time, when I almost gave up the hope of going farther. I cannot prove that this extraordinary thing actually happened to me. I cannot prove that this flower I saw was a real *udonge*. I cannot prove my life changed because of this flower. But I know deep down that I saw it with my own eyes.

27 In his book, *The Varieties of Religious Experience* written in 1902, the American psychologist William James talks about *personal* religion. He contrasts it with *institutional* religion in which the theology and the ceremony and the ecclesiastical organization are the essentials. In contrast, personal religion is based on the relation that goes directly from heart to heart, from soul to soul, between man and the Divine. It has features of the strong mystical state of consciousness, and places the emphasis on the individual's first-hand experience in contrast to the 'second-hand' experience which is ingrained and sustained by tradition and habit in institutional religion. First-hand experience requires tremendous honesty and courage to trust in the Divine and in oneself. It requires the determination to fight against anything that prevents the process of pursuing one's own first-hand experience: against following the ideas of others; against the authority of dogma; against even one's own fear of facing the truth and the corruption of his own consciousness. Often people in this personal religion have a strong tendency to live in deep existential suffering and agony. Inner peace cannot be reached through a simple process of adding up the pluses and minuses in life, as institutional religious people seem to believe. In fact, James views the "plus" element in that algebra with suspicion. Instead, people who embrace a personal religion need to be 'twice born'. In the life of the twice-born, virtue is no longer calculated as if the usual algebraic sum of pluses and minuses gives the person's total worth. James did not use the exact phase 'upside-down', but I realized that he was talking about the same thing. The turning around, the turning upside-down, of virtues has to happen. Consciousness and awareness of your own desperation is required. James discussed concrete examples of individuals with personal religion. Among them were Tolstoy and George Fox, the founder of the Quaker religion. James described how these geniuses had all those qualities of personal religion, how to an extreme degree they both expressed their passion and devotion to the truth and suffered intense agony to find their way. He spoke of them with the highest understanding and admiration. He viewed this personal religion as the experience most deeply rooted in the essence of religion. And he added that there are some people who must have this twice-born experience in order to continue living. When

I read these words, I said to myself: "This is it—I am one of them, one of those *some people*, no matter how small-scale I am. No matter how miserably I have just struggled to arrive at this point, this is my way." The spiritual teacher who helped me and the old lady in New Hampshire who was helped by him had both gone through this experience too. Now I understood clearly that this was the reason I had to leave the church where I was called a "bride of the church," and this was the reason that I heard the voice saying that I would pursue my aspiration towards God in my own way—the voice which came from the transparent cathedral rising up in the narrow rift which opened between two eaves that almost overlapped in the winter sky. I also realized that my art stemmed from the exact same root as this personal religion, from the radical upside-down root which spreads its branches deep down into the ground instead of into the sky.

28 My mother visited from Japan to see my works at a gallery in New York. It was the first time I had seen her after many years since I had come to America. She exclaimed in a whisper in front of one of my works, "So you remember the masterpiece in the Motoyasu mansion. You re-created it!" One of my works in the show consisted of three panels. It looked like a Japanese *Byoobu*—a Japanese partition. Was it those panels that my mother was talking about? But if so, it could look like a triptych of medieval or Renaissance artists who used the same kind of panels. It was the final work in a long series of dead flower drawings. It was born in that special state of consciousness, that deep psychic state of mind which I finally reached after years of staring at dead flowers and drawing countless studies of them. It was drawn with a fine-point pen, its thousands and thousands of strokes created a cloud-like effect on paper, and its delicate gradation came very much from studying the 16th-century German artist Altdorfer's drawings. When I strongly denied her idea to her, she pulled my hand and said, "But if you step back like this, see, you will see exactly that masterpiece, exactly the way I remember it." My heart darkened. Doesn't she know that I had gone through a long journey by myself in order to avoid slipping into the world of Japanese tradition? Now she was celebrating me because she thought I had re-created the masterpiece of the Edo period that hung in the mansion of Motoyasu, the source of traditional authority in her mind, believing that her remarks should make me happy. Didn't my mother remember that her words cast a curse on my life many years ago? Her words forced me to choose between the two: between being accepted by my mother but killing my own soul, or going alone with my own soul on my own severe journey. I chose to go with my own soul, which included creating revolutionary work of my own. Certainly not re-creating the old Edo period masterpiece. Is that why my heart sank? Was it because my 'vengeful triumph' over her by having the show was not quite realized in the way I had hoped? I realized I still had unresolved anger towards her whirlpooling in my depths. *I have started a new life now, and I have a lot of homework to do,* I thought.

29   In 1978, a Japanese master artist, Ichiro Fukuzawa, received a medal from the Emperor for the contribution that he made to the development of Western art in Japan. He was famous for having brought the new art form of surrealism to Japan with his avant-garde works when he returned from France in 1931, where he had studied for nine years. In 1924, when he went to Paris, Andre Breton had just made his declaration of "surrealism". Master Fukuzawa found in surrealism the springboard he needed to free himself from the bonds of realism. He created works under the influence of Ernst and de Chirico, but because he believed that the artist needed to have strong autonomy, he did not accept the idea that the unconscious invades art automatically, and this was the essential credo of surrealism. He was outrageously 'different' in Japanese eyes at that time. And under the Japanese fascist government, notorious for its horrifying judicial system, he was arrested and imprisoned under the charge of being a Communist and of refusing to stop painting in this new style. Ironically he never was a true surrealist or a Communist, but in a completely different way, which people could not see at that time, he was in fact much more dangerous to the Japanese system than the surrealism they accused him of, if only they could have recognized the essence of his work. He was a vital humanistic artist who believed in freedom and individuality. His humanism manifested itself in his mind as a burning desire to tell human dramas: the inner experiences of human beings. He was aware for a long time that modern art had forsaken human narrative and that he was working for its recovery. His humanism went beyond the sarcasm of postmodern art, which is the direction the West took.

30   He was one of the very few who established the tradition of cultural humanism in Japan, which survived throughout history but at a high cost: the persecution was severe. My grandparents and my mysterious priest friend were part of it in spirit, and my former father-in-law and the father of my Communist leader friend paid a severe price for it in jail. All of them were born in the Meiji period and exposed to the West in some form or another. They were all transformed by the power of humanism, and they kept that torch burning in the isolated and barren land of Japan by believing in themselves and being honest to their center. The passion for human existence and vitality they got from the West kept renewing them. My mother visited this artist and arranged for me to visit him in his studio.

31 His huge series of works after Dante's *Divine Comedy*, still wet, were radiating in his *atelier* when I visited him in a suburb of Tokyo for the first time, carrying with me from America a few small collages. He was eighty years old at that time, still actively producing a tremendous amount of work. It was a brilliant, dignified Meiji man, standing straight, wearing a sophisticated, subtly colored tie in the French taste, having just changed out of his studio clothes, who received me. Responding to my tense greeting, he smiled and said, "I have been doing only the things I've wanted to do in my life, but this funny nation of ours has been busy putting me in a pigsty for it and sometimes giving me a medal for it." He was imprisoned when I was just two years old and since then he had been fighting all alone for his artistic integrity. He was famous for not belonging to any group or movement. He had been an outsider until he was decorated at the age of eighty. He stared at the work of mine that I had brought to him and said—groaned—"This is real. You have educated yourself. Many artists go to art school and all become funny. You have done it by yourself, which is what an artist must do. There must be a person who sees this and realizes the meaning of it in the world: he has to help you. I don't have the power to bring this to the world but I can do that in Japan." He immediately arranged a one-person show for me and arranged all the publicity and promotional opportunities for me. Right in front of me, the moment he saw my works, he picked up the phone and did it all. He saw the same torch that those fighters had been carrying in my works—those humble, still dark, almost gruesome works. One year later, the show materialized. It was my first one-person show in Japan after nine years in America: my works were exhibited in Tokyo and the show traveled to Osaka.

32   Many people came to my opening, some carrying big shopping bags with them, many carrying briefcases after the long business day. Most of them held the article clipped from the newspaper that was written after a five-hour interview with me, which the editor, our family friend, arranged for me. He said, "The decorated master has taken care of the art world; let me handle the social journalistic part." The gallery was filled with enthusiasm. During the shows in both Tokyo and Osaka, many viewers waited in line to talk to me. The majority of them were women. I immediately noticed that almost everyone wanted to talk about their own lives, their own sufferings, their struggles. Their need to be understood, each as an individual person, was deep and urgent. Their frustration pointed to many cultural issues, and gender issues, in Japan, where men and women lived in two separate worlds and did not understand, respect, or love each other. Those viewers saw and understood my art as an expression of, or result of, my struggle towards individuation and self-actualization—even though no one used that specific language directly. But they did use those words as purely artistic, stylistic terms. It was surprising to me that the culture I had to leave in order to become myself could understand my art so well. But the truth is that if I had not left Japan, I could not have reached this level of expression.

33 After the opening day, a young man pulled a chair in front of one of my works, "Mandala", and started meditating. He repeated his meditation for several days. One evening I received a call from an inpatient of a psychiatric institution saying that she was not allowed to go out so she could not visit my show, but the newspaper's interview became the hope of her life because she learned that from the darkest abyss one can still come out of it and became an artist like this. The dark memory of stormy nights in my childhood tuberculosis days, my premonition of standing in the very narrow alley between the so-called normal world and the so-called abnormal world for the rest of my life, was affirmed. And the decision I made when I read *Jane Eyre* when I was fourteen years old, that I would not escape too far into either world, flashed back strongly. For many years since those times I had paid attention to this issue seriously: 'art and abnormal psychology', you might call it. But I did not talk about this issue during the five-hour interview for the article in the paper that she read. Yet she seems to have realized that I was willing to stand in this narrow alley, or otherwise she would not have called. I could not do much for her, but the fact that my art, or the discussion of my art in this case, attracted a person who had been in a dark abyss moved me deeply. It reminded me that we are standing together in the deep mystery of life—both so-called normal life and abnormal life. Both lives are much deeper and wider than people usually assume. This kind of experience has continued in all my shows for many years now.

34 A man walked into the gallery whom I recognized instantly. He was well built, still slender, and his hair that I once thought looked like a jellyfish was not as fluffy as it once was but it was still there. My math teacher was looking straight at me and smiled. It was as if we were continuing our conversation from yesterday—natural and pleasurable. Responding to his cheerful congratulations for my show, I expressed my congratulations to him: I had read a big article in the international edition of the Japanese nationwide newspaper about him some time before in America. He had been chosen to be the principal of the school where he was teaching and where I was a student. In that role he had opened a new school in France to address the complex needs of many Japanese businessmen's children in that foreign land. The newspaper was saying that thanks to my math teacher's approach, Japanese traditional education and international sensitivity had reached a higher level of integrity. It was a new revolutionary approach that Japan had never taken—and it was successful. He replied to my congratulations saying, "I thought you would be the only person in the world who would give me condolences instead of congratulations." It was just like him, I thought: he could make fun of himself.

35 But I understood what he meant very well and my heart was warmed that he mentioned me that way. In order to achieve this institutional accomplishment, he had to cut many aspects of himself. His love for Rilke, to which he introduced me, and his own poetry, which he was writing while I was with him, must have been two of the aspects he had to cut. And his grief, which no one he shared with him, remained. My heart was warmed that he thought about me as the only person who might express sympathy for his grief. I smiled at him. But the fact that he had grief showed that he had still not lost those qualities: they must have poured into his work as an educator. Just as he had a deep influence in my life by respecting his and my inner world, he must have given something precious to many students who were having hard lives in that foreign land. I did not throw away my own encounter with Rilke, even though the heavenly cathedral from which

Rilke spoke to me had almost been destroyed once and for a long period after. But now it had come back and was rooted deeper and stronger in me than ever. Does he see it in my artworks? I was so grateful to my math teacher and seeing how he had grown so magnificently, I experienced enormous pleasure. With that pleasure, one part of my life quietly closed.

36 It was near closing time in the gallery in Osaka when a man came into the gallery flaunting a long black robe with scarlet stripes. He introduced himself as the son of my mysterious priest friend and as the abbot of Kobe Abbey. He told me that he had come on behalf of his late father, thinking how much he would have wanted to see me on this important occasion of mine if he were alive. Tears rushed to my eyes out of affection to my 'friend' and I was moved and honored by his son's sensitivity to it.

37 After that day, warm letters were exchanged between the abbot and me for some years until I received a printed letter from his monastery telling me of his sudden death by heart attack and that the mass the monastery conducted for him had been performed. I had no one to share my affection for my friend with anymore. Is it too much of an indulgence to let my imagination go so far as to say that I wonder sometimes whether my priest friend was a son of my great-grandfather, the proud aristocrat, the superb calligrapher, and a geisha? Isn't it possible that because of the strict taboo against mixing the two worlds, the world of sensuality and the world of family honor in Japanese culture, he never identified himself? Identifying himself would be a demand for respect as a member of the Motoyasu, and at the same time would automatically degrade its name by his birth. He remained an outsider all his life, and from there he exerted an enormous influence on the mind of the Motoyasu. He was an outsider not only as a family member, but also as a Christian: he did not have his own church. He lived among condemned criminals and juvenile delinquents most of his life.

38   Did he know that they who gathered in his hut could not have done anything that I had not myself almost done or contemplated doing, and yet some thin line prevented me from doing it—almost by accident? Did he know that my desperation was as dark as theirs? It was, not because I too had become an 'ex-convict', a woman who divorced in that society, but because I was born with a mind that could not take any idea as a given—because I had to go deeply into my own inner world, and as an individual listen to God, and I had to do what I believed in strongly even if it required me to go against the whole tradition, against the way it should be even if it hurt good, serious people and violently slashed their lives. God was away at the furthest edge of the universe, further than at any time in my life. I had lost Him when I was "the bride of the church," as I was called when I lived in the peaceful home in the churchyard. The yard was covered with delicate flowers that my husband planted to make his teenage bride happy. I worked for the church day and night, taking care of my aged parents-in-law who had healed my wounds with their deep love towards me. "My friend" had honored our friendship in the noblest way that I can think of. And now, even after his death, he sent me his proud son, who chose the opposite way of his father, the more mainstream path in this world, the more traditional way, the more glorious way, as abbot of the Abbey, to celebrate the start of my new life. This was a celebration I had wanted to share with my 'friend', with the deepest gratitude towards him.

39 This was the trip that made my parents realize that their view of me up to that point had been inaccurate and inappropriate. They recognized what kind of artist their daughter Junko had become and was still longing to become, and they felt genuine respect for it. They said my husband saw something which they did not see in their Junko, and that they saw that he had been greatly supportive of her creating art and bringing it to the world. They told me that they could not sleep with their feet toward my husband ever again—a Japanese expression of deep respect. My mother told me that my father saw his idealized self in my husband: he said to my mother that he realized that the idealized man he wanted to be all through his youth was a man just like my husband. He said he had failed to become that man, but Junko had found him and married him so he was deeply happy. It sounds somehow a little weird, but it is true that I have seen a strong resemblance in both men. My husband's affection—towards dogs, other animals, even lizards—reminded me of my father's unconditional love and strong sense of responsibility towards my Q, which saved me from falling into an abyss of depression at losing Q. Both of them showed soul-to-soul sincerity, and respect towards every living soul. In my father, this unconditional commitment towards life was manifested in his being a doctor, and gave him tremendous energy to help so many who were injured in the disaster of the war. My husband and I were happily together with my parents for the first time after my marriage. I enjoyed Japan. We visited many shrines and many ancient temples and we experienced incredibly sublime nature in Japan. This trip to Japan deepened and widened my husband's view of the world drastically—and it was while we were in Japan that my husband decided to leave the computer field and become a lawyer. He saw computers as a technical enterprise which fascinated him, as a branch of speculative philosophy he wanted to pursue, but he saw law as a helping profession. This was a theme which he and I kept thinking about together, and discussing together since we got married, and now he had come to the conclusion that he was going to be a lawyer—because he believed that law was a more direct way for him to help people.

40 My husband had almost finished law school by that time. While he was running his own artificial intelligence company, at the same time he also kept going to law school. He often rushed to the school from the airport the moment he arrived from his business trip to be on time for some examination. He finished law school, finished up his business contracts, and closed his office. We decided to move to California, to open his new private law office in Los Angeles. He passed the Bar exam in California, and we were set to begin a new life. We decided to use this time for crossing the continent by car, so that we would have plenty of time to be together and talk a lot. I put some of my new works into two metal cases we rented from the moving company: one case was for sending to California with the moving company and the other I attached to the roof of our big Buick. We wanted to carry at least one case ourselves to avoid the risk of losing all of my works. We started to drive on a snowy day in December. It was our own covered wagon journey, like those that pioneers took more than 100 years earlier when they moved west for a new life. We shared the same hopes and the same fears, and journeyed with the same courage and prayers that they must have had. The Grand Canyon, the Rocky Mountains, the snow country—we passed through them all.

When we finally arrived in Los Angeles, suddenly the sky was blue. In Beverly Hills, between tall palm trees on both sides of the street, gold poles were set like an arch. And on top of those poles were reindeer and Santa Claus in red clothes shining, reflecting the bright sunlight, racing even higher into the bright blue sky in the mid-day's dazzling light. Here, I thought, you can do anything, any shameful thing, any shocking thing! Nothing surprises, nor offends people! I felt deep relief. I could start a new life here and I would start a new kind of art. We moved into a new condominium in Santa Monica, and we set up the sunny upstairs master bedroom as my studio. My husband rented an office independently for his new practice in the big Beverly Hills office building where his elder brother had his own law office. There was none of the feeling of hippies or even students that surrounded us when we were in Boston. My husband and I both started a new life with great intensity.

41 My husband's elder brother and his wife, my new brother-in- law and sister-in-law, welcomed us with a big party. It was not planned as a welcome party for us, but happened to be a gathering they hosted regularly in their living room. It was a vast living room in their big residence, covered with white carpet, which made me somehow nervous even though my shoes were perfectly clean and shining. Many chairs were circled against the walls in the beautifully, professionally decorated room. One by one or in small groups, family friends came in and gathered with drinks in their hands. Against the high fireplace, my mother-in-law was sitting with a full smile. When I approached, she stood up with both arms fully opened to hug me. "Oh, Junko darling, I am so happy you came!" We had met already before this event, but today was her special day, I knew. More than seventy friends were gathered to read Shakespeare aloud and tonight's program was *The Tempest*. My mother-in-law was a theatrical acting major while attending university and she won many contests, a sort of semiprofessional actress on stage, so this was her stage, and she was extremely happy and excited. And one of her sons was a professional actor in the theater, so they got together to produce this project. "Sit here, Junko darling." She pointed to the chari next to her. "Yes, Ema," I answered, using the Hebrew word for "mother' as I was told to do. Everyone sitting in a chair read one line, with no formal casting. Some were good and some were not; my husband was superb. For me, following where they were reading was the best I could do. I saw some lines:

> Sir, he may live; / I saw him beat the surges under him / And ride upon their backs; he trod the water / Whose enmity he flung aside, and breasted / The surge most swollen that met him; his bold head / 'bove the contentious waves he kept, and oared / Himself with his good arms in lusty stroke / To the shore...

What an image! Isn't it about life itself, struggling with the surges, fighting with obstacles and new things one after another? What is the surge, which wanted to struggle with a human? What a difference between this image and the image of my dysfunctional boat, showing the red inside of its body and barely arriving on the shore of Yokohama.

42   I passed up my turn. No one cared. Many did not even notice. *I wish this were a gathering to read Kokinshu,* I was thinking vacantly. That is an anthology of Japanese poetry, compiled by imperial order in the 10th century. I can recite many of those poems with the special ancient melody and rhythm in the way it had been done throughout history. My father trained me when I was in elementary school. I did not know that it was a special skill until I found that even many Japanese literature professors cannot recite in that way. It was the 10th century and Shakespeare was 17th century, so it cannot be so impossibly difficult. Someday I wanted to join this group. I was somehow daydreaming. The night became deep. Reading was over. My brother-in-law and beautiful sister-in-law were talking to everybody, introducing friends to friends, sweetly and with dignity. *What an elegant host and hostess they are! I have so many things to observe, learn, and master* here, I thought.

43   Within a few days, my mother-in-law called me to attend a luncheon garden party at the synagogue. She wanted to introduce me to her late husband's congregation. A young rabbi was talking to the congregation from some high spot in the garden. I could not hear well but I caught some words: "From now on, more and more, the mixed racial marriage will be increased." The audience reaction was negative: I heard some booing. After lunch, my mother-in-law put her arm around my waist, and walked around, and said to many people one by one, "This is my daughter-in-law Junko." Some warmly smiled and shook hands, some nodded with stiffened faces. I said to myself, "I have to think, truly think, about Judaism, and I have to become clear about my own religious belief and how to present it to the world." That evening, I asked my husband, "What will Judaism contribute to the 21st century?" He responded, "I was waiting for a person who would ask me that kind of question. I will write a book and the answer to that question will be in that book. Wait for me."

CHAPTER 15

1 Throughout the seven years that we lived in Santa Monica, my husband and I could barely wait for the weekends when we could drive through Topanga Canyon. Driving up the Coast Highway, the ocean on our left, just a 20-minute drive, we would turn into the Canyon and find our different world. The sunlight was reflected in the leaves of every tree, and we were wrapped in the light which filled the whole mountain. Sometimes the Canyon was covered with a deep fog; huge rocks suddenly jutting towards eaven loomed into view in our car window and then walls of rock striped with fossils came quietly into view. Our driving escalated; we added some of the weekday evenings. We talked and talked to each other and sometimes kept a long silence in our dark car staring at the winding road emerging ahead of us in the headlights. Topanga Canyon had become for us a source of strength. When our life demands expanded because more large works were created and more and more people were invited, our Santa Monica condominium became too small to handle it all and we had to move. The idea of moving to Topanga did not even float up into our heads at first. Pilgrims, no matter how passionately they seek out the holy land, would never dream of lugging all their personal possessions into that sacred spot and sitting there for the rest of their lives. The same psychology was at work here. But finally we decided to move into this "sacred land" and make an ideal studio for me there.

2   The first night in our new place, we were awakened by the sound of sirens. We heard one siren at first, but then we heard what sounded like a dozen patrol cars following it. We jumped up and stuck our bodies out of the wide-open window of our third-floor bedroom. The ocean of trees spread gently under the moonlight down the slope into the valley below. It was from that valley that the strange siren sounds were coming. We listened carefully and realized that sound was the howling of coyotes. Each time one howling rose up, it drew out other howling and there was a chain reaction. Quickly the voices of the coyotes filled the entire mountain. And again, suddenly, quietness fell.

3   The next-door neighbors gave a welcome party for us, and invited everyone who lived on the block. The conversation flowed and we talked about animals. Every one of the neighbors had some animal story to tell. One woman said mountain lions had showed up on her property a few days earlier. "Mountain lions! Are you sure?" I exclaimed. "Yes, I'm sure, I saw their footprints. At night our horses started making strange cries and they would not quiet down, and I found mountain lions' footprints scattered all around." The conversation turned to the brush fires in those mountains 15 or 16 years earlier. "The fire spread right into this Canyon: the wild flames came just over to there, but suddenly the wind changed direction and the fire stopped abruptly." The neighbor pointed through the picture windows to the hollow in the mountain ridge where the sun comes up. "Just like the Indian legends say, this mountain is protected," someone added. But Nature started showing us its real face every day. It created emergency situations each day as if to say, "Take that! And take that!"

To begin with, a huge dead pine tree had to be cut down immediately because it was about to fall on our house. And it drew me out of my "ideal studio" and made me deal with construction people. And as if that were not enough, a huge mountain fire actually came over the hill and close to our house, and we had to evacuate twice, carrying my artworks with us. But this is the place where finally the decision I made a decade before became concrete reality, that I would "put my roots down in America" and build up my life in this place. I became a permanent resident with a green card and then, married to an American citizen, I was given the opportunity to become a citizen: I went through a process of study and testing, gave up my Japanese citizenship, and became a US citizen. I set up my office in another room of our house, and hired a full-time executive assistant. I organized all my works and slides into big, heavy binders: some held my studio diaries, some held my sketches and slides of my works; other binders held my essays and writings about my philosophy of art. With my assistant's help, I applied to many contests in various states and many of my works earned me opportunities to show in galleries and museums. I won first prize in a contest at New York University, mounted a big one-person show at a gallery in SoHo, and received a Distinguished Woman Artist award from a California museum. Sending my art out into the world so that it would remain after my life was over had now become a serious task.

4 A long time ago, when I came to America for the first time, while I was auditing classes at the school for the ministry, I watched mock psychotherapy sessions that were conducted in one of the seminars. They were held at a dark stone church built in the medieval style in

San Francisco, and led by a professor in a tweed jacket who was holding a pipe and cleaning it all the time. I wanted to play the client role, rather than just being in the audience. To be more precise, I actually wanted to be a client. I was fascinated to see that someone's real life was used as a sort of textbook for us to examine, to think about and discuss and learn from. And actual people were showing us how they had been dealing with the materials of life—the everyday things that happen, the incidents we all have to deal with—and showing us how they made decisions about big things like marriages, divorce, and having babies. In short, the course was about the question, 'What is your system of values?' We need a system of human values to which we can turn to make decisions. Is that something religion provides to us? Do they—I was thinking about the people in that ministry school—follow the system of values that already existed? Is that why they came to this school? Is it written on paper for them? Do they use what is written down as a manual? And then there was a more delicate issue: how do we relate to the Divine? (Because it was a graduate university for the ministry, that must be especially significant.) How did their lives turn out after the decisions they made with those life materials? How did their system of values work? These were exactly the things I wanted to know. When I had a friend in the ministry school, "a woman of divorce" as my former husband called her, these were the questions I wanted to ask her. But my English was too undeveloped at that time to even form these questions. Even if she had answered, I would not have understood. For myself, I do not have any written manual for my life—nor for my art—to follow blindly. How my inner voice or my inner images reach me and help me decide how to handle outside life materials was the only thing I was absolutely serious about. But I have always wanted to understand my own life: where am I standing? How am I doing with all of my own materials?

5 Are we so frightened to see reality? I remember that being honest was considered one of most serious issues in the therapy. In order to avoid confronting the painful reality, don't we press the lid closed and cover things up with a pretty surface, and try to live in a false peace in the relationship with a married partner, with friends, and most of all with ourselves? The society which does not encourage its members to confront the truth is frightening. The society that requires a pretty, superficial covering lid, in the name of 'harmony', is frightening. Thus, in Japan, insider informers, and victims of bullying including students who received corporal punishment, were all forced into silence, and often ended up in suicide. Integrity and honesty have to be manifested in the individual life and in society. Deeper analysis of what really motivates you to stay in dishonesty is crucial. No matter how painful it may appear, without trying to find an easy way out, psychotherapy is a way to make you confront the truth. Psychotherapy is the constant, ongoing process of following the truth: no matter what happened you should never try to manipulate the truth. Finding the truth is what I had been trying to do throughout my life. Someday I wanted to go into therapy and see with my own eyes what things really look like under the sun, things that I had been dealing with myself, in the dark.

6 But I was fully aware that this required a very high level of language skill and sensitivity. In fact, the practice of therapy itself is based on the belief in the power of language. It came out of a long tradition of religious confession, I believe. The skillful use of language is related to religious authority, and related to the whole Western history of thought. After fifteen years or so had passed since I saw it in the ministry school, I felt that the time had come: now I had to start psychotherapy. My father had just died and my mother had just suffered a stroke. Japan, which had looked like a still solid rock and an inexhaustible source of safety and mutual affection for me, was now swaying. I made a call to a psychologist, who came highly recommended by an American friend I trusted, to set up the first appointment with her. An intelligent, warm, sincere voice responded. After I introduced myself, she said, "I am not unfamiliar with your country and culture. I lived for a while in Okinawa and we will have no problem of any communication gap in the first step. My office is in a building which has a Korean restaurant on the street level. You will have no problem finding it."

7   It was a Japanese restaurant instead of a Korean one. "She is an American woman, so I should not judge harshly. The important thing is that she has enough flexibility of mind to throw away her identity as a woman who knows Japanese culture, and if she can see me as a primary experience, not as a *Japanese* woman, and go straight into the core of the matter. I have to speak to her entirely in English. It will be hard work, but it is crucial to learn how to talk to someone whether or not he or she actually knows Japanese culture. It requires me to deal with my own prejudice, too."

8   It was a sunny clean office—it did not look like a medieval style church at all—and she was dressed in a rather fashionable cream-color suit and high-heeled shoes, with not a tweed jacket or a pipe in sight. It did not have the atmosphere of an alchemy laboratory at all. During the fifteen years since I had my first glimpse of it, psychotherapy had changed in America. And so had I. I liked her and respected her immediately. We had deep, serious, intelligent sessions weekly for many years to come. During those sessions I learned with astonishment and deep remorse that I had covered up and hidden many truths without confronting them in my life. In spite of my big efforts toward extreme honesty throughout my life, this process of revealing hidden truths to myself, one by one, was painful, but at the same time I felt a quiet pleasure at finding the way to the truth. And I also learned the deepest power of language: it could be intrusive, which is inevitable in therapy, and yet respectful; severe and yet most loving; vulnerable and yet safe. The person who has reached a strong individuality talks in this language, and this language creates true harmony between speaker and listener, between individual and community. It is entirely the opposite of the 'harmony' created by covering up and pressing the lid, for gaining power, for keeping loyalty to your group, your institution, or your tribe.

9   One bright sunny day in a beach town in California, I bought in a junk store the ugliest thing I had ever laid eyes on. It was a handmade arch-shaped object about one foot high. On the top and both sides, stuck into it were roses made of tin, whose ugly pink had turned into the color of rotten meat through age and the accumulation of dust; and equally ugly leaves also made of tin were sticking out from the arch. So it became clear that the whole thing was meant to be a tree of roses. But whatever it was, the main theme of this weird object was the bird that hung inside the arched tree, supported on both sides by wires running to the arch. Here was a bird which seemed to have been made of plaster, engraved by some sharp instrument to make it look like the surface was feathered (and apparently this effort failed), and painted dark green, almost black, like a burned chicken just come out of the oven. And there was no head for this bird. When I looked at the part of the neck where the head should be, I saw a glass bottle buried inside of the bird. This was a wine decanter! But instead of wine, packed with darkness up to his neck, this bird was round and swollen. The wire which supported the bird was actually stuck into both sides of his fat belly, so that the bird could turn his neck down when you wanted to pour wine from this decanter. And in fact right under him, there was a slight shallow hole made by the cap of a mayonnaise jar buried face up in order to hold a wine glass.

10 It was a coarse, ugly object from every conceivable aspect, however, one thing hit me deeply. There was a subtle tone of yellow, which was the background of the arched rose tree, and it was obviously made from the flat bottom of a bucket, which was cut in half in order to fit inside the arch. On its tin surface was a cheap amateur painting of a house and a few trees. Behind the house and trees was what must have been intended as the sky, but it was painted yellow. It is a most unusual phenomenon for yellow to recede into the background so quietly: wasn't it like a halo for the bird? But of course, it was just the ugly color of the gray tin appearing underneath and through the yellow. And the paint was aged, covered with dust, so the yellow had lost its glittery quality and gained a special subtle tone. The shape of the half circle looked like a celestial chart with some circled lines on it, which came from the grooves of the bottom of the bucket, and looked like the orbits of the planets on a chart. Because of this yellow background, this bird, ugly as it was, had gained a profoundly tragic tone, standing solemnly in the eternal light, embracing unfathomable sorrow in his fat belly. The old man in the store, seeing me paying attention to this object, said it was made as a wedding gift. If I dusted it or wash it, it would come back to its original bright colors. Unfortunately, he said, the cap, which was the chopped bird's head itself, was missing: because of that, he would sell it to me at a discount.

11 A half century had passed since I witnessed the execution of a bird in my faraway homeland during the war. I reencountered him today, in this sick shape, under the bright sky, in a beach town in California. When I set it down in my studio, though, the whole studio seemed to darken slightly.

12 The bird represents freedom, aspiration, and transcendence. This bird was created to fly and be free. It had been slaughtered not for anything it had done, but because of what it was. I saw it as a punishment: a cruel and unjustified execution. I was overcome by a phobia of birds of all kinds for nearly fifty years. Later on, the many experiences I had of abuse of authority, of violence against the individual, of the taboo against being who you are, became part of this experience. My journey towards freedom and individuation became a struggle against this phobia.

13 Another old terror came back: the terror of the Japanese fascist government authority that we lived with all through the war. I was afraid of our neighbors because we were all forced to spy on each other. As little as I was, I saw very clearly the essence of totalitarianism without any intellectual knowledge of it whatsoever. It is the hatred and destruction of freedom. By commanding blind obedience to an irrational authority and through torture and execution, it accomplished its goal. All through my short life until the end of that period, I was in terror of revealing who I was. The slaughtered bird crystallized this terror for me instantly. When my uncle killed a beautiful bird, my whole terror of fascism took on a most realistic material form.

14 It started the 26th day of May, 1991. After two weeks of intense reading of my diary and notes going back ten years, I was emotionally ready to go deeper. With bursts of crying in my chest, I entered the studio in the morning. Just like a flood, art rushed in to me. I was crying in my mind. It rushed at me so fast, my hand couldn't catch up with it. I heard my own loud crying voice burst and it echoed in my bones, and yet my horror and pain were circling wildly as if it were joy. All at once the first six works were completed on the Arches paper in my studio, painted with acrylic.

15 My altered state of consciousness ran deep. When I came up to work No. 22, the red roses I was already painting next to the bird in work No. 20 presented themselves to me as stained glass, and all of a sudden I realized that this bird was in a cathedral and that by painting this work I was singing a requiem for him. *This whole series of works is a requiem for the Bird! This is a requiem for the executed Bird!* It was June 16th. Until then, I did not even know the meaning of this series. One image after another, the Bird loomed up from the depths in the painful figures. However I tried to comfort him, with red roses, the Bird showed his most helpless figure. *Oh God! Only you can comfort him!* One after another, the cry came up from the depths. *This is a requiem for my Bird!*

16 "With tears of gratitude, I am writing this," I wrote in my studio diary. My hands were trembling. Works 24, 25, 26, 27, 28, were born so quickly. God responded to my prayer. He let me work through this. I felt I was rewarded for all the suffering I had undergone. The violent tone is fading and a glorious gold tone appeared. "Transcending has just started," I thought. For the first time I added Japanese letters on the artwork. "The bird is dying," I wrote, and then my hand started writing on a piece of paper on the floor nearby. This time I wrote: "The Bird is dying. The Bird is dying. The helpless Bird, the wings that are made to fly into the expanse of the sky, are bent down and hang down powerlessly. The feathers are stained with blood and tremble. The Bird is dying. Being executed, deprived of freedom, wailing, weeping; the world is listening. The world cries bitterly. The Bird is executed. The Bird who wanted to fly to the broad sky of freedom has been executed...However decorated with red roses, however lamented with the melody of crying, the Bird is in pain. The world continues to sing this pain, forever singing this pain. The Bird is executed. The Bird who wanted to fly to the broad sky of freedom, has been executed."

17 Suddenly my consciousness level shifted down even deeper: I could not breathe well. With every breath I am saying "whhhhh" and I was pulled into a darkness darker than any darkness I ever experienced. I felt that an unknown, urgent danger to my psyche lay ahead of me and the floor swayed. It was like quicksand: if I stepped in once I would be sucked into this abyss. I saw the unfathomable abyss under the floor, which was already sharply slanting towards the depths. I would never come back and continue life as normal person, but even if I would not come back, still I might be able to see and paint what I experienced in the bottom of the abyss. Am I afraid to be insane, and running away from this incredible opportunity? I was tempted and yet I was struck by terror.

18 A strange vibration came into my head. *Don't be afraid of this melody. Draw this melody which rises up; bring these words singing into the light. Then you will know that this darkness is the light. Light is gushing up everywhere, Light is gushing up everywhere.*—I wrote in my studio diary: "What a freedom I feel now. I am singing the requiem for my wounded ego which was filled with pain and fear, and You are celebrating me, a newly born me. I am writing this with deepest gratitude." Two new circles almost appeared on the artwork.

19 The work continued for the next two weeks. Many circles and half-circles appeared: some were swinging, some were standing high. A circle was completed with quiet dignity and the Bird exists in that circle. "His feathers are now spotted with gold, not red: golden air, golden space, and he exists there, He is finally free. The transcending process has happened and is almost completed."

20 I felt my mind was so empty. I realized this series was coming to an end. I thought it had ended yet still I felt something—not emotional, something different from the earlier feelings that I had. So I thought I had to paint one more. I went to Sycamore Beach. Sycamore Beach is in a state park where you have to pay to get in. It is quieter than other beaches along the Pacific Coast Highway. Being afraid that a sudden change of scenery might make my altered state of consciousness fade away, I walked on the sand as if I were carrying my body in a big container filled with liquid up to its brim, being careful not to spill even one drop from it. The sea looked different from the way I saw it in everyday consciousness. It was vivid: every edge of each wave looked sharp and bright. The sound of the waves rising far away from the beach reached my ears with clarity. The light dancing on the top of each wave, which moved constantly, was brilliant, delicate, and overwhelmingly complicated. But overall, the thing that struck me most was the undoubted feeling of assurance that I understood the meaning of this whole scene. The whole sky and the sea, the air and the light, had tremendous meaning for me. I had a sudden realization: that the most serious divine process of Creation was in progress right now, in this moment, and through creating my art I was participating in that process in some way, no matter how small. It was a most solemn realization that moved me to awe.

21 I walked for about an hour and then I went to Malibu and had a coffee alone. I did not meet anyone I knew; I was able to stay as if I were invisible. Then I became decisive. I went back to my studio and finished four more works: strong, not emotional. This is it! I came to the end. Looking at the four beautiful works, I felt extreme happiness. I prayed: *Thank you very much, God, for letting me work such a long time. I am extremely grateful. I have to go back to the world and the time to study my work will begin. I will think about this work. I will write about it in order to understand your mystery much more deeply than I do now.*

22 After I went through the experience of creating "*Requiem for an Executed Bird*", I found my phobia had gone. Resolving my phobia had been huge, serious homework that I had been carrying for fifty years. Death in wartime is different from death due to natural disasters.

It involves distinctly intended hostile killing. We felt the hostility all around us: as if it soaked through our skin, it hurt us. We knew, even though we were so little, that the twenty-six nations which Japan fought against in the world burst out in applause every time our enemies hit us. And yet we personally had no power to identify them and deal with them. The bombs always fell from the sky and annihilated the whole city; still children, we never understood why. That caused a sense of absolute fundamental powerlessness towards impersonal hostility. Death in wartime is also different from death caused by a criminal act or by natural disasters. The tremendous scale of mass killing and destruction are beyond human conception. We could not take it in. It involves all the people to whom you are related and those whom you have never known. There is no ambulance to call, no help to rely on, no place to hide. Eating, sleeping, keeping yourself warm, any kind of support to keep you strong, even turning on the light at night—all were denied to us, knowing that twenty-six nations of the world were now giving the enemy thundering applause. The Bird thus became a symbol of the total powerlessness of my own existence.

23 And there was another fear at the same time. Throughout the war, we lived in deep fear of our own government's fascistic authorities. We were afraid of them almost more than we were afraid of the enemy. And we were afraid of all our neighbors and of the people in our community because of a systematized group unity which we were forced to form with them to enforce rules against each other by checking every conceivable detail of each other's personal lives. I saw very clearly the essence of totalitarianism without having any intellectual knowledge of it: it was hatred and the destruction of individuality and the commanding of blind obedience to an irrational authority. We were in deep fear of showing any difference from others and any sign of who we were, and we were in terror of being punished for our ethical honesty, for our independent minds: we were in terror of being tortured for being ourselves. Thus, the Bird became a symbolic victim of the irrational authority of totalitarianism, a victim who was executed because of its own nature. When I saw the Bird hanging upside down, made powerless by my uncle who was feared as the authority in his community, I myself was slaughtered, and I had been dead ever since then. I was in the darkness of tormented death, until the phobia was over.

24 Phobia is like a wall preventing the phobic person from seeing the reality beyond the everyday reality, the reality that is too threatening for her ego to deal with. *What I am terrified of is only a bird!* Thus she does not have to face the real issue which is her biggest terror of all. Furthermore, the wall becomes increasingly high, and the fear of all birds, the fear of photographic images of them, becomes an obstacle and prevents her from keeping herself going in everyday life. It prevented her from achieving the further integrity of her personality. Facing a wall retards human growth and facing a phobia is an ugly setback for psychological integrity. And yet when I looked back, it was a blessing, very likely the greatest blessing for a most vulnerable little girl such as me at that time to receive. Thanks to this phobia, that little girl was able to keep enough of her sanity to keep living in the midst of an absolutely insane society, a society to which one should never adjust. Four years had passed since I had finished my psychotherapy. Psychotherapy by itself could not bring me up to the stage of being healed. But I strongly believed that without that complex and deep task of psychotherapy—descending and exploring the unfathomable depths of the dark underground world, a process I went through for ten years altogether with a brilliant loving woman psychologist—I would never have come to the point of encountering that ugly wine decanter. To see anything related to a Bird would have been too frightening to me. To hold that ugly thing in my arms, to come back to my studio with it, was already a triumph of the therapy. I do not consider this experience of creating the series only a matter of art. It was also entangled with the profoundness of the psychotherapy. Together they formed a mass of magma, boiling inside the volcano, and finally artistic strength forced an eruption and the magma boiled out to the surface to come to its artistic and psychological completion.

25   After all this discussion of the phobia, still I have to say that the phobia was not the point of this series of artworks. The phobia was a wall between me and reality which was too frightening to deal with. Phobia was my personal experience, but these fear-based walls can be found in everyone's unconscious. The artistic process that the artist undergoes is the process of breaking and penetrating her walls. The intensity of this whole process stems from the battle between her own sincere desire for the truth and her resistance to assure her survival. But when you penetrate deep enough you will reach a reality which is in itself universal. In my own case the fear I experienced during the war is very personal, but the mortality and vulnerability of human existence, pain, and indignation against the forces which destroy individuality and demand blind obedience—that is universal and eternal. The secret of creation is that the more personal your experience is, the more universal and eternal your art becomes. If you failed to reach what is universal and eternal, your art will remain as art which is created as art therapy, which may very well heal the patient who painted the trauma for herself. But the viewer would not get any spiritual benefit from that painting.

26 As I had prayed at Sycamore Beach, I studied and I thought and I wrote about this experience of creating the series "*Requiem for an Executed Bird*". This series was exhibited in galleries, museums, universities, and other institutions. In some places all forty-five works were shown together, and in some places only part of the series was exhibited. Many people came to me, some talked to me about their own tormented experiences and their phobias, and some only cried— their tears flowed but their experience was not yet verbalized. One of the shows was at a big annex in the industrial area of downtown Los Angeles. The gallery director was impressed with my husband's ideas for the show, and allowed him to design the exhibit. He had a concept of the exhibit as a narrative. He set up music stands throughout the gallery, with pages displaying the story of the series. The gallery was filled with Mozart's Requiem. And many of the works were suspended from the ceiling instead of the walls, so that the birds actually jumped out at the viewers like birds. And he set up a desk with a writing pad and encouraged all the viewers to write their reactions to the show. Many people wrote about their own experiences of phobia and spiritual growth, and he mailed copies of those statements to all the viewers. The show was reviewed, and not just the art but the whole presentation was favorably reported in an art magazine.

27 One woman came up to me after a slide show of the series. She was young and beautiful, but horribly skinny. She said she was suffering with AIDS, and she expected to die any day. "Today looking at these paintings, I resolved months of the agony I had felt. My life had meaning, deep meaning; I realize that now. I can die peacefully at any moment." The serious realization that we are reaching each other's souls through art came over me. The Artist comes from behind the painting, and the viewer approaches from the front. Thus our souls encounter each other.

28 Things started changing drastically. Completely new artworks rushed out of me one after another and deep emotions, sharp insights, and fragmentary thoughts were gradually growing and forming into my own philosophical ideas. Those ideas became my base and later on my structure of thought. As for my language problem, I gave talks on many occasions—sometimes with my artworks and sometimes without them. I could not believe that I was giving talks in English to groups, sometimes of 20, or 150, or even more people in museum auditoriums. It was far beyond what I had expected I could do with my heavy language limitations. My English was still a burden for me. Every time I had to make a public presentation, I needed extreme preparation: my papers were edited over and over by my husband, and I needed hours of practice with reading and pronunciation. But every time I did it I was always surprised to see how warmly people responded.

29 Once I was talking about the "Requiem of the Executed Bird" at a lecture in the department of theology at a graduate university, with 11 works of the series hanging on the wall of the library behind me. During the question-and-answer session I could not find the right words to express exactly what I wanted to say. When I said I was looking for a word, many hands shot up instantly because everyone in the audience had a suggested word they thought I was searching for.

We discussed each suggestion together to see if it was accurate to use that word or not—sometimes seriously, sometimes with bursts of laughter. All were more engaged in my talk than they would have been just sitting as listeners. They did not allow even my limited language skills to become an obstacle to communication: they used that limitation to stimulate and raise the level of communication. The desire for communication through language is so strong in American culture, it is not confined to intimate groups, as it tends to be in Japanese culture: it is extended to the public and to strangers. They were sharing the desire to communicate with each other using the powerful tool of language: they were working to break the wall that stands between 'us' and 'them'. To share that task with love is the key to solving the various problems of language that I had suffered, I realized. All the students of one particular class I attended, a class studying the theme of Crucifixion, used my series to understand and seek another interpretation of that theme.

30 Still we had not given up driving around through Topanga Canyon on many evenings. And my husband kept his promise to answer my question: he wrote his first major book, *The Jewish Attitude Towards Justice and Law*, and published it. It was a beautiful book. A friend told us that one of the justices on the California Supreme Court mentioned it favorably in a speech he was giving. In that book my husband wrote that the Judaism which arose after the Jewish state was destroyed is the last surviving Alexandrian mystery religion: Justice is the mystery and law is the secret art. This was his unique interpretation of Judaism and this was his answer to my question: this attitude, he said, is what Judaism has contributed and will contribute to the 21st century. When I heard this, I exclaimed: "He is a mystic, just as I am a mystic. That is not a category of religion: it is something deeply internal and it appears in every religion. There is light, but for human beings it is recognized only as darkness, and creating art is the secret craft of making that light visible to human eyes. No wonder we understand each other and are attracted to each other as if we were twins, deep down believing the same thing. And we both are suffering to manifest the core of our selves in the world." My husband published other books, but it took him many years to make the painful journey from his first book to his most recent one, *Grieving the Loss of Religion*. This book is his declaration of how he had outgrown his Judaism, and transcended it. Our discussions of the mystery of art, and the mystery of law, and of personal religion, individuation, self-actualization, transcendence, psychology, philosophy, world affairs, and fascism still continue, probably more urgently and with even greater intensity than before. We drove around, discussing all these things, until finally our odometer showed the mileage of having gone three or four times around the globe.

CHAPTER 16

1 Just as I took a long ride along Mulholland Highway through the Santa Monica Mountains to the beach when I started writing this long memoir many years ago, today I took a long ride along almost the same route as I did at that time. But instead of driving in the sunny afternoon by myself as I did then, this time I took the ride with my husband, driving after midnight and before the dawn. I was not quite confident enough to drive by myself. It was in complete darkness, only the headlights of our car showing the way: to the sides and to the back of the car, everything was jet black. The curving, winding road suddenly appeared and disappeared at the top of the cliff: it was like sticking out on a high stage, with no railing, nor a fence, around where our car proceeded.

2 I have been writing about the things that happened in my life—things that I encountered, things that I created–for many years now in this memoir. Those things are like countless stars in the night sky. They are scattered, seemingly disordered, and most of all they are countless. The act of writing makes each of those things clear. When you write, that particular experience becomes your own. Writing it down is the beginning of consciousness. To create lines among the scattered stars in the sky from one star to another and to boldly create some recognizable picture in the sky—which is a constellation, just like the ancients created: the Big and Little Dipper, the ram, the swan—had been my desire. As you place each experience into your constellation, it takes on universal meaning for you. This is what I have been doing. In fact, when I was listening to Beethoven's Ninth Symphony in the bomb shelter, I already had that strong desire. But I had an image of a solid structure: a great cathedral. I have been designing that cathedral since I was a little child. Come to think of it, when I was suffering from tuberculosis, when I was eight years old, my only prayer was that I wanted to know the meaning of my sickness. Many years later, my prayer was rephrased as the question, "Where does this sickness fit into my constellation?" The whole structure became something more flexible and organic: every time even a tiny detail changed, the whole structure changed slightly. Once it occupied the right place inside of my constellation, I was resolved and my experience of tuberculosis became a constructive part of my life structure. The ancient constellations are presented as if the sky is one flat canvas, but the reality is different. The connections are never just single lines or straight lines. To move from one star to the next might involve a movement into a tremendous depth. The universe is three-dimensional or even multidimensional. In that deep space I am drawing my constellation, as if it were a three-dimensional wire-frame diagram. I am drawing it in the sky. I never tried to alter the things that happened in my life, nor did I create any illusional stars that were not there. And yet the meaning of the particular stars often changed, and I drew different lines and I re-created my own constellation. And that constellation is my mythology. It is rooted between and includes both consciousness and the deep unfathomable unconscious, between and including both my ego and my self.

3   To live in America as an immigrant was not exactly something I had planned to do; it was not a premeditated act. The decision was made upon my second marriage. But it took a long time to understand what it involved. I was told a story about a man who suddenly and unexpectedly became blind. Accepting that he was a blind man, and accepting the idea that he had to live accordingly, took him seven whole years. But when I heard that story, I thought, what would I think if I were in the same position, if the same thing happened to me? I would have to figure out what it means for me to become blind. In other words, how would I place this profoundly significant incident into my own constellation without bringing about the total destruction of my whole constellation that I have already placed in the sky? Becoming blind is a passive experience: it happens to you. Becoming an American immigrant, and an American citizen, is a totally autonomous decision I made. And yet, it took me far more than seven years to understand what it meant and to commit to it with full conviction.

4   I was fully aware that I had to leave my land, the land I was so deeply in love with, in order to grow and keep growing to become an individual. I needed to create a new category of immigrant: there are a huge number of economic immigrants and there are also some political immigrants in America. But I wanted to use the word 'refugee', which is a word much closer to my experience. According to the Convention signed in 1951 at the United Nations Conference on the Status of Refugees in Geneva, the word "refugee" is defined. One of the conditions is "a person who has a well-founded fear of being persecuted for reasons of race, religion, nationality, membership in a particular social group, or holding a political opinion." More precisely, the reason for the persecution has to be some violation of fundamental human rights. In this way, the concept of "refugee" is related to notions of fascism, dictatorship, and totalitarianism, all of which are forces destructive of humanity.

5   I finally arrived at my own new concept of 'spiritual refugee', borrowing from those concepts of the United Nations Geneva Convention. There are some people who leave their native land only to preserve their integrity and live with honesty towards themselves. One must have, after all, a certain amount of freedom to be honest as an individual. Without this freedom there is no way for one to take responsibility for one's own actions and thoughts and therefore there is no inner life, no place where one experiences himself as an ethical being. Without that private place, others are mere strangers and one is a stranger even to himself.

6   In a society that does not allow for the existence of individuality, the effort to become an individual invites persecution. Although this sort of persecution is not as visible as political persecution, it is nevertheless fatal to one's spiritual being, so the persecuted person becomes an exile—a spiritual refugee. One usually goes into this sort of exile only after a sustained battle against the cultural system in which one's whole life is wrapped up. The battle is painful. Wounded and bleeding, one becomes an exile. These people I call 'spiritual refugees', and I consider myself one of them.

7   The suffering that refugees in general have to endure is intense: terror, outrage, misery, humiliation, pain, remorse—and these are beyond the power of words to express. So it may seem outrageously insensitive and arrogant to use the word "refugee" for my own identity. But I believe that it is crucial for anyone who values his or her own inner life to understand the concept of spiritual refugee. To identify oneself as a refugee does not degrade refugees; it is to stand on common ground with them. For me, it is to see myself naked, after everything that I thought I had and belonged to has been scraped away, and to accept this as the true base of who I am.

8 Being an artist and being an exile at the same time is no coincidence, for there is an intrinsic and essential relationship between art and the status of 'refugee'. Art is the means for searching out the truth, and creating art is itself the process of reaching integrity. The process of creating art has become a process of individuation. So art creates individuality and, at the same time, art needs tremendous freedom to let individuality grow. For many decades now, artists have been engaged in a fight for the freedom to reach individuality, and this is the essence of being a spiritual refugee.

9 I finally made a connection, drawing lines among the scattered experiences of the persecution which I had experienced and witnessed in Japan to the concept of 'spiritual refugee'. Finally I placed 'spiritual refugee' into my constellation as one of my basic concepts.

10 What happened to my illegitimate baby? I have not talked about him too much recently. He came back from under the debris and soil which had buried and covered him for a long time. He survived. Protecting him from the blind, unconscious art educators had made me strong. He is now mature, grown up and independent. He does not need protection from me anymore. Rather, he is leading me with his adventurous spirit of art. I don't know where this baby came from but

I have a strong feeling that he was the baby who was shot at by the enemy plane through the bamboo forest. He was that baby, who died by the bullet that was meant for me: instead of the bullet penetrating me, the baby in the little basket placed a few feet away from me in the bamboo forest, which no soldier could have possibly seen, was shot and killed. His little body had already been taken away by the time I was told of his death. I embraced him with my deep lament, but only inside of my mind. Yet he was born again from me. Is that because I invited him, killed as a substitute for me, to give him the opportunity to live once more? Or did he come to me of his own accord, because of a strong desire to fulfill the life he could not realize? He became my mythological child. He occupied the right place in my constellation now.

11 Now let us take a sudden turn, like a flying eagle, leaving the vast starlit sky behind; let us fly down through space and time, and focus our eyes on the ground, on the ground of the small island country named Japan.

12 Once more my grandmother surprised everybody by demolishing the old mansion and selling it to be replaced by a parking structure. This was after the grandson she raised had married and left to Tokyo, and after years of carefully sorting out to whom everything should be donated: to the church, the university, the library, the museum. Every single tree in the yard was donated and not one was wasted.

13 People in the village, now part of the city, saw her cheerfully orchestrating the pickup trucks driving in and out of the gate of the mansion of the Motoyasu. She really looked like the conductor of an orchestra: she stood up in front of the truck with both hands high, and her hands moved to invite it towards her and she turned her hands around to stop it. Some drivers followed her gestures, saying, "Thank you, Grandma"; some said with a laugh, "You don't have to do that, Grandma." She was excited to move around in the dusty old garden, as if she loved the process of destruction as much as she loved construction: these were two aspects of one thing. It was a huge construction for her new life. She built a new house in Tokyo with part of the money she received from the parking structure company. That house was for her grandson, whom she raised, and for his new family, and she turned the upstairs into her own living quarters with a tiny kitchen attached, planning that after her death those rooms would belong to the young family's children to come. She left the community of her Episcopalian church where she played a leading role and came up to Tokyo to live, and she started attending a Catholic church in Tokyo. No one knows why she changed from an Episcopalian to a Catholic, but she was decisive. "Start from the beginning!" she said. She enrolled in a Bible class in that church. She mastered the most complicated subway map and bus system of Tokyo, with just a few rehearsals with her new daughter-in-law, and then she was set: she could go to the church by herself. She now started her new life in the new city, in her new house and new church, when she was over eighty years old.

14 The last time I saw her was the year before her death. She welcomed my husband, who had come from a faraway land. In the tradition of Judaism as the son of a rabbi, and having been raised to be a rabbi himself, he carried a heavy burden by marrying her granddaughter, a woman of a different race and religion, without asking her to convert to Judaism, with only a stranger as a witness, in a strange town in a foreign country, and who embraced his wife's illegitimate child with her—her art—and gave him steady room to grow strong. My grandmother welcomed him with the greatest affection. Did the memory cross her mind that she had to work so hard against the aristocratic men by herself for the love marriage that her son wanted to enter before his death? Her dignity, her cheerfulness, and her slight shyness, which a well-bred lady in Japan is supposed to have, were all woven naturally into her manner. She astonished my husband with her beauty and the elegance of her manner; and it was true, the way she moved was almost mysterious. She looked as if she had no weight in her body at all; she moved freely, gently, and femininely in her silk kimono with its exquisite pattern of gold underneath reflected on the surface of subdued gray. This kimono I had been so familiar with, which she wore only on special occasions when she wanted to express her pleasure and respect. I had loved this kimono since my childhood and yet now it still looked brand new because of her ceremony of taking care of kimonos. And suddenly I noticed that the *obi*, the sash she was wearing, had a big splendid white chrysanthemum dyed out on the black background with a special hand-dyeing skill, *shibori*. It was unusual for an old lady to wear such a bold design, and yet it was nothing but elegant. And her collar came down to her chest; she was showing a very subtle color of water, reflecting the sky. And it was almost invisible but my eyes caught a delicate wild chrysanthemum of pink embroidered on it. *Of course, it was the beginning of the season of the chrysanthemum in Japan!* I exclaimed in my mind. *She is celebrating my marriage with him in the highest way her language could express.*

15 She told me that the classes she was now teaching in her church as a volunteer, in flower arrangement and tea ceremony, were so packed that she was teaching every day. Smiling, she said: "I am preparing for death every evening before sleep, but I am always surprised to wake up in the morning. I must still have something to give to others. When I have taught everything I have learned on this planet, God will come to pick me up." My memories rushed into me. How precious what she taught me was. My affection towards her saved me from missing this precious moment. I was there only because I wanted to be with her. Her young students at the church, perhaps without any dark association with tradition, must have been happily learning everything she offered.

16 She had met a gentleman of my age, she told me, at a bank in Tokyo. When she showed her name to him, he asked with surprise, "By any chance are you the wife of Dr. Motoyasu?" When she said yes, he stood up, being moved, and said, "I am one of the babies he saved. Of course I don't remember him, but my parents told me that I should never forget his name, for without him I wouldn't be here." She told me, smiling and with tears in her eyes, "Even in Tokyo, in such a faraway city."

17 Both of my grandparents wanted to be God's pipe. That had been their burning passion all their lives. But this pipe was not just an empty one. It was like a furnace with all their suffering, thoughts, efforts, pain, joy, and tradition that they inherited so heavily—all went into the furnace. In the highest temperature of the flaming fire, they were transformed. Their work, their teaching, is fully working because of this transformation and now everything is powerfully pouring into the next generation. They had been doing this work since the first day they were together, and God gave them a great furnace to work with. Just like she said, "after teaching everything" all day in church, surrounded by affectionate students, she came back home, satisfied. She wanted to take a long, long bath, she said. Too long a time passed, and her daughter-in-law opened the bathroom door and found grandmother dead in the bathtub. Without having even one day of sickness, she died at the age of eighty-six.

18 I was thinking about my own marriage. My marriage with a person who had an absolutely Western background, was trained in Judaism, Greek classics, Western philosophy, and law, and had no familiarity at all with Eastern culture, played an important role in my personal journey towards individuation. Through severe struggle and conflict, which we had, every issue of individuation rose to the surface and had to be defined, identified, and tackled. And every part of that work had to be done through a good command of the English language. Marriage became a private battlefield in the midst of the huge battlefield from which I could not even see the horizon. But we had been given a huge furnace too. We were thrown into this huge furnace, each with our own cultural identity, each with our own religious sensitivities, each with our own quest for integrity and our own aspirations—and all these became burning, fluid, refined, and purified. We came out as transformed, and transcended. This is the furnace from which new language is born and from which creativity grows.

19 Since I completed the "*Requiem for an Executed Bird*" series, I came to believe more strongly that the most personal thing has to become the most universal. If the artist succeeds in going through this most difficult, dangerous process truthfully, only then, encountering the art, the viewer might follow a journey to his or her own transcending. This is the mystery of art. It is through this mystery that God reveals Himself at the center of each of us. Isn't it what my spiritual teacher in Japan meant by saying "God is painting through Junko"? Nothing I received in my life was ever in vain. Even the darkest thing like the head-chopped-off bird had a most profoundly constructive meaning for me. Because I went through the difficult, dangerous process truthfully, I could pour the powerful images into the paintings. *After pouring the deep meaning of everything I experienced on this planet, God will come to pick me up.* I wanted to say exactly the same thing my grandmother had said to me.

20   It was late one morning in early winter, a few days after my mother came back from her long year of hospitalization. My husband and I were visiting her from America. My father had died years ago, and during her mourning period, she had a stroke and had been hospitalized. The stroke left her paralyzed on her left side, and she had spent a long, difficult year at the hospital and then at a nursing home. "I will play Nocturne," she suddenly said to me. "You will assist me with the left hand, won't you?" Did she forget that I could not play the piano? Was she confusing me with either of my sisters? She continued: "I raised two pianists but neither of them wants to play the piano with me. They said *no*." A harsh tone was there. "They have complicated feelings about piano, you know," I replied. "I know they do, but you don't. Would you play with me?" I said, "But I cannot play the piano, you know that." She said, "Yes you can."

21 I sat next to her wheelchair at the piano. Her body was slanting to the left in the chair towards me, and her right hand on the keyboard was small and powerless, like a wrinkled shrunken glove had been left there and forgotten. I opened the sheet music and she started playing weakly but correctly. My ability to read music did not help with the coordination of my left hand, and in spite of my intense desire to help her I could not keep up with her right hand. *A miracle has to happen to make me go through this,* I thought. Then an arm stretched over my left shoulder and a big hand appeared on the keyboard. It was my husband, who had just come back from outside and walked into the room. His hand started assisting her right-hand melody firmly and sensitively and the music suddenly came to life. The intense sadness of Chopin's Nocturne started to fill the room. I played some notes once in a while. Three hands made it through to the end.

22 It was the first time I heard my mother play the piano for her own pleasure. I heard her teaching my sisters all the time when I was a child, her cheeks red with excitement, and she sang with the piano, her body moving like she was dancing. I heard her playing this fragment and that fragment to join the discussion and analysis of the pieces and to assist their research, and I heard performance experiments while they were young when they attempted many ambitious, contemporary pieces. Her voice, which used to come out from the door of the music room, was loud and animated, and the discussions lasted forever, often to midnight, dinner forgotten. And much later, she played pieces for young students while she was teaching them at home. She was a strict, effective teacher, although she could not really control her frustration or conceal her contempt for the untalented ones—which included everyone but her daughters, in her mind. But I had never seen her playing alone for herself, for her own pleasure.

23 Once in a while I asked myself why my father prohibited my mother so strictly from playing the piano. It was because when his bride, the young princess who looked like a flower—so delicate and fragile—played the piano, she turned into a monster-like creature. In her playing, he saw a demonic power. He realized that for her, music was never simply a source of pleasure, nor enjoyment, nor comfort: instead, she surrendered herself to the frightening passion of the demon in Western music. My father forbade her to play the piano not from any lack of sensitivity towards Western music: no, it was the opposite, from his extreme sensitivity, because something inside of him resonated with that demonic power. But his fear of the demonic power was so deep that he had to camouflage it, by pretending that he was just exercising the traditional power of the Japanese husband over his wife. Through the years my mother's piano teaching became very intense, but teaching music with extreme intensity is still different from surrendering to the demon. My father knew the difference, and so did my mother. She was drawn to the demon, but she did not have the courage to go to the severe battlefield where the artist must go. So she too camouflaged her lack of courage as mere obedience to her husband, and lived in anger as a victim of her husband's command.

24 Since she had come back from hospital just a few days ago she could not get anyone to assist her to play the piano and she now had to rely desperately on other people to play. Today was the first day that she had the freedom to play piano for herself, after she was told not to play piano anymore by her husband on their honeymoon. Half a century had passed since then, and she had obeyed her husband's command as Japanese wives were supposed to do. What would have happened if she had not obeyed his order and not repressed her intense artistic passion this hard, or at least not this long? If the dragon who lived in her interior did not tumble about, had not taken her over with anger and desperation, what would have happened? No one knows but every one of our family members' lives would have surely been quite different.

25 The brilliant young man, who was the son of my father's professor and now a high-level editor of one of Japan's major newspapers, visited my mother's house to see me when I was in Japan. His wife had contacted me in America about her husband's tragedy: he had become seriously sick. She warned me not to be shocked at seeing him. He came with his wife, who was driving, and his son and daughter, both teenagers. He walked slowly into the room, with a cane, concentrating so hard on walking that he did not see me until I rushed up to him, and then he looked at me and nodded slightly. We all sat and had lunch. He did not pay attention to the conversation; he was only staring at the plate in front of him, and sometimes he slowly lifted a small amount of rice to his mouth. At some point, when his son said something funny, I looked at my friend seated next to me and recited some quotation, as a response to his son's remarks. The quotation came from a cartoon book which my friend and I almost memorized from cover to cover. I was such a dark girl all through my youth, and yet this cartoon book was a source of laughter for us. Now, the moment I quoted the passage, he laughed. It was so quick and his laugh was so weak, but it was a real, spontaneous laugh. Everybody was shocked. His wife said, "We have never heard his laugh since he came back from the hospital, which was over a year ago." His daughter added, "If Aunt Junko [that is what both of his children called me] stays in Japan our father will laugh every day," What did I do? Did I touch something buried deeply in his mind? But then he returned to concentrating on his plate, all through the lunch.

26   While I was sitting on the sofa looking at him, in front of me, in the living room, a deep sadness finally came over me. Tears ran from my eyes uncontrollably. He looked at my face and my tears and a puzzled expression appeared on his face. I suddenly realized that this was the expression I must have had on my own face, when his tears fell on the velvet chair that time he came to my parents' house as a guest of honor, when I was 14 years old. I was experiencing exactly the same scene only the roles were reversed: he became me and I became him. I saw his deep pain at having lost all his quickness, humor, liveliness—but clearly he did not notice any of this at the conscious level, and he had no idea why I was in tears. I was just like that: I was puzzled at why he was crying. I could not grasp the whole picture of my own situation at that time. But his tears had awakened me. It was on that very night that I started to see the truth of my family. But now I did not understand his situation as clearly as he had grasped mine at that time. I stood up and ran upstairs to repair my makeup. My tears ran down furiously and I could not stop them. Suddenly a faraway childhood fantasy came back to me without any preconception: *I should borrow him. I should ask his wife to lend him to me, only tonight. I will embrace him with tears and sweet words. I will make him warm in my two embracing arms, and talk to him tenderly, things*

I had never done with him during our whole friendship. Oh, how much I can talk to him. I know his memory will come back. I will be just like that prostitute, Kannon Bosatsu, who appeared in my childhood fantasy. Suddenly my thoughts were interrupted when I noticed I had lost myself completely for a few seconds. I repaired my makeup and came down to the first floor. He had saved me and helped me to grow in the most crucial time of my life. But I failed to reach him today. He never recovered until his death took him away, some years later.

27   It was 1988, the year the Emperor was dying in Japan. The black hole around him started opening up. The Mayor of Nagasaki was shot by a terrorist for saying "yes" when he was interviewed and asked whether he believed that the Emperor was responsible for the war. He replied "yes" and he added that it is clear from historical records that if the Emperor, in response to the reports of his statesmen, had resolved to end the war earlier, there would have been no Battle of Okinawa, no nuclear attacks on Hiroshima and Nagasaki. He added that he too was responsible as a soldier during the war, for encouraging young men to die. Trucks with loudspeakers on top rolled into the city and blasted threatening words at him into the air. A mountain of letters and phone calls contained numerous death threats; packages of bombs were rushed to him and his family. He was under 24 hours' police protection, his family was not allowed to be near him, and he was shot.

28   Who was this man who dared step into the black hole? Finally a man uttered one word against this darkest ancient black hole, tradition, and sure enough, he was shot. But he shook all of Japan: letters of both threats and encouragement numbered 7,300. Some of them were published and the compilation sold 36,000 copies in a few months.

The publisher identified itself, but the printer and bindery, contrary to the usual custom, did not make the letter writers' names public, considering themselves to be in danger of bomb threats. This 67-year-old man who survived the shooting was interviewed and asked the same questions over and over, and various organizations demanded he withdraw his words, but his answer was always the same. He said he could not betray his own beliefs. He said, "I am a Catholic. I cannot tell a lie." And he added that he came from a family of "Secret Christians."

29 My grandfather's document on Secret Christians was lost forever. But the Secret Christians, who continued to have faith despite persecution, survived through the generations. This Mayor who was raised by his grandfather, whose legs were crushed by the torture of persecution in the Meiji period, had stood up against the biggest irrational authority in Japan. He was shot just as his ancestors were persecuted. The one who was most afraid of clarity of thought shot the bullet into the depths of the darkness of the black hole, the Japanese Unconscious.

30 The Showa Emperor died. And the new Emperor, his son, who was a 9-year-old child during the war—just like other 9-year-olds who were torn away from their families and sent to remote backwaters with other classmates and young schoolteachers, following the government decision to protect these future soldiers—went through a series of esoteric enthronement ceremonies held throughout the dark night until dawn in the closed sacred spaces of the Imperial Palace, and became the 125th Emperor of Japan. And he and his wife, the Empress, began the deep, serious, silent prayers and ceremonies to put the spirits of the war to rest: they did it without any particular religious color, even without any music, without any governmental involvement, without any discrimination among the war dead. They prayed for the dead soldiers of Japan's defeated allies and of Japan's enemies alike.

31 One early evening while I was visiting Japan, I came back to my mother's house from a meeting with a friend. When I opened the door of her bedroom, my mother said, "Where did Mendel go? He came to see me just a moment ago. I told him to wait just for a while because I was still too sleepy to talk to him. Then he said, 'I will be back soon,' and he left. Could you look around the house? He might still be here." The Mendel my mother was talking about was the young boy she had put into the little room next to mine. He played Mendelssohn's Violin Concerto every single evening and that is why we called him "Mendel." I went out of the room and asked my mother's live-in nurse whether Mendel had come by. "Today your mother did not have any visitor," she replied. When my younger sister came to visit, I told her that Mendel had come to see our mother earlier that day. She was stunned. "Mendel died a few weeks ago. He drowned at the mouth of the bay, you know, where the lake and the ocean meet." She mentioned the name of the bay: it was the beach we all went to with my grandmother and cousin, with 43 rice cakes that we made, a long, long time ago. I remembered very well that the smoke-like spray stood on the horizon and that my grandmother told me that it was a dangerous spot, but we were all playing well inside the bay so we didn't have to worry about it. Just before Mendel went to the bay for vacation, my sister continued, she ran into him at the university where she and Mendel were both teaching and he said to her out of the blue: "I am very grateful to your mother. Without her great help I would never have had such a wonderful life." My sister said: "I did not tell mother about his sudden death. I did not want to upset her, you know." And she added, "Mother will go with him the next time he comes."

32   He had been picked up by a well-known violinist who came to give a concert in Japan after Mendel had been under my mother's wing for some years. That violinist took the teenage Mendel to America and gave him the opportunity to perform and teach at a university on the East Coast. Behind all this was my mother's tremendous ability and intelligence, as she arranged everything from the introduction to this violinist to the departure to America. After some years, Mendel came back and started teaching at the university my mother helped to build.

33   Many years ago, his emotional, dark, and yet splendid sounds of Mendelssohn hit me almost like violence. That was a big part of the reason I had to run away from my own home and marry outside. Those sounds of torment were a symbol of the cult my mother had established. I remembered Mendel's mother saying, "Thank you very much for all your kindness" and dropping her son on Mother's lap. I often asked myself if my mother had said the same words to my home-room teacher, and had dropped me on his lap before he became my husband. Suddenly I realized that Mendel was my shadow, or parallel 'other self'. While I was silently painting in my little upstairs room, with all my sadness and all my torment, I wanted to bring my work up to the highest exaltation so that I could create artwork that was the most intense. But at the same time, through the thin wall in the next room, Mendel cried loudly and screamed his torment through his violin. I was threatened. I felt my internal organs would be ripped out of me and dispersed in all directions. My mother wanted to do the same thing to me that she did to him, if I allowed her to do it. He accepted everything she offered, and followed everything she wanted him to do. If I ever allowed her to do that to me, it would have led to my losing my own soul. I somehow knew it. I chose a different way and paid a big price for it. But in his case, did the whole thing really lead him to such a "wonderful life"?

34   I was in silence thinking about how peculiarly different the creative artist is from the performing artist. The creative artist creates her own universe by herself, grabbing the root of this universe and radically pulling it out and building a universe of her own with it, however young and immature she is. The only thing she can rely on is her own soul. *Learning* about art has a different meaning to her: Rembrandt's fantastic skill and the skill of the prehistoric drawings on the walls of caves are examples of two different ways artists connect to their own souls. And you have to create your own way to connect to your own soul. It has nothing to do with historical, technical progress. Learning skills means learning how to touch your own soul with material. But the performing artist has to step into the universe that a creative artist, the composer, has already built and inside of that building he has to express his soul. Even the experience of listening to Beethoven's Ninth Symphony against the sound of bombs exploding could never make me want to be in this huge structure, and live in it and participate with it and express it as my sacred place, as a performing artist would do, as Mendel did for Mendelssohn's Violin Concerto. Instead, I wanted to create a universe of my own, like Beethoven created his universe in the Ninth Symphony. I wanted to create my universe by my own hands with my own soul, and it would be completely different from Beethoven's. This outrageous, and yet extremely humble, honest, almost desperate yearning, I can almost trace, breathing inside of me, although I was just a tiny frightened little girl.

35 European classical music requires tremendous learning, training, and methodical discipline: unless you master all those things, and master the composer's contemporary historical technique, you cannot even step into the universe that the composer built. Learning and discipline play a different role for the creative artist. My mother could not see the difference between the creative artist and the performing artist. Or should I say that my mother, like most of the people I have met in this world, could not imagine the yearning of the creative artist. I was grateful to Mendel: because of his sweetness, my mother might need it in her new life on the new shore—gratitude she deeply deserved. She knew precisely what this boy needed the moment he played Mendelssohn for her for the first time. She trusted him to go through it all, and he did. But for myself, I had to find what I needed in order to build my own universe in my own way with my own soul in the dark.

36 My mother started talking about the garden of the Motoyasu with me. She continued, "I had waited for you to come. I knew I could talk with you about the mansion of the Motoyasu, which no one else here remembers or cares about anymore. But I knew you would, because you were always that way: you observe, feel, think, remember, since you were so little. I have not noticed that quality of yours for a long time, have I? I have been too busy to think about anything, so busy with everything, with the war and with music, with everything, but Jun-chan [which she called me as if I were a little girl]. From now on, I will live like you, I will think. I want to think about the mansion of Motoyasu and all that."

37   She was not quite right saying that she never thought about anything. Her thoughts were in her letters that she wrote to me after she visited New York to see my art: she kept writing for fifteen years. Her intense letters were sometimes more than twenty pages long, and my responses were equally long. Our dialogue was a kind that only writing can reach; the words that she wrote led to her deeper thoughts.

38   When she fell by stroke, five weeks after my father died, I was with her in her house in Japan: I had visited from California alone. I rode in the ambulance with her to the hospital, and came back to my mother's house by myself. I found all my letters that I had sent to her, which she kept organized neatly in her room. I took them back to my home in America, before anyone threw them away. They joined with the letters I had received from my mother and kept. They consisted of thousands of pages altogether. It was a precious dialogue, a dialogue of two souls' intense regrets, pain, understanding, forgiveness, compassion, affection, and joy. And there was one more person behind her letters: my father was present. My letters were all addressed to both of them, without exception. My mother's were sometimes from both of them, always written and signed by her hand. But I perceived his presence behind the letters. I was right: on top of every air-mail envelope I found a little title written which summed up the contents of each letter I wrote just as in a table of contents, for further reference. These contents were in my father's hand. It was like Hamlet looking up at the ghost of his father, a dim figure in the night sky above the castle. Receiving his image was receiving the whole secret of his mind. Sometimes it was just like the memory of him in the white gown of a doctor, who could not come close to me. I was not allowed to touch him, but it was the sweetest moment with him. The dialogue that I craved to have with my parents so eagerly from the bottom of my desperation when I was a teenager was finally completed here.

39 My father's death was dignified and beautiful just like his father's, as my father had wished it to be. He treated his patients at his home office with his tremendous will power and my mother's devoted assistance until the day before his death. He had cancer and died of a heart attack. When he finally fell, he told the paramedics who were going to carry him to the hospital that he would die at home, now, right on this spot, and he lost consciousness and then he woke up, explained what was happening in his heart during the short time he was in coma—and then told them that the emergency treatment they used during that time was right—clearly, attentively, and with the voice of an elderly doctor talking to younger medical people with authority and sweetness. He knew what it was like for a doctor whose patient died on him, and it was as if he was determined to give this assurance to this young medical person in the last moment of his life. And then he expressed his love and gratitude to my mother, and died. His simple funeral was held at home without eulogy and without any religious involvement—"No man of cloth, please"—as he wished. But his former patients came to pay their respects in long, long lines, and that lasted for many days and weeks.

40 "It was a beautiful garden, wasn't it?" my mother repeated slowly with a voice as if she were trying to pull up the paralyzed side of her body to talk. It was a voice I had never gotten used to for thirteen years. She said that she noticed that grandfather and grandmother were visiting her and standing near her bed watching her lately. She looked up. The garden of the summer evenings in the mansion of Motoyasu was there, and my grandparents and I joined her together looking at it. The darkness was falling and the lanterns were lit up one by one.

41   Her two days' funeral was held in the Episcopalian Church near her house in a suburb of Tokyo. Since she had forgotten her own Christian name long ago and none of us knew it, they gave her a new one. The epithet "great mother of pianists" was repeated in the eulogies. Her intense regrets and the pain over her life which she expressed in her letters—those were not there. Her real self was not there in people's minds just as I did not exist there as one of her daughters—as I had never been. Her strength to admit her mistakes and her courage to face reality, and the sweetest embrace she and I had, were all sealed in the letters she had written to me over fifteen years. In spite of all her agony, pride, and tormented ambitions, her passion for truth was real, and it poured powerfully into me. I will stand as an only witness, if it must be, of her beautiful soul, which I saw through the thick black clouds of her torment, if she needs a witness.

42   I saw my cousin, who my grandmother raised, at the funeral after a long time of not seeing him. He was now in his mid-fifties, the father of a grown daughter, still showing the sensitiveness of the child who never knew his parents. Not becoming a doctor was so traumatic a decision for him that to find what he wanted to do after that did not seem to be in his script. He smiled and told me with a little shyness that he still painted oil paintings when his governmental office job was not too busy. "Only on the weekend, only some weekends," he added almost apologetically. When we visited the Motoyasu mansion during summer vacations when we were little, we rushed upstairs. "The greeting ceremony is not yet over," my grandmother's voice always followed as we ascended the stairs, and we painted together for hours and hours without talking to each other. Oil painting must be the only tie that connects him to his father and mother, to re-create the original family that he never experienced. And my uncle, the second son of Motoyasu, affectionately talked to my husband and me: he looked peaceful but was very skinny from many relapses of tuberculosis in his life. He died sometime after the funeral. My sisters were still teaching at the university which my mother worked hard to build, as before. The elder one had not performed for a long time after coming back from America, where she taught piano at many universities. The young one, who was just about to become a grandmother herself, was performing a little here and there. Neither of them seemed to remember or think much about the Motoyasu. There are some new descendants of the Motoyasu, but they are either too young or they just do not care about it. They all seem to think everything is over.

43 It is true that everyone and everything is gone. Only a huge parking structure is standing high in the busy district of the city 200 miles from Tokyo where the garden of Motoyasu with a red bridge over the pond, its many lanterns lit up in the beautiful summer evenings, welcomed people to stroll along the winding path on the small hills. Do the dead see things differently in a bigger perspective, just like when you climb a big steep hill and suddenly the familiar view appears new in front of your eyes? Would they finally understand the whole meaning of the beautiful garden of the Motoyasu from their new perspective? Is my mother starting to think about it, as she wanted to do? Meanwhile, still belonging to the living, I have to think and figure out the secret of this landscape inside of my own limited perspective. I still wonder if the image of the beautiful summer garden is my own memory or just a reflection of the dead. It radiates in my mind, almost like a pain, and it glows more intensely as time goes by.

44 And there is one more memory: of the Presence who appeared out of the artworks of the silk sliding doors and enveloped me in the dim light, my experience in the big display room in the mansion of the Motoyasu. I could not confirm this memory with anyone because it happened only between the unknown and me. I did not share this image with anyone, because it is unexplainable. I see it sometimes coming back, out of the artworks, sometimes when I am alone in the big rooms in the dim light in quiet museums far away from the mansion of the Motoyasu, or sometimes when I am working alone for long hours in my studio it comes quietly out of the work I am working on and stands high in front of me. Its presence is as solemn and powerful as it was the first time I experienced it. It fills me with a feeling of awe; it does not confine itself in my memory of the past anymore. It speaks to me urgently of what I hold in trust for the future.

EPILOGUE

1 Since my mother's two-day funeral, almost 25 years have passed. Meanwhile some people with whom I had deep relationships have also crossed over the shore to the other world. I found my first husband's death mentioned in the periodical of the school where I attended some parts of middle and high school. My first husband had been promoted to university professor after two years of study in England, which happened after his two years in America with me. His book had been published a few years before his death. I read his book. It was about his father as a pioneer scholar and revolutionary religious person who had a profound influence on Japanese culture. He gave his father a higher place in the history of religion and ideas in Japan than had been previously accorded. This was the book he really wanted to write and even felt he was destined to write. Because I listened to his talks about his father in many Unitarian churches in America, I had always thought so. In the afterword of his book, he wrote that he had a heart attack during the time he was writing. When everything seemed to be at an end, he received a letter and article from the Rutgers library in America: that letter arrived at his hospital bed. The librarian wrote in response to his inquiry that he found an article written by his father in the stacks. That gave him the strength to continue and finish writing his book. Through his book I was able to glimpse his peaceful life with his new wife and his daughter in the little house in the churchyard, and the death of both of his parents was deeply moving. My former husband had completed his life: this was what he really wanted to accomplish. I was convinced of that and it made me deeply happy.

2 My mother-in-law in America passed to the other shore when she was ninety-six years old. Many friends, family relatives, and former students from the college where she had been teaching visited her in her ward in the hospital in Santa Monica. Every day it seemed like a huge party was going on. One day when those party guests were gone, only two of us remained in her ward. In that precious moment, I told her that she had been so sweet, and without her sweetness my life in America would have been very difficult. She said, "You are the one who has been so sweet to me: I learned from you what sweetness is, thank you, Junko." And she held my hand. When again another cloud of party guests came in her ward, she pointed everyone to which chair he or she should sit in, and then she pointed to the closest chair next to her pillow and said, "Sit here, Junko darling." It was the same thing she had done at the first Shakespeare reading party on the evening I came to Los Angeles. She said she saw an Angel coming down into her ward. She whispered that to me with an expression of overwhelming joy. Her eyes fixed on the area between the ceiling and the top of the door, she counted every Angel that came in one by one, following the first one. She wanted me to repeat her counting, to make sure she was not making any mistake of the numbers. "Yes, Ema, now six..." I responded to her, without seeing the angels myself. When she had counted up to twelve, her consciousness faded away with a smile and she slipped into a coma. Now I have a group of more and more people towards whom I have deep affection in the world of the other shore.

3 My husband found and arranged a very large space in an industrial building for my art studio far over the mountains from Topanga Canyon. I was collaborating with a dance company on a program called "Fathom—Kukai, The Body as Temple." I contracted to create forty-two huge panels as stage art: I was the only artist for the whole project and I needed a huge space to work in. My husband helped me day and night to create prints of computer images on a drum printer—prints I then used to make the huge panel works. In the studio his suits were hanging so he could change and rush to the court downtown on short notice. He was in the middle of a big trial, and might have to go to court any moment. The dance program in a big theater in San Diego was very successful. Since then I have used that studio for myself and created new series of large works. *Lift the Curtain, Mass Killing, Integroids*—all were created there. And I must add, in front of that building is a huge garbage bin just like the one our landlady at the house in Boston described so vividly—the one in which she used to throw away the piles of manuscripts in her attic. It is as if it were set there to remind me every day that I have a very big task to accomplish before I complete my life.

4   I was born in the middle of a serious rising up of fascism seventy-eight years ago. I was stricken with the phobia of the bird at the age of four. It took me more than a half a century before my phobia of birds—my terror of Ffascism—was finally healed by creating the series of forty-five works of' *Requiem for an Executed Bird*. And now again I am hearing the rumbling of the volcano many places in the world, the rising up of fascism gradually coming closer. I see visions. The confessional phase of my art is over, and the new phase, my 'declarational' period, has started. Now I have to actualize the visions I have been receiving into creative actions before I conclude my life on this plane.

5   Fascism is not just one of those bad political systems constructed by evil leaders in some foreign countries. Fascism is the system that hates your freedom to be yourself, and wants to thoroughly eradicate you. Hitler did not do that work by himself. He was elected by the citizens through a legitimate election in a democratic system of government. And records show that millions of citizens passionately followed and supported his system of thought and wanted to be part of it with full knowledge of what he was doing. In addition to the problems of the economy and the social conditions that gave encouragement to fascism in those days, we have deep serious human problems here, even today, which we have to examine: the hatred of being yourself, the obedience to irrational authority, the willingness to submit to a fate determined by outside forces outside of your own self, the burning desire to be identified with a larger group with blood and soil, the readiness to become an automaton just like everyone else and go into a cycle of destruction and desperation, the readiness to act according to the power of sadism and masochism and their interaction. And there is necrophilia, which hates life itself, which is at the very core of fascism. Those neglected dark problems create a big hotbed where fascism is incubated. Those are problems we cannot solve simply with propaganda and posters. Our good religions which have prevailed and covered the surface of the entire globe for thousands of years have failed to recognize these problems and to treat them as serious human inner problems, as the sickness of the soul of our time.

6 Only through a deep understanding of our problems, and with love and an affirmation of your life, and by living creatively and productively, can you as a viewer and I as an artist together start changing our consciousness. For destructiveness is the outcome of an unlived life.

ACKNOWLEDGMENTS

I began writing this book in 1998, and I have been working on it for nearly twenty years. During those years many friends have read earlier drafts. I was able to share drafts only with friends who read books in English comfortably: I myself know all too well that to have an assignment to read a book in a foreign language is an enormous burden, so I did not ask any of my Japanese friends to read the drafts—either those who live in Japan or those who live in this country. I will have to wait to share my book with them until after it has been translated. But all the friends here that I asked to read the book did read it and I am grateful to all of them for their enthusiastic support and precious suggestions.

Dr. Lou and Barbara Breger were close friends of ours for many years, and both of them encouraged me after they read an early draft. Lou's book, *Dostoevsky: The Author as Psychoanalyst*, gave me a crucial idea for my art: the notion of the "observing ego"—that is, as someone who lives his life and observes it at the same time. This idea is basic to my book, as well as to my art. And his wife Barbara, who was a student of Russian history, saw my work through the lens of her sharp insight into Totalitarianism and Fascism. Her reaction expanded my own view about what I was going to do in my work. She passed away before I finished, so I could not show her this book after it had grown into its final shape, but I want to express special gratitude to her.

Friends of ours at Claremont Graduate University read earlier drafts and were most encouraging. I am particularly grateful to

Professor Dennis MacDonald, who responded enthusiastically to the book as a document of spiritual seeking. Professor Karen Torjesen encouraged me to develop the focus on the extraordinary women I describe in the book. Now she is in the Congo helping to eliminate gender violence there. She kindly sent us a comment to this book, which you may see on the back cover and inside pages.

Dr. J. Harold Ellens, who is both a psychologist and a theologian, and who served as a chaplain in the military, read an early draft and gave me many helpful suggestions.

My husband and I became friends with Dr. Jack Miles through Claremont in the late 1990s, a little before he received the Pulitzer Prize for his book, *God: A Biography*. His encouragement for my work, though it was still a very short piece when I gave him an early draft, has been sustained through all the long years and until it grew into the huge work it is today. His many emails and our discussions in meetings over the years are exalting, and what I have learned through those has become a special treasure in my life. He also introduced this work to Dr. Ted Fowler, an emeritus professor of East Asian Language and Literature at UC-Irvine, who checked the historical details in my manuscript and corrected some of my factual and historical errors, for which I am most grateful.

My mother-in-law, Judith Chodos, taught English as a Second Language to foreign students at L.A. Trade Tech. Although she told me that she did not like, and never undertook to read and edit students' personal manuscripts, still, at the age of 93, she kindly offered to read my manuscript. She corrected many of my English errors, and made suggestions. Tracing her delicate pencil marks on the pages of my manuscript became a warm memory in my heart after she passed away at 96.

My niece, Hannah, is an actress. She was just 15 years old when she stayed at our home for a week, as she played a part in a production of Midsummer Night's Dream at a professional theater in Topanga, her first professional role. While she was staying with us, she read the manuscript with great enthusiasm. I was surprised that my writing had such an impact on such a young person. A few years after that, she made a professional audio recording of the opening chapters.

A neighbor of ours in Topanga Canyon at that time, Rachel Resnick, was herself an accomplished author and the founder of WritersonFire.com. When I had completed a first draft of the opening PART ONE of my book, she read it carefully and made many suggestions—all of which I adopted and for which I remain grateful.

In 2014 and 2015, the outline of the book took nearly-final shape in my mind and I began showing drafts to neighbors and friends. Every single one of them took the time to read the manuscript deeply and comment. I am particularly grateful to Alisa Chodos, an interior decorator for large-scale hotels, for her comments; and to my neighbor, Dorothy Storer, a former therapist who was born in England and lived through World War II in Europe. She invited me to her house for English tea at 7 o'clock in the morning before I left to drive to my art studio to work. She gave me precious comments as we sat in her beautiful living room, watching a heavy fog cross over Topanga

Canyon through her big window. Suddenly the radio, which was playing faint background music started playing Chopin's Nocturne, the piece I mentioned in PART THREE of the manuscript—and the very piece my mother tried to play with her paralyzed hand shortly before she passed away, after she had been prohibited from playing it by my father for a long time.

My therapist, Dee Barlow, read an early draft and commented about my discussion of language, and passed away a few years later. Additional "pre-readers" include Laura Godorecci, a young lawyer and movie producer who has worked closely with my husband; Mark Estren, a publicist; Patti Burris, an art educator; Joe Matza, founder of a Hollywood postproduction company; Bruce Kerner, a TV producer; Leah Diaz, my studio executive assistant for many years; and Bill Barnett, the public relations manager for my art and himself a playwright—now deceased.

Suzanne Lummis, whom I asked to write a comment for the back cover, is a widely-published and admired poet. In 1990 she wrote a long article in a local newspaper about how my art reaches the deep core of the self. In that same year she invited me to read translations of my short poems (tanka) at a poetry reading she had organized at a museum in Pasadena.

My husband, Rafael, helped me with the book from the very start. Ideas often came when I was pushing a shopping cart in the grocery store. I often began handwriting in Japanese on the reverse side of my shopping list, sitting at a small table in the corner of the market. When I got home, using only my index finger, I typed those scribbles into the computer in English. Rafael corrected my English with great patience, but was careful never to change my writing. While I was writing, he was working hard on legal matters, and on his own books and articles, many of which were published during these 20 years. As my book came close to completion, he took charge of the publication process entirely. He has been a great driving force, and without his help I probably would have been buried under a huge pile of crushed shopping lists covered in Japanese scribbles.

The cover photograph dates from when I was about 25 years old, and was taken by a friend of mine at Waseda University, Gaiji Kawaguchi. Jeanette Hsu Zamora, the designer responsible for many books and art promotional designs for Rafael and me for eight years, helped with the cover design. Rafael and I are both grateful to Bob Cooper, who edited my completed manuscript and turned it into the final manuscript published here; and to Jim Shubin, at bookalchemist.net, who handled the page design and the initial cover design, and who helped us carry the final manuscript into publication.

By writing this book, and receiving all the comments and encouragement that so many people have given me, I have come to realize how blessed I have been to have these people in my life. These are the people who helped me put my roots deep into American soil, to grow.

Junko Chodos
November 2017

THE ARTIST
JUNKO CHODOS

(mysteryofart.com) was born in
Tokyo in 1939, just as WWII
was starting. She received her
B.A. from Waseda University,
majoring in mysticism and the
philosophy and history of art.

She has had one-person shows
at several museums and her
work is in over 50 collections,
including public collections
and museum permanent
collections in the United States,
Japan and Europe.

She has lectured about what art
can do for mankind and about
her notions of "spiritual
refugee," "constructive
outsider" and "centripetal art"
at museums, galleries and
universities internationally,
including Claremont Graduate
University and the Getty
Museum.

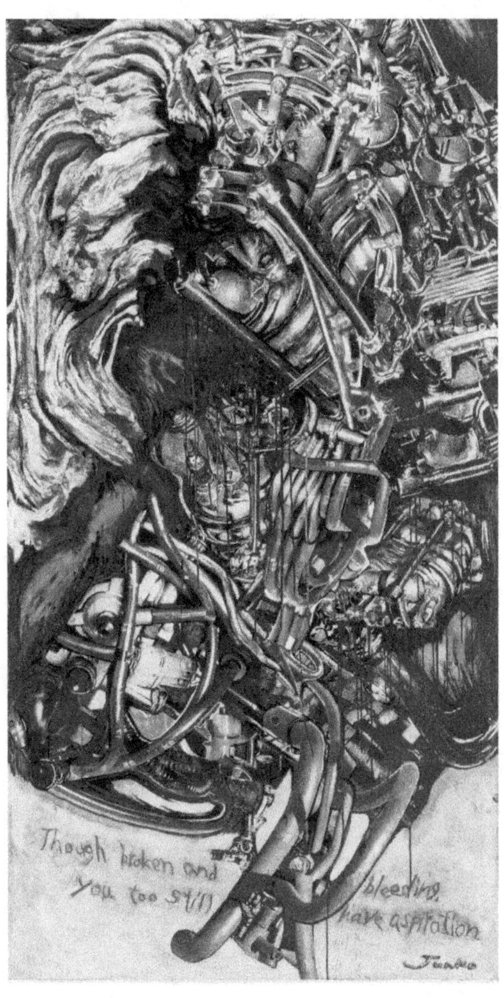

Lift the Curtain, No. 3 by Junko Chodos,
Completed July 2012, 84" high x 36" wide.

*Though broken and bleeding you
too still have aspiration*

www.ingramcontent.com/pod-product-compliance
Lightning Source LLC
Chambersburg PA
CBHW081247130726
47998CB00010B/2701